Early Christianity in South-West Britain

Wessex, Somerset, Devon, Cornwall and the Channel Islands

Elizabeth Rees

WINDgather PRESS

Windgather Press is an imprint of Oxbow Books

Published in the United Kingdom in 2020 by
OXBOW BOOKS
The Old Music Hall, 106-108 Cowley Road, Oxford, OX4 1JE

and in the United States by
OXBOW BOOKS
1950 Lawrence Road, Havertown, PA 19083

Paperback Edition: ISBN 978-1-91118-855-1
Digital Edition: ISBN 978-1-91118-856-8 (epub)

A CIP record for this book is available from the British Library

Printed in the United Kingdom by Short Run Press

Typeset in India for Casemate Publishing Services.
www.casematepublishingservices.com

For a complete list of Windgather titles, please contact:

United Kingdom
OXBOW BOOKS
Telephone (01865) 241249
Fax (01865) 794449
Email: oxbow@oxbowbooks.com
www.oxbowbooks.com

United States of America
OXBOW BOOKS
Telephone (800) 791-9354
Fax (610) 853-9146
Email: queries@casemateacademic.com
www.casemateacademic.com/oxbow

Oxbow Books is part of the Casemate group

Front cover: Three early Cornish sites. Baptistery, St Levan (*top*); churchyard cross, Mylor (*bottom left*); St Nun's well, Pelynt (*bottom right*).
Back cover: Relief of St Antony of Egypt, Padstow church (*left*); Churchyard cross, St Buryan (*right*).

Contents

Introduction

The focus of the book will be Christianity in south-west Britain before the Norman Conquest. Christianity came to Britain with the Romans, and we shall begin with an examination of two Roman villas in Dorset that were also house churches: their mosaic floors demonstrate a sophisticated understanding of theology as well as the profound faith of the villa owners. Clues in St Patrick's fifth-century *Confessio* offer hints about how members of a villa house church lived in rural Britain. By way of comparison, we shall consider an early Christian village community in southern Greece, closer to the epicentre of Christianity. We shall also examine models of early Christian ministry in the broader Church.

The first surviving Life of an early Christian who worked in south-west Britain is the eighth-century 'Life of Samson'. It describes his monastic formation in Wales and his travels across Cornwall to Brittany as a *peregrinus*, or 'pilgrim for the love of God'. We shall examine this text, which offers us unique insight into an early Christian leader and his way of life. At this date, monks also carried out pastoral care: in sixth-century Britain and Brittany they celebrated eucharist for the people. Women have mostly been airbrushed out, but we know of a few individuals and groups: a women's monastery at Lamyatt (Somerset) will be described, and what we know of a highborn Anglo-Saxon woman, Lulle, who lived and prayed nearby.

We do not yet know the degree of continuity between the Church in Roman Britain and that of Saxon times: when we read documents concerning the Church as an institution in Anglo-Saxon England, it looks very different from earlier models, and more highly organised, as one would expect. However, Saxon monks trained in pre-Saxon monasteries: Cuthbert, probably a highborn Saxon, began his monastic life at *Mailros* (Old Melrose) in the Scottish Borders, an early monastery with a British name, that may have pre-dated the establishment of Lindisfarne in AD 635.

Bede's account of Cuthbert's life and the autobiographies of later individuals such as Christina of Markyate indicate that vowed life in Saxon times retained much of its earlier framework: Cuthbert, like Samson before him, was a monk, a bishop and, at certain periods, a hermit; like Samson, he was based with fellow monks, but often travelled in his exercise of pastoral care. Christina, a Saxon in a Norman world, learnt vowed life by living with other hermits, both male and female, and eventually established a community.

Few early texts survive until Saxon times, but archaeology is gradually yielding more clues about the pre-Saxon Church. The sites of small monasteries and churches in central Somerset are almost all found on the sites of pagan temples; using evidence from excavations, we shall explore the transition from paganism to Christianity in this region. Next, we will consider some coastal sites in Somerset and Devon: many early Christian sites are on the coast and its offshore islands. One significant example is Lundy Island, off the Devon coast, which provides evidence of early Christian settlement.

In the final three chapters we shall survey early sites in the various regions of Cornwall; although pre-Norman evidence of Christianity is quite fragmentary, a large number of clues survive. Inscriptions on memorial stones provide our earliest glimpses of Cornish Christians, while place names and a study of church sites offer more hints. Many are named after a single, often unknown, individual. Excavations at the Breton monastery of Landévennec indicate how a group of hermits gradually embraced a communal lifestyle: it offers a possible model for less well-documented Cornish monastic life. We shall also consider sites in Guernsey and Jersey – many of them at prehistoric sacred places – and on the Scillies, which became a focus for pilgrims in the medieval period.

The book is largely illustrated with my own photographs; thank you to Margaret Rees, Paul and Gillian Johnson, Monica Watson, Martin Valatin and Ros Marsden, who have kindly alowed me to include photos they have taken. I am grateful to my teachers, Professor Jonathan Wooding, Dr Karen Jankulak and Professor Tom O'Loughlin. I thank Dr Oliver Padel, Dr Patricia Rumsey and Jerry Samson, a cathedral archaeologist, for their many helpful suggestions, which have significantly improved the text of this book. My thanks also to Annette Wilson for her artist's impression of the monastery of St Mawgan in Meneage, and to my sister, Dr Frances Jones, for her help with preparing the illustrations. Any errors are my own.

CHAPTER 1

House churches in Roman villas of rural Wessex

The name Wessex denotes the area conquered by the West Saxons, which includes parts of Wiltshire, Dorset, Gloucestershire, Devon and Somerset. One might also consider Cornwall as part of Wessex: it was conquered by the Anglo-Saxons in the reign of King Ecgberht (reigned 802–39), but not fully absorbed into the administrative system until the reign of Æthelstan (924–39), by which time Wessex was in process of being subsumed into England. In this chapter we shall examine the evidence for Christianity in the Roman villa house churches of rural Wessex, and also consider the type of worship that took place in them and the styles of Christian leadership that we might expect to find.

Although written evidence is relatively sparse, archaeology provides considerable evidence of Christianity in Roman Britain, particularly from the fourth century onwards. A useful synthesis of discoveries prior to 2003 is made by David Petts in his book *Christianity in Roman Britain*, his end-point being the mid-fifth century.[1] Christianity was forbidden until it became the imperial religion under Constantine (reigned 306–37), and so public churches in towns are unlikely to have existed before then.

At this point, there is little conclusive evidence for urban churches, apart from the discovery in 1992 of a large and impressive mid-fourth-century basilica that is likely to have been a church on Tower Hill, in the south-east corner of Roman *Londinium*.[2] We know, however that there were bishops in the principal towns of late Roman Britain: in AD 314 three British bishops attended the Synod of Arles in southern Gaul. Small churches are found in northern Britain on Hadrian's Wall (at *Vindolanda*, for example) and at former pagan shrine complexes in the south-west, including Chedworth and Uley, which will be described below.

Over the last fifteen years, ongoing study and discoveries have deepened our knowledge of early Christianity, and this is particularly true when we focus on Wessex. During the Roman occupation, starting in the first century AD, numerous rural villas were established across Wessex; the earliest detailed evidence of Christianity in south-west Britain is found in what appear to have been Roman villa house churches. In the villas at Frampton and Hinton St Mary in Dorset, the highly developed theology of their fourth- and fifth-century occupants can be seen in the complex imagery depicted on the mosaics of their chapels and baptisteries. The fact that these two villas are only 15 miles apart suggests a network of Christians who were theologically aware; other villas in the region present similar but more fragmentary evidence of this.

Symbolism in the mosaics

The significance of the mosaics at Frampton and Hinton St Mary was first seriously explored by Jocelyn Toynbee in the 1960s.[3] Thirty-five years later, the villas that contained them were thought to be less significantly Christian. Petts considered these rooms 'unlikely to have been churches in which Mass was celebrated', although he conceded that 'they may have had other quasi-religious functions on occasions'.[4] Writing in the same year, Dominic Perring assessed the imagery in the mosaics as arcane examples of Gnostic heresy, favoured by an unorthodox Christian elite.[5] Neither author fully addresses the fact that there were by now very many Christians in rural Britain, who would have celebrated the eucharist in appropriately decorated indoor spaces.

Today, fifteen years on, we are more aware of the extent to which Christians drew upon pagan symbolism, and used it to illustrate their own beliefs. This is largely the result of more detailed analysis of symbolic art in Western religious contexts. There has been ongoing study of how Christians developed a symbolic code whereby pagan gods symbolised aspects of Christian theology. As well as pagan mythology serving as a teaching tool, it is also possible that by depicting Christ as Orpheus or Bacchus, for example, persecuted Christians could conceal their faith more easily, at a time when Christianity was a forbidden religion.

Parallels in Israel and Greece

At the same time, our understanding of Judaeo-Christian art and theology in the Near East has deepened. Italian Franciscan archaeologists working in Judaea and Galilee collated surviving early Christian visual evidence with texts from the same era, including the *midrashim*, rabbinic literature containing commentaries upon the Old Testament and other sources, which covers a wide variety of subjects such as angels, or how God created the universe.[6] Common images in villa mosaics such as rosettes are widespread in eastern as well as western early Christian art; for Judaeo-Christians, for example, rosettes often symbolised angels.[7]

Meanwhile, archaeologists in Greece began to focus on early Christian sites, in a country where previous British and French governments had largely funded the excavation of classical sites in the hope of discovering more statues and temples. Thus in Ancient Corinth, Christian material had been blasted away in order to reach classical remains beneath them. It is largely due to the patient work of a Cornishman, Dr Guy Sanders, Director of Excavations at the American School of Classical Studies in Athens, and his training and supervision of students and scholars, that a more detailed understanding of early Christianity in Greece is beginning to emerge.[8]

Early Christian leadership

Again, it was unclear how Christian leadership functioned in its diverse forms in the early Church. In the twentieth century, some historians still thought in terms of 'bishops' and 'monks', and often looked to the Desert Fathers of Palestine, Syria and Egypt for the origins of the latter, following Derwas Chitty's seminal *The Desert a City*.[9] Certainly, the Lives of the Desert Fathers, as conveyed through the writings of John Cassian, were widely read in early monasteries, and their subjects became heroes – models, even – but Syriac scholars such as Robert Murray and Gabriele Winkler have presented us with evidence for a wide variety of styles of ministry and service in the first Christian centuries,[10] which correspond in some degree to the hints that we find nearer to the western edge of the Christian lands. In this chapter, these various developments will be taken into account as we survey the rural house churches of Roman Wessex.

The earliest account of a British Christian's conversion, call and subsequent ministry is the fifth-century *Confessio* of St Patrick. Its title employs a word frequently found in the psalms, and means 'Acknowledgement [of God's marvellous works]'.[11] Near the beginning of the *Confessio*, Patrick relates:

> My family own a small estate near the village of Bannavem Taburniae. My father was Calpornius, a deacon, and my grandfather was Potitus, a priest.[12]

This presents a rural model of church, not an urban one. It describes a house church in the countryside (though we do not know the location of *Bannavem Taburniae*), with its priest(s) and deacons, since Patrick later tells us that he, too, became a deacon.[13]

This Christian community was in existence for at least three generations; its spirituality and theology were of sufficient depth to produce a Christian of Patrick's calibre, though he tells us that he did not begin to pray to God until his conversion while he was a slave in Ireland.[14] Patrick tells us that in Ireland 'the Lord opened my understanding to my unbelief', when 'at that time I was ignorant of the true God'; previously, he had ignored priestly teaching, presumably including that of his grandfather.[15] Since only adults were baptised, after rigorous preparation, it is possible that he was not baptised until after his conversion. Patrick does not tell us where he was born: one possibility is Birdoswald on Hadrian's Wall; another is the area of western Scotland near Dumbarton, in the Romanised area south of the Antonine Wall. A slightly greater weight of probability suggests somewhere in the south-west, perhaps Wales or Cornwall.[16]

A house church in Frampton, Dorset

Frampton is 4 miles north-west of Dorchester, while Hinton St Mary is 8 miles north-west of Blandford Forum. We know that both villas served as house churches because of their unique mosaic floors. Frampton's mosaics are now lost, but were carefully drawn by Samuel Lysons in 1813; they came from the same workshop as the mosaics at Hinton St Mary. In both villas, the mosaics

ILLUS. 1. The apse mosaic, Frampton Roman villa, courtesy of Dorset Natural History and Archaeological Society.

are closely ornamented, and not intended to be covered with couches or dining room furniture. The designs are arranged to be viewed from different positions, and suggest a dynamic use of space involving movement, procession, and the designation of some spaces as more important than others (see colour plate 1).

The larger room at Frampton was shaped like a church: there was an apse facing east, with a *chi-rho* symbol of Christ occupying a place of honour on its threshold (illus. 1). During the eucharist, the priest is likely to have stood before a portable altar in the apse, facing the gathered Christians across the *chi-rho* symbol. In the apse mosaic, a large *cantharus* or chalice forms a centrepiece. This was originally the wine cup in which an aristocratic host mixed wine with water for his guests. By the mid-fourth century it symbolised the mixing of wine and water during the eucharist.[17]

Neptune, Bellerophon and Bacchus

When the mosaic is viewed from the opposite direction, close to the *chi-rho* symbol one can see a mask of Neptune, the water god. A Latin couplet describes his functions, and a procession of dolphins round the entire edge of the room converges on Neptune. In pagan art, Neptune and the sea beasts symbolised the voyage of the dead to the Isles of the Blest, and Christians adopted this imagery to depict the journey of the soul to paradise: we are dolphins swimming through the perilous sea of death into risen life.[18] There are painted masks of Neptune in the Roman catacombs, and a representation of Neptune's trident accompanied by a procession of dolphins appears on a Christian sarcophagus discovered beneath the pavement of St Peter's in Rome.[19]

At the centre of the large room in Frampton, a damaged roundel portrays the Greek hero Bellerophon mounted on his horse, Pegasus, and slaying the three-headed monster, the Chimaera. Bellerophon slaying the monster represents Christ's triumph over death and the forces of evil. The myth was similar to the story of St George slaying the dragon: it symbolised Christ's struggle with evil and ours also. Since one of the chief purposes of Roman domestic art was to provide an appropriate setting for philosophical discussions, poetry and literature, it is unlikely that we are reading too much into the symbolism of these villa mosaics.

At the eucharist, after the readings from scripture, the candidates for baptism probably withdrew to, or remained in, the side room, which may have been curtained off along the decorated panel; the same feature can be seen at Hinton St Mary. In the central roundel of this side room at Frampton, where the candidates spent the second half of the eucharist learning more about their faith, the god Bacchus is depicted, riding a panther. Bacchus was understood as a saviour-god, a symbol of triumph over death and a blissful afterlife.

In mythology, Bacchus was born of a divine father and a human mother, as Christ was both human and divine. Bacchus was honoured with excessive drinking of wine to induce ecstasy, while Jesus invited his followers to share bread and wine and so enter divine life. For Christians, pagan myths were understood as hints foreshadowing the true revelation of Christ, and so there are painted masks of Bacchus in the catacombs. On either side of the Bacchus roundel at Frampton, a panel depicts a hunting scene for the candidates to ponder as they reflected on their own struggle with their pursuing sins.

A possible baptistery at Frampton

At the north end of Frampton villa there was another elaborate mosaic floor. At its corners, the busts of four men are depicted; they have wings, and windswept hair. People at this time believed that the earth was square, and the human figures depicted here are the four evangelists taking the good news of Christ to the four corners of the earth. They resemble in style the heads and shoulders of the four evangelists at each corner of the Hinton St Mary mosaic, who also represent the four winds. Writing in about AD 185, St Irenaeus relates the four gospels to the four chief winds and the earth's four corners, to which the winds convey the life-giving message of the word of God.[20]

The mosaic in this northern room also contains a hunting scene in which deer represent Christians pursued by the hounds of sin and pleasure. The mosaic's central figure is Neptune; dolphins reappear as souls sailing through the waters of baptism into everlasting life. The mosaic has borders of stylised waves, and is surrounded by light blue tesserae; with its watery theme, this may have been where baptism took place.[21]

Hinton St Mary's house church

The mosaic at Hinton St Mary was found in 1963; it dates from AD 350–55, and, since most of the villa was destroyed, the mosaic was transferred to the British Museum. Like the main mosaic floor at Frampton, it is designed as a continuous floor in two large panels, to fit two connecting rooms, although Charles Thomas also considered it possible that the central roundel depicting the youthful head of Christ might have fallen from a ceiling mosaic, intended to be viewed from below.[22]

The larger of the two rooms at Hinton St Mary faced east, as churches traditionally do. They face the rising sun, a symbol of Christ rising from the darkness of death. The smaller room could be screened off with a wooden folding door, or by a heavy curtain suspended from an arch above the threshold. In this way, as at Frampton, after the scripture readings and the sermon, candidates for baptism could be separated from the initiated Christians, who then gathered around the altar to share the eucharist.[23]

At the centre of the larger room, in front of a *chi-rho* symbol, Christ is depicted as a young hero with a composed expression and large, dark penetrating eyes. His head is flanked by pomegranates: these were a symbol of his resurrection, and refer to the Greek myth in which Persephone was taken to the underworld and ate six pomegranate seeds. For six months each year, she returned to life from the kingdom of the dead. In Christian tradition, pomegranates symbolised Christ's resurrection as late as the Renaissance, when Italian artists painted the Virgin Mary holding the infant Jesus clasping a pomegranate as he ponders his future death and resurrection.[24]

Images of struggle with sin

The heads and shoulders of human figures appear at each corner of this large square mosaic. With their red hair blowing in the wind, they symbolise the evangelists, as at Frampton. Between the heads of the four evangelists are four half-circles, or lunettes. One at the eastern end depicts the tree of life in paradise (Gen. 2. 9); the other three contain lively scenes in which a hound chases or confronts a deer. No human hunters are depicted, and the hounds do not wound or kill the deer. In Christian art, as we have seen, a hunting scene represented our struggle with the forces of evil.

When viewing the mosaic upside-down, one can see that the central roundel in the smaller room depicts Bellerophon's fight with the evil monster, as at

Frampton. On each side of the central roundel, a panel depicts a hunting scene, like those in the larger room that surround the head of Christ. The candidates were still struggling to rise with Christ at Easter, and were given instruction during each Sunday eucharist. The earliest training manual for candidates was the *Didache* (or 'The teaching of the Lord to the nations by the twelve apostles'), a late first-century compilation of sixteen short chapters, of which the first six, the 'Two Ways', describe the way of Life and the way of Death; they summarise how to live as a Christian.

In the larger room at Hinton St Mary, the head of Christ occupies a central position of honour. It is possible that the priest stood sideways on the mosaic panel between the two rooms during the Liturgy of the Word, praying with and reading to the people in both rooms, before the candidates were separated from the rest of the congregation. There is space for a portable altar where the mosaic is discoloured, between the panel and the image of Christ's head. The priest could stand behind the figure of Christ and face east as he celebrated the eucharist, surrounded by the baptised Christians. The people might look across the icon of Christ on the floor to the altar, where he was sacramentally present.[25]

Liturgical vessels

The mythological scenes on mosaics in the villa house churches of rural Wessex indicate a concern with life as a struggle between the forces of good and evil, through death and resurrection, expressed through hunting scenes and the myths of Bacchus, Neptune, Orpheus[26] and other classical gods and heroes. This symbolism can also be seen on vessels for liturgical use that formed part of two Roman hoards of silver and pewter found in Norfolk at Mildenhall and Water Newton.

The Mildenhall treasure features Christian symbols and inscriptions, yet also contains a magnificent silver dish adorned with a central mask of Neptune and an outer border in which Bacchus features. The Water Newton utensils were used in the celebration of baptism during the eucharist, and resemble those used in eastern, rather than western rites: they include picks and prongs that may have been used to dip the communion bread into the wine, and strainers that could have been used to retrieve the dipped bread from the wine.[27]

The silver hoards, together with the mosaics, suggest an educated Romano-British elite who were familiar with Gnostic thought, with its emphasis on inner spiritual wisdom rather than on the external authority of the Church. There may have been a difference in style of Christianity between that in city churches and that in aristocratic country houses. Villa house churches may have been fairly independent from urban bishops and their authority.[28] By the fourth century, much of upper-class society was probably Christian, but we know little about Christianity in the countryside: we do not know whether the eucharist in house churches was presided over by their home owners (who may have been ordained), by a priest chaplain or by visiting clergy.

Octagonal baptisteries

Early writings describe Christians being baptised in public baths, and we can guess that, when a Roman villa became a house church, candidates might be baptised in its bath suite. In the fourth century, monumental cold plunge baths were added to villas at Lufton near Yeovil (Somerset) and Dewlish, north-east of Dorchester (Dorset), each in octagonal form. In late antiquity, guests could be entertained in ornate bath houses, so these impressive plunge baths might have been intended for secular purposes, but why were these cold plunges eight-sided, as baptisteries often were?[29] An octagonal baptistery symbolised the seven days of creation (Gen. 2. 3), followed by the 'eighth day' (Sunday) on which Christ rose from the dead, into which the new Christian entered on Easter night: the Church Fathers thought of this eighth day as the start of eternity.

On the final page of *The City of God*, written between 413 and 426, St Augustine wrote poetically:

> The seventh day shall be our Sabbath, which shall be brought to a close, not by an evening, but by the Lord's Day as an eighth and eternal day, consecrated by the resurrection of Christ, and prefiguring the eternal repose, not only of the spirit, but also of the body. There we shall rest and see, see and love, love and praise.[30]

Pope Gregory the Great (540–604) explained more succinctly:

> Seven days represent the present time, the eighth day designates eternal life, which the Lord revealed to us through the resurrection.[31]

The octagonal baptismal font used by St Ambrose (*c.* 339–97) in Milan cathedral, constructed in 387, can still be seen. According to a pilgrim visiting Milan, an eight-line inscription ran along the eight sides of the baptistery; its text was attributed to Bishop Ambrose. It may be translated thus:

> Eight-niched soars this church, destined for sacred rites.
> Eight corners has its font, which befits its gift [of risen life].
> Right it is thus to build this fair baptismal hall
> according to the sacred number eight
> for here true salvation returns to the people
> by the light of the risen Christ
> who scatters the confines of death
> and raises the dead from the grave.[32]

Chedworth's healing shrine

How were people baptised in rural Wessex? While some communities were centred upon house churches in Roman villas, other sites tell a different story. Chedworth in Gloucestershire appears to have been a magnificent pagan healing centre that was later Christianised. Nine miles south-east of Cheltenham, Chedworth is situated at the head of the sheltered valley of the River Coln. In the fourth century it appears to have been a rich and important rural sanctuary, probably dedicated to a water god.

There are similar healing shrines in Britain (at Lydney and Great Witcombe in Gloucestershire and perhaps Blunsdon Ridge in north Swindon, Wiltshire) and Germany (at Heckenmünster and Hochscheid in the Rhineland).[33] Features of their layout recall the most famous healing centre of the ancient world, that of the Greek god Asclepius at Epidaurus in the Peloponnese. A large healing sanctuary dedicated to the water goddess Sulis-Minerva in Bath, Somerset, will be examined in chapter two; again, it offers some evidence of Christianity.

The Chedworth villa includes a large complex of baths in its north and west wings, while the south and west wings also contain a series of small guest rooms. It appears to have been a sanctuary with extensive accommodation for pilgrims, with its dining rooms, large baths and ample accommodation, and with the extensive latrines required for many people. There are also cubicles that appear to be typical sleeping chambers in which the god would visit patients through healing dreams. Beyond the main complex there are shrines: a circular temple-like structure 150 m north-west of the main site and a second possible temple, half a mile to the east; both would have been in woodland clearings. A great number of religious objects were found at

ILLUS. 2. Octagonal pool of the *nymphaeum*, Chedworth Roman villa.

Chedworth, including carved stone figurines and more small stone altars than at any other British villa.[34]

In its declining years, when Christianity was replacing pagan beliefs, this may have become a smaller farming community. The villa's source of water is a spring that flows through a *nymphaeum*, or shrine to the local water spirit, where it is contained in an octagonal pool surrounded by paving slabs (illus. 2). An apsed shrine containing a small pagan altar had been built over it, but three of the slabs that surrounded the pool have the *chi-rho* and other Christian symbols carved on them. This suggests that subsequently the pool was used to immerse candidates for baptism. It seems that Christianity continued to flourish at Chedworth, for there appears to have been a post-Roman cemetery nearby. A small stone cross designed for a grave, only 15 cm high, was found, bearing an incised cross of Saxon design: it can be seen at the villa (illus. 3).

ILLUS. 3. Small Saxon cross for a grave, Chedworth.

Uley: a temple and a church

Eighteen miles south-west of Chedworth, a complex of shrines at Uley also includes an octagonal baptistery. In contrast to Chedworth, excavation at Uley has revealed an unusually complete picture of evolution from paganism to Christianity at the site. Uley is on a scarp near the edge of the Cotswolds, close to one of Britain's largest hill forts, Uley Bury, 5 miles south-west of Stroud. Immediately to the north, Hetty Pegler's Tump is an early Neolithic long barrow, a communal burial mound dating from about 3800 BC. Roman burials at the tump indicate that the site continued to be venerated by newcomers who honoured its history. The nearby village of Nympsfield recalls the sacred site, since its name means 'tract of open country belonging to the *nymed*'; this is an early British word for a shrine, sacred grove or holy place. The *nymed* appears to refer to Uley, where a ditched enclosure that may date to the third millennium BC occupied a clearing within the virgin forest.[35]

The name Uley (*Euuelege* in Domesday Book) means 'Yew Wood'; the yew tree was considered holy by ancient peoples, who perhaps considered it to be immortal, on account of its longevity. Towards the end of the Iron Age, in the first century AD, the enclosure was extended to include a sequence of timber shrines. In the early second century a square stone Roman temple was erected on the site of its central building. The temple was surrounded by buildings of one and two storeys, perhaps including guesthouses, and booths where pilgrims could purchase gifts to offer at the shrine.[36] Nothing can be seen today at the site, which is across the road from Uley long barrow.

The chief deity venerated in the Roman temple was Mercury: there are two statues and six figurines of the god, and he is named on two altars, on at least twenty lead tablets and on other items. His cult involved the veneration of goats and cockerels; the bones of large numbers of male goats and male domestic fowl were recovered. The birds were prepared away from the site, while the goats' horns were removed near the temple; their carcasses were probably eaten after the goats were sacrificed. They were fed on hay and kept in stalls nearby; they were mostly sacrificed between August and September.[37]

Uley's church

In the late fourth century, the front of the temple collapsed, and what remained was converted into an L-shaped building with four rooms. In the fifth century this was replaced by a two-aisled rectangular wooden church which partly overlay debris from the temple. In front of the chapel's central doorway was a stone pavement approached by a step that incorporates a segment of a large Roman altar depicting Mercury, positioned face downwards. Two more pieces of the altar and a second complete altar that also bore a sculptured figure of Mercury were placed in inverted positions in an apse at the north-east end of the church, which probably contained a baptistery.[38] The disrespectful treatment of the two altars dedicated to a pagan god may signal his replacement by Christ.

In the late fifth or sixth century, an embankment was constructed as an enclosure around the new church. It is likely that a Christian cemetery lies nearby. Fragments of glass drinking cups and metal vessels may have had a liturgical use; they are also found in Anglo-Saxon cemeteries in eastern England. The church was rebuilt in stone, perhaps in the seventh century. Pieces of plain and red-streaked glass found at the site may have formed its windows, or adorned the front of a reliquary.[39]

The apse was remodelled as a freestanding baptistery that was probably octagonal. It had a dry stone perimeter wall of unknown height, and appeared to be lined and faced with a thick layer of white plaster. Three postholes suggest timber supports for a covering of cloth or leather, or a more permanent shelter of wattle and timber. The candidate might have stood in the font, while water was poured over the head and flowed down the body.[40] Four miles north-east of Uley, the parish church of Woodchester is built over a Roman palace with a magnificent mosaic depicting Orpheus taming animals and birds, but a historical sequence between the two cannot be determined.[41]

A baptistery inside a villa at Bradford on Avon

As we saw at Frampton, baptism might also take place in the villa's living rooms. In 2002–4, excavations in the playing field of St Laurence's School, Bradford on Avon, Wiltshire, revealed a lavishly designed double villa dating from the late third century. While its owners lived in this large villa, which had fifteen rooms on the ground floor, uniquely, the façade of a second villa of the same proportions, immediately to the west, disguised the complex where the slaves lived and worked, with a smithy, grain drier and a smokehouse for curing food. In the mid-fourth century, its Romano-British owner converted the chief reception room of his stately home into an apsed chapel with a high-quality mosaic floor.[42] He might have been the local priest, or indeed Bradford's bishop, since baptism was conducted by bishops at this time.

However, after the withdrawal of the Romans from Britain around AD 410 and the subsequent economic decline, money was becoming scarce, and the villa's new owner built a rather simple baptistery on top of the fine mosaic floor of the reception room, partly destroying the mosaic. The baptistery consisted of a font made of stone, lead or, perhaps, wood; a shallow pit acted as a soakaway or drain. The font would have been large enough to allow the candidate to stand knee-deep in water, while the bishop poured water over his or her head. It was surrounded by a low circular dry stone wall, 5 m in diameter, which stood 1 m high (illus. 4, 5); its crude, unplastered finish contrasts poorly with the elaborate mosaic on which it stands. This late Roman baptistery within a villa is unique in Britain, but there are parallels in fifth-century Gaul and Italy; there is a similar baptistery at Rennes in eastern Brittany.[43]

ILLUS. 4. Archaeology students from St Laurence's School uncover the baptistery wall in Bradford on Avon villa. To the right is the apse mosaic.

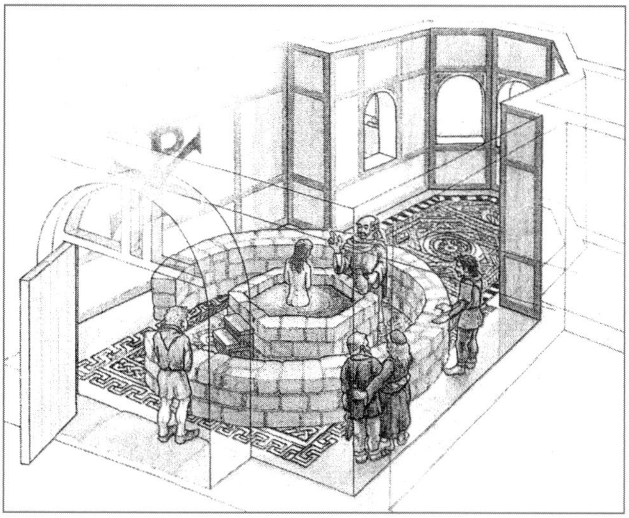

In contrast to the humble baptistery, the fine earlier mosaic on which it stands is reminiscent of those found in Tunisia, in North Africa. Its imagery recalls Christian themes, which suggests that the space had already been designed as a Christian chapel. At the northern end of the mosaic in the apse is a *cantharus* or wine cup, flanked by dolphins representing human souls (illus. 6). This adjoins a larger square patterned area, at the centre of which a rosette, symbolising eternity, stands at the centre of an octagonal figure.

This chief room in the villa was approached from the outside by a pair of doors flanked by two pillars. The approach on the right side is

ILLUS. 5 *(top)*. Artist's impression of the baptistery, Bradford on Avon, by Alan Gililand.

ILLUS. 6. Mosaic floor with wine cup, dolphins and rosette, Bradford on Avon villa.

PHOTO: MARTIN VALATIN.

worn down, in contrast to that on the left. This suggests that the left door was kept shut, and that the faithful approached the chapel through the other door, walking across the right side of the mosaic, which is similarly worn.[44] The baptistery may have remained in use from about AD 450 until perhaps as late as 650, when St Aldhelm (*c.* 639–709) is thought to have established the small church that can be seen today, on a separate site above the river. Two fragments of stone table-tops (or *mensae*) were found at the villa, one in the bath house and the other in the slave quarters; it is possible that they formed part of an altar. Graves were discovered, indicating a late Roman or post-Roman cemetery. A small bronze *chi-rho* pendant found at the ford over the River Avon in Bradford also indicates a Christian presence.[45]

Who owned the villa?

It is unclear if the owner of the villa at Bradford on Avon was a bishop. Letters survive written by Christian clergy and laymen in fourth- and fifth-century Gaul, describing wealthy landowners who became bishops. It appears that, after the collapse of central Roman authority, some owners of large estates in Gaul entered the Church, in order to legitimise their status and position. Many continued to live on their country estates, and turned part of their villa into a church serving the rural community. There are accounts of baptisteries within these villas, suggesting a vigorous Christian church, joined by new members.[46]

In Britain, many villas developed on or beside Iron Age settlements; such villas are likely to have been the homes of wealthy Britons, possibly of high status, who became Romanised. As they grew wealthy, they began to re-model their homes in a Roman style.[47] After the Romans withdrew, a villa often became the nucleus of a village, as the name implies, and if the villa's owners were Christian, its chapel or burial ground might become the site of a later church, as at Lullingstone (Kent) and Wells in Somerset.

Worship in house churches

What Christian ceremonies were enacted in the villas of rural Wessex? The two most important rituals were baptism and the eucharist: new candidates joined the community through baptism, and believers deepened their union with God and one another by blessing the Father during their weekly communal meal, in which they shared a loaf and a common cup.[48] In the New Testament, this is described as taking place within the context of a family home. In Mark's gospel, perhaps written in about AD 64, Christ's followers ask him where to prepare their final Passover meal and are told to follow a man carrying a pitcher of water – a task usually assigned to female slaves. Jesus continues: 'Follow him, and say to the owner of the house which he enters, "the Master says, 'Where is the room, for me to eat the Passover with my disciples?'" He will show you a large upper room, furnished with couches, all prepared' (Mk 14. 14–15).[49]

ILLUS. 7. White marble *agape* table found near the *Asclepieion*, Ancient Corinth.

There are depictions of the Last Supper eaten reclining, as in a second-century fresco from the Roman catacomb of St Domitilla. Low semicircular tables around which participants reclined (known as *agape* tables, or *sigma* tables) were used for the eucharistic meal; they have also been found in cemeteries, where meals were eaten to commemorate the dead. There are three magnificent later examples of *agape* tables, dating from the sixth or seventh century, in the Archaeological Museum at Ancient Corinth, including one carved from white marble (illus. 7), found near the *Asclepieion*, the sanctuary dedicated to Asclepius, the god of healing. In secular society, a party of a dozen people could recline for a meal around such tables.

It is not known when full meals were abandoned by Christians, in favour of a symbolic rite, in which 'eating' was reduced to a minimal amount of bread, and the meal became a ritual approximating to the one that we are familiar with today.[50] For the first three centuries, Christians gathered around a table for their weekly eucharistic meal, much as Jewish families celebrate the Sabbath at home. In the early third century, the Latin theologian Minucius Felix explained that, unlike the pagans, Christians had neither 'shrines nor altars'. In Roman and Greek society, altars were necessary to offer sacrifice to the gods, in contrast to the early Christian practice of blessing the Father as Jesus had done, in the context of a communal meal. However, by 306 the assembled bishops at Elvira in Spain were using earlier pagan concepts and language to describe how ritual specialists – the clergy – celebrated eucharist on behalf of the people. The common table came to be replaced by an altar of sacrifice.[51]

Baptism on Easter night

Baptism normally took place on Easter night, after intense preparation during the forty days of Lent. One might question whether rites practised in rural Wessex resembled those in the Near East, but early accounts written by pilgrims from Europe indicate a remarkable degree of similarity. The 'Pilgrimage of Egeria' (*Peregrinatio* or *Itinerarium Egeriae*), is a long letter written in about 380 by a woman from western Europe (perhaps Gaul or north-west Spain), addressed to her 'sisters' back at home; her 'sisters' may have been a convent of nuns or, equally, her local Christian community. Egeria spent three years in Jerusalem, where she describes the celebration of Holy Week in great detail. She notes that the Easter Vigil was observed 'in the same way that we do', with only one addition derived from the specific nature of the place: when the candidates emerged from the baptismal pool, they were led with the bishop to the Holy Sepulchre, where the bishop went inside the railings, and prayed with them.[52]

It is likely that the ceremonies witnessed by Egeria were conducted by St Cyril (*c.* 313–86), who was bishop of Jerusalem for nearly forty years. We are fortunate that twenty-three of the daily sermons that he preached at the Church of the Holy Sepulchre during Lent and Easter week have been preserved; they offer a unique insight into baptismal preparation in the fourth century. Cyril informs us that candidates often came for years before deciding to be enrolled for baptism:

> Brothers and sisters, welcome to the Church of God! Not that you are total strangers to the Church; some of you have been catechumens for years now, coming regularly to the first part of the liturgy, hearing the scripture readings, taking part in the prayers, and listening to the sermons. But you have put off making the total commitment to Jesus Christ which baptism demands. Now you have made up your minds. You have given in your names and been enrolled. Your hearts are full of hope and longing, and rightly so; God's word can never deceive you.[53]

The sessions were held each morning: this implies that both the candidates and their catechists gave up work for about two months, in order to focus on such a life-changing experience. Before the daily teaching, candidates were to go to the exorcists, to be prayed over and cleansed from whatever impeded them on their journey to God. After their exorcism, they were to read or pray quietly in groups, or discuss what they had been learning. Meanwhile, Cyril observed them and assessed their readiness for baptism.

The Easter ceremonies were designed to enable a radical transformation: the candidates fasted for three days, and were led into a darkened chamber where they renounced 'with their fists raised against the north-west, the kingdom of darkness, Satan and all his works'. The Holy Spirit was breathed onto them; they were exorcised, and their foreheads marked with chrism in the sign of a cross. They were then stripped naked, anointed with oil from head to foot and immersed in the water three times. After emerging from the water, they were dressed in white garments. During their first eucharist they received the blessed bread and wine, and a cup containing milk and honey. Anyone who had prepared well during Lent could not avoid a deep experience on every level of the psyche. Cyril describes the ceremony on Easter night:

> On that night, heaven will be opened to each one of you. You will go down into those wonderful Christ-bearing waters; you will receive the name of Christian, and the capacity for understanding and making your own the things of God. In the next step of the rite, you strip completely… So then, the deacon or deaconess takes you by the hand and leads you down into the water.
>
> One of the priests standing there lays his hand on your head and asks you: 'Do you believe in God, the almighty Father?' You reply: 'I do believe'. Then he gently pushes you down into the water, immersing your head. When you lift your head again, he asks you: 'Do you believe in Jesus Christ, his only Son, our Lord, who died for you and rose again?' You reply: 'I do believe', and he immerses you a second time. Finally he asks: 'Do you believe in the Holy Spirit?' For the third time you

> reply 'I do believe', and for the third time your head is plunged in the water. By these symbolic actions, you are buried and reborn.[54]

An early baptistery in Nazareth

While Bishop Cyril performed the Easter Vigil in the church of the Holy Sepulchre, excavations at Nazareth indicate that the Easter Vigil was also celebrated in house churches. The modern basilica of the Annunciation in Nazareth is built over an extensive early site, including a cave honoured as the home of Mary, its walls scratched with early graffiti prayers. Beneath the later chapel of St Joseph, storage cellars were enlarged in early Christian times by chipping away rock in order to create a cave into which candidates descended down rock steps for their exorcism and enlightenment.

They then climbed up the steps out of the cave and descended into a rectangular baptismal basin, its seven steps decorated with gold tesserae (see colour plate 2). They crossed a small channel, which was purely symbolic, for it does not empty anywhere. It may represent their crossing the River Jordan to enter the Promised Land of heaven. The candidates were guided by a deacon who represented Michael the Archangel – this is perhaps the origin of godparents in our baptismal ceremony today.

At the far end of the baptismal pool, a hollow is carved out, which could be filled with water brought from a nearby cistern. A small hole at the centre enabled the water to drain away. The candidate must have stood in the hollow, in order to be baptised.[55] The new Christian then ascended the seven steps. This was an exciting moment for the newly baptised person, who was taught that, at this point, the Holy Spirit would descend in power, in the same way that the Spirit descended on Jesus as he clambered out of the River Jordan. In Mark's gospel we read: 'And at once, as he was coming up out of the water, he saw the heavens torn apart, and the Spirit, like a dove, descending on him' (Mk 1. 10).

For early Christians, this was the beginning of a new life. It was aptly described a century before Cyril of Jerusalem by St Cyprian (*c.* 200–58), a pagan orator who converted to Christianity. Two years later, he was elected bishop of Carthage in North Africa. In a letter to a friend named Donatus, he wrote:

> At last I made up my mind to ask for baptism. I went down into those life-giving waters, and all the stains of my past were washed away. I committed my life to the Lord; he cleansed my heart and filled me with his Holy Spirit. I was born again, a new person. Then, in a most marvellous way, all my doubts cleared up. I could now see what had been hidden from me before. I found I could do things that had previously been impossible... By living according to my new birth in the Holy Spirit, I had already begun to share God's eternal life.[56]

St Patrick baptises converts

Their experience of risen life motivated Christians to share their newfound gift of faith, which Cyprian proceeded to do with great energy. In Britain two centuries later, St Patrick describes the thousands whom he baptised after his own conversion:

> It is proper to spread abroad the name of God,... so that even after my death I may leave something of value to the many thousands, my brothers and sisters, sons and daughters, I have baptised in the Lord... I have travelled everywhere for [God's] sake; I have gone amid many dangers, and to places beyond where anyone lived. I have gone where no one else had gone to baptise people, or ordain clergy, or complete people [in their faith].[57]

Since Patrick baptised such large numbers of people, it is unlikely that their preparation was as lengthy as that required by Bishop Cyril in Jerusalem. Like Cyril, Patrick describes his candidates radiant in their white robes and fragrant with the oil of chrism with which he had recently anointed them. We learn about them from Patrick's second surviving work, a short letter to the soldiers of a tyrant named Coroticus, a leader of British warriors, of uncertain date, who lived by slave-trading perhaps in north-east Ireland, or Ceredigion in south-west Wales or Strathclyde in western Scotland.

The aim of the letter was to obtain the release of Christians who had been sold into slavery to the Picts by Irish pagans. In his *Epistola*, Patrick describes the cruel murder of some of his 'anointed neophytes, still wearing their white baptismal garments, and with the fragrance of the chrism on their foreheads still about them', and laments the death of his 'radiant brothers and sons... to whom I have given birth in Christ'.[58]

Various types of early Christian communities

While we are familiar with later Benedictine-style monasteries, it is more difficult for us to imagine life in earlier Christian communities that were not monastic, and they are relatively undocumented. St Patrick's account of his family home suggests that villa house churches might be owned by clergy families, who may have formed the core of a local Christian community. Some villas may have developed into monasteries; this is perhaps what happened at Llanilltud Fawr in the Vale of Glamorgan, where a famous monastery was built on the site of a villa. There were earlier models for this practice: in the late fourth century, at several points in his life, Augustine withdrew with his friends to various country estates, to spend time with them in prayer and study.

The boundary between monastic and non-monastic communities was also somewhat blurred: in the following centuries, celibate monks might live in monasteries alongside married clerics in minor orders, and a range of craftsmen and their families. Peter Hill subtitled his detailed account of the evolution of Whithorn in south-west Scotland 'the Excavation of a Monastic Town'.[59] It includes a sketch of the monastery as it might have appeared in about AD 700, when it resembled a village with a church at its centre, encircled by small dwellings surrounded with farmland.

In chapter two we shall focus on various models of church found in Somerset. In Wells, a Roman villa's mausoleum became the nucleus of a Saxon monastery; at Cannington, an extensive cemetery contains the shrine of a young woman who appears to have been a local saint: her tomb was a focus for other burials; iron ore and slag at Carhampton suggest a community where smiths and their families were engaged in smelting on an industrial scale. From the New Testament onwards, Christian communities evolved almost by chance. The author of the Acts of the Apostles recalls:

> All who shared the faith owned everything in common; they sold their goods and possessions and distributed the proceeds among themselves according to what each one needed. Each day, with one heart, they regularly went to the Temple, but met in their houses for the breaking of bread; they shared their food gladly and generously; they praised God and were looked up to by everyone. (Acts 2. 44–47)

Lullingstone villa house church

ILLUS. 8. Fourth-century figure praying in a house church chapel, Lullingstone villa, Kent; reconstruction from plaster fragments by David Neal.

The Roman villas at Frampton and Hinton St Mary were largely destroyed by farming, and we can only guess how their Christians inhabitants practised their faith. However, there are more substantial remains of a villa house church at Lullingstone in Kent near Eynford, 11 miles east of Croydon. A small yet elaborate villa was constructed here in the late first century AD. It was rebuilt by Christian owners in about AD 360, when it was decorated luxuriously with wall-paintings and mosaic floors. The owners blocked off three or four rooms to create a self-contained house church with its own access from outside. Earlier residents had converted the cellar beneath the church into a shrine to the local water spirits, for a niche still contains a painting of three female water deities; blue water flows from the breasts of the central figure and green reeds sprout from her hair.[60]

The newly converted family decorated the upper room over the cellar as a Christian chapel; fragments of its wall-plaster have been painstakingly pieced together. Along the west wall, separated by columns painted onto the plaster, were six painted figures, a third of life-size, their arms outstretched in prayer. Their rich, flowing tunics with pearl-edged stripes are those of fourth-century Roman nobility; they were perhaps portraits of the family who owned the villa. When the worshippers were no longer present, symbolically they were still at prayer in the chapel. A figure in an orange tunic striped with blue stands in front of a curtain, perhaps to indicate 'passing beyond the veil' into the next life (illus. 8).[61]

The praying figures faced a large painted *chi-rho* symbol of Christ on the east wall (illus. 9), encircled by a gold wreath that represents eternity. The Greek letters *alpha* and *omega* painted between the arms of the cross convey that Christ is the first and the last; he existed before time began and lives for ever. This powerful representation of Christ in heaven floats on a blue river of paradise; doves on either side represent human souls, as we find in the mosaics of Ravenna's baptisteries. In Lullingstone's chapel, when the worshippers faced east to celebrate the eucharist, they would gaze at this symbolic depiction of eternal life.

ILLUS. 9. Wall-painting of a *chi-rho* symbol of Christ in the chapel, Lullingstone villa, Kent; reconstruction from plaster fragments by David Neal.

The artist painted two more wreathed *chi-rho* symbols: one on the south wall and another in the anteroom. Fragments of possible glass lamps for use during services were found at the villa. Decorating the dining-room floor is a mosaic of Bellerophon slaying the Chimaera, like those in the Dorset villas. The evidence of later coins suggests that Lullingstone continued as a house church when the villa's domestic quarters were no longer in use, after they had been gutted by fire. The villa was abandoned by about AD 420. A mausoleum had been built in its grounds in the early fourth century: a solid vaulted tomb-chamber, surrounded by a wall. It housed the family's dead, and was subsequently incorporated into Lullingstone parish church in the late Saxon period.[62]

ILLUS. 10. Jug used for the liturgy, Nemea.

A rural Christian community in southern Greece

How do the house churches of Wessex compare with models of church nearer to the epicentre of Christianity? To answer this question, we shall examine a rural Christian community in the Peloponnese, at Nemea, 17 miles south-west of Corinth. Around the ancient sanctuary of Zeus at Nemea, the soil is yellow and dry, ideal for vineyards, which have been cultivated here from early times; they are famous for their full-bodied red wine. The first recorded pan-Hellenic Games at Nemea were held in 573 BC; a sacred way led

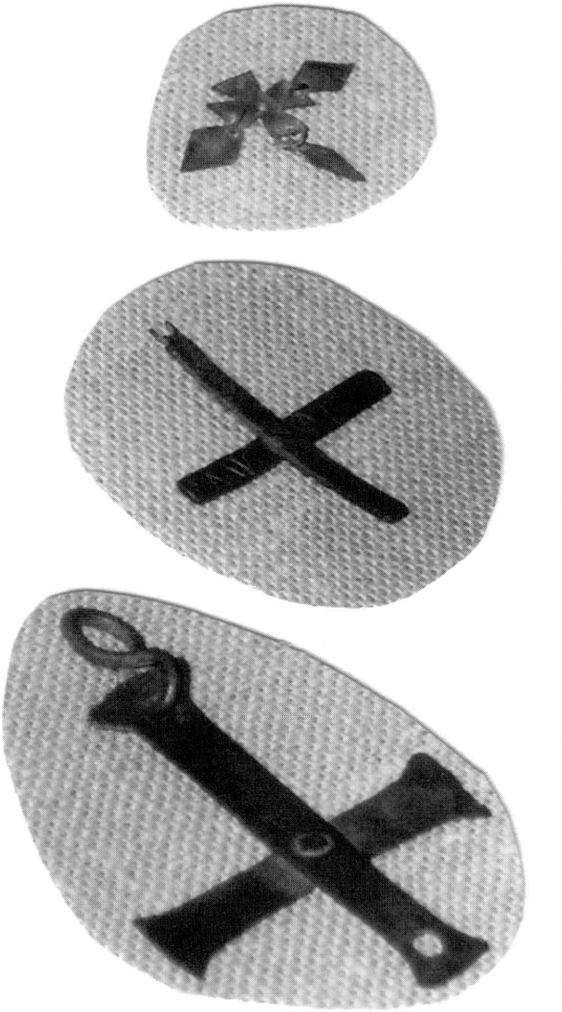

ILLUS. 11. Crosses found in Christian graves at Nemea. Top: silver cross with diamond-shaped pendants. Middle: bronze cross with suspension hole, pivot for closing and inscription. Bottom: bronze cross with suspension hook and pivot for closing.

to the stadium, which was built into the hillside 500 m away. After the enormous temple of Zeus fell into ruin, a small agricultural community lived in its shadow.

Meanwhile, Christianity spread to the region; there is a fifth-century basilica at nearby Kleonai, and another at the peak of Evangelista Hill beside a present-day transmission station, high above the sanctuary at Nemea. By this time, the settlement at Nemea was Christian; its families grew vegetables by digging rows of narrow, oblong trenches between the plants. The trenches were then filled with water, which soaked into the ground alongside the vegetables, a technique still employed in Greece. Unfortunately, the use of this method of farming has destroyed much of the archaeological evidence at Nemea.[63]

Grain provided a basic part of the diet of its inhabitants; fragments of two disc-shaped grinding stones were found, and a eucharistic bread stamp made of terracotta, which indicates that some of the bread was set aside for use in worship. The bread stamp is circular, and engraved with a superimposed cross and a *chi* symbol for Christ. Today, nuns make altar breads by stamping them in a similar way. A jug was found, impressed with the same symbol: it may have contained wine or blessed oil for the liturgy (illus. 10).

These Christian artefacts can be seen in the museum at Nemea, together with numerous everyday implements, such as sickles, bronze pruning hooks and spindle hooks. Oil lamps were found, many of them decorated with Christian symbols. A basilica was erected; the size of the community can be estimated from the fact that over 200 Christian graves were excavated, north-west and south-west of the basilica. A number of the dead wore a cross round their neck. The crosses are of various designs: they remind us that the residents were not monks who wore identical clothing – they were individual laymen and women (illus. 11).

Nemea's basilica

The Christian community erected their basilica beside a ruined bath house, whose water flowed into the River Nemea, which runs alongside it. The basilica was small, but substantial nevertheless. Its ruins stood to a considerable height when it was excavated in 1924, but unfortunately the archaeologists, who were keen to uncover the classical Greek remains surrounding it, removed much of the basilica's stone walls to construct a protective shed for their finds.

The nave of the church was separated from its north and south aisles by a row of columns, probably five or six on each side, made of drums recycled from the temple of Zeus that dominates the site. In the church, the columns rested on a raised stylobate, or row of column bases with a low parapet; these prevented movement between the nave, where the clergy processed to the sanctuary, and the aisles in which the people stood.[64]

At the eastern end, the sanctuary contained the altar and, against the back wall, the *synthronon*, which was a long, semicircular throne for officiating clergy. The altar may have been a plain rectangular marble table, supported on four legs or small columns. The sanctuary was separated from the nave by a low wall or screen, decorated with patterns incorporating the cross and other Christian motifs, executed in relief or perforated latticework.

Baptism at Nemea

Soon after the church was built, a baptistery was added on its north side: this was dated by coins to the reign of Theodosius II (402–50) or later. It is rectangular, with a circular pool at the centre of its inner chamber. The baptismal pool (illus. 12) is a shallow stepped concrete basin, sunk into the ground. It was originally paved with white marble from a recycled ritual dining table; the four broken pieces of the *agape* table had been turned upside-down. The candidate stood in the pool, while the bishop poured water over his or her head from a small vessel.[65]

ILLUS. 12. Baptismal pool when first excavated, Nemea.

A narrow room between the baptistery and the church may have been the *chrismarion*. As its name suggests, here candidates were chrismated, or anointed with blessed olive oil, and signed with the cross. The word chrism derives from Christ, whose name means 'the Anointed One'. At baptism, the bishop anointed each candidate as a sign that they were now united with Christ. A row of small square rooms adjoining the basilica's south wall may have served as the *diakónikon*, or sacristy, one of whose functions was to house the community's offerings. In the fifth and sixth centuries, members of the congregation brought offerings of grain, olive oil and wool, as well as bread and wine for the eucharist. A large sixth-century house south-west of the church may have provided accommodation for its clergy; a fifth piece of the broken-up *agape* table was found here. The residence was built, occupied and abandoned over a few decades in the mid- and second half of the sixth century.[66]

Parallels between Christians of Nemea and Wessex

It is instructive to consider the parallels between the people of Nemea and those of the house churches in rural Wessex. Like those of Wessex, the inhabitants of Nemea were a Christian community: the central element of their common life was their shared worship. They invested time and energy in creating a significant space for worship – in this case a small basilica and a baptistery. As in the Wessex villas that are surrounded by farmland, faith was integrated into normal agricultural life at Nemea, where a wide variety of objects used in daily life were found as well as vessels and other objects marked out for use in worship, as we have seen. The inhabitants of Nemea formed quite a large community, more like a village than a villa. They were not monastic: the burials indicate normal families. They were served by a group of clergy, to judge from the layout of the residential quarters.

The Latin word for God, *Deus*, derives from that of the Greek king of the gods, Zeus. The inhabitants of Nemea did not consider their pagan heritage as something to be avoided – they were content to live beside the ruins of an enormous temple dedicated to Zeus. Perhaps their attitude to the Greek gods was comparable with that of the Wessex villa owners, whose mosaic floors were decorated with mythological scenes. Early Christian theologians disagreed over the value of their pagan past. This can be seen in their attitude to Asclepius, whose cult lasted long into the Christian era. Early Christian theologians compared his healing work with that of Christ. To purists such as Justin of Alexandria, writing in about AD 150, Asclepius came from the devil; to other theologians, like Clement of Alexandria (*c.* 150–*c.* 215), Asclepius was a forerunner of Christ the healer, sent to the pagans to prepare them for Christianity.[67]

Leaders in early Christian communities

Leadership in the first Christian communities was startlingly countercultural. Even today, we view leadership in the early Church through the lens of authority and power, yet Jesus challenged his friends: 'Who is greater, the one who reclines at the table, or the one who serves? Is it not the one who reclines at the table? But I am among you as the one who serves' (Lk. 22. 27).[68] St Paul outlines the abolition of hierarchy: 'All baptised in Christ, you have all clothed yourselves in Christ, and there are no more distinctions between Jew and Greek, slave and free, male and female' (Gal. 3. 27–28).

We can easily look for Christian leadership in the wrong place: a bishop (*episkopos*) was simply an overseer, or superintendent of the congregation; the title was used interchangeably with that of presbyter (*presbuteros*). Jerome observed: 'Indeed with the ancients these names were synonymous, one [*episkopos*] alluding to the office, the other [*presbuteros*] to the [senior] age of the clergy'.[69] We might translate *presbuteros* as 'elder', though not as 'priest' since, at this early date, it was understood that Christ was the one High Priest and all Christians shared in his priesthood.

Before we focus on early Christian leadership in south-west Britain, it will be helpful to examine how it is described in early writings from the Syriac-speaking Jewish-Christian communities of Syria and Mesopotamia. The Church in this region arose from the preaching of the first followers of Jesus who brought with them a radical expectancy of the coming of the Lord. Wandering apostles went like the seventy-two (Lk. 10. 1) from village to village, preaching the Good News, following Jesus who had nowhere to lay his head (Lk. 9. 58). In early Syria, celibacy first developed as an outcome of baptism: rebirth in the Spirit demanded a radical uprooting from previous origins and ties, and so for these Syrian Christians, poverty, asceticism and celibacy were seen to be natural.[70]

The Syrian 'single ones'

The history of celibacy is complex, and a voluntary single lifestyle was considered heretical by some. However, in the Christian communities of Syria, while marriage was upheld as a positive good, single people came to be regarded as the core of the Church. Known as the 'single ones', they might vow singleness either in virginity or in marriage, which entailed abstinence from sexual intercourse.[71] Why was celibacy valued by early Syrian Christians? One reason was their intense awareness of Jesus as life-giver. They called Jesus 'Saviour', as did the Greeks, but preferred to call him 'Life-giver'. In the Syrian scriptures 'your faith has saved you' (Mt. 9. 22) appears as 'your faith has made you alive'. 'To you is born this day the Saviour' (Lk. 2. 11) is rendered 'To you is born this day the One who makes you alive'.[72]

The Greek and Pauline concept of dying to sin and rising with Christ in baptism is not found in Syria for the first four centuries. There is a crucial difference between the negative approach of being rescued or saved from something and the positive approach of receiving freely bestowed life. In the Syriac New Testament, the equivalent of the Greek verbs meaning 'to deliver', 'to redeem', 'to save' are not used; instead, they are rendered in Syriac by the terms 'to give life', 'to make alive', 'to cause to live'. Baptism meant going down into the Jordan with Christ and being filled, like him, with the Spirit of God.[73]

The 'single ones' followed the 'Bestower of Life', the 'One who causes to live' by turning away from all that was merely human. In their theology, Jesus had pronounced these things as dead when he declared, 'Leave the dead to bury their dead' (Lk. 9. 60). In their great love, these Syrian Christians felt called to uproot themselves from what constituted the essence of their humanity, to become newly rooted in the lifegiving Spirit of Jesus.[74] One might justifiably ask whether such a spirituality is healthy, but it was typical of one strand of early Christianity.

The letters of Pseudo-Clement

Two letters of Pseudo-Clement written in the third century describe how men and women in Syria lived out this theology. One is an exhortation to virgins and the other describes where wandering ascetics are to sleep. The first letter opens:

> To virgins [male and female], blessed and holy in God, who have dedicated themselves to preserve virginity for the sake of the kingdom, greetings! Any men or women who have truly and sincerely dedicated themselves to virginity are obliged to accommodate themselves to the kingdom of heaven in all things ... Do battle with the holy, tame the appetites of the flesh ... [and so] remain in Christ Jesus, strengthened by his teaching and divine eucharist.[75]

Pseudo-Clement then describes their work:

> Some go and enter the home of other virgins for the sake of making a visit [i.e. to encourage them], reading the scriptures, exorcism or teaching, by which they show their concern for them ... It is appropriate and useful to visit orphans and widows, especially those poor and burdened with children ... It is honourable and glorious to visit brothers and sisters in Christ who are vexed with evil spirits and to apply exorcism on their behalf, pouring forth an acceptable prayer to God ... Let us go to a brother or sister who is sick, in order to visit them ... It is glorious in the eyes of God and of people to remember the poor, to love our brothers and strangers.[76]

The author thus describes a full life of prayer and pastoral care undertaken by the 'single ones' in the early third century.

St Ephrem the deacon

The great Syrian writers of the fourth century continue to describe the life of the 'single ones'. Chief among the Syrian theologians and hymn-writers was Ephrem (*c.* 306–73), who was a deacon (*diakonos* means 'servant'), and not a presbyter or bishop. Ephrem used the same word for Christ, the 'One', and for the 'single ones' who followed him. The term means a celibate person involved in the daily life of the Church, rather than a solitary who lives alone in a cave or in the desert. Ephrem describes how the Holy Spirit hovers like a mother bird over the waters of baptism and brings forth 'virgins and rulers, pure ones and intercessors'. He continues:

> See, people being baptised and becoming
> virgins and consecrated ones,
> having gone down, been baptised and put on
> that single Only One [Christ].
> See, the many rush at him [or her, i.e. the virgin]
> with kinsfolk, offspring and riches.
> For whoever is baptised and puts on
> the Only One, the Lord of many,
> occupies the place of many,
> for Christ becomes their treasure.

This text appears in Ephrem's eighth Hymn for the Feast of the Epiphany;[77] in the Eastern Churches, baptism often took place on this feast. The poem is part of Ephrem's exhortation to candidates for ascetical vows at baptism. At this time it was common for people to become 'virgins and consecrated ones' at baptism. They entered a special relationship with Christ, which enabled them to represent the 'many' and to intercede for 'the many who rush at them'.[78]

Marriage and singleness

Although the Syrian theologians affirmed the goodness of marriage, they were more enthusiastic about the single state to which they were committed. The 'single ones' were so named because they had left their family and not married, because they were single-minded in their commitment to Christ and because they had put on Christ, the 'Only One', in order to possess him as their treasure. They were also called 'the standing ones' because they stood in self-commitment at baptism, and also stood in union with the ceaseless worship of the heavenly 'watchers' or angels. By the fourth century these 'sons and daughters of the covenant' were a recognisable body within the Church, although they were not yet called monks and nuns. Some lived at home while others lived in small groups, but not isolated from their local community.[79]

The wandering ascetics mentioned by Pseudo-Clement were sometimes called 'the praying people'. They were the forerunners of the wandering preachers (or *gyrovagi*, a derogatory Late Latin term which means 'wandering in circles') mentioned with disapproval in the Rule of Benedict,[80] and of the later medieval preaching friars established by Dominic and Francis of Assisi. The life of consecrated celibacy soon spread westwards through the Christian lands, facilitated by the common languages of Greek and Latin.

Married couples also became wandering preachers: St Paul names a number of them as his colleagues. He also describes married couples who led house churches: 'Aquila and Prisca, with the church that meets at their house, send you their warmest wishes in the Lord' (1 Cor. 16. 19). The inhabitants of Nemea and of the villa house churches in Wessex are likely to have been married, and some of them ordained. Presbyters normally married, and in early British monasteries married clerics in minor orders (or *manaig*) lived alongside celibate monks. As late as the ninth century, there were *clas* communities in Wales: monasteries of non-celibate clerics, although other communities were reorganised and restricted to celibate monks who followed a more structured Rule, such as that of Benedict or Augustine.[81]

The Greek term for 'single one' was *monachos*, or monk, and early descriptions of monks describe them in a village setting. The first known reference to a monk is found in a secular document, an Egyptian papyrus dated to 324, which records how a *monachos* named Isaac and a *diakon* named Antoninus saved a man from death by assault.[82] Both Isaac and Antoninus were evidently known and respected in their local community.

The first chapter of the Rule of Benedict[83] describes an interesting variety of Christian vocations and lifestyles. It begins, 'There are evidently four kinds of monks': these include hermits, wandering preachers and others living in groups of two or three (termed *sarabaites*, a word of uncertain meaning). Benedict's strong words of disapproval for the latter two types of monk hints that they were common forms of vowed life in his day, that rivalled his preferred, fourth kind – those who lived in a monastery under an abbot.

All four models of Christian leadership will be focused upon in later chapters of this book. In chapter four, we shall examine the Life of Samson, a fifth-century monk who became in turn abbot, bishop and then hermit, before setting out with members of his family as a *peregrinus* (or 'wanderer'). His life is documented as he crossed Cornwall, en route from Wales to Brittany, where he became abbot of Dol.

St Patrick's varied roles

The *Confessio* of Patrick also demonstrates that different types of vocation were not mutually exclusive. Like Samson, Patrick knew a variety of lifestyles: he appears to have trained at a monastery in Gaul, for he writes, 'I was all set to go [to Britain], and wanted to go, for it is my homeland and where my family is – and [to] Gaul to visit the brethren and to see the face of my Lord's saints – God knows how much I wanted to do this'.[84] He tells us that he was a deacon and, by the time he writes the *Epistola*, Patrick relates that he is a bishop;[85] he was also a wandering preacher. Like others in the early Church, he was engaged in a variety of ministerial roles as he served his brothers and sisters.

As a sixteen-year-old, Patrick had been taken from his home, and sold into slavery in Ireland. It is likely that he had not yet been baptised, because he tells us it was while looking after his master's flocks in all weathers that he learnt to pray and came to experience God. He planned his escape after hearing God say: 'Well have you fasted! Soon you are to travel to your homeland'.[86] Years later, perhaps in mid-life, Patrick relates: 'I was again with my parents in Britain who welcomed me home as a son. They begged me in good faith after all my adversities to go nowhere else, nor ever leave them again'.[87] If he had learnt monastic life from monks in Gaul, his family may have hoped that their son could assume leadership of their house church.

But this was not to be. The situation changed dramatically when Patrick heard 'the voice of the Irish' inviting him to 'come again and walk among us'. With his father a deacon and his grandfather a priest, we can imagine the discussions that ensued as the extended family reclined on their couches in their rural villa, and the earnestness with which his parents prayed in the chapel of their house church as they discerned God's will and struggled with their grief at letting their son depart to follow his new vocation.

In the *Epistola*, Patrick describes his call to leave his home at the invitation of God's Spirit as follows, beginning with three dramatic rhetorical questions:

> Was it without God, or according to the flesh that I came to Ireland? Who forced me to come? I am one bound in the Spirit, so that I cannot see any of my relatives. Is it from within me that the holy mercy arises which I show towards this people – a people who once took me prisoner and destroyed the servants, male and female, of my father's estate? I was a free man according to the flesh, my father a decurion [a member of the local council, or senate], and I sold my status for the benefit of others. I am neither ashamed of this nor sorry, but thus I have arrived at this point: I am a servant in Christ to a foreign people for the ineffable glory of the eternal life which is in Christ Jesus our Lord.[88]

The *Confessio* of Patrick and his *Epistola*, or 'Address to the Soldiers of Coroticus', are the only surviving texts from early times that allow us to glimpse the life of a British Christian family in a villa house church. The paradox of such a Roman villa is that it existed for the honour of God. Patrick would have been its natural leader when his parents were no longer able to fulfil this role but, following God's call, he left it behind, to preach and die in a foreign land.

Notes

1 David Petts, *Christianity in Roman Britain* (Stroud: Tempus, 2003).

2 *Ibid.*, pp. 62–65.

3 See Jocelyn Toynbee, 'Pagan Motifs and Practices in Christian Art and Ritual', in *Christianity in Britain, 300–700*, ed. Maurice W. Barley and Richard P. Hanson (Leicester: Leicester University Press, 1968), pp. 108–86.

4 Petts, *Christianity*, p. 82. Thirteen years later, Petts presented a less positive view of the surviving evidence in his chapter, 'The Evidence for Christianity in Fourth-Century Britain', in *The Oxford Handbook of Roman Britain*, ed. Martin Millet, Louise Revell and Alison Moore (Oxford: Oxford University Press, 2016), pp. 77–87.

5 Dominic Perring, 'Gnosticism in Fourth-Century Britain: The Frampton Mosaics Reconsidered', *Britannia – A Journal of Romano-British and Kindred Studies*, 34 (2003), pp. 97–127.

6 See Ignazio Mancini, *Archaeological Discoveries Relative to the Judeo-Christians* (Jerusalem: Franciscan Printing Press, 1984); Bellarmino Bagatti, *Ancient Christian Villages of Judaea and the Negev* (Jerusalem: Franciscan Printing Press, 2002); Bagatti, *Ancient Christian Villages of Galilee*, (Jerusalem: Franciscan Printing Press, 2003).

7 Bagatti, *Ancient Christian Villages of Galilee*, pp. 192–93.

8 See Guy D.R. Sanders, 'Problems in Interpreting Rural and Urban Settlement in Southern Greece, AD 365–700', in *Landscapes of Change: Rural Evolutions in Late Antiquity and the Early Middle Ages*, ed. Neil Christie (Aldershot: Ashgate, 2004), ch. 5, pp. 216–22; G.D.R. Sanders, 'Archaeological Evidence for Early Christianity in Corinth', in *Urban Religion in Corinth: Interdisciplinary Approaches*, ed. Daniel Schowalter and Steven Friesen, Harvard Theological Studies, 53 (2005), ch. 16, pp. 419–42. See also William Caraher, 'Church, Society and the Sacred in Early Christian Greece', PhD diss., Ohio State University, 2003; Rebecca Sweetman, 'The Christianization of the Peloponnese: The Topography and Function of Late Antique Churches', *Journal of Late Antiquity*, 3, no. 2 (Fall 2010), pp. 203–61.

9 Derwas J. Chitty, *The Desert a City: An Introduction to the Study of Egyptian and Palestinian Monasticism under the Christian Empire* (Oxford: Blackwell, 1966).

10 See Robert Murray, *Symbols of Church and Kingdom* (London: Bloomsbury, 2004); Gabriele Winkler, 'The Origins and Idiosyncrasies of the Earliest Form of Asceticism', in *The Continuing Quest for God*, ed. William Skudlarek (Collegeville, MN: Liturgical Press, 1982), pp. 9–43; Kathleen McVey, ed., *St Ephrem The Syrian, Selected Prose Works*, trans. Edward G. Mathews and Joseph P. Amar (Washington, DC: Catholic University of America Press, 1994), General Introduction, pp. 3–58.

11 Thomas O'Loughlin, *Saint Patrick: The Man and his Works* (London: SPCK, 1999), pp. 48–49.

12 Patrick, *Confessio* 27, in O'Loughlin, *Saint Patrick*, p. 69.

13 *Ibid.*, 1, p. 52.

14 *Ibid.*, 12–16, pp. 58–61.

15 *Ibid.*, 1–2, pp. 52–53.

16 For an interesting contribution to studies concerning Patrick's identity, see John T. Koch, 'The Early Chronology for St Patrick (*c.* 351–*c.* 428): Some New Ideas and Possibilities', in *Celtic Hagiography and Saints' Cults*, ed. Jane Cartwright (Cardiff: University of Wales Press, 2003), pp. 102–22. Koch starts from the premise that Patrick was a very unusual name in a Romano-British context.

17 Perring, 'Gnosticism', pp. 105, 109.

18 James Hall, *Dictionary of Subjects and Symbols in Art* (London: Murray, 1986), p. 105.

19 Toynbee, 'Pagan Motifs', p. 182.

20 Irenaeus of Lyons, *Against Heresies* (*Adversus haereses*), bk 3, ch. 11. 8, in *Ante-Nicene Fathers*, vol. 1 (Lexington, KY: Ex Fontibus, 2010).

21 Perring, 'Gnosticism', p. 113.

22 Charles Thomas, *Christianity in Roman Britain to AD 500* (London: Batsford, 1981), p. 182, following Kenneth S. Painter, 'The Roman Site at Hinton St Mary, Dorset', in *British Museum Quarterly*, 32 (1968), pp. 15–31. The mosaic will soon be returned to Dorset.

23 Toynbee, 'Pagan Motifs', pp. 180–86.

24 Hall, *Dictionary of Subjects*, p. 249. There are fine examples by Fra Angelico (*c.* 1387–1455), Sandro Botticelli (*c.* 1444–1510) and Pinturrichio (1454–1513).

25 Toynbee, 'Pagan Motifs', p. 185.

26 There are paintings of Christ as Orpheus taming creation with his grace-filled music in the Roman catacombs of Domatilla (third century) and of Marcellinus and Peter (early fourth century).

27 Perring, 'Gnosticism', pp. 119–21.

28 *Ibid.*, p. 122.

29 Perring, 'Gnosticism', p. 113.

30 St Augustine, *The City of God*, trans. Marcus Dodds (Peabody, MA: Hendrickson, 2009).
31 St Gregory the Great, *Moralium libri* 25. 8, Jacques-Paul Migne, *Patrologia Latina* (Paris: Imprimerie Catholique, 1841–49), vol. 76, col. 759.
32 Ludovico V. Geymonat, 'The Parma Baptistery and its Pictorial Program', PhD diss., Princetown University, NJ, 2006, pp. 9–10.
33 Bryn Walters, 'Chedworth: Roman Villa or Sanctuary?' in *ARA: The Bulletin of the Association for Roman Archaeology*, 9 (Summer 2000), pp. 10–13.
34 *Ibid.*
35 Ann Woodward and Peter Leach, *The Uley Shrines: Excavation of a Ritual Complex on West Hill, Uley, Gloucestershire, 1977–9* (London: English Heritage, 1993), pp. 32, 303, 305.
36 *Ibid.*, pp. 310, 314–16.
37 *Ibid.*, p. 333.
38 *Ibid.*, pp. 318, 322. See pp. 324–25 for a discussion of the use of portions of Mercury's cult statue around the church site.
39 *Ibid.*, pp. 321–22, 334–35.
40 *Ibid.*, pp. 322–23.
41 Carolyn Heighway, 'Not Angels but Anglicans – The Origins of the Christian Church in Gloucestershire', in *The Land of the Dobunni: A Series of Papers Relating to the Transformation of the Pagan, Pre-Roman, Tribal Lands into Christian, Anglo-Saxon Gloucestershire and Somerset*, ed. Martin Ecclestone, published jointly by the Committee for Archaeology in Gloucestershire and the Council for British Archaeology – South West (2003), p. 61.
42 Mark Corney, *The Roman Villa at Bradford on Avon: The Investigations of 2002* (Bradford on Avon: Ex Libris Press, 2002), p. 22.
43 Mark Corney, *The Roman Villa at Bradford on Avon: The Investigations of 2003* (Bradford on Avon: Ex Libris Press, 2003), 'The Roman Villa', p. 18.
44 *Ibid.*, p. 15.
45 Martin Valatin, personal communication, 11 July 2004.
46 Corney, *The Roman Villa 2003*, p. 19.
47 *Ibid.*, p. 8.
48 Thomas O'Loughlin, *The Eucharist: Origins and Contemporary Understandings* (London: Bloomsbury, 2015), pp. 84–88.
49 Quotations are from the *New Jerusalem Bible*, ed. Henry Wansbrough (London: DLT, 1985), unless otherwise stated.
50 Paul Bradshaw and Max Johnson, *The Origins of Feasts, Fasts and Seasons in Early Christianity* (London: SPCK, 2011), p. 25.
51 O'Loughlin, *The Eucharist*, pp. 98–100.
52 Egeria, *Itinerarium Egeriae*, 8. Vigil of Easter, f. 79. See Anne McGowan and Paul F. Bradshaw, *The Pilgrimage of Egeria: A New Translation of the* Itinerarium Egeriae *with Introduction and Commentary* (Collegeville, MN: Liturgical Press, 2018).
53 St Cyril of Jerusalem, *Catechesis Mystagogia*, Prologue, in Jacques-Paul Migne, *Patrologia Graeca* (Paris: Imprimerie Catholique, 1857–66), vol. 33; translated in Anne Field, *From Darkness to Light* (Ann Arbor, MI: Servant Books, 1978), pp. 19–20.
54 *Ibid.*
55 Jean Briand, *The Judeo-Christian Church of Nazareth* (Jerusalem: Franciscan Printing Press, 1982), pp. 36–64.

56 Cyprian of Carthage, *Letter to Donatus* 3–4, in Field, *From Darkness to Light*, pp. 190–92.
57 Patrick, *Confessio* 14, 51, in O'Loughlin, *Saint Patrick*, pp. 60, 83.
58 Patrick, *Letter to the Soldiers* 3, 16, in O'Loughlin, *Saint Patrick*, pp. 94, 102.
59 Peter Hill, *Whithorn and St Ninian; the Excavation of a Monastic Town, 1984–91* (Stroud: Sutton, 1998).
60 David Neal, *Lullingstone Roman Villa* (London: English Heritage, 1981), pp. 8, 10, 24.
61 *Ibid.*, p. 23.
62 Warwick Rodwell, *Wells Cathedral: Excavations and Structural Studies, 1978–93* (London: English Heritage, 2001), vol. 1, p. 46.
63 Stephen Miller, *Nemea: A Guide to the Site and Museum* (Athens: Ministry of Culture Archaeological Receipts Fund, 2004), pp. 106, 108.
64 *Ibid.*, pp. 100–01.
65 *Ibid.*, pp. 101–02, 104.
66 *Ibid.*, pp. 72, 106, 166.
67 In his *Dialogue*, Justin of Alexandria writes: 'And when he [the devil] brings forward Asclepius as the raiser of the dead and healer of other diseases, may I not say that in this matter likewise he has imitated the prophecies about Christ?' (*Dialogus* 69. 3). St Ambrose viewed Asclepius in a more positive light. He accepts that Asclepius raised the dead, but reminds his hearers that, unlike Christ, he could not raise himself. He writes: 'To Asclepius let them grant that he revived the dead, provided only that they admit that he himself did not escape being struck dead by lightning' (*De Virginibus* 3).
68 The Lockman Foundation, ed., *New American Standard Bible* (Cambridge: Cambridge University Press, 1977).
69 Jerome, *Letter* 69. 3, in *The Principle Works of St Jerome*, trans. William Henry Fremantle, in *Nicene and Post-Nicene Fathers*, 2nd series (Grand Rapids, MI: Eerdmans, 1952), vol. 6, p. 143.
70 Winkler, 'The Origins and Idiosyncrasies', pp. 9–43, esp. pp. 16–17.
71 Robert Murray, 'The Features of the Earliest Christian Asceticism', in *Christian Spirituality: Essays in honour of Gordon Rupp*, ed. P. Brooks (London: SCM, 1975), pp. 65–77.
72 Winkler, 'The Origins and Idiosyncrasies', pp. 16–17.
73 *Ibid.*
74 *Ibid.*
75 I am grateful to Professor Richard Price for translating these two letters from the Syriac for me.
76 *Ibid.*
77 St Ephrem, 'Hymns for the Feast of the Epiphany', no. 8, trans. A.E. Johnson, in *Nicene and Post-Nicene Fathers*, 2nd series (Grand Rapids, MI: Eerdmans, 1989), vol. 13, pp. 265–89.
78 Robert Murray, 'The Exhortation to Candidates for Ascetical Vows at Baptism in the Ancient Syriac Church', *New Testament Studies*, 21 (1975), p. 59.
79 Murray, *Symbols of Church and Kingdom*, p. 14.
80 St Benedict's *Rule for Monasteries*, ch. 1, in *RB 1980: The Rule of St Benedict in Latin and English with Notes*, trans. Timothy Fry (Collegeville, MN: Liturgical Press, 1980).

81 The word *clas* derives from the Latin *classis*, meaning a group, or gathering, of people. For *clas* communities, see Elizabeth Rees, *Celtic Saints of Wales* (Stroud: Fonthill, 2015), pp. 27, 28, 44, 151, 158.

82 The Petition of Aurelius Isidorus of Karanis, described in Edwil A. Judge, *Jerusalem and Athens: Cultural Transformation in Late Antiquity* (Tübingen: Mohr Siebeck, 2010), pp. 156–57.

83 Based on the *Rule of the Master*, which was compiled between AD 500 and 530, the *Rule of Benedict* was written between 530 and 560 in southern Italy. It is three times shorter than the *Rule of the Master*; chapter 1 is found in both rules. Benedict's Rule is also based on that of Augustine. See Adalbert de Vogüé, *A Critical Study of the Rule of Benedict*, vol. 1, *Overview*, trans. Colleen Maura McGrane OSB (New York: New City Press, 2013), pp. 10–13, 103–04, 114.

84 Patrick, *Confessio* 43, in O'Loughlin, *Saint Patrick*, p. 78.

85 Patrick, *Epistola* 1, in O'Loughlin, *Saint Patrick*, p. 93.

86 Patrick, *Confessio* 17, in O'Loughlin, *Saint Patrick*, p. 61.

87 Patrick, *Confessio* 23, in O'Loughlin, *Saint Patrick*, p. 66.

88 Patrick, *Epistola* 10, in O'Loughlin, *Saint Patrick*, pp. 98–99.

CHAPTER 2

Roman Christian sites in central Somerset

It is a striking fact that most of the early Christian sites of Somerset originate within a Roman context. This is in marked contrast to Somerset's south-western neighbours, Devon and Cornwall: in Devon there are few pre-Saxon sites, while in Cornwall there are many pre-Saxon sites, but few that developed from a Roman context. Somerset is not far from the great Celtic monasteries of south Wales across the Bristol Channel, and one might expect the Welsh monks to have had some impact upon the development of Christianity in Somerset, but little evidence survives to suggest this.

In Somerset, most evidence of early Christians is found in rural settings, particularly on the sites of Roman villas. A few early church sites in high places, such as Lamyatt Beacon and Brean Down, replaced isolated Roman temples. The only significant Roman town that offers some evidence of early Christianity

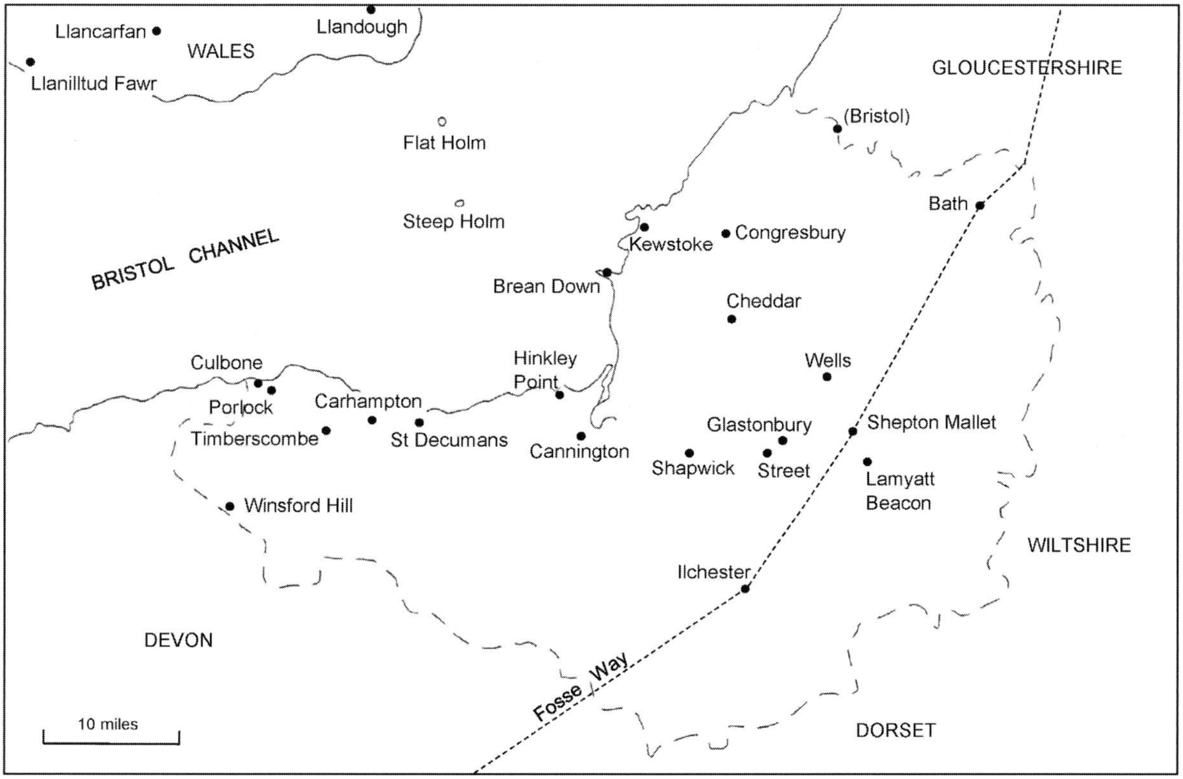

ILLUS. 13. Early Christian sites in Somerset.

is Bath, although the evolution from a Roman healing sanctuary to a Saxon monastery is still unclear. There is further evidence of Christianity in two small towns, Ilchester and Shepton Mallet, both on the Fosse Way.

In the mid-fourth century, Somerset was calm and relatively prosperous. Along with other cults, Christianity had been brought to the area by the movement of peoples in the Roman empire, chiefly through trade and the army. The Fosse Way, running from Lincoln to Exeter, bisects Somerset from the north-east to the south-west (illus. 13). There were subsidiary Roman roads leading to the port of Combwich and to the mines at Charterhouse, where silver was extracted from lead and used to pay the Roman army.

The many Roman villas in the region grew into villages. Some villas contained house churches, and their Romano-British owners and those who joined them in worship handed on the faith through their families. As we shall see, villas at Cheddar and Wells provide possible examples of this. The large Christian cemeteries on the various emerging Saxon estates in Somerset suggest a sizeable Christian population already working the land.

Bath, a pagan healing sanctuary

Our earliest evidence for Christianity in Somerset is found in Roman Bath, which was by then a famous healing sanctuary. The hot spring of mineral water in the deep valley of the River Avon, now at the centre of Bath, had long been a subject of wonder to ancient people. It emerged into a marshy pool, overhung

ILLUS. 14. Model of the Roman baths and temples at Bath in the second century AD.

ILLUS. 15. A Roman channel conveys steaming water from the reservoir to the great bath.

with steam on winter days. Mesolithic flint blades found in the hot spring indicate that in about 5000 BC nomadic bands of food-gatherers were attracted to the hot water. By the first century BC, this area was ruled by the Celtic tribe of the Dobunni, who believed that the spring was sacred to the goddess Sulis. A causeway of gravel and boulders was built out across the mud, and offerings of coins were thrown into the pool.[1]

In AD 44 the holy site was swallowed up in the heavily patrolled Roman military zone beside the Fosse Way. In about AD 60, the Roman authorities turned the native sanctuary of Sulis into a magnificent healing shrine (illus. 14); they enclosed the spring within a massive reservoir, lined with sheets of lead from the Mendips, and made the ground stable with oak piles. They quarried limestone from the Downs overlooking the site, to build a complex of baths and temples.[2] A channel conveyed steaming water from the reservoir containing the spring to the great bath (illus. 15).

Bath was known as *Aquae Sulis* ('The Waters of Sulis'); pilgrims came from France, Spain and Germany. They equated Sulis with the Roman goddess Minerva. Such conflation was common in Roman provinces: it appeased native feeling, made obscure local cults intelligible to visitors and reassured those who believed in the classical pantheon. Fourth-century pilgrims to the wondrous hot springs and temple of Sulis Minerva followed the custom of the time by writing prayers to the goddess on small, rolled-up sheets of lead, and some were thrown into the healing waters. The curse in the illustration was written by or for a supplicant named Annianus, who was angry because someone had stolen six silver coins from his purse. He wanted Sulis to recover his money from this pickpocket, 'whether man or woman, boy or girl, slave or free, pagan or Christian' and listed 18 suspects (illus. 16).[3] This is a unique reference to the presence of Christians in the community.

The inner precinct of the great temple of Sulis Minerva was resurfaced many times. In the late fourth century, part of the portico to the great pool had been converted into a small room, which may have served as a shrine. In the fifth century, timber structures were built against the walls of the portico. The temple of Sulis was now in a dilapidated state; repairs continued into the early fifth century, using slabs from the temple pediment, including the impressive relief of the Gorgon's head. The upper part of the building containing the sacred pool was not demolished until the sixth or even the seventh century.[4]

Early Christian Bath

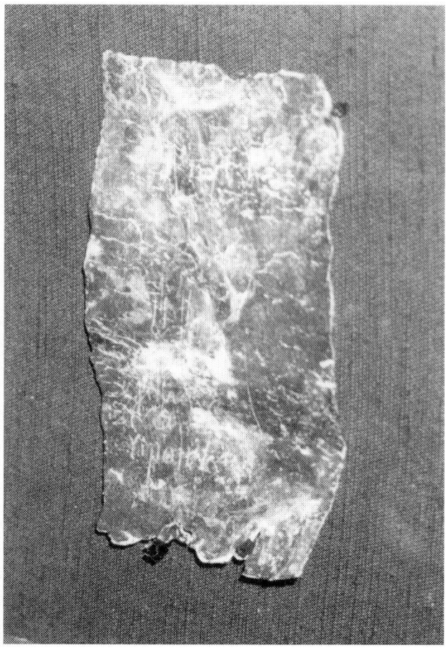

ILLUS. 16. Roman curse on a tiny sheet of lead, Bath.

In 2000, excavations elsewhere in Bath revealed the graves of a man and woman who may have been Christian. Two late fourth-century burials were set against the wall of an imposing yet decaying Roman town house with colonnades, beside Walcot Street, the busy road at the north end of Bath, leading eastwards towards London. In one grave was the first lead coffin to be found in Bath; it contained the body of a man aged about forty-five, possibly a wealthy trader. In the other grave was the wooden coffin of a woman, aged around thirty, of slightly lower rank. The absence of grave goods and the east–west orientation of the graves suggest that these were fourth-century Christians living at the end of the Roman occupation of Bath.[5]

From AD 367 onwards, barbarians attacked Britain. Villas were destroyed and their inhabitants thrown down wells; people fled from the cities. In Bath, the temple and the baths became increasingly derelict. Periodic flooding of the River Avon in the fourth century caused the drainage system to break down, and gradually the water rose until by the fifth century black mud covered everything. Yet the spring continued to flow, and the shrine continued to be revered. In 675, Osric, King of the Hwicce, a sub-kingdom of Mercia, granted land to Abbess Berta to establish a monastery of Frankish nuns at the centre of Bath, immediately to the east of the temple. The convent may have replaced the Roman temple, reusing its stones.[6] In 757–58 we hear of land being made over to the monks of St Peter's Church. It is likely that these two communities lived close to the spring, since Saxon burials have been found above the east end of the Roman baths, just north of the spring.[7] The earliest Saxon name for Bath was *Hat Bathu*, or 'Hot Baths'.[8]

A poem survives, an elegy perhaps written by a monk in the adjacent Saxon monastery, which appears to describe the ruined Roman baths. He begins by depicting their destruction:

> Splendid this rampart is, though fate destroyed it,
> the city buildings fell apart, the works
> of giants crumble. Tumbled are the towers,
> ruined the roofs, and broken the barred gate,
> frost in the plaster, all the ceilings gape,
> torn and collapsed and eaten up by age...[9]

The poet recalls their former glory:

> Resolute masons, skilled in rounded building,
> wondrously linked the framework with iron bonds.
> The public halls were bright, the lofty gables,
> bath-houses many; great the cheerful noise,
> and many mead-halls filled with human pleasures,
> till mighty fate brought change upon it all...

> ... And so these halls
> are empty, and this red curved roof now sheds
> its tiles, decay has brought it to the ground...[10]

Finally, he describes the hot stream, the round pool and the baths:

> Stone buildings stood, and the hot stream cast forth
> wide sprays of water, which a wall enclosed
> in its bright compass, where convenient
> stood hot baths ready for them at the centre.
> Hot streams poured forth over the clear grey stone,
> to the round pool and down into the baths...[11]

Bath's famous monastery

The monastery flourished: by 781 it was described as 'most famous'. The earliest charter from Bath, issued in 796,[12] exists in two versions of which one describes it as 'the famous minster' and the other 'the famous *vill* (or "town")'; at this time Bath appears to have been both a monastery and a town. There was a royal assembly at Bath in 796 in the reign of King Ecgfrith. In 794, Charlemagne had moved close to the hot springs of Aachen, where his great stone palace was being built. This may have inspired King Ecgfrith to imitate the emperor in the town of Bath, with its own hot springs and monumental ruins. A charter dated 864 (S 120) describes Bath as 'that famous town (*urbs*) which is called "at the hot baths"'.[13]

King Edgar (*c.* 943–75) ascended the throne in 959; fourteen years later he was crowned King of England in Bath abbey, together with his consort, Queen Ælfthryth. The ceremony was devised by Dunstan who was then archbishop of Canterbury; it forms the basis of today's coronation rite. In the twelfth century, the Norman bishop John of Tours built a fine new abbey on the site. The monastic infirmary was constructed above the temple precinct north of the spring, and the Roman walls of the hall that once enclosed the spring were used to create a new bath, fed by the hot spring.[14] Medieval medicine encouraged bathing in hot water for gout, palsy, colic and leprosy (a term for any skin complaint).[15] A monastery at a healing shrine reminds us of a similar development in south-west Scotland at Whithorn, in Galloway, at the opposite end of Britain.[16]

Ilchester: a small town with a large Christian population

There was another Roman town at Ilchester, also on the Fosse Way, 30 miles south-west of Bath. If there was a Roman bishop in Somerset, he is likely to have lived either in Bath or perhaps Ilchester, on account of its location on the Fosse Way and the size of its Christian cemetery.[17] Ilchester developed from a short-lived Roman fort, which was built just to the north of a large Iron Age settlement established by a Celtic tribal group, the Durotriges.

Ilchester is at the lowest crossing-point of the River Yeo, a common river name in Somerset which means 'flowing water', as opposed to the water of rhynes or drainage ditches; it is a dialect form of the Old English for 'river'.[18] The fort may have existed for no more than a decade; by the end of the first century, it had become a thriving market town, though one of the smallest in Britain. It reached the height of its prosperity in the mid-fourth century, with perhaps 2,000 or 3,000 inhabitants. It lay within a wealthy region, surrounded by villas and their estates.[19]

There were a number of cemeteries on its outskirts; beyond the boundary of the town, a large one on the north bank of the River Yeo was probably Christian, with at least 1,500 burials oriented east to west. Many bodies were buried in shrouds or wooden coffins, but some of the town's wealthier inhabitants could afford lead or stone coffins. Some graves contained late fourth-century coins from the reign of Theodosius (379–95); later burials were cut into these earlier graves, which suggests continuing Christian activity.[20]

The large number of burials in the cemetery suggests a flourishing and well-organised church; this was a stable worshipping community, lasting for several generations at least. The skeleton of a woman who was buried in the Roman cemetery can be seen in the small museum in Ilchester High Street. She was aged about forty, and bore signs of osteoma, a bone tumour in the skull.[21] The woman was wealthy, since she rests in a lead coffin, although the family were careful with their money, since the coffin had been recycled.

During the fifth century, Ilchester gradually ceased to function as a town on the Roman model; it became part of the Saxon kingdom of Wessex in the seventh century. The Roman cemetery continued in use after the Romans departed, but fell into disuse in the Anglo-Saxon period.[22] To the north of the cemetery, the church at Northover is built on a small outcrop (illus. 17); it would have dominated the low-lying land alongside the river. It appears to have become a Saxon minster dedicated to St Andrew, perhaps with a community of clerics.

The word 'minster' is a broad term, deriving from the Latin *monasterium*; its meaning varies according to its context. The minster at Northover was well endowed with land, although the church and its estate were controlled by a Saxon landowner, Brictric, who held the property from Glastonbury abbey. The revived Roman town of Ilchester came to be known as Givelcestre. A reference in Domesday Book (1086) to St Andrew's as the church of Givelcestre indicates that it served not only the population north of the river, but also of Ilchester itself.[23]

Shepton Mallet, a Roman garrison town

Shepton Mallet lies beside the Fosse Way, almost midway between Bath and Ilchester. In 1990, excavation uncovered a small Roman town here which was perhaps a *vicus*, or garrison town, that developed to service an as yet undiscovered fort. Within the town were three small cemeteries, the largest of which was used by the local Christian community. Here, seventeen bodies were buried

ILLUS. 17 *(opposite)*. St Andrew's church on an outcrop, Northover, Ilchester.

facing east, mainly in wooden coffins set into rock-cut graves, within a ditched enclosure. A silver-alloy pendant in the form of a cross was found here, although it is considered a forgery by some (though not by all) archaeologists. At its centre is a disc on which a late form of the *chi-rho* monogram has been crudely punched. A loop at the end of the pendant enabled its owner to hang it from a chain round his neck. If genuine, its style would date it to soon after AD 400.[24]

The occupants of the other two cemeteries appear to have been pagan, buried prone, oriented north–south, with some bodies decapitated. Unlike Christian graves, these included coins, animal remains, nails from hobnailed boots and pottery vessels, suggestive of pagan burial rites; two were radiocarbon dated to the fifth or even sixth centuries.[25] This suggests that pagans coexisted with Christians at a late date: evidence from cemeteries in various parts of Britain suggests that pagan burial practices, and therefore, presumably, beliefs, persisted into the eighth century.[26] This is because the Saxons, who conquered large areas of Britain, were pagan, so much of the country had to be re-converted to Christianity.

A temple and a church on Lamyatt Beacon

Four miles south of Shepton Mallet, a Romano-British temple on Creech Hill, a wooded section of Lamyatt Beacon, was excavated by Roger Leech in 1973. It was constructed in the late third century AD and continued in use until the early fifth century. The temple was built of mortared stone, and paved inside, with limestone roof slates. There were two annexes on its eastern side and a sunken room to the south. In about AD 300 a road was constructed to connect the temple with the Fosse Way. Shallow niches (*aediculae*) built into the temple's inner walls contained figures carved in relief, and a tall statue, larger than life, stood either inside the temple or on a podium against its east side; it may have depicted the god Mars.[27]

Numerous votive offerings were found, including miniature arrows and spears appropriate to the god of war, small pots, beads and a brooch. Nine antlers were buried in shallow pits, and other antlers had been excavated previously; this suggests that Mars was here conflated with a British horned god, perhaps Cernunnos.[28] In a letter written in the 680s, Aldhelm, then abbot of Malmesbury, described the worship of stags at pagan sites; he also recounts how he has established churches and study-houses in their place, alluding to the foundations that he made at Frome (Somerset) and Bradford on Avon (Wiltshire), before becoming bishop of Sherborne (Dorset). He rejoices that

> where once the crude pillars (*ermula cruda*) of the … foul snake and the stag were worshipped with coarse stupidity in profane shrines (*fana profana*), in their place dwellings for students, not to mention holy houses for prayer, are constructed skilfully by the talents of architects.[29]

This suggests that a substantial re-conversion from paganism was taking place. Pope Gregory the Great's decision to send a group of missionaries to Britain in 596, under the leadership of Augustine, the prior of Gregory's monastery in Rome, to convert the Saxons, formed another part of this process. The last of Augustine's missionary group died in 653, some thirty years before Aldhelm's letter.

A possible women's monastery at Lamyatt

Just to the north of Lamyatt's temple, a small rectangular Christian church was later built, within a boundary bank. It had stone walls made from mortared limestone, with a floor of limestone paving slabs. Inside were traces of three stone benches, offset from the north, west and south walls. The church faced west–east, with a probable entrance in the east wall. A small adjacent cemetery contained at least sixteen burials, eleven of them female, carbon-dated to between AD 559 and 782; these burials were therefore some 200 years later than the temple.

The bodies faced west–east, and were buried with no grave goods. The eleven women were above average height and showed few signs of hard manual labour; they are therefore likely to have been of high status, and brought up on good food.[30] Such highborn women had the opportunity to enter religious life, unlike lower-class women who had no rights and often spent their lives working in harsh conditions. The female burials suggest a possible monastic cemetery of women, dating from the sixth or early seventh centuries.

ILLUS. 18. Norman font in Lamyatt village church.

Of the remaining skeletons, one was male and the others too fragmentary to assess their gender; at least one male cleric would have been required to celebrate eucharist for the community. The more complete female skeletons were of women aged from about twenty-one to over forty-five; their average age of thirty-two was relatively young, though if the fragmentary skeletons had survived intact this might have altered the picture.[31] Evidence for a possible women's monastery is rare at this early date. By Norman times, the Christian community had moved down the hillside to the present site of Lamyatt village. There is a plain Norman tub font with cable moulding in the small thirteenth-century church (illus. 18).

The springs of Wells

Five miles west of Shepton Mallet, in a sheltered spot on the southern slopes of the Mendips, the cathedral town of Wells takes its name from five large and several small springs, which rise in a small cove close to the medieval bishop's palace, beside the river bank. Three of them now lie beneath the water of St Andrew's Pool; one can still be seen through an aperture in the wall of the Camery garden, east of the cloister (illus. 19).

Excavation in the Camery has yielded a scatter of Roman material: some first-century samian ware from southern Gaul which is likely to have reached the area via the Roman army, followed by objects from the second to the fourth centuries – pottery, wall plaster, clay roof tiles and tiles from hypocausts for underfloor heating: all these indicate domestic structures. A villa with its agricultural estate probably lay under or near the bishop's palace, straddling St Andrew's stream.[32]

Excavation here in 1894 and 1978–80 revealed the foundations of a late Roman mausoleum: an underground tomb chamber large enough for one or two coffins, with perhaps a funerary monument above them, probably dating from the fourth or fifth century. Posts appear to have supported either a canopy or an elevated shrine. The villa's owner(s), or possibly the founding saint(s) of a house church, appear to have been buried in a grave chamber, enclosed within a small chapel. There are similar chapels dating from Roman times at St Martin's church, Canterbury, at Lullingstone in Kent, at St Mary de Lode church, Gloucester, and elsewhere on the European mainland.[33]

ILLUS. 19. St Andrew's well, with the tower of the cathedral reflected in the water, Wells.

A funeral chapel at Wells

The sepulchre at Wells was of profound local significance, since it was preserved and venerated until the mid-tenth century. The site of the future minster seems to have been chosen because Christians owned and were buried at the villa. When we recall the model of house church described by St Patrick (see chapter one), it is possible that the villa's first priest might have been buried here, perhaps with his wife.

The funeral chapel at Wells continued as a focus for Christian worship. A seventh- to eighth-century Middle Saxon cemetery containing over 200 burials developed around the mausoleum. What appear to be the bases of two Saxon crosses were found along the eastern boundary of the cemetery. The fragment of what may be a Saxon cross shaft was also found, with interlaced ribbon-like stems.[34] The mausoleum was emptied and re-used as an ossuary, with hundreds of bones stacked fairly neatly inside. They belonged to about fifty men, women and children, all of whom were well-nourished; they were therefore families of fairly high status. The ossuary was sealed in the mid-tenth century; the infilling was dated by a silver coin, a penny of Anlaf Sihtricsson, ruler of the Viking kingdom of York, minted between 941 and 944.[35]

There were now timber buildings standing nearby. A small late Saxon chapel was built in the tenth century, partly over the mausoleum. It was evidently intended as a memorial chapel to enshrine the Roman tomb, which must have been considered exceptionally important, and still worthy of veneration.[36] In the tenth or eleventh century, a major structure with deep and curving foundations was constructed a few metres to the west of the mausoleum. It appears to be the eastern apse of the minster church of St Andrew, with a crypt beneath it; the church would have extended diagonally across the present cloister garth, beside the river bank.

The Saxon cathedral

The entire complex was aligned with the river bank and the holy wells, and so faced north-east. However, these buildings were later destroyed, and the medieval chapel of St Mary was built above them, aligned east-north-east, like the cathedral beside it. A series of extensions and redevelopments culminated in the thirteenth century with the construction of a Lady Chapel beside the present cloister. Some of the Saxon structures must be associated with the founding of a church, possibly by St Aldhem, in 705, during the reign of King Ine.[37]

A document dating from 766 is the first to mention the 'holy well' and minster church of St Andrew. In 909 the minster was raised to diocesan status by King Edward the Elder, with Aldhelm as the first bishop of the new cathedral. The sequence of early Christian burials and chapels is unique in the history of English cathedrals, although there are parallels in mainland Europe. At the same time, though, it is part of a broader pattern: almost 200 English churches and chapels are built over or alongside Roman villas, often with an adjoining sixth- to eighth-century cemetery; this indicates the extent to which noble families valued ancestral memorial shrines.[38]

The Saxon font at Wells

In about 1175, construction began on a wholly new church in the Early English style, immediately north of the old cathedral. The cloister was laid out, and the memory of the earlier holy place was kept alive by a succession of chapels that were incorporated into the new development. The tub font from the Saxon cathedral (illus. 20), complete with its stone arcading, was brought into the new church, and is still in use. Its bowl dates from the beginning of the tenth century, or even earlier. It was subsequently re-cut, and probably transferred from the old cathedral into the new one in the 1190s. It was brought to the south transept and placed on a new plinth; its wooden cover is Jacobean.[39]

The font's unusual location may be due to the fact that the new church was incomplete, and in the late twelfth century the south transept entrance was

the only doorway into the completed portion of the church. In this location, the font was also near to the dipping well in the cloister, which presumably provided water for baptism. The font was originally decorated with carvings of saints, standing beneath round arches; traces of their haloes can be seen. At some time the figures were chipped off and the arches re-shaped, to better match the font's new setting.[40]

Cheddar: a villa and a Saxon palace

Like Wells, Cheddar lies at the foot of the southern slope of the Mendips; it was an ideal situation for a Roman villa, where vines could be grown on the sunny hillside. Cheddar is an ancient settlement at the base of a gorge that was a route through the Mendip hills in ancient times, as we can tell from the artefacts left by cave-dwellers near the lower end of the gorge. The caves show evidence of occupation from at least 12,000 BC. In Roman times, several caves in the gorge were inhabited: pottery and tools were found here, and over 200 Roman coins. There were several small settlements along the valley's edge, and field systems indicate farming.[41]

Where the land levels out, beside the Cheddar Yeo, parch marks observed in the vicarage garden in 1975 revealed a building plan that probably represents part of the living quarters of a Roman villa. A coin dating from the Emperor Domitian's reign (81–96 AD) was found in the churchyard, and flat red Roman bricks were later incorporated in the medieval church tower. Further portions of the villa may lie beneath the modern graveyard to the east of the church. Part of a mortarium for pounding corn was found beneath the path alongside the church.[42] These are circular Roman kitchen bowls made of pottery, with coarse sand or grit embedded into their internal surface, to grind the corn.

The existence of a villa was confirmed by many Roman finds in the area, including wall plaster, tesserae from mosaic floors, burials, much ceramic pottery and metal objects. A rescue dig adjacent to the site in 1970 indicated a metalled access road and evidence of industrial working including hearths and furnaces, dating from the second century AD. Excavations in a ditch at the Old Showground gave a radiocarbon dating of AD 350–550, which suggested continuing occupation of the area.[43] Excavation in 2007 prior to the creation of a cycle path west of the parish church and south of the Kings of Wessex School produced further Roman material spanning the first to the fourth centuries.[44]

A possible Christian villa at Cheddar

ILLUS. 20 *(opposite)*. Tub font from the Saxon cathedral, Wells.

Cheddar is one of four Somerset towns, including Wells, Glastonbury and perhaps Street, each of which may have originated as a Roman villa complex; all four were also associated with a religious site. Their location may have been chosen because Christians had owned the villa and were buried there. Although Cheddar was probably not a Saxon town, its palace and church indicate a significant settlement around a royal manor.[45] Two early documents offer clues concerning the status of its church, the first being King Alfred's will, composed in about 850. This includes an unusual phrase, 'I [Alfred] am petitioner to the families/communities at Cheddar …', which suggests that there was perhaps a double community established at this time, whose members had special rights to choose their own royal protector.[46]

A forged charter of 978, which may be based on genuine material, also refers to a double religious house at Cheddar minster.[47] A century later, Domesday Book records *Cheddarmynster*, which indicates a community of priests by this date. It has been suggested that a large monastic property stretched southwards to the canalised river Yeo; the enclosure would have been entered from the north-east, where the fifteenth-century market cross now stands.[48]

Cheddar's Saxon palace

In 1960 Philip Rahtz discovered remains of the Anglo-Saxon palace in the grounds of the Kings of Wessex Community School. The building was made of wood, and had a thatched roof. This first timber hall was dated to the end of King Alfred's reign in the late ninth century. According to the Anglo-Saxon Chronicle, the Kings of Wessex met here in 941, 956 and 968. The site can be visited: outlined in the grass are the positions of a twelfth- to fourteenth-century great hall and a twelfth-century *witan*, or council chamber.

There are substantial remains of a tenth-century chapel (illus. 21) dedicated, unusually, to Columbanus: the discovery of a tenth-century coin helped to date the building. Its dedication to an Irish missionary in Europe may be explained by intermarriage between the Saxon royal family and that of Lotharingia, a region now split between eastern France and western Germany, where Columbanus had worked. In the eleventh century, Bishop Giso of Wells (d. 1088) came from Lotharingia.[49] It is not known who would have prayed in the chapel, but the Rule of Columbanus was popular, and was often conflated with that of St Benedict. The chapel was rebuilt in the eleventh century and again in the thirteenth, when the bishops of Wells restored both the chapel and the east hall. By now, the complex was probably no more than a royal hunting lodge with a hall, a chapel and a domestic annexe.

Roman Glastonbury

On lower land 10 miles south of Cheddar, Glastonbury was an island, at least in winter, in Iron Age times; a wooden boat and possible lake villages have been found in the surrounding marshland. Somerset was a region of summer pastures; in winter, when the land was flooded, the animals would have been slaughtered or moved to higher ground. Roman material has been found at a range of locations in Glastonbury, in particular, on the slopes of Wearyall Hill

ILLUS. 21. Chapel of St Columbanus, Cheddar.

on the south-western edge of the town. At Glastonbury abbey, St Joseph's well in the crypt of St Mary's chapel could be of Roman date: the stonework of its lower courses resembles that of other Roman wells excavated in the region. St Joseph's well would have been adjacent to the seventh-century 'old church' described below; later builders went to some trouble to incorporate the well into the Norman crypt (illus. 22).[50]

In the area around St Joseph's well, fragments of Roman pottery, glass, coins and building materials including tiles have been found. The Saxon glass kilns described below were partly constructed of Roman box flue tiles, which probably came from a Roman building of some quality, perhaps a villa.[51] Two rough-tooled Roman coffins of Bath stone were also found during early excavations. One was of a size suitable for a small adult; the other was for a child. The former was found beneath the crossing of the abbey church; both are preserved in the abbey museum.[52]

In the fifth or sixth centuries there were high-status buildings that may have been religious or secular on the site of the later abbey; this could have been a trading station or a Celtic monastery, or both. At the royal monastery of Lyminge in Kent, an imposing hall complex preceded an Anglo-Saxon monastery. At Glastonbury, fourteen sherds of late Roman amphorae were recovered, dating from about AD 450 to 550; they would have contained wine and oil. The amphorae were associated with a roughly trodden floor and postholes for perhaps one or more timber halls that may have been in use for several centuries; they were destroyed in the eighth or ninth century.[53]

ILLUS. 22. St Joseph's well with its Norman arch, Glastonbury abbey.

Glastonbury's Saxon monastery

There was a sequence of stone churches at the Anglo-Saxon monastery, laid out on a single axis, as was customary. In the eighth century there were at least three churches on the same alignment; that at the western end was the 'ancient church' (or *vetusta æcclesia*) popularly associated with Joseph of Arimathea. There is an early boundary ditch to the east of the 'ancient church'; material found at the bottom of the ditch dates from the late sixth and early seventh centuries. It might have formed one side of a large rectangular monastic precinct, bounded at the western end by St Benedict's church in Benedict Street. To the south lies a large cemetery that was constructed before the tenth century. It included at least three chapels and also freestanding stone crosses, between two of which was a small tomb chamber, giving rise to the story that Arthur and Guinevere were buried here.[54]

There were three phases of construction dating from early, middle and late Saxon times. The first Saxon church, constructed in about AD 700, was in three sections, with a detached crypt. The church walls were built of shallow courses of limestone, and there were traces of a pink *opus signinum* floor, created by mixing crushed recycled Roman tile or brick with mortar; similar floors are found in Saxon churches in Kent. A large number of E-ware fragments were also found – pieces of jars, bowls and jugs of a hard, granular consistency, produced in Gaul and distributed across western Britain during the sixth and seventh centuries.[55]

In the mid-Saxon period, during the eighth or ninth century, a square east end was added to the church, above the crypt. The absence of metal objects and other artefacts from the second monastery suggests that the mid-Saxon monastic buildings may lie to the north of the church, an area so far unexamined. In the late Saxon period, during the tenth century, the crypt was partly destroyed and a substantial tower was built over it. A large stone coffin was placed at the entrance to the crypt; it contained the carefully arranged bones of seventeen individuals.[56] The late Saxon church was associated with St Dunstan, under whom monastic life spread from Glastonbury across parts of southern England.

Saxon glass furnaces

Five glass furnaces were constructed in the early Saxon period; their floors were preserved, and provide unique evidence for early medieval glass technology in Britain. Radiocarbon dating from samples of charcoal indicates that glass manufacture lasted only a few decades, in the late seventh or early eighth centuries. It took place during the reign of King Ine of Wessex (688–726) who, according to William of Malmesbury and the Anglo-Saxon Chronicle, established or re-founded the monastery. In the furnaces, window glass was produced for the first stone church and glass vessels for use by the monks. The craftsmen re-melted old Roman glass, which was possibly imported as cullet, or crushed glass, from mainland Europe.[57]

An early Irish manuscript

An early Irish fragment of the *Etymologiae* by Isidore of Seville (560–636) survives as the two fly-leaves of an account of Glastonbury abbey's properties, compiled at the time of Henry of Sully's election as abbot in 1189. The *Etymologiae* is an encyclopedia containing extracts of many books from classical antiquity; the fly-leaves date from about AD 700. There are glosses in the margins employing Irish spellings and grammar. The Latin text contains errors, and seems to have been rather carelessly copied by a monastic scribe.[58]

The manuscript must have arrived in Glastonbury by 1189, when it was discarded and its pages used as fly-leaves, but it could have arrived much earlier: by the mid-seventh century, English monks went to Ireland to study, and monks from southern Ireland travelled to south-west England.[59] Under the date 664, Bede describes how Englishmen went to Ireland,

> either for the sake of Divine studies or of a more chaste life; and some of them presently devoted themselves to a monastic life; others chose rather to apply themselves to study, going about from one master's cell to another. The Scots [i.e. Irish] willingly received them all, and took care to supply them with food, and also to furnish them with books to read, and their teaching, without payment.[60]

In a Life of St Dunstan (*Vita S. Dunstani*) composed around 1000, the author indicates the presence of Irish monks at Glastonbury by the time of Dunstan's birth (*c.* 909), and that they possessed books. The author relates that Dunstan read the philosophical books in the library belonging to the 'wandering Irishmen' (*Hibernensium peregrini*) who resided at Glastonbury. It is possible that the fly-leaf comes from one of the books read by Dunstan as a student.[61]

Glastonbury's Norman abbey

By the late Saxon period, there were several freestanding monastic buildings built of stone; they remained in use into the twelfth century. A Norman church was erected in 1080, and in turn replaced by a larger one in the first half of the twelfth century. The late twelfth-century chapel of St Mary stands on the site of the 'ancient church', a wooden building which, before the fire of 1184 was the most revered part of the complex. Its foundations were destroyed by the later chapel and medieval crypt.[62]

The enormous medieval church (illus. 23) and its surrounding buildings housed up to sixty men. Celtic monks including Ke, Fili, Rumon and Collen were revered at Glastonbury, but many Somerset dedications to Celtic saints date from the eleventh century, when the monks of Glastonbury created a new interest in the lives of their holy predecessors. After the great church was destroyed in 1184, Glastonbury's superiority among English monasteries was threatened, and enterprising monastic historians developed a legend describing how Joseph of Arimathea, the disciple who buried Jesus in his family tomb, came to Glastonbury and built its first church. In 1191, after the monks

ILLUS. 23. The ruins of Glastonbury abbey's great church.

'discovered' the tomb of King Arthur and his consort Guinevere beneath the floor of the 'ancient church', the supposed relics of the royal couple were entombed in a shrine; they were probably moved into the chancel in 1278.

Hermits on Glastonbury Tor

There may have been a pre-Saxon monastery at Glastonbury, but there is stronger evidence that early hermits lived on the Tor above the settlement, where excavations conducted by Philip Rahtz in 1964–66 revealed what appear to have been the remains of monks' cells, cut into the rock below the summit, in the sixth century. In these layers, Rahtz found sherds of amphorae, perhaps containers for wine or olive oil, imported from the Mediterranean. There were a great many animal bones, mostly of cattle, with a few sheep or pigs. These were the residue of joints brought to the site from animals butchered elsewhere. The remains of so much meat led Rahtz to at first conclude that this was a secular site, perhaps a defended stronghold, until the discovery of large quantities of meat bones at Whithorn and Iona provided evidence that pre-Saxon monks were meat-eaters.[63]

Two graves on the Tor contained leg bones of young people, well under twenty years old, of undetermined sex. Were they young hermits, who perhaps died of exposure in a severe winter? There was a medieval tradition of a monastic foundation on the Tor in early times, with two hermits. Metalworking hearths with crucibles and copper alloy slag suggested a small-scale, perhaps specialised, smithing industry; a bronze head mask was discovered, which could have been the handle of an elaborate pail, possibly for use in the liturgy. Smithing was often undertaken at religious sites, since metal items were required both for worship and for everyday use.[64]

A later Anglo-Saxon complex on the Tor included two square monastic cells, one of which was half underground, with a timber superstructure. The location of this monk's dwelling had been chosen with some thought, for it was well protected from the prevailing winds, and had a pleasant view to the south. There were signs of a small chapel or communal building, while the base of a wheel cross and what may have been its head were found just below the summit of the Tor. The cross stood 1.7 m feet high, tall enough to be visible from a distance.[65]

There was no source of water on the Tor, but there was some arable land. The ridges round the Tor (illus. 24) indicate that it continued to be farmed in medieval times, for there was little land available for agriculture except for that on the steep-sided hills, since all the low-lying l and was marsh. A later church was destroyed by an earthquake in the thirteenth century; the tower visible today dates from about 1400, and incorporates material from the church.

Beckery: one of Britain's earliest monasteries

On the south-western edge of Glastonbury, overlooking the River Brue, there was a monastery at Beckery, situated on a small low-lying hill whose summit was above the flood waters. Excavation by Philip Rahtz in 1974 revealed two

ILLUS. 24. Glastonbury Tor from Wearyall Hill, showing late medieval terraces.

rectangular buildings; that to the south was a church containing a stone-lined grave of a man aged twenty-five to thirty-five, who may have been the founder of the monastery. To the north and east were some fifty to sixty burials. The site was excavated again in 2016 by Richard Brunning and, to his surprise, radiocarbon dating of the remains of seven individuals revealed that the monastery was occupied from the fifth or early sixth century. It thus pre-dates both Iona, founded in the late sixth century, and Glastonbury, established in the seventh.[66]

Most of the burials excavated by Rahtz were adult males, except for two juveniles, perhaps novices. A female skeleton might have been that of a visiting nun or patron. There were only a small number of monks, which suggests a group of hermits rather than a large monastery. Its location on a small island just outside Glastonbury, surrounded by wetlands, enabled a degree of solitude. There were a few rudimentary buildings of wattle and daub, before the construction of the two medieval buildings. The cemetery remained in use until the ninth century, after the Vikings attacked Somerset, when perhaps monastic life at Beckery ended. Further tests are planned to determine whether the monks were local or came from abroad. The early chapel was rebuilt a number of times, the last construction dating from the thirteenth century. Beckery's name may derive from the Old English for 'bee-keeper's island'.[67]

A monastery of St Ke in Street

The name of Street, 2 miles south-west of Glastonbury, indicates that it was built on an ancient 'hard road'. This was the route from Glastonbury southwards, towards the ridgeway along the top of the Polden Hills and the estuary of the River Parrett, where pilgrims could embark from the port of Combwich and head for the Bristol Channel. The causeway linking Glastonbury to Street crosses some 600 m of marshland surrounding the River Brue. In the eighteenth century a pre-Norman causeway was found under the turf, 12 m east of the present road: it consisted of layers of stones set on brushwood, held in place by upright piles.[68] Radiocarbon dating assigned materials to the eighth century AD.

The church of Leigh in Street is dedicated to saints Gildas and Ke (illus. 25). In a charter purporting to date from 680, though it is likely to be later, the church is described as belonging to Glastonbury abbey.[69] It names the church as *Lantokay*, or 'church site of Ke'; this is the only use of the prefix *lan* in a Somerset place-name. The *Liber Terrarum* (*c.* 1075–*c.* 1140) states *Lantokay id*

ILLUS. 25. Church of Gildas and Ke at Leigh in Street.

est Leghe ('Lantokay, which is to say Leigh'), while Domesday Book mentions Leigh but not Street, which was evidently of less significance at the time.[70] The dedication to the more famous figure of Gildas is likely to date from medieval times; it is now named Holy Trinity church.

The large churchyard was oval (illus. 26); its unusual size indicates the probable presence of a monastic community here. An oval monastic site is typical of a pre-Saxon monastery, but also occurs more widely in Saxon Britain, northern Gaul and monasteries of English monks in Germany.[71] The medieval church of Street is not at the centre of the enclosure; this suggests that it might be the site of one of several early chapels within the monastery compound. Before its renovation in the Victorian era, there was an Anglo-Saxon arch on the north side of the present church, which strengthens the possibility that this was the site of an original chapel.[72]

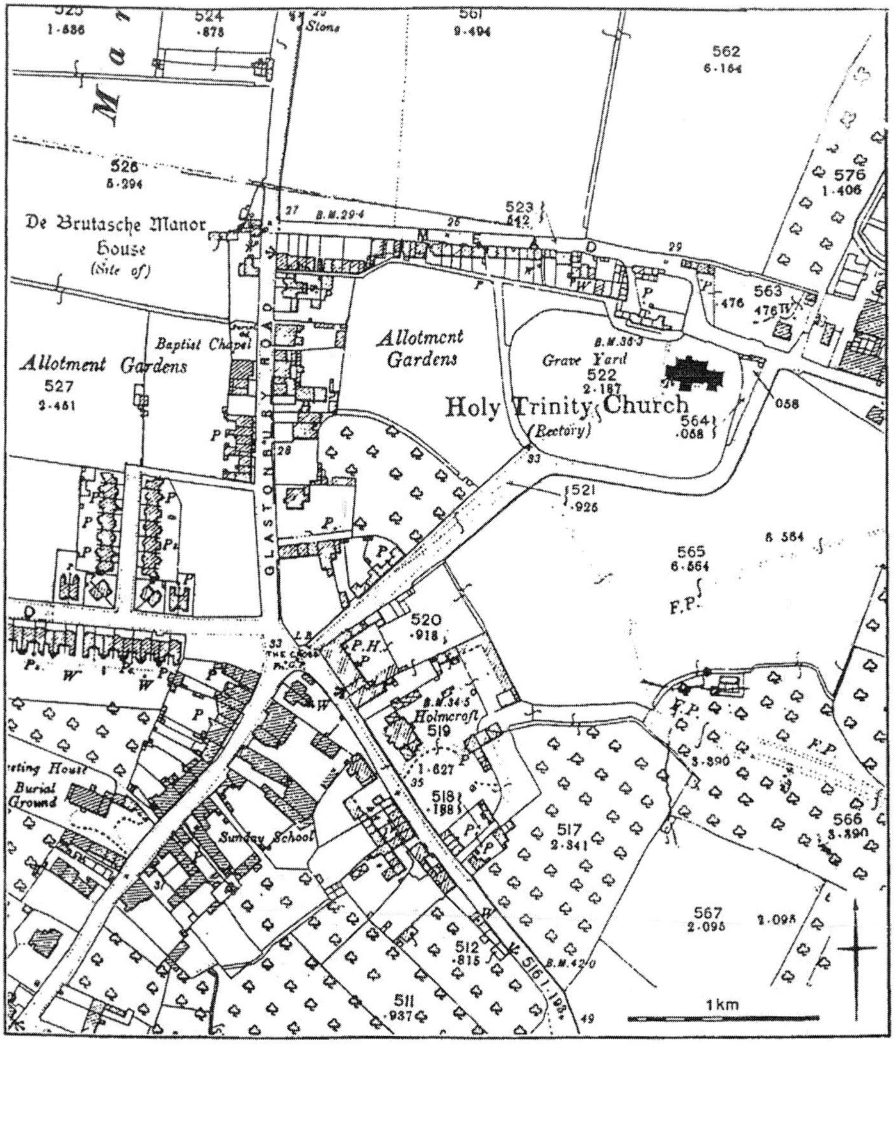

ILLUS. 26. OS map (1904) showing the monastic enclosure at Leigh in Street.

Ke could have been a Romano-British monk with the Latin name Caius. There are dedications to Ke at Landkey in north Devon, alongside the Fal estuary in Cornwall and also in Brittany; Sir Kay in the Arthurian legend may also derive his name from Ke. In 1503 the first enclosed plot beyond the church was named 'Ankerhey' or 'anchorite's enclosure', which suggests that a hermit lived beside the church.

To the west of the church, a manor house was named *Brutessayshe*, meaning 'Brutus's ash tree' in Middle English: Brutus is a literary figure in the legendary history of Britain popularised in the twelfth century by Geoffrey of Monmouth. Three ash trees were recorded as growing here in 1503.[73] In earlier times, however, the ash was regarded as a holy tree: in a twelfth-century charter purporting to be Saxon, the charter-bound area around Taunton church, 18 miles south-west of Street, was marked by an 'ash tree which the ignorant call holy'.[74]

Laws issued under the Saxon King Ine (688–725) describe the British as *wealas*, from which our word 'Welsh' derives; the word probably means 'foreigners'. After the Saxon conquest, it appears that pockets of local Britons remained in this region. The name of the village of Walton (*Waltone* in Domesday Book), 2 miles west of Street, is likely to mean 'Welsh tun' or 'Foreigners' town'.[75] This would denote a British settlement in a predominantly Anglo-Saxon area, as does the village of Wales, 10 miles south-east of Street. Walton was a daughter church of Street.

Shapwick and St Indract

St Indract is associated with Shapwick which is just north of the Polden ridge, 5 miles west of Glastonbury and Street, on an ancient route from Glastonbury to the coast. Indract's story may be genuine: the Irish *Martyrology of Tallaght*, written around 800, described him as 'a martyr for the faith at Glastonbury'. According to his Life, which was probably compiled in the tenth century, Indract was the son of an Irish prince. When he was a deacon, he visited Rome with twelve companions. On the way home, bringing sacks of celery seed, presumably to plant in their monastery back in Ireland, they stopped at Glastonbury. They stayed for the night near Shapwick, where a thegn of the King of Wessex murdered Indract and his companions, thinking that their sacks contained gold.

His Life relates that Indract was buried at Shapwick. Since the Life dates from the tenth century, this implies that Shapwick's church was already in existence by this date. Subsequently, according to the Life, Indract's relics were taken to Glastonbury abbey, where they were enshrined beside the high altar of the old church, which was destroyed by the fire of 1184.[76] This story may have been invented by the monks of Glastonbury, or it may be based on an earlier tradition.

A Roman road ran from the Fosse Way past Shapwick to the sea. There was a Romano-British villa at Shapwick; in 1988 Britain's largest hoard of early Roman coins was found here. It was buried around AD 230, and was the equivalent of about ten years' pay for a legionary soldier.[77] The original settlement and its church lay some 650 m east of the present village, in East Field at Old Church Farm. Excavation here has provided evidence of Roman habitation and of a large medieval building lower down the field from the site of the former church.

The photo (illus. 27) shows the excavation of the large medieval structure; in the foreground is a Roman boundary ditch. Near the church there was evidence of a Bronze Age hut, and a powerful spring emerged on the east side of the church; it is likely to have been used for baptisms. There was continuous settlement at the site over a long period. A track led diagonally across East Field, where St Indract's holy well is in the verge opposite, though overgrown and often dry, since the water table is now lower.

The estate of Shapwick was probably owned by Glastonbury abbey from the early eighth century onwards, when its church may have been established. Domesday Book indicates that the estate extended some 10 miles west along the Polden Ridge. The church probably served as a minster for the whole estate; in the later medieval period, Shapwick was still the mother church of the area. The original church was not abandoned until perhaps the fourteenth century, when a church was erected at the centre of the new village.[78]

ILLUS. 27. Excavations at Old Church Farm, Shapwick, summer 2000.

While John of Glastonbury's Life of St Indract in his *Cronica sive antiquitates Glastoniensis ecclesie* (chs 50–51) relates that Indract and his companions were murdered at Shapwick, an account in the Digby Manuscript states that they were killed at *Hywisc* (Huish). This appears to refer to a portion of Shapwick's estate about 7 miles to the west, where Withy Farm now stands, just south-east of the M5 as it crosses the Huntspill River. This would have been marshland close to the pilgrim route to the port of Combwich and the Bristol Channel.[79]

St Cyngar of Congresbury

Of the pre-Saxon saints who are said to have worked in Somerset, Cyngar is the most likely to have existed. He gave his name to Congresbury, and may have been associated with the nearby hill fort of Cadbury, half a mile to the north. This is one of five hill forts in the south-west to be named 'Cadbury' or 'Cada's fort'; it was probably occupied by members of the Dobunni tribe, who were based in the Cotswolds. The fort was abandoned during the Roman occupation, from AD 43 to 410, when the lowland region around it was under stable Roman administration, as the region grew and flourished. The hill fort was later reoccupied from 410 to 700; perhaps it was now no longer safe to live in the lowlands below the fort.[80]

Cadbury Camp is the only fortress in the region to have been reoccupied after the departure of the Romans. Amphorae were found here, still imported from Mediterranean lands, as they had been in Roman times. The people living here were wealthy: the fort has produced the second largest collection of fragments of early medieval glass from any western site. There were at least sixty vessels; the only site that has so far produced more is Whithorn, which yielded pieces of some eighty vessels.[81]

There may be evidence of Christianity at Cadbury: an elegant Latin cross is carved on a piece of African red slip ware dating from the mid-sixth century.[82] It is possible that the monk Cyngar lived near the people in the fort, for on the neighbouring hilltop of Henley Hill at Yatton is what appears to have been an early Christian cemetery. There had been a Roman temple here, which fell into ruin in the third century. Later, perhaps in the sixth century, between fifty and a hundred Christian graves were dug through the site.

Congresbury's Saxon minster

In Saxon times, the settlement of Congresbury grew beside the River Yeo (the Congresbury Yeo is different from the Cheddar Yeo) that flows at the foot of the fort, half a mile to the south-west. Here there was a minster, or Saxon monastery. The large oblong site of 10 acres is bounded by deep ditches, and probably dates from the late seventh or early eighth century. There was a second church within the enclosure, dedicated to St Michael. Since the

Archangel Michael is associated with the souls of the dead, this was probably a mortuary chapel.[83]

The church at Banwell, 4 miles south-west of Congresbury, lies close to the site of a Roman villa, which might argue for a continuous Christian presence there, too. There could have been pre-Saxon monasteries at both Congresbury and Banwell: there was a hill fort and a substantial post-Roman settlement near to each of them.[84] Congresbury is mentioned in the *Life of King Alfred*, attributed to Asser, but this text may have been written at the end of the tenth century, and not by Bishop Asser.[85] Later, King Cnut (990–1035) gave the two monasteries of Congresbury and Banwell to a priest named Duduc.[86]

Cyngar's shrine at Congresbury

There were several saints named Cyngar; the monk honoured at Congresbury may have originated in Pembrokeshire, where Llanwngar, near St Davids, is named after him. He is listed in many Somerset church calendars, and his relics were honoured in the minster church at Congresbury.[87] In 1996, in the floor of a barn at Brinsea, a mile south of Congresbury, stones were discovered which had formed part of Cyngar's eleventh-century shrine, including a piece of one of its corner pillars. It would have been a substantial monument, over 2 m high, and was perhaps donated under King Cnut. Two sculptured figures depict Christ and a tonsured saint, perhaps St Peter. A large torso fragment may have come from a statue of Cyngar.[88] The sculptures are now in Taunton Museum.

The shrine probably stood near or behind the high altar of the minster church. However, Cyngar's cult may have waned, for in 1217/18 the church was rebuilt and re-dedicated to St Andrew. The great east window was constructed at this time. St Cyngar's shrine was now seen to be in the way, and his relics were relegated to a side chapel off the south aisle. Some of the stone foundations of his shrine were reused in the new east wall of the church, which was rebuilt yet again in the fourteenth and fifteenth centuries.

Eleventh- and fourteenth-century pilgrim guides describe Cyngar's body enshrined in Congresbury church.[89] Next to the church there is a fine thirteenth-century priests' house (illus. 28), built to accommodate the clerics who ministered to the pilgrims visiting the shrine. In the churchyard, an ancient yew stump growing inside a great beech tree is known as 'Congar's Walking Stick' (colour plate 3). According to his legendary Life, Cyngar planted his staff here, where it took root; this miracle persuaded King Ine of Wessex to grant land for a monastery here. Yew is still a traditional wood for carving walking sticks.

The *Vita S. Cungari* was composed at Wells cathedral, probably in the twelfth century; it survives in fragmentary form. A later, more complete version was added to the 1516 printed edition of John of Tynemouth's *Lives of the Saints*. The Life tells of a dream in which a wild boar shows Cyngar where he should live. On waking, he sees a boar in a reed bed, and builds an oratory on the site. A wild boar features in a number of Anglo-Norman Lives of early saints; often a white sow indicates where a monk's chief monastery

ILLUS. 28. Thirteenth-century priests' house, Congresbury.

should be built. Swineherds lived on the edge of settlements, where a monk could combine solitude with accessibility to local people. Medieval Christians familiar with the classics would recall that Virgil described how a huge white sow showed Aeneas where to found the great city of Alba Longa, the forerunner of Rome.[90]

Lulle of Baltonsborough

We know little about the holy men and women who peopled early Christian Somerset, but there are records of one who, unusually, was a woman. Baltonsborough is a village 4 miles south-east of Glastonbury; it is mentioned in four charters in connection with Glastonbury abbey, in each of which we are told that an early Saxon holy woman named Lulle in Baltonsborough sold land to the abbey. The *Landbook* (or *Liber Terrarum*), compiled between about 1075 and about 1140, speaks of 'Lulla de Baltenesbeorge'. William of Malmesbury's *Antiquity of the Church of Glastonbury* written between 1129 and 1139 and expanded by others up to about 1247 records that Lulle gave *Baltenesbeorthe* and *Scrobbamurht* to Glastonbury. *Scrobbamurht* refers to meadows in Baltonsborough beside the River Brue. One of John of Glastonbury's charters possessed by the abbey in 1247 describes 'Lule femina de Baltenesbeorge' who grants land to 'Alberto abbati'.[91]

We learn more, however, from the fourth document, the Great Cartulary (GC 766), compiled in about 1348, which is more accurate than the preceding three sources. It informs us that in 744, on 10 July, Lulle sold ten hides (meaning the land that supported ten peasants and their families) of her land to Glastonbury abbey, together with its farm labourers; she also placed some of it at the disposal of Æthilbald, King of Mercia.[92] A section of the charter explains the need for a written record of boundaries, in order to prevent disputes 'between your servants and ours' (*inter tributarios uestros nostrosque colonos*). An endorsement is added, which confirms King Æthilbald's consent, and includes a sanction and a blessing. There are two lists of witnesses.

We are given valuable information about Lulle: she is 'a warrior for Christ, a humble maidservant' (*militancium Christo, humilis ancilla*). This is a typical description of an early monk or nun: a man or woman of God who is both strong and gentle. She possesses a great deal of land, so she is likely to be a noblewoman. Since she negotiates as an equal with an abbot, a bishop and two kings, as we shall see, she may well be an abbess. In early Saxon times, a wealthy noblewoman might enter a monastery if her husband died, leaving her a widow, or if she was past the age of childbearing, and therefore no longer of dynastic value.

Lulle makes a petition on behalf of herself and her community, 'for the redemption of my soul and of those joined with me through the bonds of association and necessity'.[93] She uses the masculine gender, which suggests that she is describing a double monastery, containing both monks and nuns. Lulle sells her land to Tunberht, abbot of Glastonbury, 'with the knowledge and royal licence granted by Æthilbald, king of Britain'.[94] King Æthilbald was certainly involved in the abbey's affairs at this time: he had given a grant of land to the abbey two years previously and he confirmed King Ine's grant of land at Brent Knoll.[95]

The two lists of witnesses give us more valuable information. The first list includes Abbot Tunberht, together with Bosa, Urta, Walcstod and Tidbert, priests, with two laymen, Tida and Cuthwin. These are early Saxon names: short names were rarely used by the tenth century, and no names starting with 'Cuth' except for Cuthbert.[96] The two laymen were perhaps tenants or local nobility. The second list of witnesses endorses the king's consent, and includes men of high profile: the Mercian King Æthilbald himself, the West Saxon King Cuthred, together with King Æthilbald's brother, and Bishop Herewald of Sherborne among others. The business transaction was completed in the 'church dedicated to Saints Peter and Paul', which may refer to the 'great church' at Glastonbury abbey, since this was its dedication by the eighth century.

It is interesting that the charter leaves some unfinished business: while Lulle sells to the abbey ten hides of land at Baltonsborough, she reserves the sale of another ten hides at nearby Lottisham and Ledenford (Lydford) to the discretion of King Æthilbald, apparently leaving him to make the decision. This indicates that the charter is likely to be genuine: a forger would either have claimed that Lottisham and Lydford belonged to the abbey, or would not have bothered to mention them. Again, these very specific arrangements made in the mid-eighth century could not have been known by a scribe from a later period.[97]

If Lulle was a nun, and possibly an abbess, where did she train for her role in the Church? The church of Lamyatt was 8 miles to the east; as we have seen, its cemetery contained the bodies of at least eleven highborn women. This could have been a double monastery; it was still in existence when Lulle drew up her charter in 744, and was easily reached from Baltonsborough. Lulle's land bordered the Fosse Way where it crossed the River Brue at Lydford; it was an easy journey north along the Fosse Way, and east on the track leading to Lamyatt.

Lulle might have lived in either or both places. She could have lived alone or with a community in Baltonsborough; if so, this would probably have been

ILLUS. 29.
Baltonsborough church.

PHOTO: MONICA WATSON.

near the fifteenth-century church, beside a leat off the River Brue (illus. 29). If she lived in Baltonsborough, she is likely to have come from the same family as St Dunstan, who was born in the same village in 909 and was a later abbot of Glastonbury. It is unlikely that there was more than one noble family in such a small settlement.

Women's monasteries in Wessex

Women's monasteries in seventh- and eighth-century Wessex are chiefly found in Somerset, Dorset and Devon, three counties that became the diocese of Sherborne in 705, under its first bishop, Aldhelm. Lamyatt was originally a British community, but, as we know from Lindisfarne and other monasteries, Britons and Saxons studied and prayed alongside each other. In earlier centuries, the British landowning aristocracy formed the link between Roman villas and churches, and this situation may have continued in Saxon times. British churches and estates were taken over by the Anglo-Saxons, but King Ine's laws indicate that the British survived at all levels of society, living alongside their new Saxon neighbours.[98]

Towards the end of the eighth century the West Saxons were consolidating their control of the former British provinces in the west, but British churches and monasteries continued to be held in respect. Women religious did not all live in conventional double monasteries, however. In about 760, a nun named Sulca, meaning 'handmaid of God', gave property at Culmstock (Devon) to Glastonbury abbey.[99] There were religious women associated with Glastonbury abbey in the tenth century when St Dunstan was abbot, and Cheddar's minster contained both religious men and women.[100]

The evolution of Christianity in Somerset

Having examined a range of sites that demonstrate the presence of early Christians in Somerset, what conclusions can we draw from the evidence that remains? It is likely that there were Christians in the Roman towns of the region, but the end of Roman administration caused a dislocation of the economy, and towns declined in the first half of the fifth century. When urban society collapsed, perhaps wealthy townsfolk retreated to the countryside, taking their faith with them. Monasteries were beginning to be established, the earliest in the region, so far as we know, being that of Beckery. If there were bishops in the former towns, they may have moved into the monasteries, for priests still needed to be ordained by bishops, if the Church was to continue.

The rural population was probably Christianised in the fifth century, and it is possible that the attacks of pagan Saxons encouraged this process: it was now patriotic to be a Christian. The Saxons entered Somerset in 658; the local population would have soon learnt to speak English in order to survive in the new dominant culture. But in Somerset, British and Anglo-Saxon society were quite similar. The two peoples were distinct ethnically but not politically in Somerset, or in Wessex as a whole, where there were relatively few Anglo-Saxon foreigners from abroad. In this region, Britons were quite well integrated into Anglo-Saxon society, and by the ninth century Old Welsh was spoken only in pockets.

Under the Saxon kings, minster churches developed in the large estates across rural Somerset. A minster could house monks or nuns or both, like Cheddar minster, or it might consist of a group of priests serving the laity, like those at Congresbury who cared for pilgrims coming to visit St Cyngar's shrine. A minster could be administered by a powerful family; it might be large or small. Lulle of Baltonsborough is an example of a Saxon nun who may have trained in a large minster elsewhere, or in a local British community such as Lamyatt. It is unlikely that she was influenced by monastic life in the great Welsh monasteries or those of Ireland. She demonstrates that, in the Saxon era, it is probable that Christianity continued to be home-grown in the region of Somerset.

Notes

1 Barry Cunliffe, *The Roman Baths at Bath* (Bath: Bath Archaeological Trust, 1993), pp. 3–4.
2 *Ibid.*, pp. 5–9.
3 Charles Thomas, *Celtic Britain* (London: Thames & Hudson, 1986), p. 52.
4 Barry Cunliffe and Peter Davenport, *The Temple of Sulis Minerva at Bath*, vol. 1, part 1: The Site (Oxford: Oxford University Committee for Archaeology, 1985), pp. 66, 68–70, 74.
5 *Meet the Ancestors* Series, BBC 2, December 2000, presented by Julian Richards, produced by Suzanne Daggar.
6 Peter Leach, *Roman Somerset* (Wimborne: The Dovecote Press, 2001), pp. 112–13.
7 Cunliffe, *The Roman Baths*, p. 35.
8 Stephen Bird and Barry Cunliffe, *The Essential Roman Baths* (London: Scala, 2006), p. 46.
9 From 'The Ruin', in *The Exeter Anthology* (Exeter Cathedral Library MS 3501), ed. and trans. Richard Hamer, in *A Choice of Anglo-Saxon Verse* (London: Faber and Faber, 2015), lines 1–6.
10 Hamer, 'The Ruin', lines 19–24, 29–31.
11 *Ibid.*, lines 38–43.
12 Peter H. Sawyer, *Anglo-Saxon Charters: An Annotated List and Bibliography* (London: Royal Historical Society, 1968), charter S 148.
13 John Blair, *The Church in Anglo-Saxon Society* (Oxford: Oxford University Press, 2005), pp. 274–75 (S 120).
14 Cunliffe, *The Roman Baths*, p. 35.
15 Bird and Cunliffe, *The Essential Roman Baths*, p. 46.
16 Peter Hill, *Whithorn and St Ninian: The Excavation of a Monastic Town* (Stroud: Sutton, 1997), pp. 19–10, 27, 128; E. Rees, *Celtic Saints of Scotland, Northumbria and the Isle of Man* (Stroud: Fonthill, 2017), pp. 51–57.
17 Michael Costen, *The Origins of Somerset* (Manchester: Manchester University Press, 1992), p. 48.
18 Eilert Ekwall, *The Concise Oxford Dictionary of English Place-Names*, 4th edn (Oxford: Oxford University Press, 1970), entry: 'Yeo'.

19 Leach, *Roman Somerset*, pp. 58, 63–64.
20 *Ibid.*, p. 114.
21 Juliet Rogers, 'Human Skeletal Remains from Northover House 1982' (2.8), in Peter Leach, *Archaeological Excavations and Fieldwork to 1984* (Sheffield: John Collis, 1994), vol. 2, Cemeteries, p. 197, skeleton HB 5.
22 Sam Turner, *Making a Christian Landscape* (Exeter: Exeter University Press, 2006), p. 134.
23 Mark McDermott, *St Andrew's Church, Northover, Somerset* (Horncastle: Cupit, 1995), p. 1.
24 Peter Leach, *Shepton Mallet: Romano-Britons and Early Christians in Somerset* (Birmingham: Birmingham University Field Archaeology Unit, 1991), pp. 9, 24.
25 Leach, *Roman Somerset*, pp. 114–15.
26 R. Fleming, *Britain after Rome: The Fall and Rise, 400 to 1070* (London: Allen Lane/Penguin, 2010), pp. 136–51.
27 Roger H. Leech, 'The Excavation of a Romano-Celtic Temple and a Later Cemetery on Lamyatt Beacon, Somerset', *Britannia*, 17 (1986), pp. 259–328, at pp. 270–72.
28 *Ibid.*
29 Aldhelm, Letter to Heahfrith: *Aldhelmi Opera* no. 489, in *Aldhelm: The Prose Works*, ed. Michael Lapidge and Michael W. Herren (Cambridge: Cambridge University Press, 1979), pp. 160–61.
30 Leech, 'The Excavation of a Romano-Celtic Temple', p. 268.
31 *Ibid.*, p. 272.
32 Warwick Rodwell, *Wells Cathedral: Excavations and Structural Studies, 1978–93* (London: English Heritage, 2001), vol. 1, pp. 37, 53.
33 Rodwell, *Wells Cathedral*, vol. 1, pp. 47–48, 85.
34 Rodwell, *Wells Cathedral*, vol. 1, pp. 61–62, 74; vol. 2, pp. 489–90.
35 *Ibid.*, vol. 1, pp. 77–78.
36 *Ibid.*, pp. 79–83.
37 Michael Aston and Ian Burrow, eds, *The Archaeology of Somerset* (Bridgwater: Somerset County Council, 1982), p. 121.
38 Tyler W. Bell, 'The Religious Re-use of Roman Structures in Anglo-Saxon England', PhD diss., Oxford University, 2001, pp. 52–95, table 6.
39 Rodwell, *Wells Cathedral*, vol. 2, pp. 149–60.
40 *Ibid.*
41 Miranda Richardson, *Cheddar Archaeological Assessment: Somerset Extensive Urban Survey* (Taunton: Somerset County Council, 2003), p. 5.
42 It was found by Jeremy Sampson (personal communication with the author, 10 August 2018).
43 Richardson, *Cheddar Archaeological Assessment*, p. 6.
44 Janice Grove, Lorraine Mepham and Rob Goller, 'Archaeological Recording at the Kings of Wessex Playing Fields', *Proceedings of the Somerset Archaeology and Natural History Society*, 150 (2007), pp. 182–86.
45 Richardson, *Cheddar Archaeological Assessment*, pp. 4, 7.
46 King Alfred's will (BL, Stowe MS 944) states '… and I [Alfred] am petitioner to the families/communities at Cheddar that they will choose him [a royal protector] on the conditions of which we have already spoken …'. See Richardson, *Cheddar Archaeological Assessment*, p. 7.
47 John Blair, 'Palaces or Minsters? Northampton and Cheddar Reconsidered', in *Anglo-Saxon England*, 25 (1996), pp. 97–121, esp. p. 118.
48 Blair, 'Palaces or Minsters?', p. 112.

49 Men from Lotharingia were appointed bishops from the latter years of King Cnut's reign. These included Giso, who was bishop of Wells from 1061 and Bishop Walter of Hereford. Lotharingia, on the western fringe of the empire, offered excellent academic and administrative training, and the Englishman Leofric, bishop of Exeter, trained there. See Emma Mason, *The House of Godwine: The History of a Dynasty* (London: Hambledon, 2004), p. 51.

50 Clare Gathecrole, *Archaeological Assessment of Glastonbury* (Taunton: Somerset/English Heritage Extensive Urban Survey, 2003), pp. 14–16.

51 *Ibid.*

52 Rodwell, *Wells Cathedral*, vol. 1, p. 49.

53 Roberta Gilchrist, 'Glastonbury Abbey: The Archaeological Story', *Current Archaeology*, 320 (November 2016), pp. 24–25.

54 Aston and Burrow, *The Archaeology of Somerset*, pp. 119–20.

55 Gilchrist, 'Glastonbury Abbey', p. 25.

56 *Ibid.*, pp. 25, 27.

57 *Ibid.*, p. 26.

58 The manuscript is preserved at Longleat House (NMR 10589). See James P. Carley and Ann Dooley, 'An Early Irish Fragment of Isidore of Seville's *Etymologiae*', in *The Archaeology and History of Glastonbury Abbey*, ed. Lesley Abrams and James P. Carley (Woodbridge: The Boydell Press, 1991), pp. 135–61.

59 *Ibid.*, pp. 149–51.

60 Bede, *Ecclesiastical History of the English People*, trans. L. Sherley-Price, rev. R.E. Latham (London: Penguin Classics, 1990), bk 3, ch. 27.

61 Carley and Dooley, 'An Early Irish Fragment of Isidore', p. 152.

62 Aston and Burrow, *The Archaeology of Somerset*, p. 119.

63 Philip Rahtz, *The English Heritage Book of Glastonbury* (London: Batsford/English Heritage, 1991), pp. 54–57.

64 *Ibid.*

65 *Ibid.*

66 BBC News, 5 December 2016, www.bbc.co.uk/news/uk-england-somerset-38187299.

67 *Ibid.*

68 Rahtz, *The English Heritage Book*, p. 112.

69 Sawyer, *Anglo-Saxon Charters*, S 1249.

70 Michael Costen, *Anglo-Saxon Somerset* (Oxford: Oxbow Books, 2011), p. 182.

71 Blair, *The Church in Anglo-Saxon Society*, p. 198.

72 It was sketched by John Skinner, Rector of Camerton, in 1829 (BL, Add. MS 33712), reproduced in Michael McGarvie, *Sir Stephen Glynne's 'Church Notes for Somerset'* (Stroud: Sutton, 1994), p. 330. I am grateful to Jeremy Sampson for drawing my attention to this.

73 Rahtz, *The English Heritage Book*, p. 112.

74 Charter S 311, … *ad quendam fraxinum quem imperiti sacrum vocant*: Blair, *The Church in Anglo-Saxon Society*, p. 477.

75 Ekwall, *Dictionary of English Place-Names*, entry: 'Walton'.

76 Michael Lapidge, 'The Cult of St Indract at Glastonbury', in *Ireland and Early Medieval Europe: Studies in Memory of Kathleen Hughes*, ed. Dorothy Whitelock, Rosamund McKitterick and David Dumville (Cambridge: Cambridge University Press, 1982), pp. 184–88.

77 David Millward, 'Finders Keep Roman Coins', *Daily Telegraph*, 10 November 1999.

78 Turner, *Making a Christian Landscape*, pp. 39, 48.

79 *Ibid.*, p. 55.

80 Philip Rahtz suggested that Cadbury-Congresbury was an extensive Christian complex (see 'The Dobunnic Area in Post-Roman Times', in *The Land of the Dobunni: A Series of Papers Relating to the Transformation of the Pagan, Pre-Roman, Tribal Lands into Christian, Anglo-Saxon Gloucestershire and Somerset*, ed. Martin Ecclestone, published jointly by the Committee for Archaeology in Gloucestershire and the Council for British Archaeology – South West, 2003, pp. 27–29). However, this is considered doubtful.
81 William J. Watson, *The Celtic Place-names of Scotland* (Edinburgh: Birlinn, 1986), p. 311.
82 Hill, *Whithorn and St Ninian*, p. 297.
83 Philip Rahtz, 'The Dark Ages, 400–700 AD', in *The Archaeology of Somerset*, ed. Michael Aston and Ian Burrow (Taunton: Somerset County Council, 1982), p. 103.
84 Costen, *Anglo-Saxon Somerset*, pp. 181, 183.
85 Alfred P. Smyth, *The Medieval Life of King Alfred the Great: A Translation and Commentary on the Text Attributed to Asser* (Basingstoke: Palgrave, 2002), pp. 64–91, 108–31.
86 Simon Keynes, 'Giso, Bishop of Wells', in *Anglo-Norman Studies no. 19, Proceedings of the Battle Conference, 1996* (Woodbridge: Boydell, 1997), p. 220.
87 David Hugh Farmer, *The Oxford Dictionary of Saints*, 2nd edn (Oxford: Oxford University Press, 1987), p. 98.
88 Catherine Oakes and Michael Costen, 'The Congresbury Carvings – an Eleventh-Century Saint's Shrine?', in *The Antiquaries Journal*, 83 (2003), pp. 281–309.
89 *Ibid.*, p. 289.
90 Karen Jankulak, 'Alba Longa in the Celtic Regions? Swine, Saints and Celtic Hagiography', in *Celtic Hagiography and Saints' Cults*, ed. Jane Cartwright (Cardiff: University of Wales Press, 2003), pp. 272, 274.
91 Stephen C. Morland, 'The Glastonbury Manors and their Saxon Charters', *Somerset Archaeology and Natural History Society*, doc.130104Morland.pdf, p. 68. The three documents are, respectively, LB 370, WM 46 and JGA 375.
92 Aelred Watkin, 'The Great Cartulary of Glastonbury', *Somerset Record Society*, 3 vols (1947–56), pp. 41–45 (S 1410, Longleat House, Manuscript 39, ff. 153v–54).
93 … *pro redempcione mee anime eorumque videlicet qui michi contribulium ac necessitudinum nexibus conglutinati sunt.*
94 … *cum consciencia videlicet ac regalisque regni regmina gubernat. Athelbaldi.*
95 Heather Edwards, 'The Charters of the Early West Saxon Kingdom', PhD diss., University of Glasgow, 1985, p. 70.
96 *Ibid.*, p. 71.
97 *Ibid.*, pp. 74–75.
98 Barbara Yorke, 'The Bonifacian Mission and Female Religious in Wessex', *Early Medieval Europe*, 7, no. 2 (Oxford: Blackwell, 1998), pp. 164–65.
99 Nicholas Orme, ed., *Unity and Variety: A History of the Church in Devon and Cornwall*, Exeter Studies in History no. 29 (Exeter: Exeter University Press, 1991), p. 10.
100 Yorke, 'The Bonifacian Mission', pp. 165, 167.

CHAPTER 3

Coastal sites in Somerset and Devon

Having examined a number of early Christian inland sites in Somerset, we shall now focus on those nearer to the coast in both Somerset and Devon. At these sites there is less evidence of a Roman pagan presence; in contrast, more are dedicated to pre-Saxon saints. We know very little about most of these holy men and women who were called saints; for the most part their Lives were written centuries after their death, not as accurate historical records but as edifying accounts to be read aloud on their feast day.

The first Christians to be honoured as saints were martyrs, but by the fourth century people who had shown their faith by the goodness of their lives began to be considered saints, including Ephrem the Syrian in the East and Martin of Tours in the West. A holy man or woman could be honoured publicly with the approval of their local bishop, after he had examined their life. After this, their relics might be transferred to a church, and an altar could be erected over their tomb. St Augustine (d. 430) described the procedure that was followed in his day for the recognition of a martyr.[1] While the formal recognition of a saint applied only in a bishop's own diocese or ecclesiastical province, if a saint's fame spread, he or she was often venerated elsewhere.

St Kew's Steps, Kewstoke

St Kew is a pre-Saxon female saint who may be commemorated in the village of Kewstoke, a mile north-east of Weston-super-Mare; it is situated on the lower slopes of Worlebury Hill and overlooks the sea. Since Kew is relatively obscure, it is unlikely that her cult owes its origin to later medieval interest in famous saints of the past. At Kewstoke, the church and graveyard form part of a roughly oval enclosure that appears to pre-date the surrounding landscape; this might suggest the presence of a small community here in early Christian times. Its size closely resembles that of the monastic enclosure in Street, described in the previous chapter.

In Domesday Book, Kewstoke appears as *Chiwestoch*. The suffix *stoc* is an Old English place-name element which can mean 'a religious place'. It sometimes appears as 'stow' or 'stoke', to replace the lost British name of an early church site.[2] The small parish church at Kewstoke is now dedicated to St Paul; no record survives of an earlier dedication to St Kew. The late medieval church may reflect an Anglo-Saxon design in its dimensions, height and floor plan. Saxon openings may have been enlarged to become what are rather unusual clerestory windows.

A remarkable flight of steps leads from the churchyard up the steep cliff of Worlebury Hill; it is now known as Monk's Steps, but on earlier maps the flight is named St Kew's Steps. A century ago, they rose dramatically between the bare rock face on either side of a gully, as we can see from an engraving attributed to T.H. Hair (illus. 30).[3] The hillside is now gently wooded; a rare piece of early British metalwork, a large silver penannular brooch designed to fasten a cloak, was found in 1853 at the top of the steps (illus. 31).[4]

On a platform halfway up St Kew's Steps are the remains of a small stone building enclosing a pit which was probably a well; the building appears to have been an early well chapel or baptistery. When it was excavated in the late nineteenth century, finds suggested ritual activity in the Iron Age, and continuing use into the late medieval period. The closest parallel to this site is at St Levan in Cornwall, near Land's End, where the remains of two stone structures, possibly St Levan's chapel and cell, are connected by an ancient flight of over sixty stone steps to a holy well and baptistery, higher up the cliff.[5]

Kewstoke church and well chapel site may be related to the hill fort of Worlebury Camp, which faces the sea at the summit of Worlebury Hill, at its western end. This impressive Iron Age hill fort was also occupied in the Romano-British period: a hoard of Roman coins dating from AD 450 was found here, together with Roman pottery, glass beads and fragments of bronze.[6]

There is an early dedication to this saint in Cornwall at St Kew near Padstow, where she is connected with Docco. A charter of Edgar dating from about 962 refers to the monastery of St Dochou and St Cywa at the Cornish site and

ILLUS. 30. St Kew's Steps in the mid-nineteenth century.

ILLUS. 31. St Kew's Steps today.

claims that her relics were at the church. This is the monastery where, according to his seventh-century Life, St Samson hoped to stay with his companions, but was dissuaded from doing so by its monks, apparently because they had grown lax, and did not want to incur Bishop Samson's disapproval.[7] It will be discussed in more detail in the following chapter.

Domesday Book contains the phrase *Honore S. Chei* ('in honour of St Kew'),[8] and she is mentioned in two later martyrologies, or calendars of saints' feasts, one at Exeter cathedral dating from the twelfth century which names her as *Kiwa*, and a Welsh calendar from around 1200 where she appears as *Kigwa*. A chapel in St Kew churchyard, Cornwall, was described in 1373 as being dedicated to her; this may have been the chief centre of her cult.[9]

Brean Down: a church overlooking the sea

Until medieval times, Brean Down was an island; people lived, farmed and worshipped on the Down for 4,000 years (colour plate 4). A Romano-Celtic temple was built here in about 340, but it appears to have been in use for only thirty years. Its plan was similar to that on Lamyatt Beacon described in chapter two, though the temple on Brean Down was erected some forty years later.

On a clear day one can see Brean Down from Lamyatt Beacon. At both sites, antlers were found, which suggests that a local horned deity was venerated. At Brean, antlers were found in the ambulatory surrounding the temple, in its south annexe and in late layers above the small church. Antlers have also been found in Roman religious contexts at Wookey Hole, 18 miles to the south-east, at Maiden Castle and Woodyates (both in Dorset) and at Lydney (Gloucestershire).[10]

The temple on Brean Down was partly demolished in order to build a small rectangular church with an eastern entrance. It was constructed towards the end of the fourth century or a little later, without mortar, using stone robbed from the temple. Coins were found here dating to the fifth century, and the floor is worn, suggesting a long period of use.[11] Like the church at Lamyatt Beacon it faced west–east, with three stone benches inside the chapel. Nearby were five graves dating from the fifth to the seventh century; these were oriented east–west in the Christian manner.

In 1976, Martin Bell found the footings of round stone houses, bones and pottery dating from the Bronze Age, below Brean Down, in the flat land 100–200 m offshore, indicating that sea level was lower in earlier times than it is today; perhaps this was the site of the original village of Brean. Further excavation in 1983–87 revealed much more, including two gold bracelets from the late Bronze Age, and a salt extraction site from the same period, one of the earliest in Atlantic Europe.

There was a larger post-Roman Christian cemetery on the southern shoulder of Brean Down: its graves appeared from time to time in the eroding sand cliff. Ten skeletons had been uncovered in the 1950s; a further eight were uncovered in 1983–87, buried east–west, with the heads facing west. One was a baby less than six months old, two were juveniles or teenagers, and four were adults – two in their thirties and one a very old person; all of them were fragmentary.[12]

Three skeletons yielded a range of radiocarbon dates spanning the period between the departure of the Romans in the early fifth century and the conquest of this area by the Saxons in the second half of the seventh century: the first was dated AD 415–600, the second 560–660 and the third 654–786. The third dating suggests that the cemetery may have continued in use into Saxon times; perhaps the church, with its worn floor, also continued as a centre for worship.

At least five graves had stone linings; similar post-Roman examples were found at Ilchester, Glastonbury and Cannington. There are examples further to the south-west at Mawgan Porth in Cornwall, Beacon Hill on Lundy Island and several sites on the Scilly Isles. Some blocks of stone in the cemetery on the shoulder of Brean Down appear to have been grave markers. The graveyard may have been abandoned after the Saxon conquest, when the settlement moved a mile to the south, around the church of St Bridget in the village of Brean.[13] The present church dates from the thirteenth century.

Two islands in the Bristol Channel

The small islands of Steep Holm and Flat Holm lie off the Somerset coast. Steep Holm is 3 miles west-north-west of the tip of Brean Down, and is considered to be part of Somerset. Flat Holm is 2 miles north of Steep Holm and now belongs to Glamorgan; the two islands were not far from the great Welsh monasteries. Steep Holm (colour plate 5) was associated with Cadog of Llancarfan by the twelfth century.[14] In medieval times it was claimed that he used the island as a Lenten retreat.

Flat Holm is named in the Anglo-Saxon Chronicle (AD 918) as *[æt] Bradan Relice*, meaning 'broad, or flat, graveyard', and Steep Holm is similarly named *[æt] Steopan Re[o]lice* in the Anglo-Saxon Chronicle (versions B, C, D) in AD 915. Both derive from Old Irish *reilic*, meaning 'cemetery', which originates from the Latin *reliquae*, or 'relics'.[15] This indicates that in Saxon times the islands were considered to have been Christian burial grounds, but no early Christian remains have been found. The Anglo-Saxon Chronicle records that the mother of King Harold II stayed on Flat Holm before travelling to St Omer in France, after the Norman Conquest in 1066.[16]

Unlike Flat Holm, Steep Holm was visited from early times: prehistoric flints have been found here, and a variety of Roman artefacts dating from the second and third centuries AD. Fragments of roof tiles and box flue tiles suggest a bath house; a signal station or watchtower is also a possibility. According to the Anglo-Saxon Chronicle, a Viking fleet from Brittany took refuge on Steep Holm during the summer of 914 and then carried out raids on the Somerset coast at Watchet and Porlock. They were repelled by the Saxons and took refuge on Flat Holm. By the late twelfth century there was a small priory of canons on Steep Holm; they may have introduced the wild peonies that are a feature of both islands.[17]

A cemetery with a shrine at Cannington

There are a number of extensive post-Roman cemeteries in Somerset, the largest of which is at Cannington, 2 miles north-wert of Bridgwater, on a limestone hilltop overlooking the estuary of the River Parrett. The name Cannington means 'settlement by the Quantocks':[18] the medieval village lies at the foot of the Quantock Hills. In early times this was an important location, near the Parrett, which provides access to the Bristol Channel. Its hill fort was occupied from late Roman times, and there was a post-Roman settlement just outside the walls of the fort. During excavations in 1962, 523 graves were examined on the hillside to the east of the fort, although many more had been destroyed by quarrying. All the graves are oriented within the northern and southern limits of sunrise or sunset. The cemetery may have contained over 2,000 burials; it appears to have served a large populated area over a long period.[19]

A young woman's shrine

Radiocarbon dating suggests burials from the fourth century until the seventh or eighth, and from at least the sixth century the burials appear to have been Christian. The graves were carefully aligned in family groupings. An early pre-Christian focus was a small circular shrine near the top of the hill, containing the grave of a young man. This may have been a late Roman shrine, temple or mausoleum; there are a few graves on either side. A later significant burial was that of a young woman, radiocarbon dated to around AD 621. She seems to have been a local Christian saint; imported stone was used to create what may have been a memorial chapel over her tomb. There was evidence that her grave was frequently visited; her tomb provided a focus for many other burials. It was approached by a path from the north-west.[20]

The girl's rock-cut grave was marked out from the others: it was covered by a low mound, on the surface of which was set a box-like structure of stone slabs, aligned on the grave below. At the east end of this structure, one stone was decorated with a circular motif and perhaps runes. The path indicates that the grave was frequently visited, but later the mound was cut into by other graves. After the Anglo-Saxons conquered Somerset, the population moved south to the present village of Cannington, where there may have been a church and a burial ground by the eighth century.[21]

A cemetery at Hinkley Point

Early in 2015 a Saxon burial ground was found at Hinkley Point on the coast, 8 miles north-west of Bridgwater. Excavations in preceding years had already established the existence of Bronze Age, Iron Age and Roman farming communities close by. Roman levels provided evidence of salt making, with paddocks for cattle and plots for arable farming. Discarded limpet shells indicated an additional source of food, and there were clay pits for storing liquids such as wine and oil. At some point the population converted to Christianity. A Saxon cemetery included about 100 graves containing about 200 individuals, some buried in family groups and others singly. Most were east–west burials with the head at the western end, which suggests that they were Christian. Evidence of a post-Roman building with a sunken floor was also found; it could have been a chapel.[22] Somerset's large cemeteries may each have been associated with an Anglo-Saxon estate.

St Decumans, Watchet

St Decumans is a mile south-west of Watchet, on the north Somerset coast. It is situated on high ground above the town, and served the large Saxon estate of Williton. Decuman's name might derive from the Latin *Decumanus* (meaning 'tenth'), in which case he could have been a Romanised Briton; however, this could be a later Latin version of a British name. He may have been Welsh: a saint Degyman is patron of Roscrowther parish (or Llanddegyman) in south Pembrokeshire, where a monastery named after him was listed in the *Laws of Hywel Dda* ('Hywel the Good', *c.* 880–950) as one of the 'seven bishop houses in Dyved', or south-west Wales, along with St David's and Llandeilo Fawr.[23] There are other dedications to Degyman in south Wales and Cornwall.

ILLUS. 32. Holy well at St Decumans, Watchet.

Michael Calder has proposed that St Decumans is a pre-Saxon church site, in a typical location high above a river, with partial evidence of a surrounding oval enclosure. A *follis* of Justinian I, dating from AD 540–41, was found here – a coin of low value, made of bronze coated with silver. It was issued by the mint of Constantinople and was found in 'St Decuman's garden', which appears to be the same as 'St Decuman's acre', a curved field parallel with the church, mentioned in the fourteenth century.[24]

In Saxon times, the church may have been relocated to Daw's Castle, a conjectured Anglo-Saxon *burh* on the opposite river bank, closer to the sea, where burials were found; early maps name an adjacent field 'Old Minster'. However, the *burh* was abandoned due to coastal erosion, perhaps in the early eighth century, and worshippers may have returned to the original site, further inland.[25]

The church at Watchet was dedicated to St Decuman by about 1190; his legendary fifteenth-century Life was probably written at Wells cathedral, to which St Decumans belonged. It relates that he lived as a hermit and was murdered one day while at prayer.[26]

Decuman's holy well is inside a well-house off the lane below the church on the steeply sloping hillside (illus. 32). The water is contained in a semicircular basin and until recently it flowed into two pools, before continuing underground. In 1914, the Benedictine monk Ethelbert Horne noted a record from around 1100 that states: 'The fountain of St Decuman is sweet, healthful and necessary to the inhabitants for drinking purposes'. He added that 'The water is still sought after by the inhabitants, or was when I saw this curious spring in Sept 1914'.[27]

ILLUS. 33. Ancient yew tree outside the church of St Dubricius, Porlock.

Porlock and other late dedications to early saints

The church at Porlock is named after the early bishop Dubricius (or Dyfrig in Welsh), but it is not known how early this dedication may be. The church is called *ecclesia S. Dubricii* in the foundation deed of the Harrington chantry chapel in 1476. The yew tree in the churchyard (illus. 33) dates from early times; inside the church are two fragments of a pre-Norman cross. The church was formerly closer to the sea, which has now receded. Its stocky tower, perhaps dating from the thirteenth century, may have had a light on top of its spire to guide boats into the harbour.

There are other churches and chapels in Somerset that are likely to have been dedicated to early saints in the high medieval period, though probably not before, such as those of Nectan at Cheddar, Benignus (or Beon) at Meare, Carantoc at Carhampton, Paternus (or Padarn) at Nailsea and Gildas at Street, who was also claimed to have chosen Flat Holm as a Lenten retreat. Timberscombe was named after St Petroc because it belonged to St Petroc's priory at Bodmin in Cornwall.

There are a number of early church sites in the area surrounding Porlock. One is a small church with a late dedication, possibly to Columbanus, in the hamlet of Culbone, a tiny settlement in a deep valley above the sea, 4 miles west of Porlock. Breton variants of the name of Columbanus include Coulomb and Coulban.[28] Culbone's earlier name was Kitnor (or 'Kite Slope', referring to these small birds of prey): this name is recorded both in Domesday Book and in a lawsuit of 1225.[29]

ILLUS. 34. Saxon font, Culbone church.

According to Domesday Book (f. 88) there were only four inhabitants: two villeins (villagers), a bordar (owner of a smallholding) and a serf (slave). The ground plan of the tiny church is Saxon; it may have developed from an earlier hermit's chapel. There is a Saxon font (illus. 34) on a Victorian base; the porch dates from the thirteenth century; the nave was rebuilt in the fifteenth. A so-called 'lepers' squint' set into the north wall does not in fact allow those outside to view the altar; it is designed to throw light on the pulpit.[30]

Two miles south-west of the church is the Culbone stone, a slab of local Hangman grit, decorated with a wheel cross in the seventh to the ninth century. The stem of the cross was extended, perhaps later. The stone appears to mark the parish boundary between Culbone and Porlock, and may have been removed from a prehistoric stone row, 40 m to the north. There is another inscribed cross on one of the stones in the stone row, which is now about 340 m long, and was probably once greater in length. It runs east–west in woodland near the A39, west of Porlock. There are about twenty-one stones remaining, but many are overgrown.[31]

Early Christian memorial stones commemorating individuals are a notable survival of this period in parts of western Britain. The only stone in Somerset, near the border with Devon, stands on Winsford Hill, Exmoor, 8 miles south of Porlock (illus. 35). It is just off the B3223 at OS 889335, and is inscribed CARATACI NEPUS, or '[the stone] of the grandson [or immediate descendant] of Caratacus'. It has been dated to the last third of the sixth century; no grave has been found at the site. Caratacus is a heroic British name.[32] Such memorials may indicate a literate Christian elite at this date.[33]

The Caratacus stone is less than a mile south-east of five Bronze Age round barrows (three were named the Wambarrows by the twelfth century, when they are mentioned as boundary markers), which are also close to the route across the summit of Winsford Hill, broadly in a line running from north-west to south-east. These high-class deceased leaders, including the descendant of Caratacus, could therefore be remembered by those who passed by.

ILLUS. 35. The Caratacus stone, Winsford Hill.

Carhampton: a monastery with a smelting industry

Another medieval church was dedicated to Carantoc at Carhampton, 8 miles east-south-east of Porlock. The name Carhampton is formed from the Old English words *carrum* and *tun* ('rock town'), but the sixteenth-century antiquary John Leland thought that the place-name derived from the saint, drawing on information from a twelfth-century Latin Life of Carantoc. By Leland's time it was known as *Carntoun*, which he explained as 'Carantokes towne'. Leland describes two churches, one being the church of St John the Baptist that survives today, and the other 'a chapel of this sainct [Carantoc] that sumtyme was the paroch chirche'.[34]

The location of Carantoc's church remained unknown until 1993, when Charles and Nancy Hollinrake excavated an early medieval building at Eastbury Farm on the eastern edge of the village. The site is typical of a pre-Saxon monastery, in an undefended location, on the edge of the alluvial levels, with easy access to the sea. There are suitable landing bays and beaches within half a mile, yet its location renders it invisible to pirates. Unfortunately, torrential rains hindered the Hollinrakes' exploratory excavations, but, nevertheless, significant discoveries were made.

Most of the features investigated dated from the sixth to the tenth centuries: timber buildings, a cemetery and enclosures bounded by ditches. There were four pieces of sixth-century pottery imported from the Mediterranean, including the handle of an amphora, and a piece of seventh-century pottery, probably imported from Gaul. Two fragments of early glass were also found: all these artefacts suggest a high-status site. Nearby was a later enclosed cemetery, in use from the twelfth to the sixteenth centuries. All this probably lay within a large oval enclosure, about 350 m long and up to 250 m wide.[35]

The position of the early medieval church was deduced from holes for posts, stakes and perhaps timbers. There were early cobbled floors and possible cobbled tracks. A number of finds dated from the fourth to the fifth centuries, suggesting that this was a very early site. Its most unusual feature was a large quantity of iron ore and slag. Iron was smelted here, mainly in the sixth and seventh centuries, but continuing into the tenth century. Some of the iron may have been used for smithing in the monastery, but most of it was worked into billets for export. This is the only early British smelting site in south-west England; it could be one of the largest in England and Wales.[36]

In Saxon times, the three royal estates of Carhampton, Williton and Cannington encompassed the entire north-west Somerset coast between Minehead and the River Parrett. The Anglo-Saxon Chronicle records successful Viking raids on Carhampton in the ninth century; the site would have been easy to capture if Carhampton were an undefended monastery, yet, despite the raids, it continued to be occupied through the Saxon period into the thirteenth century.[37]

A cemetery on Lundy Island

There is less evidence of early Christianity around Devon's two coastlines, but Lundy Island in the Bristol Channel, 12 miles north-north-west of Hartland Point, is one of the most significant early Christian sites in Devon. The island is 3 miles long and half a mile wide; it is a well-defended plateau, protected by steep cliffs. As the arrangements at the modern landing stage show, landing on the island would not have been easy (colour plates 6, 7).

From about 2500 BC, Neolithic people created a ritual landscape on Lundy, with cairns, burial mounds and standing stones. Near its northern end, Bronze Age hut circles and low field walls may date from 1000 BC. By about 450 BC, Carthaginian traders had established links with the silver mines along the coast of the Bristol Channel. There is little evidence of Iron Age or Roman activity on Lundy, though a small amount of pottery was found dating from the third and fourth centuries AD. It was made in Dorset or south Devon, which indicates that Lundy was in contact with the Devon mainland.

By the fifth century, there was a small Christian settlement at the south-western end of Lundy. No church has been found, and few dwellings, but a cemetery at Beacon Hill yielded substantial evidence when it was excavated by Charles Thomas in 1969. Four inscribed memorial stones enabled the site to be accurately dated.[38] It could have been a secular or a monastic site, though Thomas considered it to be the latter. There were few clues to indicate where or how Lundy's Christians lived; perhaps they used little pottery, apart from occasional Mediterranean imported ware. The inhabitants may have reclaimed Bronze Age huts: one hut circle on Beacon Hill was reused in Roman times.[39]

The cemetery was originally enclosed by an oval bank and ditch, which can still be seen at its south-west corner; Thomas viewed this as the *lan* enclosure of an early monastery. There could be a church in an unexcavated portion of the cemetery. Twenty-three cist graves were found, but only a small area of the cemetery was uncovered; it was estimated that 100 people had been buried here. Some of the early Christian graves were small, as if for children. Use of the cemetery on the island had perhaps ended by the seventh century; no community is mentioned in later written records.[40]

Lundy's possible shrine grave

The cemetery stands within an extensive field system, with huts dating from the later centuries BC and the first few centuries AD.[41] The cemetery's inscribed stones date from the fifth or sixth century AD. Three of the four are inscribed with single names; this suggests that they perhaps belonged to monks or nuns who had renounced their earthly families. An early Christian slab-lined (or cist) grave was situated within a stone enclosure filled with small granite pebbles that may have been intended as prayers to a holy person; this could have been their grave (illus. 36). No bones have survived in the acidic soil, but the grave had been opened, perhaps a century later, possibly to transfer the relics to a monastery on the mainland; the nearest would have been that of St Nectan at Hartland.[42] Two other burials to the west of the shrine grave, also in cists made from stones taken from an earlier Romano-British hut, may be contemporary with the shrine grave; they were contained within the same rectangular enclosure.[43]

Inscribed stones on Lundy

The inscribed stones (illus. 37) offer unique insights into the Christian settlement. The earliest slab dates from the last third of the fifth century, and is inscribed [OP]TIMI, Latin for '[memorial of] the Best One'. No example of this name has been found elsewhere; it is a Latin name of a male. A stone dating from the first third of the sixth century commemorates a woman: below a circle, perhaps enclosing a cross, is carved the Latin name RESTEVTAE or '[the memorial] of Restieuta'.[44]

A third stone dates from the second third of the sixth century, inscribed with a cross incised in a circle, followed by POTITI, or '[the stone] of Potitus';

ILLUS. 36. Early Christian shrine grave, Beacon Hill cemetery, Lundy Island.

ILLUS. 37. Four inscribed stones in Beacon Hill cemetery, Lundy Island.

this was also the name of St Patrick's grandfather, a priest.[45] The final memorial slab dates from the last third of the sixth century and reads ...IGERNI [FIL]I TIGERNI, meaning '[the stone] of ...igernus, son of Tigernus'.[46] The British name-element *tigern* or 'great prince' is found in a number of names of the period, such as the warlord Vortigern and St Kentigern of Glasgow. Tigern might have been a high-born abbot or a secular leader prominent in the community.

The *Orkneyinga Saga* describes a Viking fortress on Lundy in the mid-twelfth century.[47] In 1199 King John confirmed an earlier grant of the island to the Knights Templar, although this was contested by the Norman Marisco family, who apparently owned Lundy. King Henry III built a castle on the island; the foundations of a thirteenth-century chapel can be seen in Beacon Hill cemetery.

Early Christian sites on the Devon mainland

There is less evidence of Celtic Christianity on the Devon mainland, because the Anglo-Saxons conquered the region at an early date. There was considerable continuity, however: it is likely that the Saxon minsters of Cornwall and west Devon developed out of pre-Saxon monasteries. There are also standing stones with Latin inscriptions like those on Lundy Island, dating from the fifth to the seventh centuries. They commemorate the dead from the local aristocracy, mainly men, who had become Christian. About forty of these can be identified, eleven between the River Exe and the Tamar in what is now Devon, and thirty-one west of the

River Tamar, in Cornwall.[48] The earliest of these may pre-date churches; often they were erected beside ancient tracks, where they could be seen by travellers.

Early Christian place-names in Devon

In Devon and adjacent regions conquered by the Saxons, a small group of place-names ending in *-stow*, *-ciric* and *-burh* may indicate the presence of an early hermit or monk, although by the mid-tenth century *-stow* had become a generalised term for a religious establishment. The earlier usage may apply to the Devon settlements of Stowford, Jacobstow and Instow, each of which stands within an oval enclosure.[49] Stowford is a village 11 miles south-west of Okehampton, with an inscribed stone in its churchyard dating from around AD 700; Jacobstow is named after St James of Compostella and Instow is dedicated to St John the Evangelist. Listed in Domesday Book as *Johannesto*, it is in a typical location for an early religious site, close to the sea but protected from pirates, on a tidal river estuary where the Rivers Taw and Torridge meet. It is 6 miles west of Barnstaple.

The name-element *cirice* means 'church'; it, too, can indicate the presence of an early foundation. There are two instances of *ciric-stow* in Devon, including Cheristow (*Chircstoua* in Pipe Rolls, 1168), now a farm near Hartland abbey, associated with St Wenn. She was said to be one of the twelve daughters of Brychan, a semi-mythological ruler of Brecon; the parish of St Wenn in Cornwall is also named after her. As we saw at the beginning of the chapter, the suffix *-stow* may replace the lost British name of an early church site.

There are four examples of Cheriton (*ciric-tun*, or 'church town') in Devon, including Cheriton Bishop, 9 miles west of Exeter; it was so named because it was held by the bishop of Exeter. A farm in Cheriton parish is named Treable; this is one of the few British place-names to survive in Devon and suggests a pre-Saxon settlement. Treable means '*trev* (or homestead) of Ebel', who was a landowner with a British name. Although it is first recorded quite late, in 1242, it is described as an estate called 'Hyple's [meaning Ebel's] old land' granted by King Edward in 976 to his vassal Æelfsige. The estate's boundaries are described in the charter; its eastern boundary is marked by a hollow way and two massive earth banks that still survive. This is an unusual example of a church site close to a pre-Saxon farmstead.[50]

Nectan of Hartland

One of the most likely sites on the north Devon coast for a pre-Saxon hermitage, or even a monastery, is Hartland. However, no evidence survives from early times, though St Nectan was later claimed to have been a local hermit. At earlier sites in Gaul, such as Lérins, hermits often lived in association with monasteries; if they came to be known as holy, they might be honoured as a local saint. By the eleventh century, Hartland (*Nectanstoc*) had become a significant Saxon minster, centred on the cult of Nectan.[51]

He was believed to be a son of Brychan, the semi-legendary dynastic founder of the early kingdom of *Brycheiniog*, or Brecon, in south-east Wales, perhaps in the fifth century. Churches supposedly named after Brychan's children are found in Wales, south-east Ireland, Devon, Cornwall and Brittany. Some of these may date from early times, but Brychan was popular in the late medieval period, and many more churches were then named after his so-called family.

Claimed to be the eldest of Brychan's twenty-four children, Nectan is the subject of three documents probably dating from the twelfth century and written at Hartland abbey, preserved in the fourteenth-century Gotha manuscript: a short Life (the *Vita S. Nectani Martyris*), an account of the rediscovery of his body in the tenth or eleventh century and its interment in a shrine in Hartland church (the *Inventio*), and a description of fifteen recent miracles (the *Miracula*), which include cures of diseases such as paralysis, and madness.[52] Some of the cures occurred at Hartland, and others elsewhere, for Nectan's relics were taken as far afield as Marhamchurch in Cornwall, 15 miles to the south, and to Barnstaple, 25 miles to the south-east. A knight from Dunster in Somerset came to Hartland on pilgrimage and was said to have been cured of a paralysed arm as he approached the abbey.[53]

Nectan is not mentioned in Welsh accounts of Brychan, although a monk named Nectan occurs in medieval Welsh genealogies. His *Vita* is short and lacks detail, which suggests that little was known about Nectan, even at the centre of his cult. It relates that Nectan crossed the Bristol Channel and settled at Stoke in Hartland as a hermit. We are told that Nectan's brothers and sisters settled in Wales, Devon and Cornwall, and that they met together at his cell every New Year's Eve; in this way, the monks of Hartland claimed authority for their foundation over those of his brothers and sisters.[54]

In the *Vita*, many of Nectan's brothers and sisters are given the names of patron saints of parishes in north-east Cornwall and Devon, though only two or three of these occur in Welsh traditions, so the names of the rest seem to derive from local saints known in the twelfth century. Nectan was said to have been beheaded by two robbers; he was widely venerated in south-west Britain, largely through promotion of his cult by the clerics of Stoke at Hartland.

Hartland's status

Hartland's minster was in a position to benefit from its connection with a royal *vill*, 1.5 miles away. Saxon *vills* were centres for royal estates and played an important role in the collection of royal dues, in rural administration and the provision of justice. The West Saxon kings established or confirmed minster churches close to royal settlements.[55] According to the *Miracula*, Gytha, widow of Earl Godwin (d. 1053), greatly honoured St Nectan's church at Stoke, giving it lands and precious objects, and installed two clerics named Æthelmann and Leofmann, whose descendants continued to hold the property.[56]

ILLUS. 38. Norman font, Stoke church, near Hartland.

Exeter Domesday Book relates that in 1066 there were twelve canons at Hartland, each holding a ploughland – an area able to be ploughed in a year by a team of eight oxen.[57] A Norman cleric named Gerald was later imposed on these Saxon clergy by King William I; in 1086 Gerald the chaplain held two hides 'which the canons of that house used to hold … the same twelve canons … now hold them of Gerald and pay him 40s. yearly'.[58] This was a very large sum of money.

Nothing is known of the earliest church at Stoke. Bishop Lyfing of Crediton (d. 1046) authorised the erection of a shrine to contain St Nectan's relics, for which he donated bells, lead for the roof and a carved reliquary. Nectan's staff was said to be preserved there, decorated with gold, silver and jewels. The shrine was supported by Saxon kings and Norman lords. An elaborate Norman square arcaded font (illus. 38) is thought to date from about 1170, with carved heads at the corners.

The collegiate church was replaced by a house of Augustinian friars at nearby Hartland abbey in the twelfth century. The friars restored Stoke church and its shrine, which they continued to tend until their dissolution at the Reformation. The large and impressive church visible today was built in the fourteenth century (illus. 39), and a statue of Nectan placed on the east face of the tower: his head was removed at the Reformation, and has been replaced. Hartland abbey was later rebuilt; only its cloister remains.

The twelfth-century document containing the Life of St Nectan hints at church politics: it appears to record an attempt by the community at Hartland to extend its influence over other churches of north-west Devon and north-east Cornwall, named after Nectan's brothers and sisters. While it claims authority over these sites, it does not mention churches dedicated to well-known saints, such as David and Petroc, or other saints of superior status.[59]

From the tenth century, guilds arose associated with larger churches. These were lay groups who promoted the spiritual welfare of their members: they provided candle wax or money for the church at major feasts, brought members' bodies to the church for burial and gave money for Masses after their death. They also engaged in festive jollity: the *Vita* describes the guild brothers at Hartland struggling to boil the pot in their house beside the cemetery at St Nectan's minster, because it was occupied by the miraculous eel from St Nectan's holy well.[60] The well (illus. 40) is 100 m from Stoke church, down a steep path off Stoke's main street; it is enclosed in a stone well-house.

Fish and eels in wells were regarded with awe and respect from pre-Christian times onwards. They are associated with holy wells in Ireland, Scotland and Wales, and appear in the Lives of Celtic saints. Eels were associated with St Cybi's wells at Llangybi (Caernarvonshire) and Holyhead, for example. If the patient stood barelegged in the former well, and a large eel coiled itself around their legs, it was believed that a cure would follow.[61]

There is another dedication to Nectan at Welcombe, a hamlet 4 miles south-west of Hartland. It was a dependent chapel of Stoke, and eventually became a parish church. It, too, was established by Norman times: there is a Norman tub font in the church. St Nectan's holy well is near the church, at a junction of lanes. It is contained within a substantial stone well-house with a steeply pitched roof and a niche which may have contained a statue of St Nectan, above its lintelled doorway (illus. 41).

St Brannoc of Braunton

Braunton is near the coast, 17 miles north-east of Hartland. It is one of Devon's earliest recorded Christian sites, described in the mid-ninth century as *Brannocminster*, or Brannoc's monastery, in a charter which states that the King of Wessex granted ten hides of land at *Brannocminster* to Glastonbury abbey.[62] Ælfgar the priest and the priests of Braunton are mentioned in Domesday Book.[63] Thus in early Saxon times it was a major church still dedicated to its pre-Saxon saint. Later it diminished in importance and became a parish church which was appropriated by Exeter cathedral in 1221.[64]

Details of Brannoc's life, as recounted by the Devon antiquary Thomas Westcote in 1630, are taken from the Life of Brynach of Nevern in Pembrokeshire, a better-known saint, whose Life is preserved in a twelfth-century Welsh

ILLUS. 39. St Nectan's church, Stoke, near Hartland.

ILLUS. 40 *(left)*. St Nectan's well, Stoke, near Hartland.

ILLUS. 41 *(right)*. St Nectan's well, Welcombe.

manuscript; we therefore know nothing about Brannoc apart from his name. The antiquary William Worcestre (1415–82) heard that Brannoc's body was preserved at Braunton. Some of his bones were presented to Exeter cathedral by the dean of the cathedral, who was also rector of Braunton; they are recorded in a cathedral inventory of 1327.[65]

The name Brannoc also appears to be an element of the name Branscombe, a coastal parish in south Devon between Seaton and Sidmouth. This seems to be an early Saxon dedication meaning 'Brannoc's combe, or valley'; it is recorded as *Branescumb* in about AD 880.[66] The ground plan of Branscombe's Saxon church can be traced, and there is Saxon herringbone tooling on stones in the tower and stonework at the base of the nave.[67]

Churches of St Ke and St Rumon

Nine miles south-east of Braunton, a third early church site is Landkey, near the tidal River Taw, a mile south of Barnstaple. The name means '*Lan*, or church, of Ke', a dedication similar to that of *Lantokay* in Street, described in chapter two. Landkey's name is not recorded until 1166,[68] but its form, *Landechai*, indicates a pre-Saxon origin, and indicates the possible presence of an early community. It is one of the few pre-Saxon church sites in north Devon.

ILLUS. 42 *(left)*. Bowl of a Saxon font, Romansleigh church.

ILLUS. 43 *(right)*. St Rumon's well, Romansleigh.

Romansleigh, 11 miles south-east of Landkey, is an early site that acquired its dedication later. In Domesday Book it is simply named *Liega*, meaning 'a wood, or a woodland clearing', from the Old English *leah*. However, it appears as *Reymundesle* in 1228, a name derived from the early Cornish saint, Rumon.[69] By this time it belonged to Tavistock abbey, which was founded in 981. William Dugdale notes that the abbey was lavishly endowed by King Edgar (reigned 959–75) with about twenty properties, including the church of *Leghe* (Latin, *Lega*), and that the donations were confirmed in 1193 by Pope Celestine III.[70]

Tavistock was dedicated to the Virgin Mary and Saint Rumon, whose relics were brought from Ruan Lanihorne in Cornwall to Tavistock abbey in the tenth or eleventh century. William of Malmesbury visited the abbey in 1120, where he saw an effigy of Rumon 'buried as a bishop, decorated with a beautiful shrine'. The church at Romansleigh contains the bowl of a plain Saxon font (illus. 42); St Rumon's well (illus. 43) is to the north of the church, just outside and below the churchyard; it stands beside a sunken medieval track into the village.

Early Christians in Exeter

The south coast of Devon also offers evidence of early Christianity. A single find in Exeter, at the southern end of the Fosse Way, hints at the presence of Christians in Roman times. During excavations in 1945–46 near South Street, a fragment of coarse black pottery was found, probably dating from the fourth century, with a form of the *chi-rho* symbol for Christ pecked on the outside; the pot was perhaps owned by humble people.[71] Excavations have revealed a cemetery south-west of Exeter cathedral, dating from the fifth to the seventh centuries, on the site of the former Roman basilica, or assembly hall. The graves appear to be Christian, and their location at the centre of the town suggests a church nearby.[72]

A post-Roman cemetery was discovered in a field at Kenn, 5 miles south of Exeter, in 1995. Radiocarbon dating suggests that it was in use from about the fifth to the eighth centuries. Over a hundred graves were found, of which forty-seven were excavated. They were mostly aligned east–west, which indicates that this might have been a Christian burial ground. Seven small clusters of graves could represent family groupings; no grave markers were found.[73] The field is named 'Long Stone', which may refer to a pre-Christian menhir (a Cornish word meaning 'stone long'); this would suggest that the field had been used for burial before the arrival of Christianity.

Exeter's monastery

When the Saxons entered Devon in the seventh century, they established monasteries, or sometimes took over existing ones that later became minsters housing a group of secular canons. The earliest known monastery is that of Exeter, where St Boniface (672–754) was educated in about 690. At this time it was still monastic in its lifestyle, for we are told that Boniface trained to be a monk, according to information from Willibald, his successor as bishop of Mainz. Exeter's abbot bore a Saxon name, Wulfheard, but because Boniface studied here so soon after the Saxon conquest, this was possibly a pre-Saxon foundation.[74]

At least two of Devon's minsters were envisaged or built during the eighth century – Crediton, 9 miles north-west of Exeter, and Axminster (or 'monastery on the River Axe'), 24 miles east of Exeter. The Anglo-Saxon Chronicle records that a prince named Cyneheard was buried at Axminster in 757. By the eleventh century there were fourteen minsters in Devon, all founded or endowed by kings, or close to royal manors.[75] This Saxon royal initiative makes it difficult to know which monasteries might have existed in pre-Saxon times.

Exeter became a cathedral only in 1050; the see was transferred from Crediton as it declined in importance, although a college of canons remained at Crediton to administer the buildings and continue the life of the collegiate church. By this time, a century of economic growth had led to the development and expansion of towns, in which churches multiplied. Four are recorded in eleventh-century Exeter, including St Olaf's church, near the street called *Irlesbyri* ('earl's *burh*'), which received small endowments from Earl Harold's mother and the king in the early 1060s.[76] It was dedicated to the Norwegian king Olaf Haraldsson (*c.* 995–1030), who had been killed in battle only thirty years earlier.

St Sidwell's shrine

Another eleventh-century Exeter church, on land owned by the cathedral outside the east gate of the town, was named after *St Sidefulle*. A document from around 1000 suggests that she was buried near the city; her Saxon name means 'full of morals', and therefore 'the virtuous one'.[77] Her relics were venerated in the church, and a nearby well was dedicated to her. An eleventh-century catalogue of relics at Exeter cathedral calls her 'the gentle virgin St Satiuola, who though innocent was killed by her father's hired man, a mower (*maedmannum*), but almighty God afterwards showed many miracles at her tomb'.[78]

Sidwell's name was later equated with the Latin *satis volens* ('sufficiently willing'); she was therefore considered, on flimsy evidence, to be the pre-Saxon Sitofolla, who is named as a sister of St Paul de Leon, in his ninth-century Breton Life. Since her cult first appears in eleventh-century Exeter, Sidwell is more like to have been a Saxon saint than a British one. A short Life of Sidwell was included in a compilation by Bishop Grandisson in the 1330s for use in the cathedral on her feast day. It recounts how her stepmother had her murdered by her father's reapers, who cut off her head. A spring arose where she died, and she carried her head to the site where her church was later built. The story resembles that of St Juthwara of Sherborne in Dorset, and it is unclear which came first.[79]

Behind the legend lies the pagan myth of the corn spirit dying at the hands of the reapers at harvest time, to be reborn the following spring. By the fourteenth century, a light burned before Sidwell's tomb, which was tended by a keeper. The parish of Laneast in Cornwall was dedicated to her by 1437, and she is depicted on benches and screens in about twenty churches in Cornwall, Devon and Somerset. Sidwell became a popular girls' name in Devon and Cornwall in the sixteenth and seventeenth centuries.[80]

Early Christians around Dartmoor

Some twelve post-Roman memorial stones dating from the fifth to the seventh centuries have been found on the fringes of Dartmoor, though none are in their original position.[81] They commemorate tribal leaders, some of whom were of the new Christian faith. The inscriptions are in Latin and/or ogham, an alphabet used by Irish speakers, consisting of horizontal lines and strokes carved at an angle, incised on the edges of the stones. One such monument is in the village of Lustleigh, on the eastern edge of Dartmoor, 12 miles south-west of Exeter, in the Wrey Valley. This area was inhabited in early times: there are remains of Bronze Age stone hut circles in the Cleave (meaning 'cliff' or 'cleft') at the edge of the valley, and an Iron Age hill fort on nearby Hunters Tor, that was probably one of a chain of forts along the eastern edge of Dartmoor.[82]

The curvilinear raised churchyard suggests an early burial ground, and it is one of only four church sites in Devon that contains an early inscribed stone, which now stands in the north aisle of the church. The memorial slab dates from the last third of the sixth century; its inscription is in two lines, to be read downwards. It reads DATUIDOCI FILI CONHINOCI, and means '[the stone] of Datuidoc, the son of Conhinoc' (illus. 44). The language is Latin, while the names are of two British males. Datuidoc may derive from *Date-Uidacos* and mean 'fortunate, lucky' (like the later Welsh *dedwyddach*), and Conhinoc may derive from the Latin *Cuno-Senacos*, and mean 'Elderly Hound', thus describing a warrior who was both experienced and fleet of foot.[83] The stone describes two local Christian chieftains prominent in eastern Dartmoor.

The Exeter Anthology

A manuscript preserved in Exeter was compiled in the second half of the tenth century in a monastery somewhere in south-west Britain, drawing on early Saxon sources. Also known as the Exeter Book, it is the largest surviving collection of Old English poetic literature.[84] The anthology contains 130 religious and secular poems, including 'elegies' or meditative poems, such as *The Ruin*, quoted in the previous chapter, in which a monk lamented over the destruction of Roman Bath, *The Wanderer*, *The Seafarer*, *Advent Lyrics* and over ninety riddles. The book was donated to the cathedral's library in 1072 by Leofric, the first bishop of Exeter; there is a copy of his will in the first quire of the manuscript. Leofric (*c.* 1016–72) was appointed by King Edward the Confessor as bishop of Devon and Cornwall in 1046.

The anthology is a fine example of tenth-century Benedictine scholarship, and of the monks' concern to preserve the heritage of previous centuries. At the time of Leofric's death, Exeter's monastery was not rich, and its library would have been enhanced by his donation of 'one great English book on various subjects'.[85] The compiler of the anthology assembled the work of various poets, whose aims were to glorify God, while teaching Christian doctrine, through sophisticated verse composed in the native language of the English people. The collection is an elegant monastic production which expresses the devout yet cosmopolitan literary culture of England during the period when Benedictine monks reinvigorated monastic life.

The copyist was a conscientious craftsman who made hundreds of corrections to his own work, inserting letters above and below the text. When he made an error, he often scraped away bits of letters or added strokes to change one letter into another: there are over 400 examples of this in the manuscript. There would have been 150 or 152 folios. Some of the parchment is defective: this suggests that a large quantity of high-quality parchment was not set aside for this manuscript, perhaps because it contained vernacular, not Latin, texts, and was not designed for use in worship. On some folios there are traces of gold leaf. This indicates that at a later date, when the text was no longer understood or valued, the manuscript was used to store sheets of gold leaf used to decorate other volumes produced in the monastery's scriptorium.[86]

The ninety-five riddles in the Exeter Book vary in length from four or five lines to over a hundred. Their subject matter is very diverse, and may be roughly divided into the religious, the obscene and those descriptive of natural or domestic objects and weapons. They range from the light-hearted to the serious. Riddle 25 is eleven lines long, and asks: 'What is smooth above and hairy below?' The answer is 'an onion'. From the fifth century, the riddle became a popular Latin exercise. In England, it reached the height of popularity in the eighth century, when riddles were composed by Bishop Aldhelm of Sherborne (*c.* 639–709), among others. Many are based on Latin originals: Riddle 35, 'Coat of Mail' is an Anglo-Saxon translation of Aldhelm's Latin *De Lorica*.[87]

A description of a gospel book

Riddle 26 describes the creation of a gospel book like the Book of Kells or the Lindisfarne Gospels, composed by a monk who was familiar with the process. First, the calves were skinned; their hides were washed and scraped to remove the blood and gore and then soaked for several days in a tawing tank, using lime to whiten them. The hides were next scraped and thinned with knives on a hard floor. They were then stretched over an oblong frame to be shaved with a curved knife, pumice rubbers and smoothing stones. Any gashes would be mended with a needle and thread.[88] All this is described in the first six lines of the riddle:

> Some enemy deprived me [a calf] of my life,
> And took away my worldly strength, then wet me,
> Dipped me in water, took me out again,
> Set me in sunshine, where I quickly lost
> The hairs I had. Later the knife's hard edge
> Cut me with all impurities ground off.[89]

Each piece of vellum was formed from the skin of a single cow or calf.

It was now cut to size and taken to the scriptorium, where the sheets would be planned, prepared and written on by more experienced monks. They folded the vellum, and used quill pens, made from 'the bird's fine raiment' (mainly the wing-feathers of geese and swans), which they dipped in ink ('tree-dye') mixed with water, to mark out the page and then inscribe the letters. The black ink was made from oak galls (or 'oak apples'): these are round balls caused by a gall wasp larva. They were combined with iron sulphate, to which gum was added, so that the ink would adhere to the parchment. This method was used from the fifth century until recent times.[90] The anonymous monk continues:

> Then fingers folded me; the bird's fine raiment [a quill pen]
> traced often over me with useful drops [of ink]
> across my brown domain, swallowed the tree-dye [ink]

ILLUS. 44 *(opposite)*. Sixth-century memorial stone, Lustleigh.

PHOTO: FRANCES JONES.

mixed up with water, stepped on me again [wrote on me]
leaving dark tracks …[91]

The pages were then stitched together, and the book fitted with a cover of wooden boards bound with leather and decorated with fine metalwork. The gorgeous gospel book now proclaimed the good news of the kingdom of God:

… The hero clothed me then
with boards to guard me, stretched hide over me,
decked me with gold; and thus the splendid work
of smiths, with wire bound round, embellished me.
Now my red dye and all my decorations,
my gorgeous trappings far and wide proclaim
the Lord of Hosts, not grief for foolish sins.[92]

Finally, the benefits of reading the gospel book are described. Readers will become bold, joyful and wise; their friends, dear ones and relatives will profit from their wisdom and goodness:

If sons of men will make good use of me,
by that they shall be sounder, more victorious,
their hearts more bold, their minds more full of joy,
their spirits wiser; they shall have more friends,
dear ones and kinsmen, truer and more good,
more kind and faithful, who will add more glory
and happiness by favours, who will lay
upon them kindnesses and benefits,
and clasp them fast in the embrace of love.
Say who I am, useful to men. My name
is famous, good to men, and also sacred.[93]

Throughout Europe, no comparable anthology dating from such an early period has been found. While the volume dates from the tenth century, Riddle 26 is likely to be earlier: the production of illuminated manuscripts declined in the ninth century and virtually ceased after Viking attacks in many regions during the late ninth century.[94] The monastery from which this poem originated would have been a large one: it has been estimated that 100 acres of pasture would be required to support the cows and their calves necessary to create one gospel book.[95] It is tantalising that no clues survive to indicate which monastery was creating such manuscripts, but the survival of the poem indicates the existence of a rich monastic tradition in south-west Britain.

Nuns illuminate manuscripts

It is, indeed, possible that the anthology was created by women: the jaw of an eleventh-century nun exhumed from a convent of about fourteen women in Dalheim near Lichtenau in Westphalia, northern Germany, revealed traces of lapis lazuli, an expensive pigment imported from Afghanistan in order to decorate vellum. Fascinating detective work revealed that she had sucked the end of her paintbrush to a fine point, leaving traces of lapis lazuli in the plaque on her teeth. Other fragments were found in her skeleton, suggesting they had been inhaled or ingested as the stone was ground into fine powder.[96]

Women's monastic communities, especially during earlier periods, were largely made up of noble or aristocratic women, and many were highly educated. Although these women would have led lives largely free of hard labour, work was encouraged within the monastery, and activities related to book production were considered worthy pursuits.[97] In Germany and Austria, nuns worked as scribes and illuminators from the late eighth century onwards.

As we saw in the previous chapter, in the seventh and eighth century there were women's monasteries in Somerset (at Lamyatt, for example), Dorset and Devon.[98] There are later traditions, though without firm evidence, of nuns living in minsters, or monasteries, at both Exeter and Bodmin in late Saxon times.[99] It is possible that manuscripts were illuminated by women at some of the monasteries in seventh- and eighth-century Wessex, and this could also be true of significant early Cornish sites dedicated to female saints, such as St Buryan and Breage in south-west Cornwall, which may have contained monasteries of women in early times.

Notes

1 Nicolas De Maeyer and Anthony Dupont, 'A Study of Augustine's Theology of Martyrdom on the Basis of Sermon 306C (Morin 15) on the Feast of the Martyr Quadratus', in *Felici curiositae: Studies in Latin Literature and Textual Criticism from Antiquity to the Twentieth Century in Honour of Rita Beyers*, ed. Guy Guldentops (Turnhout: Brepols, 2017), vol. 72, pp. 275–79.

2 Michael Calder, 'Early Ecclesiastical Sites in Somerset: Three Case Studies', *Proceedings of the Somerset Archaeological and Natural History Society*, 147 (2004), pp. 13–15.

3 Engraving by T.H. Hare in F. Warre, 'Worle Camp', *Proceedings of the Somerset Archaeological and Natural History Society*, 2 (1851), pp. 64–84.

4 Calder, 'Early Ecclesiastical Sites', pp. 11–13.

5 *Ibid.*, p. 15.

6 'Worlebury Camp: A Large Mutivallate Hillfort on Worlebury Hill', Historic England, Ancient Monuments no. 1011260, 1997.

7 The Life of Samson, ch. 45, from Tomas Taylor, *The Life of St Samson of Dol* (London: SPCK, 1925), emended by Karen Jankulak from the Latin text of Pierre Flobert, *La vie ancienne de saint Samson de Dol* (Paris: CNRS Éditions, 1997).

8 Domesday Book (1086), Exeter, f. 245v.

9 Nicholas Orme, *The Saints of Cornwall* (Oxford: Oxford University Press, 2002), p. 161.

10 Roger H. Leech, 'The Excavation of a Romano-Celtic Temple and a Later Cemetery on Lamyatt Beacon, Somerset', *Britannia*, 17 (1986), pp. 270–72.

11 Ann Woodward and Peter Leach, *The Uley Shrines: Excavation of a Ritual Complex on West Hill, Uley, Gloucestershire, 1977–9* (London: English Heritage, 1993), p. 325.

12 Martin Bell, *Brean Down Excavations 1983–87* (London: English Heritage, 1990), p. 74.
13 *Ibid.*, p. 80.
14 See David Walker, ed., *The Cartulary of St Augustine's Abbey Bristol* (Stroud: Sutton, 1998), p. 27. The Cartulary was compiled in 1270.
15 Eilert Ekwall, *The Concise Oxford Dictionary of English Place-Names*, 4th edn (Oxford: Oxford University Press, 1970), entries: 'Flat Holme'; 'Steep Holme'.
16 *Flat Holm Island* (Cardiff Council, 2004).
17 Stanley and Joan Rendell, *Steep Holm: The Story of a Small Island* (Stroud: Sutton, 1993), pp. 12–17.
18 It was Cantuctun in *c.* 880. Ekwall, *Dictionary of English Place-Names*, entry: 'Cannington'.
19 Michael Costen, *The Origins of Somerset* (Manchester: Manchester University Press, 1992), p. 62.
20 Peter Leach, *Roman Somerset* (Wimborne: The Dovecote Press, 2001), p. 121.
21 Philip Rahtz, 'Pagan and Christian by the Severn Sea', in *The Archaeology and History of Glastonbury Abbey*, ed. Leslie Abrams and James P. Carley (Woodbridge: The Boydell Press, 1991), pp. 14–15.
22 Stuart Joyce, Sian Reynish, Steve Sheldon and Charlotte Haines, *Hinkley Point, Somerset. Archaeological Works: Post-Excavation Assessment SPE1–SPE5 (Task 10.2), Cotswold Archaeology Project 9131; Report 13432, for NNB Genco on behalf of EDF Energy* (2014).
23 Heather James, 'The Geography of the Cult of St David: A Study of Dedication Patterns in the Medieval Diocese', in *St David of Wales: Cult, Church and Nation*, ed. J. Wyn Evans and Jonathan M. Wooding, Studies in Celtic History 24 (Woodbridge: The Boydell Press, 2007), p. 47.
24 Calder, 'Early Ecclesiastical Sites in Somerset', pp. 16–24.
25 *Ibid.*
26 Gilbert H. Doble, *The Saints of Cornwall*, vol. 2: *Saints of the Lizard District* (Truro: Dean and Chapter of Truro Cathedral, repr. 1980), pp. 28–33.
27 Percy Ethelbert Horne, *Somerset Holy Wells and Other Named Wells* (London: Somerset Folk Press, 1923), p. 50.
28 Michel Priziac, *Bretagne des Saints et des croyances* (Grâces-Guincamp: Ki-Dour Editions, 2002), pp. 200, 203. The nearest way to approach the church is from the Culbone Inn on the A39, west of Porlock. Park, and walk along a narrow lane opposite the inn for 1.5 miles through the woods above Porlock Bay.
29 Ekwall, *Dictionary of English Place-Names*, entry: 'Culbone'.
30 Jeremy Sampson, personal communication, 3 September 2017.
31 IMS07891: Culbone Stone, Culbone Hill, 2015.
32 Charles Thomas, *And Shall These Mute Stones Speak?* (Cardiff: University of Wales Press, 1994), pp. 288–89, 329.
33 The Historic Environment Record for Exmoor National Park, MS08534. Caratacus Stone, Winsford Hill, 2017.
34 Karen Jankulak, 'Carantoc Alias Cairnech? British Saints, Irish Saints and the Irish in Wales', in *Ireland and Wales in the Middle Ages*, ed. Karen Jankulak and Jonathan M. Wooding (Dublin: Four Courts Press, 2007), pp. 116–48.
35 Charles and Nancy Hollinrake, 'Archaeological Evaluations in Carhampton, 1993–1995', unpublished report for Somerset County Council, Somerset Sites and Monuments Register, 1997. I am grateful to the authors for giving me access to this report.

36 *Ibid.*
37 *Ibid.*
38 Christopher Webster, Lundy Field Society, 2018, www.lundy.org.uk/index.php/about-lundy/archaeology.
39 Shirley Blaylock, 'Patterns of Settlement on Lundy: Putting Lundy's Archaeology on the Map', in *Lundy Studies*, ed. Jennifer George, Proceedings of the 60th Anniversary Symposium of the Lundy Field Society (Exeter: The National Trust, 2007), p. 21.
40 Thomas, *And Shall These Mute Stones Speak?*, ch. 10.
41 Susan Pearce, *The Kingdom of Dumnonia* (Padstow: Lodenek Press, 1978), p. 70.
42 Webster, Lundy Field Society.
43 Pearce, *The Kingdom of Dumnonia*, p. 70.
44 Thomas, *And Shall These Mute Stones Speak?*, pp. 163–82, 206, 249.
45 St Patrick, *Confessio*, ch. 1.
46 Thomas, *And Shall These Mute Stones Speak?*, pp. 165–66.
47 Anthony F. Langham, *The Isle of Lundy* (Stroud: Sutton, 1994), pp. 9–18.
48 Nicholas Orme, ed., *Unity & Variety: A History of the Church in Devon and Cornwall* (Exeter: University of Exeter Press, 1991), p. 2.
49 John Blair, *The Church in Anglo-Saxon Society* (Oxford: Oxford University Press, 2000), p. 216.
50 William G. Hoskins, *The Making of the English Landscape* (Harmondsworth: Penguin Books, 1970), pp. 30–32, citing Herbert P.R. Finberg, *Early Charters of Devon and Cornwall* (Leicester: Leicester University Press, 1953), pp. 27 ff.
51 Blair, *The Church in Anglo-Saxon Society*, pp. 217, 305.
52 Paul Grosjean, ed., *Vita, Inventio, Miracula S. Nectani Martyris*, Analecta Bollandiana, vol. 71 (1953), pp. 397–414, at p. 410. English translation by Gilbert H. Doble, *The Life of St Nectan*, 'Cornish Saints' Series, no. 48 (Bideford, 1964), pp. 3–28.
53 Orme, *The Saints of Cornwall*, p. 198.
54 Sam Turner, *Making a Christian Landscape* (Exeter: Exeter University Press, 2006), p. 77.
55 *Ibid.*, pp. xiii, 66–67.
56 Blair, *The Church in Anglo-Saxon Society*, pp. 357–58.
57 Exeter Domesday Book, ff. 456–56v, in *Domesday Book: Additamenta* (London, 1816), cited in Blair, *The Church in Anglo-Saxon Society*, pp. 357–58.
58 *Ibid.*, see Blair, *The Church in Anglo-Saxon Society*, p. 364.
59 Turner, *Making a Christian Landscape*, p. 117.
60 Blair, *The Church in Anglo-Saxon Society*, p. 454.
61 Francis Jones, *The Holy Wells of Wales* (Cardiff: University of Wales Press, 1992), pp. 108, 110.
62 Peter H. Sawyer, *Anglo-Saxon Charters: An Annotated List and Bibliography* (London: Royal Historical Society, 1968), S 1695.
63 Exeter Domesday Book, ff. 66, 94, cited in Blair, *The Church in Anglo-Saxon Society*, p. 30.
64 Nicholas Orme, ed., *Nicholas Roscarrock's Lives of the Saints: Cornwall and Devon*, New Series, vol. 35 (Exeter: Devon and Cornwall Record Society, 1992), p. 117.
65 *Ibid.*, p. 118.
66 Walter de Gray Birch, ed., *Cartularium Saxonicum* (London: Whiting, 1885–93), BCS 553.
67 Philip M. Johnstone, in *Proceedings of the Congress of the British Archaeological Association at Exeter* (1927), pp. 50–53.

68 It is named *Landechai* in the Red Book of the Exchequer; see Ekwall, *Dictionary of English Place-Names*, entry: 'Landkey'.
69 *Ibid.*, entry: 'Romansleigh'.
70 William Dugdale, *Monasticon Anglicanum* (London: John Stevens, 1718 edn), 'Additions made to the Benedictines' (*i.e.* addenda to his original work), pp. 115–16.
71 Aileen Fox, *Roman Exeter* (Manchester: Manchester University Press, 1952), p. 92, pl. Xa.
72 Orme, *Unity & Variety*, p. 2.
73 Peter J. Weddell, 'The Excavation of a Post-Roman Cemetery near Kenn, South Devon', *Proceedings of the Devon Archaeological Society*, 58 (2000), pp. 93–126.
74 Orme, *Unity & Variety*, p. 7.
75 *Ibid.*, p. 9.
76 Sawyer, *Anglo-Saxon Charters*, S 1037; Blair, *The Church in Anglo-Saxon Society*, pp. 402–03.
77 Anthony Poulton-Smith, *South Devon Place Names* (Stroud: Amberley, 2013), entry: 'Exeter'.
78 Orme, *Nicholas Roscarrock's Lives of the Saints*, p. 171.
79 *Ibid.*
80 *Ibid.*, p. 172.
81 (No author), *A Guide to the Archaeology of Dartmoor*, rev. edn (Dartmoor National Park Authority, 2003), p. 39.
82 Michael J. Swanton and Susan Pearce, 'Lustleigh in South Devon: Its Inscribed Stone, its Churchyard and its Parish', in *The Early Church in Western Britain and Ireland: Studies presented to C.A. Raleigh Radford*, British Archaeological Society Report (Oxford, 1982), pp. 139–43.
83 Thomas, *And Shall These Mute Stones Speak?*, p. 281.
84 Exeter Cathedral Library MS 3501.
85 … *mycel Englisc boc be gehwilcum þingum on leoð-wisan geworht* …, as described in Leofric's eleventh-century donation list, Oxford, Bodleian Library MA Auct. D. 2. 16 (2719).
86 Bernard J. Muir, 'A Preliminary Report on a New Edition of the Exeter Book', *Scriptorium*, 13, no. 2 (1989), pp. 273–88.
87 Richard Hamer, *A Choice of Anglo-Saxon Verse* (London: Faber and Faber, 2015), intro. to the section 'Riddles'.
88 For a detailed description of evidence of these processes in an excavated monastery, see Martin Carver, *Portmahomack: Monastery of the Picts* (Edinburgh: Edinburgh University Press, 2010), pp. 55, 64, 121–25.
89 Hamer, *A Choice of Anglo-Saxon Verse*, Riddle 26, lines 1–6.
90 See Bernhard Bischoff, *Latin Palaeography: Antiquity and the Middle Ages* (Cambridge: Cambridge University Press, 1990) for a comprehensive account of the manuscript production.
91 Hamer, *A Choice of Anglo-Saxon Verse*, Riddle 26, lines 7–11.
92 *Ibid.*, lines 11–17.
93 *Ibid.*, lines 18–28.
94 Blair, *The Church in Anglo-Saxon Society*, p. 291.
95 R. Fleming, *Britain After Rome: The Fall and Rise, 400 to 1070* (London: Allen Lane/Penguin, 2010), p. 182.

96 Anita Radini, Monica Tromp, Alison Beach, Emma Tong and Camilla Speller, 'Medieval Women's Early Involvement in Manuscript Production Suggested by Lapis Lazuli Identification in Dental Calculus', in *Science Advances*, 5, no. 1 (January 2019), pp. 1–8.

97 *Ibid.*

98 Barbara Yorke, 'The Bonifacian Mission and Female Religious in Wessex', *Early Medieval Europe*, 7, no. 2 (Oxford: Blackwell, 1998), pp. 164–65.

99 Orme, *Unity & Variety*, p. 10.

CHAPTER 4

The Life of Samson

The earliest written evidence of monastic life in Cornwall is found in the First Life of Samson (or *Vita Prima S. Samsonis*). This long and interesting Life was composed by a Breton monk, perhaps in the late seventh century, and it may be based on an earlier written work. Samson lived from about 490 to about 565, and this is the first surviving account of a British wandering monk, or *peregrinus*. As the only near-contemporary record of an early Christian holy man in south-west Britain, it gives us unique insight into how such people lived. It is likely that other early Christians, though less gifted than Samson, followed a similar path, although, or course, many did not travel as *peregrini*, and many were too poor to do other than work the land for someone wealthier than themselves.

In this chapter we shall therefore focus on the First Life of Samson, despite the fact that much of it describes Samson's education in Wales and his later ministry in Brittany: the text reminds us that south-west Britain was intimately linked with these other regions, and it illustrates how these links worked out in practice. The Life contains detailed descriptions of monasteries in several locations and describes the progression of Samson through various stages of monastic life, ending in self-exile (or *peregrinatio*) from his homeland. He died in Brittany, where his relics were honoured at Dol, which became the centre of his cult.

The author also refers to Illtud and Dyfrig (or Dubricius in Latin), providing us with the earliest information we possess concerning these leaders of the Welsh Church. Samson and these other two leading figures were active at what is generally agreed to have been the monastery of Llanilltud Fawr in south-east Wales, and they were also involved with what appears to have been its daughter house on Caldey Island off the Pembrokeshire coast, 40 miles to the west. Dyfrig seems to have been a bishop rather than a monk, while Illtud seems to have been an abbot, though not a bishop.[1] It is likely that other Christians leaders working in south-west Britain received their training at the great monasteries of south Wales.

The first two-thirds of the First Life of Samson (chapters 1–52 of Book 1) describe the unfolding of his monastic life. He achieves a balance between various monastic ideals: he combines stability with a search for more remote places in which to encounter God; he obeys his abbot, but also listens to his own inner call; he is ascetic, but gentle. The Life appears to be written for a monastic audience who understand these ideals, which are also set out in the Rule of Benedict, who was a contemporary of Samson.

ILLUS. 45. Memorial to Dallus Dumelus, Llanddewi Brefi, Ceredigion.

Benedict's Rule is based on long monastic experience, and derives from the earlier 'Rule of the Master'. Monastic life was aimed at a person's transformation, in order to mirror a loving God to an increasing extent. Monks were not primarily involved in pastoral care, but Samson unwillingly assumed this role, first as bursar of his monastery on Caldey Island, then in relation to his family, who travelled across Cornwall with him, and eventually to a wider community, as he became involved in Breton politics. One answer to the question 'What was it like to be an early Christian in south-west Britain?' would be to imagine ourselves as one of Samson's extended family, as they are depicted in his Life.

Samson's name

Early British monks were often given the name of an Old Testament holy man whom they in some way resembled. Samson was sent to the monastery of Illtud at a young age, and it would be likely that Illtud gave him a new monastic name. In the Old Testament, Samson was an ancient warrior leader, born to a barren woman; his birth was announced by an angel (Judges 13. 2–7), like that of John the Baptist, the forerunner of Jesus. Samson 'began to rescue Israel' and was considered as a model for monks, although his violent exploits might cause consternation today.

While on campaign with his followers, the warrior leader came across a colony of bees making honey inside the carcass of a young lion that he had killed earlier. Pondering this sight, he observed: 'Out of the strong came forth sweetness' (Judges 14. 14). Early monks understood this as a description of their calling: a monk was a young lion with honey in his heart or, more precisely, a strong young man whose body was dead to this world's pleasures, while his heart was a honeycomb dripping with love.[2] A monk learned to become strong in virtue and sweet in manner, combining fortitude with kindness.

The monk Samson is depicted in similar terms: he is presented as a young man austerely detached from this world, yet full of the honey of God's love. He ate neither flesh nor fowl, and no one ever saw him drunk. He was praised for his ability to conquer his lust for both women and men, yet he was kind to all. Among the early memorial stones to abbots of St David's monastery at Llanddewi Brefi in Ceredigion, a seventh-century stone commemorates a monk named Dallus Dumelus (illus. 45). One possible interpretation of his double name (though other meanings have been suggested) is that Dallus means '[God's] portion', or 'an offering to God', while Dumelus is an Irish name, which derives from *dun* ('fort') and *mel* ('honey'), meaning something like 'fort of honey'.[3] Like Samson, Dumelus was strong in spirit, yet with sweetness of heart.

Why were monks given new names?

In the scriptures, people were given a new name when they received a new call from God. In the Book of Genesis, God tells Abraham, 'You shall no longer be called Abram; your name shall be called Abraham, for I make you a father of a multitude of nations' (Gen. 17. 5), though in fact his new name is not derived from this expression: there is merely a similarity between 'Abraham' and the Hebrew expression for 'the father of many'. In John's gospel, Jesus gives Simon a new name, Peter: '[Jesus] said, "You are Simon son of John; you shall be called Cephas" – meaning Rock' (Jn 1. 42).

In Luke's gospel, the author explains that John the Baptist was expected to be given his father's name, but God intervened, and gave him a name that means 'The Lord is Gracious', because he would bring such a gracious message to the people. His father Zechariah was struck dumb, and his speech returned only when he gave permission for his son's new name:

> The angel said to him, 'Zechariah, do not be afraid… Your wife Elizabeth is to bear you a son and you must name him John. He will be your joy and delight and many will rejoice at his birth… They were going to call him Zechariah after his father, but his mother spoke up. 'No', she said, 'he is to be called John'.
>
> They said to her, 'But no one in your family has that name,' and made signs to his father to find out what he wanted him called. The father asked for a writing tablet and wrote, 'His name is John'. And they were all astonished. At that instant his power of speech returned and he spoke and praised God. (Lk. 1. 13–14, 59–64)

In this way, John began, as a baby, to bring the graciousness of God to others. In the same way, a monk might receive from his abbot a name that described a gift or characteristic with which God had endowed him.

The First Life of Samson

In its plain and direct Latin style, this work is different from later saints' Lives, with their concern to present their subjects interacting with kings, princes and popes, working spectacular miracles before and after their death: all of which were considered fitting subject matter to be read aloud on their feast day, or to justify their community's expanding territorial claims. These elements are present to some extent in the First Life: Book 2 is a homily for Samson's feast day that recounts a story set in Britain, another in the Channel Islands and two legends from Dol about miracles he worked after his death. But the author also reflects the primitive monasticism found in the Lives of the Desert Mothers and Fathers, when he describes Samson's asceticism and his constant search for solitude.

In the Prologue, the Breton author explains that his source of information is a monk who lived for many years in a British monastery founded by Samson 'beyond the sea', and who now, as an old man, has come to live in the same community as the author. The elderly monk had an uncle named Henoc, who was a cousin of Samson and often talked about him. We are told:

> These words … I derived from a certain religious and venerable old man whose house beyond the sea Samson himself had founded. He led a catholic and religious life there for nearly eighty years. In times most approximate to those of the aforesaid St Samson, the mother of St Samson reported these deeds to [the old man's] uncle [Henoc], a very holy deacon, himself the cousin of St Samson; of what follows [the old man] assured me truthfully, relating to me many parts of the saint's wonderful career.
>
> And not only so, but there are also very many and delightful accounts of the amazing deeds that he performed, … which were written in suitably elegant style and taken across the sea by the said holy deacon, Henoc by name. The venerable old man, of whom we have already spoken, who lived in this monastery, caused them continually to be read piously and attentively before me.[4]

Thus the authorship of this Life is complex: the Breton author refers to an earlier Life 'written in a suitably elegant style' to which he alludes a number of times throughout the work, composed, he infers, by Samson's cousin, Henoc. The 'house beyond the sea' seems to be the monastery that Samson founded in Cornwall; it still existed, though we are not told its exact location, and it apparently possessed an account of Samson's life, upon which the first Breton Life is based.[5]

Supernatural elements in Samson's Life

The author begins in a style typical of saints' Lives, by demonstrating Samson's holiness through using phrases from the gospels. In Luke's Gospel, Mary's cousin Elizabeth is barren until an angel tells her husband that she will give birth to John the Baptist, who will be a great prophet (Lk. 1. 5–25). Similarly, in the Life of Samson, his mother Anna was thought barren until she was told in a dream of the future birth of her child and of his priestly vocation. In the dream she is told: 'Blessed is your womb and more blessed is the fruit of your womb'. This recalls Elizabeth's greeting to the Virgin Mary (Lk. 1. 42).

Jesus healed the sick, cast out devils and raised a widow's son to life (Lk. 7. 11–17). In the same way, Samson's power is demonstrated by healing the sick, casting out devils and raising a dead boy to life. Luke relates that, at Pentecost, tongues of fire came down on the disciples, who were then empowered to go and preach (Acts 2. 1–4). There is an echo of this in Samson's Life, when its author writes that, after his consecration as a bishop, fire came from Samson's mouth and nostrils. This also demonstrates Samson's power over the elements, a quality attributed to Christ in the gospels and, in some medieval Welsh texts, to magicians.

At other points in the Life, the author praises what appear to be druidic powers of Christian monks. We are told that Illtud, with whom Samson studied, was 'by birth a most learned magician (*magicus*), having knowledge of the future', though some early copyists were uncomfortable with the term *magicus* and altered the word to *magnificus* (or 'noble').[6] The author describes how, through his prayer, Samson caused the death of a witch who brandished a 'bloody trident' (ch. 27), and how on several occasions he killed or banished a large serpent.

In early Lives, saints were often depicted as killing snakes, while Patrick was said to have banished snakes from Ireland. In addition to its biblical associations with the fall of Adam and Eve (Gen. 3. 1–15), a serpent could represent a pagan deity vanquished by God's power.[7] While mythological and hagiographical elements were normal in a saint's Life, alongside these we are also offered unique and fascinating insights into Samson's extended kin-group and their role in the Church of their day, as we shall see.

Samson's youth

Samson was born into a British Church that had evolved from Romano-British roots.[8] We are told that Samson's parents were from prominent families of two kingdoms: his father Amon was the son of court officials in the kingdom of Dyfed (modern Pembrokeshire), with Carmarthen as its ancient tribal capital, while his mother Anna belonged to a similar family from the neighbouring Welsh kingdom of Gwent that lay to the east, between the River Usk and the Wye, with Caerwent as its capital. The authors of Celtic saints' Lives generally describe them as nobility, and this may normally have been the case. The theme of intermarriage between nobles of two neighbouring kingdoms might be a literary convention – it features in the later Life of David by Rhygyfarch, written in about 1090 – but, again, such intermarriage would not have been unusual.[9]

The Life relates that Samson's parents took the youngster to the monastery of Llanilltud Fawr (or 'Illtud's great church'),

> to the school of the famous master of the Britons, Eltut [Illtud] by name. Now this Eltut was a disciple of St Germanus [of Auxerre, d. *c.* 448], and St Germanus himself had ordained [Eltut] in his youth. And in truth Eltut was of all the Britons the most accomplished in the Scriptures, namely of the Old and New Testaments, and in philosophy of every kind, of form, geometry namely, and of rhetoric, grammar and arithmetic, and of all the theories of philosophy. And by birth he was a most wise magician, having knowledge of the future.[10]

The writer adds a personal comment: 'I have been in his magnificent monastery'. Illtud was a renowned teacher: his education was not only monastic but also Roman, with its emphasis on philosophy, rhetoric and mathematics, perhaps hinting that a classical education continued in some form after the Roman infrastructure had collapsed. It is questionable whether Illtud was in fact a disciple of Germanus, who would have been a very old man at that point.

St Illtud's monastery

Llanilltud Fawr (in English, Llantwit Major) is on the south coast of Wales, in the Vale of Glamorgan, 9 miles west of Barry. It is hidden in a small river valley, where it could not be seen by pirates; nearby St Donats provided a natural harbour. There are other early Christian sites in the region: there is a Roman villa and a post-Roman cemetery beside the parish church at Llandough, now a southern suburb of Cardiff, on the coast 14 miles to the east. There is another significant early church site to the east of Llanilltud Fawr at Llancarfan, 5 miles inland. The name Llanilltud Fawr ('Great *llan* or church-site of Illtud') indicates an early medieval motherhouse of Illtud's monastic family.[11] It became an influential early Welsh monastery: it was claimed that other famous monks, Gildas and Paulinus, studied here.

The First Life of Samson does not idealise Illtud's monastery: it is based in a secular world in which the abbot's nephews expected to inherit their uncle's role, but realised that Samson's holiness posed a threat to their aspirations. We are told that one of the two nephews, a priest, 'grew afraid that, because of St Samson, he would be robbed and deprived of his hereditary monastery which he hoped to possess after his uncle' (ch. 16). They tried to poison Samson; the priest went mad, but was healed by the saint. Later, in chapter 20, Samson describes Illtud's community as 'riotous and wasteful' (*tumultuosum et expendiosum*).

The author of the Life of Samson depicts a tender relationship between Abbot Illtud and the teenager:

> When [Samson] was about fifteen he exercised himself in the very frequent fasts and the longer vigils which were kept by all the brothers who lived there, so much so … that that most sensible master [Illtud] forbade him and said to him, 'It is not meet, little son, that the tender body of a youth, up till now in the flowering stage, should be broken by too many and ill-regulated fasts'.[12]

The author does not portray Samson as following his abbot in studying philosophy, arithmetic, rhetoric or grammar; instead, he adopts a strictly monastic programme as he climbs the 'spiritual ladder' (*scala spiritualis*) of holiness (ch. 13), focusing on the study of scripture, especially the psalms, which monks chanted daily. Samson's chosen focus perhaps indicates the degree of personal freedom that could be found in monasteries at this time. While each monastery reflected the spirituality of its abbot, monks were also familiar with other monastic 'Rules': the anonymous Life of St Cuthbert recounts that, at Lindisfarne, Cuthbert's rule of life was observed 'along with the Rule of Benedict'.[13]

Early monuments at Llanilltud Fawr

Today there are two late medieval churches at Llanilltud Fawr, built end-to-end. Illtud's church may have been on the site of the present west church, which now contains a fine collection of monuments to early abbots and kings; they indicate the monastery's continuing importance. There may have been a burial chapel nearby, containing Illtud's grave.[14] The twelfth-century *Brut y Tywysogion* (or 'Chronicle of the Princes') relates that Vikings destroyed Llanilltud Fawr during raids in the later tenth century; the earliest surviving structures date from the twelfth century.

A number of monuments preserved in the church commemorate kings and abbots named Illtud or Samson in honour of the two saints who had formerly lived here. In later medieval times, a number of Welsh sites were named after Illtud, but none honour Samson. As a wandering monk who left his native country, all Samson's later dedications are in mainland Europe, like those of his younger Irish contemporary, Columbanus, who has no dedications in Ireland but many in Brittany and beyond, reflecting both his travels and the monasteries that he established.[15]

ILLUS. 46. Pillar of Samson, Llanilltud Fawr.

One pillar slab at Llanilltud Fawr commemorates a later abbot named Samson and dates from the second half of the ninth century. It bears an inscription that reads: 'In the name of God most High begins the cross of the Saviour, which Abbot Samson prepared for his own soul and for the soul of Juthahelo and [for the souls] of Artmail and Tecain' (illus. 46). Juthahelo is likely to have been King Iudhail (or Ithel) of Gwent (d. 848).[16] Perhaps Abbot Samson gave orders for the cross to be erected after his death.

Another monument at Llanilltud Fawr, known as the St Illtud or Samson Cross, refers to a later king named Samson; it dates from the ninth century or the first half of the tenth century. The shaft, which is likely to have been capped by a wheel cross, contains two Latin inscriptions in three pairs of panels that perhaps represent open books or even wax tablets that were used for a range of purposes, such as learning to read or write (illus. 47). The paired panels on its east face, which can be seen in the photograph, read '+Samson has set up this cross for his soul'; it is thought to refer to a current abbot of the monastery, named Samson. The two pairs of panels on its west face read '[cross of] Iltut, of King Samson' and '[for the souls of] Samuel [and] Ebisar'. Iltud is thought to refer to St Illtud, the original found of the monastery; King Samson, Samuel and Ebisar are unidentified individuals.[17]

ILLUS. 47. St Illtud or Samson Cross, Llanilltud Fawr.

Samson departs for Caldey Island

The First Life relates that Bishop Dyfrig came to Illtud's monastery, to ordain two presbyters, and to ordain Samson as a deacon. When Samson had lived for some time in the large community at Llanilltud Fawr, he longed to spend more time alone with God and wondered how to accomplish this without upsetting Abbot Illtud. God kindly arranged for an angel to tell the abbot to ask Samson what he desired. After doing so, Illtud sent him to Ynys Pyr, which is almost certainly Caldey Island, 2 miles south of Tenby, where Samson could find more solitude, and so enjoy 'with untiring patience a wonderful, isolated and above all a heavenly life'.

Samson's Life names the island Ynys Pyr after its first abbot, an elderly holy man called Pyr, whose community allowed for the possibility of a lifestyle closer to that of a hermit:

> [Here, Samson] ceased not, day or night, from prayer and communion with God. Spending the whole day in working with his hands and in prayer, and the whole night, moreover, in mystical interpretation of the Holy Scriptures, he carried the lamp to his dwelling in order that, bent upon reading, he might either write something or exercise himself in spiritual contemplation; for though, as a man, he had need of rest for the sake of human weakness and reclined against the wall or anything hard for support, he never slept in a bed.[18]

This account of Samson's radical asceticism reflects the influence of John Cassian and the Desert Fathers.

Samson's study of the scriptures

Samson's intense study of the scriptures was in order to acquire not head knowledge but 'the mind of Christ', in St Paul's words (1 Cor. 2. 16). This was a task for every Christian, and especially for monks and nuns. St Patrick's autobiographical *Confessio* is largely made up of quotations from the Old and New Testament: Patrick believed that God's past actions, recorded in the scriptures, were mirrored in his own life, with all its adventures. In order to put the tracing paper of Christ's life over his own, he had devoted enormous energy into absorbing the scriptures; this gave him assurance and a sense of his calling, day by day.

In his study of scripture, Samson modelled himself on the young Jesus. At the age of twelve, or entry into manhood, Jesus is described as surprising his parents by going to the temple in Jerusalem, where they found him 'sitting among the doctors [of the Law], listening to them, and asking them questions; and all those who heard him were astounded at his intelligence and his replies' (Lk. 2. 46–47). In turn, Jesus modelled his devotion to the word of God on that of the Old Testament prophets. Jeremiah, for example, said to God: 'When your words came, I devoured them: your word was my delight and the joy of my heart' (Jer. 15. 16). Samson could have echoed these words; he went to Caldey in order to 'acquire the mind of Christ'.

Caldey Island

Caldey was a foundation of some significance: a piece of sixth-century Phocaean tableware from the Byzantine Empire was found in the New Orchard. Nearby, the base of a seventh-century ceramic E-ware jar from Gaul was found close to the eleventh-century parish church, now dedicated to St David (illus. 48). Here, where there are dunes, to the east of the present jetty, the tide came in almost up to the chapel, which stood beside a creek, which has now silted up. Many cist (or slab-lined) graves were found near St David's chapel, indicating an early medieval cemetery.[19]

Near the centre of the island, and close to its well, are the remains of a Norman priory, with a distinctive stone watch-tower, and St Illtud's church. Located against the south wall of the nave is an early inscribed stone that marked a grave, of red sandstone; it broadly dates from the time of Samson and was found in a field near the farm, in which there was another early Christian cemetery. It bears a fifth- or sixth-century ogham inscription on its upper edge that has been interpreted as *magla- dubr-*.

If the first element is Irish, it could mean '[the stone of] the servant [of]'. Since the Welsh word *moel*, meaning 'bald, bare-headed', is known as an epithet and a surname, it has been suggested that this might apply to the clerical tonsure, or haircut, with the front half close-shaved and the back grown long. In a monastic context, *magl-* might then mean 'the tonsured servant'; however, other scholars dispute this. The second element forms part of a personal name: Dyfrig (or Dubricius in Latin) has been suggested, since Bishop Dyfrig is associated with the island, but this attribution is uncertain (illus. 49).[20]

The grave marker also bears a later Latin inscription dating from the eighth century, which has been translated as 'And by the sign of the cross [which] I have fashioned upon that [stone], I ask all who walk there that they pray for the soul

ILLUS. 48. St David's chapel, Caldey Island.

of Catuoconus'.[21] Its use of half-uncial script (the word uncial means 'an inch') shows that the stonemason was familiar with early manuscripts; Catuoconus is an Old Welsh name.

Many fragments of imported pottery similar to those on Caldey Island, dating from the fifth to the seventh century, were found in excavations at an unenclosed settlement of high status on the mainland at Longbury Bank, Penally, just over a mile across the water.[22] Linked with the monastery, at some point there was a community of nuns on St Margaret's Island, which lies just to the west of Caldey. At that time it was possible to walk across low-lying marsh to St Margaret's Island from the mainland at Penally. There was a medieval chapel of St Margaret on the island, but in the nineteenth century it was converted into housing for miners quarrying limestone on the island.[23] The author of Samson's Life notes that horsemen could ride across to Caldey from the mainland, presumably at low tide.

ILLUS. 49. Ogham-inscribed stone, St Illtud's church, Caldey Island.

Samson converts his family

While Samson was practising his austere life, his father Amon became seriously ill and sent messengers begging Samson to return home, to give him the eucharist and prepare him for death. As a true monk who considered himself dead to the world, Samson was unwilling to respond to this request. He replied to the messengers: 'Go back to our house for, unless I am mistaken, I have already left Egypt', and began to walk away (ch. 24). In early monastic theology, a monk was called to symbolically leave Egypt and cross the Red Sea, to enter into the desert where he might contemplate the Promised Land of heaven. Samson had already done this by crossing the sea to live on Caldey Island.[24]

However, Abbot Pyr 'gently called him back' and urged Samson to do this 'work of God' (ch. 24). We are then presented with a narrative that differs from most other early saints' Lives, which focus on the separation of a saint from his earthly relatives. Samson returns home; on his sickbed, Samson's father confesses a serious sin and repents, after which the entire family dedicate their lives to God and enter religious life:

> Without more ado [Samson's father] confessed in their midst a principal mortal sin, which he had kept hidden within himself, and vowed that, from that very day until his death, he would serve God with all his heart, his wife [Anna] especially

> supporting him in his resolve. [Amon] found strength to shave his head that same hour, his wife, as I have said, very strongly urging him and saying to him, 'Let not only me and thee, as is meet and right, serve God, but let us link together all our children in the service of God and let all that is ours become wholly God's'.[25]

Amon's brother Umbraphel with his wife and their three sons, together with Anna's sister, joined the enterprise. The riches of this wealthy extended family were used to establish new churches and monasteries, and to care for the poor. Samson's parents, uncle, aunt, siblings and cousins came to form a significant part of his own vowed life, first as a monk on Caldey and then as its abbot, and still later when he became a wandering monk and bishop.[26]

It has been suggested that if, in fact, this section of Samson's Life is based on an earlier Cornish exemplar, the original work was in part devised to justify the presence of a network of family monasteries after Samson's death. Perhaps the family promoted his memory to legitimise their new position in the religious landscape of Wales and, particularly, Cornwall.[27] At this time, as we have seen in the case of Llanilltud Fawr, the male members of a kin-group generally assumed responsibility for their founder's monastery: at Iona, five out of the first nine abbots were Columba's kinsmen.

Amon and Umbraphel returned to Caldey Island with Samson; the author makes clear that they do so for spiritual, not worldly reasons (ch. 40). This is deliberately contrasted with the fate of Abbot Illtud's two nephews who featured earlier in the narrative. Samson's family, by contrast, are presented as holy men, who therefore deserve to govern Samson's monasteries. He arranges for his uncle Umbraphel to be 'full speedily ordained to the office of priest' and appoints him abbot of a newly acquired Irish monastery; later he founds a monastery in south Cornwall and appoints Amon as its abbot. One of Umbraphel's sons enters Samson's Cornish monastery, is ordained deacon and follows Samson to Brittany.

The lengthy narrative of his kin-group's religious activities, occupying chapters 42 to 52, may have formed the core of an earlier Cornish Life of Samson, upon which the later Breton author drew. The narrative would have strengthened the claims of the new Cornish monastery governed by Amon, but would have been of less interest to Tigernomalus, Bishop of Dol (d. *c.* 707), at whose request the Breton monk says he has compiled his Life of Samson. The lost Cornish Life could have been written around AD 600.[28]

The names of Samson's relatives

Unusually, Samson's closest relatives are given biblical names, which they might have received from Samson on their entry into monastic life, when Samson was a monk on Caldey Island.[29] His mother had declared that she would found churches and monasteries in which she, her sister and their children could follow a religious life (chs 29–31). She is named Anna, perhaps after two biblical women: Anna the mother of Samson in the Old Testament (Judges 13. 2–7) and

Anna the prophetess in Luke's gospel, who lived as if in a Christian monastery, since she 'never left the temple [in Jerusalem], serving God night and day with fasting and prayer' (Lk. 2. 36–38).

Samson's father Amon, whom he converted from serious sin when at the point of death, entered the monastery where his devout son was a monk (chs 22–24). He may have been named after King Amon of Judah who committed serious sin and 'did what is displeasing to the Lord' (2 Chron. 33. 22), but whose son Josiah began to seek God 'when he was still a youth' (2 Chron. 34. 3), as did Samson. Amon's brother Umbraphel is named after one of four kings who conquered five wicked kings, including those of Sodom and Gomorrah in the time of Abraham (Gen. 14. 1). In the same way, monks strove to conquer evil in their own lives and in the world around them. This may seem unduly abstruse, but the sixth-century monk Gildas also refers to the 'dire armies of five kings' in Genesis 14, and compares them with kings in his own day.[30]

Umbraphel's son – Samson's cousin – the deacon Henoc, was named after the Old Testament figure of Enoch; he is described as a holy man 'who walked with God'; he was taken up to heaven and entered the divine mysteries (Gen. 5. 21–24), as monks strove to do. If Samson gave such abstruse names as these to his relatives on their entry into monastic life, it would indicate his unusually detailed familiarity with the Old Testament, and the 'mystical interpretation of the Holy Scriptures' that occupied his nights, according to the author of his Life.

Such a focus on Old Testament names was not unique to Samson, but was paralleled in monasteries elsewhere. The first surviving folio of the Book of Kells, written by Irish monks on Iona in about AD 800, is the final section of an etymological guide to biblical proper names (chiefly Hebrew names), compiled by St Jerome in the fourth century. This is followed by canon tables, or concordances of gospel texts, also compiled in the fourth century by Eusebius of Caesarea. The creators of this gospel book were well educated, familiar with Latin and some Hebrew, and aware of international scholarship.[31] The guide to proper names and the concordances were fourth-century equivalents of computer search engines: laboriously written on parchment with quill pens, they were an immense feat of scholarship, and also a labour of love.

Samson becomes bursar, then abbot

Impressed by Samson's holiness, the elderly bishop Dyfrig appointed him as cellarer, or bursar, of the community on Caldey Island. This task required wisdom, because a cellarer had influence over the lifestyle of the monks, including the amount and quality of their food and drink, and their gifts to the poor. We are told:

> Knowing that St Samson was endowed by God, in that hour [Bishop Dyfrig] bestowed upon him the office of cellarer, saying to him, 'I ordain and above all I desire in the Lord that all the goods which abound in this storehouse by the gift of God shall be administered and shared by you'. Thereupon, acting in accordance with the old man's

> bidding, for the sake of obedience, [Samson] did all things according to God; for at every moment he seemed to dispense everything in the name of God and of charity.[32]

The author of Samson's First Life then describes Abbot Pyr's undignified death: walking back to his cell one night, the drunken abbot fell into the monastery's well, and was drowned:

> One dark night ... Pyr took a solitary stroll into the grounds of the monastery, and what is more serious, so it is said, owing to stupid intoxication, fell headlong into a deep pit. Uttering one piercing cry for help, he was dragged out of the hole by the brothers in a dying condition, and died in the night from his adventure.[33]

It is an indication of Samson's monastic virtue that he appears to have lived peacefully and patiently under the rule of an alcoholic abbot. Bishop Dyfrig then appointed Samson as abbot to replace Pyr:

> And it came to pass when the bishop heard of [Pyr's death], he made all the brothers to remain just where they were and spend the night together; and then, having assembled a council, after Matins, all the men of this monastery, with one accord, chose St Samson to be abbot. ... He trained the brothers gently to the proper rule.[34]

The author presents Samson as loved by the brothers, despite the fact that his lifestyle was stricter than theirs. While he 'trained the brothers gently', he did not follow their lifestyle: during his time as their abbot, 'the brothers regarded him as a hermit rather than as a member of an order of monks'.[35] On a visit to Ireland, Samson acquired a chariot, or light cart, in which to travel. As we have seen, he ordained his uncle Umbraphel as a priest, and sent him as abbot to an Irish monastery (ch. 40).

Samson retires to a cave

After only eighteen months as abbot of Caldey, Samson withdrew to a quieter place, a ruined fort, perhaps a prehistoric earthwork, near the Welsh bank of the River Severn. He took three others with him – his father Amon, an Irish monk from the monastery to which Samson had sent Umbraphel as abbot, and one of Illtud's nephews, the brother of the envious priest. Samson gave his companions the 'delightful fort' as a hermitage, complete with a spring of water, and returned to them each Sunday to celebrate eucharist. He chose a more isolated cave for himself where, after a week, a second spring arose to slake his thirst. We are told:

> And he caused Amon to come with him, ... four of them altogether, to a very desolate wilderness, and, having discovered a very delightful fort near the River Severn, and in it a spring of very sweet water, he set about making a dwelling for his brothers, while he prayed that the Lord would be pleased to show him some underground cave and the Lord graciously fulfilled that most faithful prayer. For, on a certain day, as he wandered through the forest he found a very spacious and very lonely cave, and its mouth being situated towards the east, he embraced it affectionately as though it had been given by God for a dwelling.[36]

We are reminded of Antony of Egypt, who first lived and prayed with others and then in AD 285 went to live in an abandoned fort in the Pispir Desert, east of the Nile. The Life of St Antony by Athanasius, bishop of Alexandria (*c.* 295–373), can be considered the prototype of Celtic saints' Lives. Athanasius observed of Antony:

> Whoever stands fast in the desert solitude is freed from three combats of hearing, chatter and of sight. Only one remains: that of the heart ... Antony was more and more certain that he desired a holy life. He went quickly on to the mountain. On the other side of a river he came to an old fort full of snakes. He went up to it and made the fort his home. Then the serpents went off as though someone was chasing them ... There was water inside the fort. So he went in as to a safe and holy shrine and stayed there by himself without ever going out.[37]

As we have seen, victory over serpents symbolises victory over Satan, reversing the story of Adam and Eve in the Garden of Eden.

The author of the First Life notes that the site of Samson's fort was known and still venerated a century after his death, though its location was later forgotten; it could have been further down the Severn, in the Bristol Channel, and thus anywhere between Shropshire and Pembrokeshire:[38]

> ... and up to the time when I was in Britain the place, in which the three before-mentioned brothers were, was always reverenced with great devotion, and also an oratory constructed therein, where St Samson was wont to come every Sunday to sing Mass and for Christ's communion.[39]

When Samson prayed that God would show him a cave, he was following an ancient Jewish and Christian tradition. The Book of Exodus in the Old Testament relates that God showed his glory to Moses in a cave at the top of Mount Sinai (Ex. 33. 18–23), and the Prophet Elijah was said to have climbed to the same cave in order to meet God (1 Kgs 19. 9–13). According to the apocryphal Gospel of James (or *Protevangelium Jacobi*), which dates from the mid-second century, Jesus was born in a cave in Bethlehem. Early pilgrims to the Holy Land believed that Jesus was born in a cave and buried in a tomb-cave outside Jerusalem.

The Letter to the Hebrews recalls Old Testament holy men who 'were too good for this world, and they went out to live in deserts and mountains and caves and ravines' (Heb. 11. 38). A cave provided a simple yet practical hermitage, warm in winter and cool in summer, and a number of caves around the British coast are associated with early monks. Hermitages in caves are difficult to date archaeologically, but their existence is often described in Lives of saints and recorded by place-names or local tradition.

Samson returns to community life

After enjoying his time of retreat in the cave, Samson returned to community life and became abbot of an unnamed monastery, either Llanilltud Fawr or elsewhere, at the request of a synod. When his brother monks fetched Samson to attend the synod, his face was 'radiant, like that of an angel', just as Antony of Egypt emerged radiant from his ruined fort, when his friends found him after twenty years: 'His friends broke the door down by force. Antony came out … radiant as though from some shrine where he had been led into divine mysteries and inspired by God'.[40] We are told of Samson:

> He came, though not with willing steps, to the synod with them. … But when the elders saw him with a countenance exceedingly joyful, as if they beheld an angel of God, they received St Samson with reverent greeting and appointed him abbot against his will.[41]

Samson sets out as a pilgrim

One Easter night while Samson, now a bishop, was praying alone in the monastery church, an angel appeared in a vision, telling him to leave the monastery and set out across the sea as a pilgrim for Christ. The angel says:

> 'I have been sent to you by my Lord; of a truth you ought to tarry no longer in this country, for you are ordained to be a pilgrim, and beyond the sea you will be very great in the Church and worthy of the highest priestly dignity.' …
>
> On the arrival of the brothers for the morning chapter, the angel gently withdrew and left; and [Samson], accepting the omen with all the eagerness of faith and keeping it carefully in his mind, when he had finished the office of the Paschal Celebration, forthwith, amid the regrets and tears of the whole congregation, directed his course towards this side of the Severn Sea.[42]

The Bristol Channel was then known as the Severn Sea – Bristol became a significant trading centre only around 1020.

As a bishop, Samson still had work to do before crossing the Channel: he blessed the work of his family (excluding his adulterous sister), consecrated their churches and healed the sick:

> On his way, moreover, he goes to see his mother and his aunt and consecrates the churches which they have already built; and he excommunicates his sister … close gathered in adulterous embraces … He thankfully rejoices … over his brothers and cousins who are leading a noble and catholic life; he sets afoot much good work in those places …; he sets free from disease many among them who are sick whether in body or in mind, and, freely bestowing the power of his blessing upon them all, with a favourable wind, after a happy passage, attended by [Amon and the two companions who had lived with him on the river bank] and many others, arrives at a monastery which is called Docco.[43]

The author thus depicts Samson sailing to Cornwall, together with his relatives and servants. Samson had now experienced communal life in the monastery of Llanilltud Fawr, semi-eremitic life on Caldey and solitary life in a cave. He had been an abbot and been consecrated as a bishop (ch. 43). He is now described as entering a new monastic phase of self-exile for Christ (*peregrinatio pro Christo*).[44] This was a recognised form of monastic life: Samson's contemporary, Columba, left northern Ireland for Scotland as a *peregrinus*, according to the ninth abbot of Iona, Adomnán in his Life of St Columba. We are told: 'Columba sailed from Ireland to Britain, wishing to become a pilgrim for Christ'.[45]

St Kew, formerly Docco

The author of the First Life relates that Samson and his travelling companions reached the Camel estuary, near Padstow; they are likely to have continued up the River Camel for about 4 miles until they reached Wadebridge, where the modern A39 probably follows the line of a Roman road. If they travelled overland 4 miles north-east along this route, Docco was then only a mile to the north-west.[46] Docco is now named St Kew; it is called *Landochou* in a tenth-century charter. Since it is mentioned in Samson's Life, it is the earliest recorded Cornish monastery. A holy well (OS 023768) in the wall of Trescobel, the former vicarage, may have been the monks' water supply. It was frequently visited by pilgrims; its well-house was restored in 1890 (illus. 50).[47]

The author of Samson's Life describes how the bishop had hoped to stay at Docco; he asked to 'rest with them for a little period' (ch. 46), but the community sent one of their number, 'the wisest of them', named Viniavus, to dissuade him. The monks had become lax, he explained, and did not wish to be condemned by the bishop. Viniavus also implied that the community would not take kindly to criticism from an outsider – it was undesirable that either party should judge the other. This was considered a monastic virtue: Jesus said, 'Do not judge, and you will not be judged; because the judgements you give are the judgements you will get' (Mt. 7. 1, 2), and the sixth-century British monk Gildas repeats this advice.[48]

Viniavus politely presented his case:

> When St Samson told him the cause of his journey and asked whether he might stay with them for a little time, St Viniavus, prudent in spirit, thus gently gave reply, saying, 'Most loving father, the journey you have undertaken is desirable for a servant of God, who in the gospel praises those who become pilgrims for his sake. But your request to stay with us is not convenient. Otherwise we, who are unworthy, might condemn you. Or, more to the point, you might condemn us as we deserve. For I wish you to know this, that we have lapsed from our former rule'.[49]

The author's portrayal of Docco's monastery as one whose standards had deteriorated could have been intended to prove a point: if the original Life was composed in a new monastery in southern Cornwall, established by Samson and ruled by members of his family, it might have been in their interest to highlight the laxity of an older monastery in north Cornwall.[50] But wherever the Life was written, the episode succeeds in emphasising the greater holiness of St Samson.

A bilingual grave marker survives from the early monastery; it probably dates from the second half of the sixth century. It is a rounded pillow-stone that marked the head of a grave; the name was probably read downwards. The

ILLUS. 50. Holy well, St Kew.

Latin inscription 'IUSTI' means '[the stone] of Justus'; the name is enclosed within a roughly carved cartouche (illus. 51). Along the edge of the gravestone, the mason inscribed the man's name in Irish ogham, a stroke alphabet that was used frequently in south-east Ireland, but rarely in Cornwall. The granite stone can be seen inside the church; it was found in 1924, having been built into a bridge over the stream that flows past the churchyard, along the valley bottom.[51]

St Docco

ILLUS. 51. Bilingual grave marker, St Kew church.

We know little about Docco, after whom the monastery was named, but his chief monastery may have been that of Landochau Fawr, or 'great church of Docco', at Llandough, a north-western suburb of Penarth, just south of Cardiff. This was established beside a Roman villa (possibly a house church), close to the 'Severn Sea'. Excavations in 1963, 1979 and 1994 at the Roman villa and the large adjacent post-Roman cemetery yielded imported ceramics and radiocarbon datings from the fifth or sixth century onwards.[52] There was a monastery here from about 650 to 1075,[53] though it is not known when it was named after Docco. A church is also named after Docco at another settlement called Llandough, 5 miles north of Llanilltud Fawr. Docco in Cornwall might have been a daughter house of Landochau Fawr.

Docco's cult was widespread: an eighth-century Irish Catalogue of Saints refers to St Docus, while another early source, the *Annals of Ulster*, notes 'the falling asleep of Doccus, holy bishop, abbot of the Britons' in 473.[54] Docco has been equated with the Breton saint Doac, after whom four settlements are named in Brittany.[55] Chief of these was the monastery of Landoac, on a headland at the mouth of the River Arguenon, 25 miles west of Dol, where Samson was to establish his chief Breton foundation. Landoac is now named St-Jacut-de-la-Mer, after a later Breton monk; in records of 1352 and 1499, it is named St-Jacut-de-L'Îsle, referring to its location on an island linked by a causeway to the mainland.[56] Situated beside the broad river estuary, extensive mussel beds accessible at low tide could have provided a valuable source of shellfish for the monks (illus. 52).

By the mid-tenth century St Cywa, or Kew, was a co-patron of Docco in Cornwall. Perhaps a chapel within the monastery had been dedicated to her, before the church came to be named after her.[57] King Edgar (reigned 959–75) granted the estate at St Kew to the monastery of Saints Docco and Kew.[58] Of the monasteries mentioned in early texts, only that of St Kew is recorded as a significant site in the tenth and eleventh centuries.[59] Landocco was abbreviated to Lanow (it is spelt *Lannohoo* in Domesday Book, 1086); Lanow farm, half a mile north of the church, was part of a secular manor in the later medieval period.[60] It is likely that Kew's cult superseded that of Docco, but later traditions claimed that Docco and Kew were related to one another: in the early seventeenth century, the antiquarian Roscarrock referred to Docco and Kew as brother and sister.[61]

ILLUS. 52. Mussel beds, Landoac (now St-Jacut-de-la-Mer), Brittany.

Church organisation

After leaving the neighbourhood of Docco, the author tells us that Samson decided 'to completely traverse the country' of Cornwall, before departing across the 'Southern Sea' or English Channel (ch. 47). He sent away the ship that had transported his travelling companions, himself and a light travelling cart (or *currus*); he then acquired two horses and arranged for a larger wagon (or *plaustrum*) to transport 'his holy vessels (*spiritualia utensilia*) and his books' (ch. 48). The 'holy vessels' would have included the utensils required to celebrate eucharist, and the 'books' would have included not only a Missal and Gospel Book but a compilation of the rites that bishops require. Even today, a bishop possesses a 'Pontifical' that includes a range of rites from consecrating a virgin to consecrating a church.

The Life affords us a glimpse of Church organisation at this time: there are bishops like Samson, who may not be attached to a single area but might travel widely, as Samson does, from Wales across Cornwall to Brittany. Samson is abbot of a Welsh monastery when he is ordained bishop, and he continues to live in monasteries, except when travelling. Dyfrig, on the other hand, is a bishop who appears not to live in a monastery, except for a specific reason: he used to spend most of Lent on retreat in the monastery on Caldey Island (ch. 33). However, Dyfrig appears to have episcopal oversight of monasteries: he brings about Samson's election as abbot of Caldey (ch. 36) and also his appointment as bursar (ch. 34), even though Caldey's previous abbot, Pyr, was still alive.[62]

There is no mention in the Life of non-monastic priests; we can only guess whether or not such priests existed. Non-priests take leadership: members of Samson's family build churches and found monasteries (ch. 31). Samson, as bishop, can consecrate the churches built by members of his family (ch. 45). Women assume responsibility in the Church: Samson's mother founds monasteries, where she, her sister and her children are able to become monks and nuns (ch. 31).

Samson crosses Cornwall

Samson and his party appear to have circumvented Bodmin Moor: the author describes them travelling through 'a *pagus* which they call *Tricurius*' (or 'land of three battalions'),[63] which seems to refer to Trigg Hundred in north-east Cornwall, between the Camel estuary and the Devon border. Here, they encountered a chieftain named Guedianus and his people, who were apparently holding games, including horse racing, in honour of their ancestors. A standing stone dominated the scene.

Samson challenged them, with little success, until a boy galloped past in a horse race, and was thrown from his mount. He seemed dead, but Samson prayed beside him for two hours, and the lad recovered. Samson carved a cross on the standing stone, and the author of his Life adds:

> I myself have been on that mountain, and with my own hand have reverently touched the sign of the cross which St Samson carved by hand with an iron tool on the stone that stands there.[64]

Crosses incised like this on ancient sacred stones were forerunners of the elaborate crosses carved in the following centuries.

After Samson cured the boy who had been thrown from his horse, the ruler told his followers to come and have their baptism confirmed by Samson: this implies that they were already Christian. The cured lad promised to become a cleric. The chieftain then asked Samson if he could solve another of their problems: an evil serpent inhabited an impenetrable cave, and terrorised the neighbourhood. Samson agreed to visit the 'terrible cave', and the cured boy showed him the way. Samson drove the serpent out of the cave and killed it.

The grateful chief and his followers asked Samson to become their bishop. He refused, but accepted the offer of the cave as a retreat. Condensation dripping from its interior provided him with drinking water:

> [Samson] commanded his own men to found a monastery near the cave; yet he himself indeed, in the meanwhile, led a heavenly life in the cave, ever giving himself to fasting and to prayer ...[65] One day [Samson] was thirsty ... After he had prayed, he saw water dripping in a continuous shower from the rocky roof of the cave ... and to this day that water does not cease flowing, day or night.[66]

Parallels with the Israelites in the desert

After symbolically 'crossing the Red Sea' of the Bristol Channel, Samson and his followers are depicted entering Cornwall as a spiritual Sinai desert. The monks at Docco had become unfaithful to their high ideals, and refused to welcome Samson, as the wandering Jews became unfaithful to God in the desert, and grew hostile to Moses, according to the Book of Exodus (Ex. 16. 1–3). The chieftain Guedianus and his people were Christians who had lapsed into pagan worship, as the Israelites fashioned and worshipped a golden calf (Ex. 32. 1–6).

Samson carved a cross on their standing stone, as Moses erected a serpent on a pole for the Israelites to gaze on and be healed of their infidelity, according to the Book of Numbers (Num. 21. 4–9). The author of John's Gospel explains that the serpent prefigured Jesus on the cross (Jn 3. 13–15). Samson expelled an evil serpent, as Moses dealt with the serpents that killed the faithless Israelites. Throughout his experience in the Cornish 'desert', Samson and his party were sustained like Moses and his followers. When Samson drove the serpent from its cave, and took up residence there himself, he slaked his thirst with water dripping from the rock. In the same way, God provided Moses with water from the rock (Ex. 17. 1–7).

Samson's Cornish monastery

We are told how Samson organised his new monastery: with a bishop's authority, he ordained his cousin Henoc as a deacon, and he instructed his father Amon concerning how to govern the newly built foundation:

> Then, when he had received his cousin – him already mentioned at the beginning of this work – and admitted him to the office of the diaconate, after giving instructions to his father for the government of that monastery by them built and completed, and having finished the works which God wrought by him in those parts, with God for his guide, he directed his course towards this side of the sea [*i.e.* Brittany].[67]

The monastery's location is unclear. Four Cornish sites are named after St Samson, including Golant (referred to in the late twelfth century) and South Hill (first recorded in 1333). Both sites are likely to have acquired their dedication much earlier than this, but not as early as Samson's lifetime; they may be later dedications as a result of Breton influence.[68] Possible sites of the 'monastery near a cave' include South Hill, Golant, and Fowey; the three sites will briefly be described below.

South Hill

The hamlet of South Hill lies to the east of Bodmin Moor; it may have been a Saxon minster, and was formerly the mother church of the town of Callington, 2 miles to the south-west.[69] South Hill's church is still dedicated to Samson, as was a nearby holy well.[70] This is an early site: there is a granite memorial pillar in the churchyard, almost 2 m high that dates from the last third of the sixth century. It reads +CVMRECINI FILI MAVCI, or [the stone] of Cumrecinus, the son of Maucus'. The name of the dead man may consist of British elements forming the title *Comreginos*, or 'Very Proud One'; it might describe a highly respected warrior chieftain.[71]

Above the inscription is a cross with what appears to be a hooked top, shaped like a shepherd's crook. This form of cross evolved from the *chi-rho* symbol for Christ, using the first two Greek letters of his name; it is one of only four memorial stones in the south-west to bear this symbol.[72] The author of Samson's Life implies that while in *pagus Tricurius* he had touched a stone decorated with a cross that Sampson had carved, though South Hill is actually 5 miles south-west of Trigg Hundred.[73] It is possible that the author had visited the inscribed stone at South Hill, and fitted it into his story.

ILLUS. 53. St Samson's cave, Golant.

Golant

The location of Samson's monastery fits better with the topography of Golant, on the west bank of the River Fowey, 2 miles from the south Cornish coast. The river is tidal at this point, and could have served as a useful departure point for Brittany. There is a watery cave down by the harbour at Golant, known to local residents, that corresponds to the author's description quoted above (illus. 53).[74]

Golant church is high above the harbour and the cave, on a bluff overlooking the River Fowey (illus. 54); the present church largely dates from the sixteenth century. In the fourteenth century, a wood carver depicted Samson as a bishop, on a panel that may once have formed part of the rood screen; it was later used as a section of the fine wooden pulpit (illus. 55). Close to the church porch is Samson's holy well in a medieval roofed well-house (illus. 56).

Half a mile to the west of Golant is Castle Dore (OS 103548), an Iron Age hill fort that was probably occupied from the fifth or fourth centuries BC until the first century BC. It was defended by two well-preserved circular ramparts; inside were many round houses. The site was excavated in 1936–37 by Ralegh Radford, who thought he had found postholes to indicate a timber hall dating from the fifth or sixth century AD, during a period of reoccupation.[75] However, later excavation in the 1980s concluded that the posts had supported earlier Iron Age granaries; there was no evidence of the fort's occupation in the early Christian period.[76]

An early Christian monument that formerly stood within a mile of Castle Dore is now beside the B3415 near Fowey – a tall granite shaft with a Latin inscription, dating to the second half of the sixth century. For a time, it was erroneously thought to commemorate a chieftain who lived at Castle Dore. It bears an inscription in two parallel lines running down the shaft, in an early medieval insular form of script derived from Roman-style capitals. It reads DRVSTANVS HIC IACIT CVNOMORI FILIVS, or 'Drustanus lies here, the son of Cunomorus'.[77]

ILLUS. 54. South porch, Golant church.

PHOTO: MARGARET REES.

ILLUS. 55 *(left)*. Carving of Samson as a bishop on the pulpit in Golant church.

ILLUS. 56 *(right)*. Samson's holy well in Golant church porch.

PHOTO: MARGARET REES.

Wrmonoc of Landévennec's largely legendary Life of St Paul Aurelian, written in about 884, mentions a 'King Marcus' ruling in Britain, 'whom by another name they call Quonomorus'. If this information is accurate, Drustanus could be equated with Tristan, nephew and heir of King Mark in the legendary story of Tristan and Isolt, assuming that the relationship between the two men had been altered to uncle and nephew, to make the story more acceptable. However, the remark in the ninth-century Life may be due to Wromonc's knowledge of the inscription on the stone.[78]

Alternatively, Cunomorus might be identified with Cynfawr, King of Dumnonia, denounced by Gildas for his evil behaviour.[79] Another possibility could be Chonomor, a sixth-century Breton prince mentioned by Gregory of Tours in his History of the Franks (*Historia Francorum*).[80] Regardless of whom the monument commemorates, it indicates a Christian presence in the vicinity of Golant, broadly dating from the time of Samson. On the upper part of the opposite face of the monument, a T is carved in relief. It is probably a late addition, since carvings in relief are not normally found in inscriptions from this early date; the T perhaps refers to the parish of Tywardreath. A mortice inserted into the top of the memorial stone, designed to receive a cross head, suggests later use of the stone as a wayside cross.[81]

ILLUS. 57. Fowey harbour.

ILLUS. 58. Norman font, Fowey church.

Fowey

A third possible site for Samson's monastery might be Fowey, 2 miles south of Golant. Its large natural harbour (illus. 57) made it an ideal departure point for Brittany, and the church is near the shore. Fowey is the site of an early Christian enclosure or *lan*; its exact location is unknown, but a site on higher ground close to the present-day church is suggested by a surviving place-name, *Langorthou*.[82]

The present church at Fowey dates from the fourteenth and fifteenth centuries, but the font from the earlier Norman church survives, carved out of hard black elvan stone from a quarry near Padstow (illus. 58). Its high quality suggests a flourishing post-Saxon church. By the early twelfth century, it was dedicated to a saint named Barry: he may have been a monk in south Wales who gave his name to Barry Island in Glamorgan, or perhaps he was a saint unique to Fowey.[83]

Samson in Brittany

Samson then sailed to Brittany with his followers and established a monastery at Dol on the north coast. His sea journey is depicted in a detail from a magnificent late thirteenth-century window in the apse at the east end of Dol cathedral. The window includes eight lancets, on which the third from the right depicts the life of Samson in quatrefoils, to be 'read' downwards, from top to bottom. The fifth quatrefoil depicts Samson and two monks in a small sailing boat; it is reproduced here in a drawing by Sabine Baring-Gould (illus. 59).[84]

The author of the Life describes their arrival in Brittany:

> And with very many monks, and above all with that deacon [Henoc]… as companions, after a favourable passage, they reached their desired port in Europe… And going forth from thence, having God for his guide, [Samson] discovered a most suitable spot in these parts and founded a famous monastery which to this day, by an appropriate use of language, is called Dol. From that place he planted the seed of many works of a wonderful character and founded many monasteries throughout almost the entire province.[85]

ILLUS. 59. Samson sails to Brittany: detail from the east window, Dol cathedral.

Samson's monastery of Dol-de-Bretagne was established beside the small River Guyoult, which may have been larger in early times; Dol's name means 'a meander'.[86] Until the tenth century Dol was on the coast, although it is now some miles inland across the reclaimed marshes. The monastery was close to a harbour at the river's mouth; it became a bishopric some time between the mid-sixth and mid-ninth centuries. In later medieval times, there were three churches near one another in the town that grew round the monastery: the Romanesque parish church of St Pierre, the eleventh-century cathedral of St Samson and the twelfth-century church of Notre Dame, which was only 100 m east of the cathedral.[87]

Pental in Normandy

Apart from Dol, Pental in Normandy is the only other monastery that the author of the First Life describes Samson as founding:

> [Samson arranged] with the help of the king that a magnificent monastery be built for him in the place [at Pental] whence he had driven out the serpent, sending with the encouragement of the king, brothers there to oversee the work.[88]

Thus Pental was a royal foundation, gifted to Samson by King Childebert. Samson may have been a spiritual adviser to the royal household: it is possible that one of King Chilperic's sons was named Samson in his honour.[89] The fact that Samson attended the Council of Paris, which took place some time between 556 and 573, suggests that during his lifetime Pental may have been

ILLUS. 60. Merovingian sarcophagi at Pental.
PHOTO: LÉON COUTIL.

more significant than Dol. The senior clergy who gathered at the Council of Paris came not from Brittany but from a wide band of territory further to the east that includes Pental. This suggests that Samson attended the Council as the founder of Pental, rather than as abbot of Dol.[90]

The Merovingian monastery of Saint-Samson-de-la-Roque at Pental is about 140 miles north-east of Dol – a considerable distance away. It is 2 miles from the mouth of the River Risle, west of Rouen, situated at a strategic point overlooking the lower reaches of the Seine before it flows into the sea. In 1922, Léon Coutil conducted excavations in the abbey. He uncovered eight enormous sarcophagi that probably date to the seventh century (illus. 60); these may have been the tombs of Merovingian royalty. One has a vigorous, though crude, hunting scene carved on it; Coutil concluded that this could be the tomb of Samson.[91] One of the sarcophagi from Pental was brought to Dol cathedral; it is now in the presbytery garden (illus. 61).

By the late seventh century, Samson's younger contemporary, Columbanus, had established communities at Luxeuil and Annegray. Influenced by the monks of Luxeuil, members of the court now supported the foundations of Saint-Wandrille and Jumièges, and Pental was eclipsed by these newer monasteries in the region of the lower Seine. Vikings probably attacked Pental, too, which appears to have declined in importance and become merely a dependency of Dol.[92]

ILLUS. 61. Granite sarcophagus, Dol cathedral.

Samson's old age

As we have seen, Samson was present at the Council of Paris, together with bishops and senior clergy gathered from a wide geographical area. Samson stands out among the other signatories for his learning: unlike all the others, he signed the acts of the council in rhyming verse, meaning 'Samson has subscribed and consented [to the Council's enactments] in the name of Christ':

> Samson subscripsi
> et consensi
> in nomine Christi.

This is an example of Leonine hexameter, using internal rhyme (*subscripsi ... consensi ... Christi*) within a line containing six feet, or strong beats; it could be an echo of his classical training in 'rhetoric and grammar' under Abbot Illtud in the monastery of Llanilltud Fawr.[93]

The author of the First Life informs us that Samson travelled throughout Domnonia (northern Brittany), where he established communities; many monasteries in other dioceses were daughter houses of Dol. We are told that he tried to free Domnonia from the tyranny of King Conomorus, whom he considered to have usurped the throne. Samson took an active part in Breton politics; in his old age he returned to Dol, and chose his first cousin, Magloire, to succeed him.

At the end of Book I of Samson's Life, the author describes his death and burial:

> With all good qualities fully and completely adorned, happy in his death, he left his wasted body to be embalmed and buried in the sacred mound in the monastery at Dol, in the hope of resurrection to eternal life... Here [the account] endeth in the name of our Lord. Up to this point we have corrected it just as we wished to do.[94]

The final two sentences could refer to the Breton monk's reworking of the earlier text on which it was based.[95]

Dol and Alet

Samson is one of a number of bishops who are described as accompanying a migrant group, rather than serving a city and its environs. He established a

ILLUS. 62. Remains of Alet's Gallo-Roman wall looking north towards St Malo.

monastery at Dol as a British bishop ministering to a group of Britons, in a region with an established bishopric at Alet, only 15 miles north-west of Dol. This could partly explain why the monks at Dol who composed successive Lives of Samson went to considerable lengths to demonstrate the validity of his consecration as a bishop and, by implication, the authority of his successors.[96]

The promontory of Alet had been the headquarters of a local Gaulish tribe, and by the late third century there was a fortified Gallo-Roman settlement at Alet; portions of its defensive wall can still be seen (illus. 62). The promontory was protected from the mainland by a fort built in about AD 340. A large administrative building was constructed inside the fort in the mid-fourth century – this may have been the *principia* (or military headquarters), or perhaps the basilica of the town's forum. The complex remained standing until the eighth century, and was taken over by the first bishops of Alet. In the ninth century a cathedral was built on the site with two small rectangular rooms, possibly sacristies, at its eastern end. In the second half of the tenth century, a larger cathedral was built, with an apse at each end (illus. 63).[97]

Alet claimed St Malo as its founder; his Life relates that he was unpopular with the local clergy, and was exiled to Aquitaine, where he died, although his remains were returned to Alet. However, the island to the north of Alet, now

named St Malo in his honour, was easier to defend from the Norse, and the bishopric was transferred to St Malo in 1144, while Alet put itself under the protection of another local holy man, St Servan.

ILLUS. 63. The eastern apse of Alet's tenth-century cathedral.

Samson and Paternus

Paternus was a local Breton saint whose monasteries, like those of Samson, were also found in the region stretching between Dol and Pental. It seems that, when Samson arrived, there were a number of monks, hermits and bishops like Paternus in the region. We know little about Paternus: according to his Life, he was the son of a noble family of Aquitaine who became a monk and hermit in Normandy, first on the Cotentin peninsula, to the north-east of Brittany and then at Sciscy (probably Saint-Pair-sur-Mer) on the coast, 13 miles north-west of Avranches. He died and was buried at Sciscy in about 564.

Samson and Paternus are both recorded as having been present at the Council of Paris. Paternus, according to his Life, was appointed bishop of Avranches by King Childebert I. He was therefore a canonically appointed Gallo-Roman bishop, unlike Samson, who was a wandering British bishop. Avranches is only

27 miles east-north-east of Dol by land, and the journey by sea is shorter, so it is possible that Paternus and Samson knew each other.

Paternus is the subject of an unusually early Life, almost contemporary with the saint: the *Vita Sancti Paterni* or 'Life of St Paternus' was composed in the last third of the sixth century by Venantius Fortunatus (d. *c.* 600), an Italian who became bishop of Avranches.[98] Paternus is a common monastic name meaning 'Fatherly', and by the twelfth century this saint became conflated with Paternus of Vannes who lived a century earlier, who in turn was confused with the Welsh Padarn of Llanbadarn Fawr, close to Aberystwyth. In Cornwall, at the north-eastern edge of Bodmin Moor, North and South Petherwin are named after one of the Padarns. Both had large parishes until the twelfth century, and one of them may have been a minster, or monastic church.[99] The name Petherwin derives from *Padarn wyn*, or 'Blessed St Paternus'.[100]

Two parallel Lives

Although it is possible that a Cornish account of Samson and his family forms the core of the 'First Life of Samson', the entire Life appears to be modelled upon the earlier Life of Paternus. There are close parallels of subject matter and some linguistic echoes: both men are born to noble parents, the mother being elderly; each enters a monastery whose abbot urges him not to exceed the Rule; both retire to a quieter island and then retreat to a cave, creating a spring by striking the ground with their staff. Each sees a vision of three holy men consecrating them as bishop; doves appear as a sign of the Spirit's presence; both intervene at a pagan festival, and later found many monasteries; each meets a king and frees men from demons at the royal court; both build a church or monastery on the spot where a serpent had lived.[101]

While many of these features are found in Lives of other saints, there is a new emphasis on spending time as a wandering monk and hermit in both of these Lives. The Life of Samson differs from its model, though, in its attention to detail, its many cross-references, its individuality and its greater length. The author of the later 'Second Life of Samson', probably composed between AD 850 and 860, includes an extended verbatim quotation from the Life of Paternus. This suggests that the monks of Dol possessed a copy of the Life – which was not, in fact, widely distributed – perhaps in the form of a *libellus*, or soft-covered booklet.[102] The relationship between the proposed 'Cornish Life' of Samson and the Life of Paternus is unclear; perhaps the latter was also available to the author of the Cornish Life.

Dol becomes a diocese

The First Life of Samson does not describe Dol as a diocese; the monastery was not proclaimed a bishopric until the synod of Coetleu in 848–49. In the 860s, King Salomon attempted to make Dol the seat of an archbishopric of Brittany. A second 'Life of Samson' was created to strengthen Dol's claim, with an emphasis on Samson as a divinely appointed bishop; some of the less relevant Cornish material found in the First Life was omitted from the Second Life.

The Vikings attacked the Breton and Norman coasts, destroying the cathedral of Dol several times, and the Breton clergy fled with their treasures. A tenth-century text describing the removal of Magloire's relics from Dol, *Translatio Sancti Maglorii*, implies that the clergy of Dol took their saints' relics, including those of Paternus, to Count Hugh the Great of Paris, for safekeeping. Rabod, Prior of Dol, sent some of the abbey's relics, including those of Samson and Paternus, as gifts to King Æthelstan of England, who reigned from 924 to 939; Æthelstan gave them to the monastery of Milton in Dorset, which he had founded.[103]

In 936 Alain Barbetorte attacked the monks of Dol while they were feasting, and in 944 King Harold caused so many inhabitants of the town to flee that the bishop was suffocated by the terrified crowd. In 1014 the town was probably burnt by Olaf Haraldsson. The town recovered: by the later medieval period, it possessed property in six neighbouring dioceses. A third Life of Samson was composed in about 1124 by the archbishop of Dol, Baudri de Bourgueil, who presents Samson as an eleventh-century wandering preacher and a hermit. At this time there was a struggle for supremacy between Dol and Tours, so Baudri took care to emphasise that the archbishopric was conferred 'not only on St Samson but also on his successor' (ch. 24).[104]

After 1203, reconstruction work began on the cathedral (illus. 64), and the vast building was completed over the next three centuries, by which time Dol

ILLUS. 64. Dol cathedral viewed from the north. From a postcard published *c.* 1910 by E. and L.-A. Neurdein, Notre Dame Photos, Paris.

was an important bishopric. Seen from the north, it resembles a fortress, and its crenellated parapet is linked to the old fortifications of the town. Near the great south porch of the cathedral is what may have been the monastery's well, which is now reached through a crypt.[105] Some of Samson's relics are contained in an eighteenth-century reliquary.[106]

There are some twenty-six sites dedicated to Samson in Brittany, and from the tenth century onwards contacts between Brittany and England helped to develop his cult in Britain, where churches including Glastonbury abbey acquired relics of Samson, commemorated him in their calendars or were dedicated to him. He was perhaps patron of a chapel on the island of Samson, one of the Scilly Isles, and a town in Guernsey is named after him.

Notes

1 Wendy Davies, *An Early Welsh Microcosm: Studies in the Llandaff Charters*, Studies in History no. 9 (London: Royal Historical Society, 1978), pp. 146–49.

2 For the significance of bees in early Christianity, see Elizabeth Rees, *Celtic Saints of Wales* (Stroud: Fonthill, 2015), pp. 16–19.

3 These stones probably commemorate abbots and holy men revered in the community. An alternative suggested translation of Dallus Dumelus as 'Blind Unfortunate' (Patrick Simms-Williams, 'The Five Languages of Wales in the Pre-Norman Inscriptions', *Cambrian Medieval Celtic Studies*, 44 (Winter 2002), pp. 1–36, at p. 27), would make little sense as a monastic name.

4 Prologue to the Life of Samson, from Thomas Taylor, *The Life of St Samson of Dol* (London: SPCK, 1925), emended by Karen Jankulak from the Latin text of Pierre Flobert, *La vie ancienne de saint Samson de Dol* (Paris: CNRS Éditions, 1997).

5 Lynette Olson, 'Introduction', *St Samson of Dol and the Earliest History of Brittany, Cornwall and Wales*, ed. Lynette Olson, Studies in Celtic History no. 37 (Woodbridge: The Boydell Press, 2017), pp. 8–9.

6 Oliver Davies, *Celtic Christianity in Early Medieval Wales* (Cardiff: University of Wales Press, 1996), p. 13.

7 *Ibid.*, p. 14.

8 Jonathan Wooding, 'The Representation of Early British Monasticism and *Peregrinatio* in *Vita Prima S. Samsonis*', in Olson, *St Samson of Dol*, p. 140.

9 *Ibid.*, pp. 141–42.

10 *The Life of Samson*, ch. 7, Taylor.

11 Wooding, 'The Representation of Early British Monasticism', pp. 146–47.

12 *The Life of Samson*, ch. 10, Taylor.

13 Bertram Colgrave, ed., *Two Lives of St Cuthbert* (Cambridge: Cambridge University Press, 1940), pp. 94–97; see Wooding, 'The Representation of Early British Monasticism', p. 143.

14 David Petts, *The Early Medieval Church in Wales* (Stroud: The History Press, 2009), p. 76.

15 Columbanus was, in fact, at least thirty years younger than Samson, but his Life was composed by the monk Jonas before the First Life of Samson was written.

16 Celtic Inscribed Stones Project (CISP), Llantwit Major, LTWT/3; Royal Commission on Ancient Historical Monuments in Wales (RCAHMW), *An Inventory of the Ancient Monuments in Glamorgan, vol. 1: Pre-Norman. Part 2: The Early Christian Period* (Cardiff: Her Majesty's Stationery Office, 1976), pp. 58–59, pl. 23.

17 CISP, Llantwit Major, LTWT/2; RCAHMW, *An Inventory of the Ancient Monuments in Glamorgan*, pp. 50–51, pls 11, 12.
18 *The Life of Samson*, ch. 21, Taylor.
19 Rees, *Celtic Saints of Wales*, pp. 58–59.
20 Kenneth Rainsbury Dark, *The Inscribed Stones of Dyfed* (Llandysul: Gomer, 1992), pp. 32–33.
21 Victor Erle Nash-Williams, *The Early Christian Monuments of Wales* (Cardiff: University of Wales Press, 1950), pp. 180–82.
22 Wooding, 'The Representation of Early British Monasticism', p. 150.
23 Pembrokeshire Coast National Park, https://www.pembrokeshirecoast.wales – St Margaret's Island, accessed 19 September 2019.
24 Wooding, 'The Representation of Early British Monasticism', p. 153.
25 *The Life of Samson*, ch. 29, Taylor.
26 Richard Sowerby, 'A Family and its Saint in the *Vita Prima Samsonis*', in Olson, *St Samson of Dol*, p. 24.
27 *Ibid.*, pp. 34–35.
28 *Ibid.*, p. 30.
29 *Ibid.*, pp. 35–36.
30 Michael Winterbottom, ed. and trans., *Gildas: The Ruin of Britain and Other Works* (London: Phillimore, 1978), *De Excidio*, 69. 3.
31 Fáinche Ryan, 'Book of Kells: A Thing of Beauty, a Song of Joy', *The Tablet*, 16 March 2019, p. 4.
32 *The Life of Samson*, ch. 34, Taylor.
33 *Ibid.*, ch. 36.
34 *Ibid.*
35 *Ibid.*
36 *The Life of Samson*, chs 40–41, Taylor.
37 *Vita Antoniae*, ch. 14, in Jacques-Paul Migne, *Patrologia Graeca* (Paris: Imprimerie Catholique, 1857–66), vol. 26, cols 839–975, trans. Mary Groves and Roland Walls, in *Life of Saint Antony* (Vauve: Aide Inter-Monastères, 1994), pp. 28–30.
38 Wooding, 'The Representation of Early British Monasticism', p. 153.
39 *The Life of Samson*, ch. 41, Taylor.
40 *Vita Antoniae*, ch. 14, trans. Groves and Walls, p. 32.
41 *The Life of Samson*, ch. 42, Taylor.
42 *Ibid.*, ch. 45.
43 *Ibid.*
44 See Jonathan M. Wooding, ed., *The Otherworld Voyage in Early Irish Literature* (Dublin: Four Courts Press, repr. 2014) for a study of this aspect of monastic life.
45 … *de Scotia ad Britanniam pro Christo peregrinari volens enavigavit*. Alan O. Anderson and Marjorie O. Anderson, eds and trans., *Adomnán's Life of Columba* (Edinburgh: Thomas Nelson, 1961), Second Preface, p. 186.
46 Wooding, 'The Representation of Early British Monasticism', p. 154.
47 Jack Meyrick, *A Pilgrim's Guide to the Holy Wells of Cornwall* (Falmouth: Meyrick, 1982), no. 78, p. 67.
48 Winterbottom, *Gildas: The Ruin of Britain*, *Fragmenta*, 4. 7.
49 *The Life of Samson*, ch. 46, in Donald Attwater, ed., *The Saints of Cornwall by Gilbert H. Doble* (Truro: Dean and Chapter of Truro Cathedral, 1960–70), vol. 5, p. 87.
50 Olson, 'Introduction', *St Samson of Dol*, p. 10.
51 Charles Thomas, *And Shall These Mute Stones Speak?* (Cardiff: University of Wales Press, 1994), pp. 240–41, 294.

52 Wooding, 'The Representation of Early British Monasticism', p. 148.
53 Davies, *An Early Welsh Microcosm*, pp. 124–25, 135.
54 Nicholas Orme, *The Saints of Cornwall* (Oxford: Oxford University Press, 2000), p. 109.
55 Michel Priziac, *Bretagne des Saints et des Croyances* (Grâces-Guincamp: Ki-Dour Éditions, 2002), pp. 290–92.
56 Alain Dag'Naud, *Guide des Lieux Insolites et Secrets de Bretagne* (Luçon: Éditions Jean-Paul Gisserot, 2002), p. 101.
57 Turner, *Making a Christian Landscape*, p. 49.
58 Peter Sawyer, *Anglo-Saxon Charters: An Annotated Handlist and Bibliography* (London: Royal Historical Society, 1968), charter no. 810.
59 John Blair, *The Church in Anglo-Saxon Society* (Oxford: Oxford University Press, 2005), p. 304.
60 Olson, 'Introduction', *St Samson of Dol*, p. 9.
61 Nicholas Orme, ed., *Nicholas Roscarrock's Lives of the Saints of Cornwall and Devon* (Exeter: Devon and Cornwall Record Society, 1992), p. 84.
62 Lynette Olson, *Early Monasteries in Cornwall*, Studies in Celtic History no. 11 (Woodbridge: Boydell Press, 1989), p. 19.
63 Thomas Charles-Edwards, *Wales and the Britons 350–1064* (Oxford: Oxford University Press, 2013), p. 23.
64 *The Life of Samson*, chs 48–49, Attwater.
65 *The Life of Samson*, ch. 50, Taylor.
66 *The Life of Samson*, ch. 51, Attwater.
67 *The Life of Samson*, ch. 50, Taylor.
68 Orme, *The Saints of Cornwall*, pp. 228–29.
69 Thomas, *And Shall These Mute Stones Speak?*, p. 278.
70 Thought to be at OS 333726: Meyrick, *A Pilgrim's Guide*, no. 172, p. 133.
71 Thomas, *And Shall These Mute Stones Speak?*, pp. 231, 278, 293–94, figs 17.15, 17.17.
72 *Ibid.*, pp. 293–94, figs 17.15, 17.17.
73 At that time, Trigg Hundred probably included the hundreds of Lesnewth and Stratton; see Charles-Edwards, *Wales and the Britons*, p. 23.
74 The cave is beside the railway track, and although the entrance is covered by brambles (which can be removed with secateurs), it can easily be located behind the third telegraph pole alongside the track.
75 Ralegh Radford, 'Report on the Excavations at Castle Dore', *Journal of the Royal Institute of Cornwall*, New Series, 1 (1951), pp. 1–119.
76 Henrietta Quinnell and Daphne Harris, 'Castle Dore: The Chronology Reconsidered', in *Cornish Archaeology*, 24 (1985), pp. 123–32. The ring fort can best be approached from the B3269, by walking along the track to Lawhibbet Farm; it is in the first field to the right.
77 Thomas, *And Shall These Mute Stones Speak?*, pp. 279–80, fig. 17.18.
78 *Ibid.*
79 Courtenay Arthur Ralegh Radford, *The Early Christian Inscriptions of Dumnonia* (Redruth: Cornwall Archaeological Society, 1975), p. 7.
80 Elisabeth Okasha, *Corpus of Early Christian Inscribed Stones of South-west Britain* (Leicester: Leicester University Press, 1993), p. 94.
81 Cornwall and Scilly Historic Environment Record, 'The Tristan Stone, Early Christian Memorial Stone and Wayside Cross, 65 m NNE of Polscoe', Scheduled Monument no. 1016287, 2018.

82 *Fowey Conservation Area, Character, Appraisal and Management Proposals* (Cornwall County Council, 2010), p. 15.
83 Orme, *The Saints of Cornwall*, pp. 68–69.
84 Sabine Baring-Gould and John Fisher, *The Lives of the British Saints: The Saints of Wales and Cornwall, and Such Irish Saints as have Dedications in Britain* (London: C.J. Clark, 1907), vol. 1, St Samson.
85 *The Life of Samson*, ch. 52, Taylor.
86 I am grateful to Luc Philament, of Forget, Casson, Brittany, for this information.
87 Pierre-Roland Giot, Philippe Guignon and Bernard Merdrignac, *The British Settlement of Brittany* (Stroud: Tempus, 2003), p. 240.
88 *The Life of Samson*, ch. 59, Taylor.
89 *Ibid.*, p. 106.
90 Ian N. Wood, 'Columbanus, the Britons, and the Merovingian Church', in Olson, *St Samson of Dol*, p. 112.
91 Léon Coutil, 'Sarcophague mérovingien du monastère de Pental, à Saint Samson-de-la-Roque (Eure)', *Bulletin de la Société Préhistorique Française*, 20, no. 11 (1923), pp. 330–36.
92 Wood, 'Columbanus, the Britons, and the Merovingian Church', p. 113.
93 John Reuben Davies, 'The Saints of South Wales and the Welsh Church', in *Local Saints and Local Churches in the Early Medieval West*, ed. Alan Thacker and Richard Sharpe (Oxford: Oxford University Press, 2002), p. 381.
94 *The Life of Samson*, ch. 61, Taylor.
95 Richard Sowerby, 'The Lives of St Samson: Rewriting the Ambitions of an Early Medieval Cult', *Francia*, 38 (2011), pp. 24–25.
96 Olson, 'Introduction', *St Samson of Dol*, pp. 11–15.
97 Giot *et al.*, *The British Settlement of Brittany*, pp. 105–09.
98 Caroline Brett, 'The Hare and the Tortoise? *Vita Prima Sancti Samsonis*, *Vita Paterni*, and Merovingian Hagiography', in Olson, *St Samson of Dol*, pp. 83–87.
99 Turner, *Making a Christian Landscape*, p. 43.
100 Nicholas J.A. Williams, '"Saint" in Cornish', *Cornish Studies*, 7, ed. Philip Payton (Exeter: University of Exeter Press, 1999), p. 227.
101 Brett, 'The Hare and the Tortoise?', p. 84.
102 *Ibid.*, p. 86.
103 *Ibid.*, p. 95.
104 Bernard Merdrignac, 'The Process and Significance of Rewriting in Breton Hagiography', in *Celtic Hagiography and Saints' Cults*, ed. Jane Cartwright (Cardiff: University of Wales Press, 2003), p. 194.
105 Dag'Naud, *Guide des Lieux Insolites*, p. 28.
106 Priziac, *Bretagne des Saints*, p. 69.

CHAPTER 5

Early Christian sites in east Cornwall

We shall now begin a selective survey of early Christian sites in Cornwall – selective because there are a large number of small sites, many of which provide a fragment of evidence that can be difficult for us to interpret within the bigger picture of Christianity across the region. We shall therefore focus on those places that tell us the most: excavated sites, early memorial stones that offer a little information about specific individuals, place-names that indicate pre-Norman religious sites or secular courts, a few surviving lists of saints and allusions to early Christianity in chronicles and other texts.

In this chapter we shall examine early sites in eastern Cornwall, between the River Tamar that forms the border with Devon, and Bodmin to the west. In the north-east, there is an interesting group between the River Camel and the coast, including St Kew, which was described in chapter four; in the south-east another group can be found between the River Fowey and the Tamar. Bodmin Moor occupies a significant area of north-eastern Cornwall, and there were a number of settlements on its lower slopes, but habitation was impractical at an altitude higher than about 200 m.

There are a number of inscriptions in Irish ogham on memorial stones in north-east Cornwall. This suggests Irish influence, either from Ireland itself, or from the Irish kingdom of Dyfed in south-west Wales (modern Pembrokeshire) or, more likely, from Irish settlers living inland in the area that later became Breconshire (or *Brycheiniog*). Later legends claimed that saints from Brecon settled in north-east Cornwall, citing as evidence church sites dedicated to the children of Brychan, the chieftain from whom Brecon acquired its name. While this is unlikely, the legends hint at links between north-east Cornwall and Brecon, which is a shorter distance by sea than either Dyfed or Ireland.

However, links of all kinds between Cornwall and Brittany have always been closer than those with Wales; this is partly because there are more safe harbours on the south Cornish coast than on the inhospitable north coast. Many saints' dedications and place-names are found in both Cornwall and Brittany, and the reasons for this are many: the travels of early monks, the spread of saints' cults, the acquisition of their relics, the preferences of Norman landowners who held property on both sides of the English Channel and the emigration of families and groups of people in both directions.

Tintagel fort

One of the most significant early sites of north-east Cornwall is the rocky headland of Tintagel, on the narrow strip of coastline to the west of Bodmin Moor; it has also been the subject of several excavations. We therefore know about the site in some detail, which enables us to set the scene to some extent for pre-Norman Christianity in this region by beginning with Tintagel. It was primarily a secular site rather than a religious one, but these two aspects of life were entwined. Repeated excavation within the area surrounding Tintagel, including the royal burial ground on the mainland opposite, has enabled us to reconstruct life at the fortress in early times in a way that has not been possible elsewhere.

Situated 3 miles south-west of Boscastle, Tintagel is almost an island; its name means 'narrow-necked fortress'. Tintagel's rulers lived in style, and more imported sixth-century Mediterranean pottery has been found here than at any other British or Irish site. The headland was occupied in late Roman times: a small hoard of coins and pottery found at Tintagel probably date from the third and fourth centuries.[1] Two late Roman stones recording road maintenance, one at nearby Trethevy and one from an unknown location, now in St Materiana's church on the mainland above Tintagel, suggest the presence of official imperial agents.[2]

Tintagel was evidently a centre for trade at a high level; Charles Thomas suggests that the wealth represented by its imports may have come from exports of tin.[3] If the residents of Tintagel traded tin, they must also have collected it and stored it, although no tin ingots have so far been discovered here. Tintagel may have functioned both as a sophisticated multicultural trading station and a fort. The rich range of imports and the number and density of Tintagel's buildings suggest a royal residence.

There are well over one hundred early rectangular structures on the summit and sides of the outcrop (colour plate 8), with still more beneath the Lower Ward of the thirteenth-century castle; most of these structures date from the fifth to the seventh centuries. Many of the less substantial buildings may have been for storage, and others could have been used for industrial processes, since probable debris from metalworking was found.[4]

Life at the fortress

The fort appears to have been more luxurious than other British royal sites. Finds include fragments of a sixth- or seventh-century decorated glass flagon from Spain, and pieces of a fine red slipware bowl from Anatolia in central Turkey, dating from the late fifth to mid-sixth century. Some sherds are stamped on the base with a Christian cross. There were pieces of amphorae designed to transport wine and oil from Cyprus or southern Anatolia, and fragments of bowls from the French region around Bordeaux.[5] The remains of cereals, especially barley and oats, suggest that a large population was fed here. Bones of cattle, sheep and goats showed signs of being butchered and cooked at the site; the residents also ate roast pork, fish and oysters. A cod bone was possible evidence of deep-sea fishing at Tintagel.[6]

In 2016, a five-year research project was begun, commissioned by English Heritage and undertaken by the Cornwall Archaeological Unit. During excavations in 2018, a slate 60 cm long, perhaps a window sill, was found, dating from around the seventh century. It is inscribed with Christian symbols and words in Latin and Greek – despite the fact that Greek was little known at this time – in a decorative script similar to those found in illuminated Gospel manuscripts, indicating that the writer was familiar with those texts. The words include what may be a Roman name (*Tito*), a British one (*Budic*), and the Latin words *fili* (son, or sons) and *viri duo* (two men). It may have been the work of a scribe practising his handwriting, perhaps prior to carving an inscription on a monument.[7]

St Julitta's chapel

Near the summit of the outcrop are the remains of St Julitta's chapel (colour plate 9). It was built in about 1000, and its east end was added around 1230, when the medieval castle was built; the chapel was granted the right to baptise and to bury. It may incorporate the remains of fifth- or sixth-century buildings in its lower courses.[8] An eleventh-century triangular panel found in St Julitta's chapel can be seen in the parish church on the mainland above; it is decorated with a six-petalled 'marigold cross' within a circle.

Unexpectedly, there are two springs and a dug well of uncertain date on the rocky outcrop at Tintagel, two of the water sources being close to the chapel: a supply of fresh water was vital for a fort and useful for a chapel. From the seventh century until the twelfth, the fortress and its chapel were apparently abandoned. Julitta may have been an early local saint or, alternatively, an early Roman martyr.[9] There are two other dedications on the north-east coast to a saint with a similar name, at St Juliot and at Lanteglos by Camelford.

St Mertherian's church above Tintagel fort

The parish church of St Mertherian (or *Materiana* in Latin) is on the mainland cliff-top above the fort, about 500 m to the south of the fort. It is one of Cornwall's earliest Christian cemeteries, set within what was perhaps a royal burial ground for the chieftains who lived in the stronghold above. The graveyard may have remained in use throughout the early medieval period, even though the settlement on the outcrop was abandoned in the seventh century. Large numbers of burials have been discovered outside the cemetery; this suggests that members of the wider community were also interred here.[10]

Graves in the earliest levels at the parish church were surrounded by spreads of burnt clay containing remains of food and fragments of imported pottery: these could indicate funeral meals eaten in memory of the dead.[11]

This practice may have derived from Mediterranean models, described in chapter one. St Mertherian's church is first referred to in a document from about 1200; she has no dedications except at Tintagel and nearby Minster.

ILLUS. 65. Minster's Norman font, carved from porphyry.

St Mertherian's church at Minster

Minster, the mother church of nearby Boscastle, is set deep in a wooded valley (OS 111906). The name Minster derives from the Latin *monasterium*, and denotes a religious community. In 1478, William Worcestre was told that Mertherian was buried at Minster; a large greenstone slab that may be the lid of her shrine now rests on the floor of the church.[12] The place-name *Merther* can sometimes mean 'grave; burial place';[13] Mertherian might have been a retrospective name for a holy woman, meaning 'the enshrined one'.

A later church was built here in 1150 by William de Boterel, lord of the manor of Boscastle ('Boterel's Castle').[14] Minster's Norman tub font dates from this time; it is carved from porphyry, and decorated with diagonal patterns (illus. 65). Porphyry is a hard rock composed of crystals of feldspar. Their tiny flecks gleam in the sunlight: this would have been a costly gift to Mertherian's shrine. The church was given to Benedictines from Angers in William's native France; their priory adjoined the church to the north. In the twelfth century, Minster was served by a community of only two or three Frenchmen; its prior was French until about 1382.[15] Twenty years later, however, King Henry IV closed all 'foreign' monasteries. On the terrace below the church is St Mertherian's holy well, now dry.

Dedications to the so-called children of Brychan

There are two early lists of Cornish saints: one is written into a tenth-century Breton manuscript and lists forty-eight saints, preserving their names in vernacular Cornish, rather than in Latin.[16] The list suggests a large number of small religious sites focused on local saints' cults. A second list enumerates twenty-four children of the legendary Welsh saint-king Brychan; it is found in the Life of St Nectan written by or for the church of Hartland, probably in the twelfth century, and contained in the fourteenth-century Gotha manuscript, as we saw in chapter three, on pages 82–84.

Since the names in the list differ greatly from those found in Welsh versions of the legend, the Hartland list is likely to provide information not about Brychan's family but about a group of churches named after local holy men and women. Their names are given in Cornish, while the remainder of the text is in Latin; most of the twenty-four saints have dedications in north-east Cornwall. The twelve daughters are named Endilient, Menfre, Dilic, Tedda, Mabon, Wencu, Wensent, Merewenne, Wenna, Juliana, Yse and Morewenna. The twelve sons are named Nectan, Johannes, Wynup, Wenheden, Cleder, Keri, Jona, Canauc, Kenhender, Adwen, Helie and Tamalanc.[17] Of these, about fifteen – mainly the women – can be matched with place-names: their churches are therefore likely to have existed by the twelfth century.

Women in leadership

It is interesting that almost two-thirds of the surviving sites named after Brychan's 'children' are those dedicated to a woman: this might be unexpected in a culture where women had little power or standing. It is an indication that Christianity was still counter-cultural: in an ideal Christian world, as St Paul urged, 'there are no more distinctions between Jew and Greek, slave and free, male and female, but all of you are one in Christ Jesus' (Gal. 3. 28). However, this was more an aspiration than a reality.

We catch glimpses of single vowed women in the British Church from very early times. In the *Confessio* of St Patrick, a fifth-century British Christian who probably trained as a monk in Gaul, he describes his missionary activity in north-east Ireland. He relates how one woman received her religious vocation soon after he had baptised her, and so he established her in this new calling to 'that life which is lived by all virgins of God', as he puts it. Patrick writes:

> The Irish leaders' sons and daughters are seen to become the monks and virgins of Christ. Indeed, on one occasion this happened. A blessed Irishwoman of noble birth, a most beautiful adult whom I had baptised, came back to us a few days later for this reason: she told us how she had received a divine communication from a messenger of God which advised her to become a virgin of Christ and that she should move closer to God.
>
> Thanks be to God, six days after that, she avidly and commendably took up that life which is lived by all virgins of God. This, of course, is not to the liking of their fathers, and they have to suffer persecution and false accusation from their parents. Yet despite this, their number keeps increasing, and we do not know the number of those born there from our begetting – apart from widows and those who are celibate.[18]

This provides us with valuable information. First, it is the earliest British account of a woman's call to single vowed life. Her parents would understandably be upset at the loss of a marriageable daughter, who could have enabled a useful tribal alliance with a neighbouring prince. Secondly, we learn that the vocation to celibate life could happen very soon after baptism. In the Syrian Church during the first three centuries, baptism was very thoroughly prepared for and celibacy was normally vowed at baptism. There seems to be an echo of this situation in Patrick's account.

Thirdly, we are told that this woman was highborn; she was therefore likely to be able to assume leadership in the local community of new Christians. Fourthly, Patrick tells us that he considered the presence of virgins and widows in the Church to be so important that he kept a record of them, for he writes that he has no idea how many people he has baptised, but he does know how many celibates and Christian widows there are. At this time, when girls married at the age of puberty, 'virgins' would often have been teenagers, and Christian widows, with a little more life experience, are likely to have assumed responsibility for them.

Writing in the late seventh century, Patrick's biographer, Tírechán, describes small Christian centres which Patrick founded and left in the care of 'three brothers and a sister' (ch. 11):

> On the Close of Easter, when Sunday was over, he went out to the Ford of the Mill and founded a church there, in which he left three brothers and one sister; and these are their names: Cathaceus, Cathurus, Catneus, and their sister Catnea, who drew milk from wild hinds, as old men have told me.[19]

Tírechán also describes Patrick placing 'two young women' (ch. 35) or even one woman (ch. 37) in charge of churches, though this pattern may not date back to Patrick's lifetime. St Samson lived in the century between Patrick and Tírechán: his biographer describes the men and women in Samson's family founding churches and communities as they moved across Wales and through Cornwall to Brittany.

These women would have dressed appropriately to their new state. In early Greek tradition, holy women prayed and prophesied with unbound hair, whereas in the Judeao-Christian tradition women wore veils, as St Paul emphasised when addressing the women of Corinth (1 Cor. 11. 4–16).[20] The earliest evidence for this custom is in the Book of Enoch, a Jewish commentary on the Book of Genesis, written in about 100 BC. Its author recalls, in Genesis 6. 4, how the giants came down and had sex with the (golden-haired) daughters of men; he therefore prescribes that women should cover their heads to protect themselves against demons. According to this theology, the veil was a sort of safety helmet, in order to keep demons out of nuns' living space, to prevent Satan from being enticed in.

St Juliot, a local holy woman

We shall now examine six of the sites named after men and women in the Hartland list of Brychan's children, including those that contain early evidence of a Christian presence. The list names one of Brychan's daughters as Juliana; we have already focused on one site that is likely to be named after her – St Julitta's chapel at Tintagel. In about 1540, the antiquarian John Leland noted that it was named after *St Ulette*, *Uliane* or *Julianes*.[21] Julitta, with its French and English forms Juliot and Juliet, are diminutives of Juliana. She may have originated as, or been named after, a fourth-century Roman martyr named Juliana, or after Julitta, another early martyr, who was usually paired with her son Cyricus.[22]

There are several dedications to Juliana or Juliot in the Tintagel area, one of which is across the valley from Minster, at St Juliot. This appears to have been a foundation associated with the small manor of St Juliot recorded in Domesday Book (1086) when it was held by one Thurstan from the Norman half-brother of William the Conqueror, Count Robert of Mortain. St Juliot's church is in an isolated location above the valley of the River Valency, on a minor road between Boscastle and Lesnewth (OS 133913). There are three medieval crosses in the churchyard (illus. 75), two brought from elsewhere and one thought to be in its original position serving as a boundary marker between the parishes of Minster and Lesnewth (colour plate 10).

Lanteglos by Camelford

The church of St Julitta at Lanteglos by Camelford was described as *Ecclesia Sancte Julitte* in 1291.[23] It is 2 miles south-west of Camelford; the settlement was named *Lanteglos* in an episcopal register of 1268. Its name derives from the elements *nant* and *eglos*, meaning 'valley church'. The first element, *Nant-* (or 'valley') later evolved into *Lan-*; the suffix *-eglos* derives from the Latin *ecclesia*, meaning 'church'. As an early foundation, Lanteglos was the mother church of both Advent and Camelford. Advent appears to be named after an otherwise unknown male saint, Adwen, who appears in the Hartland list of Brychan's children, but is more likely to have been a local holy man.[24]

ILLUS. 66. Wheel-head cross in the churchyard, Lanteglos by Camelford.

The relative isolation of Lanteglos is typical of many Cornish parish churches; it adjoined Helstone Manor, at least by Domesday Book. In 1086 the manor is named Henliston, or *hen-lys*, means 'ancient court', with the addition of the English *tún*, meaning 'farm, manorial centre'.[25] This suggests that it was a native administrative centre that became the core of an Anglo-Saxon manor. At the time of Domesday Book, the manor belonged to the count of Mortain, Cornwall's major Norman landowner. Later, Helstone became a significant manor of the earls and then dukes of Cornwall, by which time Lanteglos church lay on the northern edge of its deer park.[26]

In the graveyard is a memorial stone with a text running down two sides, written in what appears to be early Middle English; it may contain some early dialect forms in the Cornish language.[27] The inscription has been translated as 'Ælselth and Genereth made this family-stone for Ælwyne's soul and for themselves'. It dates from the late eleventh or twelfth century, and appears to have been the shaft of a cross, since it has a mortice at the base to secure it into the ground,

ILLUS. 67. St Julitta's holy well beside a hazel tree, Lanteglos by Camelford.

and another mortice at the top intended to support a wheel-head; what appears to have been the cross-head was found at the rectory. The stone may commemorate a steward of Helstone manor.[28]

Lanteglos church sits within 130 acres of glebe land, which would have provided the church with income from its rent and tenure.[29] Its Norman font was found in the rectory garden, but was subsequently moved to Washaway church, 9 miles to the south. There are four later medieval wheel-head crosses in the churchyard brought from nearby, including the upper portion of a wheel cross with typical diminutive arms (illus. 66), close to the church porch.

Julitta's holy well can be found a mile to the north-east of the church, on St Juliett's Farm (OS 093829). The farm and well were also named 'Jetwells' and 'St Gitwells' – both forms derived from the name Julitta. The water is still pure and clear; the well-house was removed and incorporated into the farm buildings, but in the nineteenth century it was reconstructed at its former site.[30] It stands above the River Allen beside an old hazel tree (illus. 67): this may be the successor of earlier hazel trees, since they were considered holy. We learn from the Second Irish Life of Maedoc of Ferns that when a king of Breifne was inaugurated, his wand, or sceptre, was to be cut from the hazel tree beside St Maedoc's hermitage.[31]

An early shrine at St Endellion

Another of Brychan's so-called daughters in the Hartland list is named Endelient. She is likely to have been a local Cornish saint, and was honoured at St Endellion, a village 1.5 miles from the north Cornish coast and 8 miles north of Wadebridge. St Endellion church is on the northern side of the B3314, an ancient hill-top route heading west towards a Roman crossing point of the River Camel estuary near St Enodoc's church, deep in the sand dunes.[32]

There was an extensive post-Roman cemetery at St Endellion. In 1977, during a rescue dig in a trench cut by the Water Board, seventeen graves were uncovered south and east of the church, across the B3314. Similar graves had been found earlier, in the churchyard. The graves faced east–west and were in two main groupings: an eastern row chiefly consisted of slate-covered dug-graves or pits, and a western group mainly of slate-lined cist-graves, some containing skeletons. There were a few children's graves among those of adults.[33]

The eastern row lay beyond the later boundary with St Kew parish: it is likely to have passed out of use by the time the manorial or parish boundary with St Kew was drawn up. No positive dating evidence was found during the excavation: the cemetery could have been in use from early Christian times

ILLUS. 68. Endelient's shrine, in St Endellion church.

until after the Norman Conquest, when the present church was built. There were indications of a flat-bottomed ditch carved out from the rock, with sloping sides. Its small size suggests that it was a boundary to the cemetery – there was possibly a boundary ditch surrounding a similar cemetery at St Kew.[34]

The church contains a Norman font; by the thirteenth century, St Endellion housed a college of priests. The probable shrine of St Endelient can be seen at the east end of the south aisle of the church; it was carved in about 1400, of black catacleuse stone from St Merryn. It contains eight deep niches, and survived the Reformation because it was reused as the tomb of a local gentleman; it now serves as an altar (illus. 68).[35]

A gold rosary that belonged to Lord William Howard, made in about 1500, contains a bead that depicts St Endelient with a martyr's palm, a cow and a well, some of which feature in the legend of her life, as recounted by the antiquarian Nicholas Roscarrock.[36] She was said to have lived on the milk of a single cow, until it was killed by the Lord of Trentinny, onto whose land Endelient had wandered. Two wells in the parish are named after her, the more distant being the one she was said to visit; according to her legend she was not martyred, but died a natural death.[37]

Sixth-century Christians at St Endellion

ILLUS. 69. Memorial to Brocagnus, St Endellion.

An early Christian memorial stone that later served as a medieval wayside cross stands at Long Cross junction, the first crossroads on a minor road running north-west from St Endellion to Portquin harbour. At the upper end of the shaft is a *chi-rho* monogram, above a transverse curved line which arches over a Latin inscription incised in two parallel lines running downwards. The inscription is in an early medieval form of script derived from Roman-style capital letters and reads BROCAGNI IHC IACIT [N]ADOTTI FILIVS, or '[the stone] of Brocagnus lies here, the son of Nadottus'.[38]

The *chi-rho* monogram, the style of lettering and the formula HIC IACIT ('here lies') combine to suggest a late sixth-century date (illus. 69). The stonemason made an error, and carved IHC instead of HIC for 'here'. Brocagnus (or *Brocagnas* in Primitive Irish) means 'Little Badger', the name of the Irish chieftain who was claimed as Endelient's father in the Hartland legend.[39] The name Brocagnus appears on several stones in this area, including one at Welltown, Cardinham, described later in this chapter; the name was evidently current in the late sixth century.

A church at St Illick in the parish of St Endellion is named after Dilic, another daughter of Brychan in the Hartland list, and other neighbouring churches are each assigned a daughter of Brychan as their patron, including those of St Minver, St Teath, St Mabyn and perhaps St Issey, on the south side of the Camel estuary. Many of the dedications are attested before the fourteenth century, when the Gotha manuscript was compiled, and there are other Welsh versions of the list of Brychan's children, with different names. It seems, therefore, that the dedications already existed and the list was edited at Hartland to give it a local north Cornish flavour.

A cliff-top site at Morwenstow

Further north, nearer to Hartland, with its parish extending to the Devon border, Morwenstow, or 'Morwenna's holy place', is named after another

ILLUS. 70. Norman tub font, Morwenstow.

daughter of Brychan in the Hartland list; it is named *Morwestewe* in 1201.[40] The parish adjoins that of Welcombe in Devon, which belonged to Hartland, but Morwenna is likely to pre-date the Hartland legend, since substantial parts of Morwenstow church survive from the early Norman period. It is in an isolated location facing the sea, with no surrounding settlement – only a farm and vicarage.

The church at Morwenstow contains a roughly shaped early Norman font decorated with cable moulding (illus. 70). There is an elaborate twelfth-century south porch, arcade and arch, decorated with zigzag and beak-head carving, with sculptures of birds, pine cones and a ram's head. Beside the church, in the vicarage garden, a well is named after St John the Baptist. The secondary dedication of the church to the Baptist was added after 1285 when it was given to the Hospital of St John the Baptist in Bridgwater (Somerset) by William de Monkton; Lanteglos church had already been given to the hospital.

Perhaps Morwenna lived on the cliff top near the present church; her holy well is almost inaccessible down the steep cliff, three fields away. On the north wall of Morwenstow church, a fragment of a late fifteenth- or early sixteenth-century mural depicts a woman holding a scroll in her left hand, with her right arm raised in blessing over a tonsured cleric; it is thought to represent St Morwenna.[41] There may have been renewed interest in St Morwenna at this time: in 1478 the antiquarian William Worcestre heard that she was enshrined in Morwenstow church.[42]

Twelve miles further south, another small settlement by the sea is called Dizzard; it is named from the nearby manor, which was *Disart* in 1086, from *di-serth*, meaning 'a steep place'.[43] In other Celtic regions, this name can also mean a 'desert' or 'empty place' for a hermitage: it can be an early loan-word from the Latin *desertum*. Examples are Dyserth in Wales (near Rhyl), Dysart in Scotland (on the Fife coast) and many instances of Díseart in Ireland.[44] However, there is no historical or archaeological evidence for this at Dizzard.

Egloskerry, 'church of Keri'

In the Hartland manuscript, two of the so-called sons of Brychan are named Keri and Cleder; their churches are in adjacent parishes on the north-eastern edge of Bodmin Moor. Keri does not feature in Welsh lists of Brychan's children; he appears to be a local Cornish saint with a single dedication, Egloskerry or 'church of Keri', 5 miles north-west of Launceston. The chapelry of *Eglescheria* is first mentioned in a document dating between 1159 and 1181, recorded in the fifteenth-century cartulary of Launceston priory.[45] By this time it was owned by the priory, to whom it was given by the Bottrell family.

The first church may have occupied part of the present building; early stonework has been discovered in the existing walls, including an unusual Norman piscina, or basin used to wash the communion vessels, and a Norman tympanum, or sculptured panel above a door, depicting Christ, the Lamb of God. The triumphant risen Lamb bears a cross; it has been reset over the south doorway (illus. 71). A tympanum over the blocked north door depicts a dragon snapping at its own tail.[46] The two

ILLUS. 71. Christ, the risen Lamb, Norman tympanum, Egloskerry.

ILLUS. 72. St Clether chapel and holy well, looking down to the River Inney.

PHOTO: MARGARET REES.

ILLUS. 73. St Clether's lower pool, with shelf for pilgrims' offerings.

reliefs could form a pair, representing the spiritual forces of good and evil.

St Cleder's chapel and holy well

Cleder features in the Hartland list as one of the sons of Brychan; his name appears next to that of Keri. Cleder's church at St Clether is 8 miles west of Launceston, on a valley slope above the River Inney.[47] The Norman church stands beside the road above the village; its oval churchyard is surrounded by an embankment. Cleder's chapel and holy well are 400 m beyond the church, on the hillside above the river valley (colour plate 11).

The chapel is built into the steep hillside, a little below a solid well-house constructed over a spring (illus. 72). The complex was rebuilt in the fifteenth century when arrangements were made to conduct water from the well through the chapel: the water flows down into the chapel through a trough behind three massive granite slabs that form the altar. The floor was lowered so that the water could flow out through the chapel into a second pool.[48]

An oblong cavity was made in the east wall beside the altar, so that Cleder's relics could be housed for veneration. The chapel was given two entrances, probably to facilitate the passage of pilgrims through the chapel. A shelf for their offerings was constructed above the pool; behind the shelf was a small wooden door, which enabled a priest inside the building to retrieve the offerings (illus. 73).[49] With these ingenious facilities, St Clether is perhaps the most complete medieval Cornish well and chapel.

Davidstow and bagpipes

The sixth-century Welsh saint, David, is unlikely to have travelled beyond south-west Wales, but David's cult was popular in Wales, and was taken elsewhere. In Cornwall, Davidstow was named after him, at least by 1244, when it is described as *Ecclesiarum … S. Davyd*. Its earlier name was *Dewstow*, or 'holy place (*stów*) of David', referring to David's Welsh and Cornish name, *Dewi*: it appears as *Ecc[lesia] S. Davidi alias Dewstow* in 1269.[50] The church stands on high ground on the northern edge of Bodmin Moor, 12 miles west of Launceston. In a field to the east of the church is a holy well (OS 151873); its pool is protected by a rectangular well-house whose stones were brought from a ruined chapel in nearby Lesnewth. The spring water is so pure that it is used by the local creamery to make mild Davidstow cheese.

There are some fine carved bench-ends in the church dating from about 1600, including a depiction of the Cornish bagpipes (illus. 74). These are rarely mentioned in early sources, but they are an ancient instrument, widely distributed throughout Europe and beyond. They are described in a first-century discourse by Dio Chrystostom (AD *c.* 40–*c.* 120), from Bithynia in Asia Minor, who lived in Rome; in a sarcastic allusion to Nero, he relates that the emperor could play a reed pipe (*tibia*) with his mouth as well as by tucking a bladder beneath his armpit.[51]

ILLUS. 74. Cornish bagpiper on a bench-end in Davidstow church.

Bagpipes form the subject of Riddle 44 in the Exeter Anthology, which was described in chapter three. The riddles are likely to date from the eighth or perhaps the ninth century, and no. 44 gives us a rare description of early medieval music. The author imagines the bagpipes held like a bird, over a man's shoulder at a banquet. Its beak is in the player's mouth, while its legs are the pair of pipes on which the tunes are played, here referred to as 'brother and sister'.

First, the author introduces this beautiful bird, perhaps the size of a goose or a swan, which can neither walk nor fly:

> Beautifully made in many ways
> is this our world, cunningly adorned.
> I saw a strange thing singing in a house;
> its shape was more wonderful than aught among men.
> Its beak was underneath, its feet and hands birdlike,
> yet fly it cannot nor walk at all.[52]

At a banquet it eats nothing, but is passed around like a harp, as nobles take turns to demonstrate their skill:

> Yet eager for movement it starts to work
> with various arts. It often goes around
> again and again among noble men.
> It sits at the banquet-board, awaits its turn
> till comes its time to display its skill
> among those who are near. It partakes of nothing
> that the men there have for their pleasure.[53]

The bagpipes can sound stirring, beautiful, even glorious:

> Brave, eager for glory it remains dumb,
> yet it has in its foot beautiful sounds,

a glorious gift of song. Wondrous it seems to me
how this very thing can play with words
through its foot beneath adorned with trappings.[54]

The inflated bellows contain the wind ('its treasure'), guarded by rings to prevent the air from escaping:

It has on its neck when it guards its treasure,
bare, proud with rings, its two companions,
brother and sister. It's a great thing surely
for a wise singer to think what this is.[55]

Cornish pipers

Cornish pipers are mentioned in sources from about 1150 onwards, when they feature in the twelfth-century Cornish Vocabulary (or *Vocabularum Cornicum*), based on Ælric's late tenth-century Latin/Anglo-Saxon glossary, but it is unclear whether or not they are bagpipers. In the Ordinalia, three medieval mystery plays dating to the late fourteenth century, mainly written in Middle Cornish, with Latin stage directions, the minstrels are instructed to 'pipe'. Pipers also feature in a play entitled *Beunans Meriasek*, or 'The Life of St Meriadek' (1504).[56]

Both halves of *Beunans Meriasek*, performed on two successive days, end with a speech urging the minstrels (*menstrels*) or pipers (*pyboryon*) to 'pipe' (*peba*) 'so that we may go dancing'.[57] The term 'piper' could refer to the pipe and tabor, also popular at this time, though since the plays were performed out of doors before large numbers of people, the instruments used in them may well have been bagpipes, with their more penetrating timbre.

Bagpipes are depicted in a few Cornish churches: on stone carvings at St Austell (*c.* 1480) and Launceston (*c.* 1515), and on bench ends at Altarnun (*c.* 1530) and Braddock (*c.* 1600), as well as at Davidstow.[58] The carving on the external wall of St Austell church tower resembles other Tudor examples, such as that at Curry Rivel (Somerset). It has been suggested that these are carved above the routes of outdoor processions, especially those that took place on Palm Sunday; the carvings appear to echo the sounds of the musicians who accompanied the singers in the procession below.[59]

Altarnun, or 'Altar of Non'

Altarnun is 7 miles south-west of Launceston, beside a fast-flowing stream, a tributary of the River Inney, on the north-east side of Bodmin Moor. Part of Davidstow's parish boundary is shared with that of Altarnun, whose name means 'Altar of Non', referring to David's mother. Nothing is known about her: she is named Non (meaning 'a nun'), or *Nonnita*, in Rhygyfarch's eleventh-century Life of David.[60] The name *Nonnita* also features on an inscribed stone dating from the sixth century in St Cuby church, Tregony, in central Cornwall, near the south coast. St Non's name was perhaps intended to emphasise her son's holiness.

Non is a rare example of a raped female saint: in the saints' Lives, many virgins fled arranged marriages, or were abducted, tortured or killed, but few were actually raped. However, particularly in medieval hagiography in the Celtic regions, the violation of a nun was sometimes deemed appropriate in order to explain the conception of a powerful male saint, while a raped virgin could be considered more heroic, in that she conceived without experiencing sexual pleasure.[61]

If Non existed, it is not inconceivable that she might have been a nun, as were most early Christian female saints in the Celtic lands. St Non was seen as holy because of her relationship with her holy son, in a role similar to that of Mary within the Holy Family. Perhaps because of her role as a maternal saint, Non offered a closer model for medieval married women than the virgin saints.[62]

Non's cult may have reached Cornwall quite early, for the church of Altarnun appears as *Altrenun(e)* around 1100, and again in the early and mid-twelfth century.[63] This suggests that the church perhaps contained a relic of St Non in its altar stone, some time before 1100: by the ninth century, even portable altars contained relics.[64] Above the altar, late medieval glass fragments may depict Non. In 1281 the commissary of the dean and chapter of Exeter cathedral carried out a visitation at Altarnun, and described a Life of St Non in a service book kept there; it no longer survives.[65] In about 1480 William Worcestre recorded in his *Itineraries* the belief that Non's body lay at Altarnun, where he also claimed that St David was born.[66] This tradition is also recorded in the calendar of the abbey of St Michael's Mount.[67]

Non's cult at Dirinon

The cult of St Non appears to have developed in a similar manner, though on a larger scale, at Dirinon in Brittany, with a relic, a 'tomb' and a play. Dirinon (or 'Oak of Non') seems to have acquired a significant relic of Non – two fragments of shin bone. They were wrapped in silk and placed in a silver-gilt shrine, perhaps made at Morlaix in about 1450. It is designed in the shape of a chapel, with stone walls, traceried windows and a tiled roof, surmounted by a silver statue of Non's son David, with mitre and crozier (illus. 75); visible in the photo behind the shrine is its original leather cover. Daoulas abbey, 3 miles to the south, developed Non's cult by claiming that she died at Dirinon, where she was 'buried' in a fine tomb. However, when it was later taken apart and reconstructed, it was found to contain only a few bones of an adolescent.

A Breton miracle play, *Buez Santez Nonn hac ez map Deuy* ('The Life of St Non and of her son David'), survives in a fifteenth-century manuscript, probably written at Daoulas abbey.[68] It expands upon the brief account of Non in the Latin and Welsh Lives of David, giving a lengthy and dramatic account of Non's rape, and relocates most of the story to Brittany. It claims that Non was born of 'powerful people from Brittany, nobles of a rich house', and that

ILLUS. 75. St Non's reliquary at Dirinon, Brittany.

she lived and died at Dirinon, where her bones were interred in a new tomb.[69] The Life was evidently composed shortly after the tomb was built, in order to emphasise Dirinon's new status and the importance of its patrons.

Altarnun's 'bowssening pool'

Returning to Cornwall, there are seventy-nine bench ends in Altarnun church carved between 1510 and 1531 by Robart Daye, two of which depict musicians playing the medieval fiddle and the Cornish bagpipes. In the churchyard there is a wheel-head wayside cross, perhaps dating from the thirteenth century or later, mounted on a modern shaft.

St Non's well is in a field above the church (OS 226816), beside an old hawthorn tree (illus. 76). The well feeds a 'bowssening pool', which was used to cure insanity by a primitive form of shock therapy.

This term was first recorded by the Cornish antiquary Richard Carew (1555–1602), in his description of the pool at Altarnun. He describes with disdain how deranged people were tumbled into the pool by a sudden blow to the chest; they were tossed up and down, accompanied by the chanting of prayers, until they were exhausted. The patients were then taken down to the church, where Mass was celebrated for their recovery.[70] The practice continued until the eighteenth century.

ILLUS. 76. St Non's well and 'bowssening pool', Altarnun.

PHOTO: MARGARET REES.

Memorial stones inscribed in ogham

To the east and west of the River Tamar there are six memorial stones inscribed in Irish ogham. As we have seen, these early stones may indicate immigration from the Irish kingdom of *Brycheiniog*. The spread of ogham-inscribed stones follows an arc that extends some 40 miles: this narrow band may indicate the main area of Irish settlement in Devon and Cornwall.[71] In Devon there was one at Tavistock and another further to the south-east at Fardel near Ivybridge.

Of the four in Cornwall, one is at St Kew, inscribed '[the stone] of Justus'; it is illustrated on page 116. Another is a pillar stone dating from the mid-sixth century, later used as a footbridge over a stream, at Slaughter Bridge near Camelford. It carries a Latin text, LATINI IC IACIT FILIUS MA[?C]ARI, or '[the body] of Latinus lies here, the son of Macarius'. The son's name, Latinus, is Roman, but the father's name, Macarius, derives from the Greek *Makarios*.[72] He may have been named after the great Desert Father, Abba Makarios, who was born in about AD 300. His life was well known in European monasteries through the Conferences of John Cassian (*c*. 365–*c*. 435), who wrote of Makarios, 'He was the first who found a way to inhabit the desert of Scetis'.[73] Makarios had been a camel-driver who traded in nitre, used as soap. After his conversion at the age of thirty, he

ILLUS. 77. Sixth-century monument to Ingenuus, Lewannick.

travelled around the Egyptian deserts as an early 'pilgrim for the love of God'.[74]

Lewannick's ogham stones

The final two ogham-inscribed stones are found at Lewannick, 4 miles south-west of Launceston; its western parish boundary adjoins that of Altarnun. Lewannick church stands within an oval graveyard, and is recorded in about 1125 as *Lanwenuc*: this means *lan*, or church-site, of someone with a name such as Guenoc, who may have been a local secular patron, a priest or perhaps a saint honoured in Wales or Brittany or both regions.[75] Its two bilingual inscribed stones provide information about its early Christian community: their inscriptions date from the first half of the sixth century and, like the other ogham-inscribed stones, they indicate Romanised Christians who were Irish immigrants.

Each stone is inscribed with a single name, instead of 'X, son of Y'; this may imply that they refer to celibate vowed men, who had forsaken worldly ties with their family of origin. One is a large, badly weathered stone of reddish granite, 1.6 m high; unusually, it includes the word 'memorial' in both its Latin and ogham inscriptions (illus. 77). The Latin is thought to read INGENVI MEMORIA, while the ogham has been taken to read IGENAWI MEMOR. Both are likely to mean 'The memorial of Ingenuus'; the personal name is Latin.[76]

The other memorial, of grey Elvan stone, is better preserved, since it was split in two and built into the walls of the north porch. Its inscriptions are more typical of the period: the Latin reads [HI]C IACIT VLCAGNI, or '[Here] lies [the body] of Ulcagnus' and the ogham reads ULCAGNI (illus. 78). Although the first words 'Here lies' are in Latin, the name, *Olcán* in Old Irish, commemorates an Irish-speaking Christian. The text of the ogham inscription contains errors, and reads UDSAGCI, because the mason became confused over which strokes were to be carved above the line and which were to be carved below.[77]

ILLUS. 78. Memorial to Olcán, Lewannick.

Lewannick's cresset stone

From at least 1428 until the Reformation, Lewannick church was dedicated to St Martin of Tours. There is possible medieval evidence of monastic life at Lewannick: a granite cresset stone can be seen in the church (illus. 79). Its seven holes would have been filled with tallow and each contained a wick, to provide light. The word cresset probably derives from the French word *craisset*, meaning an oil lamp. Other examples have been dated to between the twelfth and the fourteenth century; some twenty examples survive in Britain.[78]

This is one of Britain's finest cresset stones; they are mostly found in a monastic context, and were used to provide light to enable monks or nuns to navigate safely during the night from their dormitory to the church, in order to chant the night office of matins. There is one at Calder abbey (Cumbria), founded by Cistercians from Furness abbey, and another at the Augustinian priory of Inchmahome on the Lake of Mentieth, Stirling, for example. The 'Rites of Durham' describe their purpose:

ILLUS. 79. Cresset stone in Lewannick church.

> Also there is standinge in the south pillar … a foure-squared STONN … which had twelve cressets wrought in that stone, which was filled with tallow, and everye night one of them was lighted, when the day was gone, and did burne to give light to the Monkes at midnight, when they came to mattens.[79]

The anonymous author adds that there were also cressets at each end of the dormitory,

> fill'd and supply'd by the cooks, as they needed, to afford light to the monks and novices on their arising to their matins at midnight, and for their other necessary uses.[80]

The book was written in the mid-sixteenth century, and describes Durham cathedral's monastic traditions prior to the Reformation.

Later Irish monks

Some Irish Christians arrived in Cornwall from mainland Ireland, rather than from the Irish kingdom of *Brycheiniog*. In an entry for the year 891, the Anglo-Saxon Chronicle describes three *Scoti*, or Irishmen, who set sail 'in a boat without any oars' from Ireland, and drifted ashore in Cornwall. This suggests that they were *peregrini*, or pilgrims 'for the love of God'. They desired to live in exile in a foreign land, like Abraham in the Old Testament, to whom God said, 'Leave your country, your family and your father's house, for the land that I will show you' (Gen. 12. 1).

Their boat was made of cow hide, and would have been a small curragh. The entry reads:

> And three Scots came to King Alfred in a boat without any oars from Ireland, which they had left secretly, because they desired for the love of God to be in foreign lands [or 'in a state of pilgrimage'], they cared not where. The boat in which they travelled was made of two and a half hides, and they took with them enough food for seven days. And after seven days they came to land in Cornwall, and went immediately to King Alfred. They were named Dubslane, and Macbeth, and Maelinmun.[81]

ILLUS. 80. Wheel-headed cross decorated with trefoil shapes, St Breward.

They are likely to have been members of an Irish monastic community, who departed with the blessing of their abbot, since their venture would not have been according to the will of God unless they had received their abbot's blessing.[82] They probably set out from a monastery in south-east Ireland, and were carried by the ocean currents to the north Cornish coast. Their reason for visiting King Alfred may to have been to ask permission to settle in his kingdom and establish what was known as 'the place of their resurrection', a place where you would live and die, and so enter paradise.

St Breward, Cornwall's highest parish

On the west side of Bodmin Moor, 4 miles south of Camelford, the parish of St Breward is bounded on the north by Advent and St Clether, and on the east by Altarnun. It is a hill-top settlement, 200 m above sea level; at this high altitude, its rocky ground was unsuitable for ploughing and had to be dug by spade or used as sheep pasture. St Breward may take its name from the Latinised form of a Breton saint, Branwalader, who is thought to be commemorated at three Breton sites and at St Brelade in Jersey.[83]

Branwalader appears to have gained popularity in England when King Æthelstan founded Milton abbey (Dorset) in about 933 and dedicated it to the Virgin Mary, Samson and Branwalader; Æthelstan endowed it with relics of both men.[84] An unusual eleventh-century wheel-head cross decorated with trefoil shapes carved out between each arm, a design unique to Cornwall, stands in the lower churchyard on a modern shaft (illus. 80). This is the earliest feature of the church site: perhaps the church was established to serve the needs of farmers, when settlement expanded onto the higher reaches of Bodmin Moor.[85]

ILLUS. 81. Norman carved head on a corbel, St Tudy.

PHOTO: PAUL JOHNSON.

St Tudy, a Breton saint

On the opposite side of the River Camel, on lower ground, the parish of St Tudy is also named after a Breton saint. It is situated in a farming area between the Rivers Camel and Allen; to the west, it adjoins the parish of St Kew. St Tudy's circular churchyard is considered to be the site of an Iron Age round – a small enclosure bounded by a ditch and a bank, which often contained a farmstead.[86] There was another round at nearby Jory's Meadow, beside the Wadebridge Road.[87] About 1,400 rounds are known in Cornwall, dating from the fourth century BC to the sixth century AD.[88] They are often situated on a spur or a hillside close to good arable land.[89]

Late additions to the Leofric Missal, dating from the time of Leofric, bishop of Exeter from 1050 to 1072, state that King Æthelstan gave relics of St Tudy to Exeter cathedral. The manor of St Tudy is referred to in the Exeter Domesday Book as *Ecglostudic* and *Hecglostudic*, meaning 'church of Tudic'.[90] The earliest feature of the building is a Norman carved head on a corbel above the first pillar, removed from a previous church on the site; it can be seen as one enters from the porch (illus. 81).

There is also a magnificent tenth-century coped, or 'hogback', tombstone, brought in from the churchyard; with its scroll-like patterns on the roof, resembling vine tendrils, and its arcading on the sides, it might represent a

ILLUS. 82. Hogback tombstone, St Tudy.

PHOTO: PAUL JOHNSON.

ILLUS. 83. Gallo-Roman memorial column, east of Loctudy church, Brittany.

lord's feasting-hall (illus. 82).[91] These tombstones are more commonly found in northern Britain, in areas conquered by Vikings, but there are five similar stones in Cornwall, one each at Padstow, Lanivet and Phillack, and two at St Buryan. Since they are not found in Scandinavia, they are more likely to be an Anglo-Saxon phenomenon, an elite Christian form of commemorating the dead.[92] They are often too small to have covered a tomb, and are sometimes found together with a grave cross; they may have commemorated a kin-group or household. Like a saint's tomb-shrine, they may represent not so much a house for the dead as a doorway into heaven.[93]

Loctudy, Brittany

Loctudy, on the south-west coast of Brittany, together with Île Tudy, an island across the bay from the small harbour on the mainland, may have been the chief cult-site of Tudy. Eight Breton sites are named after him, across north and south Brittany. The prefic *loc* derives from the Latin *locus*, meaning 'the place of Saint X'. Tudy is sometimes considered to be the same person as the more popular Tudwal, after whom thirty-eight Breton sites are named.[94]

Loctudy is an ancient holy site: its first church was built beside a pre-Christian Gallo-Roman pillar, perhaps dating from 300 to 200 BC – a fluted memorial column to a Gaulish warrior (illus. 83); it was later surmounted by a cross. Loctudy was founded by the abbey of St Gildas de Rhuys, and was apparently named after the local saint. In common with other abbeys in the region, it was probably sacked by Vikings in the early tenth century; the church was rebuilt on an impressive scale between 1070 and 1130 (illus. 84).[95]

Cornwall and Brittany

As we saw in chapter four, Christian leaders like Samson and their families moved to and fro between Cornwall and Brittany. A similar pattern can be deduced from dedications of such churches as St Breward and St Tudy: like Samson, Tudy and Branwalader have Breton churches named after

ILLUS. 84. Column capitals in the Norman apse, Loctudy church, Brittany.

them, as we have seen. In the sixth and seventh centuries there was close contact between Cornwall and Brittany: it was at this time that Cornish names were given to Breton regions.

In the Roman period, Dumnonia was the tribal land of the Dumnonii, with their capital at Exeter; Britons migrating to Brittany gave the same name, Dumnonia, to northern Brittany. The name of Cornwall (or *Kernow* in Cornish) was applied to Cornouaille, a region of south-west Brittany (*Kernev* in Breton). The Breton language is closer to Cornish than to Welsh, and both countries were on trade routes from mainland Europe to the Irish Sea.[96]

Breton art and culture continued to influence the Cornish Church. Breton architectural style can be seen in the fourteenth-century spire of Lostwithiel church and the well chapel at Dupath (OS 374693), 1.5 miles east-south-east of Callington (illus. 85), built in about 1510 by Augustinian canons from St Germans. This is the largest medieval well-house in Cornwall; it houses a spring flowing into a well pool. Its granite walls rise to a roof with mock battlements,

ILLUS. 85. Well chapel at Dupath, near Callington.

four pinnacles and a large bellcote designed to house a single bell, containing sockets for the bell pivot.[97]

Many Bretons settled in Cornwall; at North Petherwin in 1523–24 'brytons' (meaning Bretons) were paid £58 to build the rood loft, and at Bodmin in 1529–30 two 'Bretouns' were hired to construct pews and dismantle the organ.[98] Bretons settled in west Cornwall, where the Cornish language, similar to their own, was strong, in parishes such as St Ives, Towednack, Zennor and Lelant. There were also Bretons on the south-east coast, at Fowey, Polruan and East Looe.[99]

Irish Christians at Cardinham

Situated on the south-western edge of Bodmin Moor, Cardinham takes its name from Bury castle, an Iron Age hill fort a mile north-west of the church. The earliest surviving form of its name is *Cardinan* (*c.* 1180), derived from two early words meaning 'fort': *dinan*, to which the Cornish prefix *ker* was later added.[100] At some point the church was dedicated to St Meubred: he is named as patron saint of Cardinham church in a subsidy roll of 1440 and from the bishop's register of 1473.[101] In about 1480, William Worcestre was told that Meubred's relics lay in the church.[102]

There were Christians here in early times: beside the gate of the raised churchyard, a tenth-century cross-head has been attached to a pillar stone dating from the second half of the sixth century (illus. 86). Its Latin inscription has been interpreted as [?R]ANOCORI FILI MESGI, or '[the stone] of Ranocorus, son of Mesgus'.[103] A second inscribed memorial stone from the same period stands at a crossroads in Welltown, a mile to the south-east. Its inscription reads VAILATHI FILI VROCHANI, or '[the stone] of Vailathus, of the son of Vrochanus' (or 'Brochanus', meaning 'Little Badger'); the names are Old Irish.[104]

Outside the church porch is a finely ornamented cross in Scandinavian style, dating from the tenth century, with the (incomplete) name of the person commemorated, ARTHI…, carved below the cross-head. Four crosses were erected at the boundaries of the church lands, possibly in the twelfth century, two of which survive. There is a holy well half a mile to the north, at Millpool: its well-house stands behind a bank adjoining the entrance to Trezance Farm. Beside it are the stones of a ruined chapel; water from the well was brought to Cardinham church for baptisms.[105]

ILLUS. 86. Sixth-century memorial stone, Cardinham churchyard.

The legend of St Sidwell

On a medieval chest in Cardinham church there is a carving of St Sidwell, carrying a sheaf of corn and a sword (illus. 87). The chest was probably

made from the rood screen, which was removed from the church to nearby Carblake at the Reformation. As we saw in chapter three, Exeter was the centre of Sidwell's cult, where a church and a holy well were named after her. We first hear of Sidwell in the late Anglo-Saxon period, and people came to her shrine in Exeter for healing throughout medieval times.[106] Her cult and its origins were described in greater detail on pages 89–90.

Her popularity may have been the reason why only a relief of Sidwell was preserved from Cardinham's rood screen; she is also the patron saint of Laneast, 12 miles to the north-east, on the opposite side of Bodmin Moor. Sidwell is more often depicted with a scythe, which also features in her legendary life. She is portrayed with her scythe on rood screens, bench ends and windows in churches in Cornwall, Devon and west Somerset.[107]

In the twelfth century, the bishop of Exeter compiled a book of liturgical readings for use in the cathedral, in which he records Sidwell's story as it was then told: her stepmother had her murdered by labourers reaping in the fields, who cut off her head with their scythes. As we have seen, a similar legend was told of St Juthwara of Sherborne; it preserves a pre-Christian myth, in which the spirit of the corn was said to die when reapers cut the last sheaf of corn. This was ritually enacted from ancient times in many countries; in England this took place on farms into recent times.

ILLUS. 87. St Sidwell carrying a wheat sheaf and a sword, Cardinham church.

The death and rebirth of the corn spirit

The earliest form of this ritual may have involved human sacrifice, when the reaper who cut the last sheaf, or a stranger representing him, would be killed on the field to restore life to the corn spirit, who was thought to retreat into the last remaining corn stalk. The last sheaf was therefore considered significant, and risky to cut. In Britain it was often thought unlucky to harm it, and the cutter would be swathed in the corn, jostled and roughly handled. On some farms, to spread responsibility for this dangerous act, the last sheaf was cut jointly. A little of the corn was left standing and its stalks were tied or plaited together; the reapers stood round it in a wide half-circle, and one by one threw their sickles at it.[108]

The ceremony of bowing to the sheaf then followed on many farms. It was called 'Crying the neck', since the last sheaf of corn was called 'the neck'. In 1826 a north Devon farmer wrote:

> I have once or twice heard upwards of twenty men cry [the neck], and sometimes joined by an equal number of female voices. About three years back, on some high grounds, where our people were harvesting, I heard six or seven necks cried in one night, although I knew that some of them were four miles off. They are heard through the quiet evening air … I think the practice is beginning to decline of late, and many farmers and their men do not care about keeping up the old custom. I shall always practise it myself, because I take it in the light of a thanks giving.[109]

How did they cry the neck? In a typical example, the captain of the reapers bent down and touched the ground with the last sheaf, crying: 'I have'n, I have'n, I have'n!' The reapers replied: 'What have'ee? What hav'ee? What have'ee?' The captain cried: 'A neck, a neck, a neck!' and they shouted: 'Hurrah, hurrah, hurrah!'[110] The tradition has been revived on some Cornish farms.[111]

This ritual may seem pagan to us, but a similar ceremony appears to have been the basis of one of Joseph's dreams in the Old Testament Book of Genesis:

> Now Joseph had a dream, and he repeated it to his brothers. 'Listen', he said, 'to this dream I have had. We were binding sheaves in the countryside; my sheaf, it seemed, rose up and stood upright; then I saw your sheaves gather round and bow to my sheaf.' 'So you want to be king over us', his brothers retorted, 'or to lord it over us?' (Gen. 37. 5–8)

Joseph dreamt that he was 'Lord of the Harvest', as he later became for the whole of Egypt, when famine struck. The concept of a cosmic harvest is described by the prophet Joel (4. 13) in which the angels are the reapers and we are the harvested corn, and early Christians preserved this vision. The Book of Revelation describes the angel's command: 'Put your sickle in and reap: harvest time has come and the harvest of the earth is ripe' (Rev. 14. 15).

Jesus applied the concept of harvest to individuals: 'Unless a wheat grain falls on the ground and dies, it remains only a single grain; but if it dies, it yields a rich harvest' (Jn 12. 24). While the legend of St Sidwell killed by the reapers focuses on the death of the corn, the north Devon farmer wrote of the harvest ritual, 'I take it in the light of a thanksgiving'. 'Thanksgiving' is a translation of the Greek word *eucharisto*, the word adopted by Christians to celebrate being fed by the bread of life. Historians might be reluctant to juxtapose rituals from such different epochs and cultures, but liturgists and social anthropologists might be intrigued by their similarities.

St Neot: a dispersed religious community

The village of St Neot is on the southern edge of Bodmin Moor; Neot is probably included in the tenth-century list of forty-eight Cornish saints, where he is named *Nioth*.[112] Domesday Book lists two manors at St Neot in 1086. The population of the two estates was small: it comprised three *servi* (serfs, or slaves), three *villani* ('men of the *vill*, or village') and ten *bordarii* (unfree peasants, with less land than *villani*).[113] It is also possible that St Neot owned rough grazing land on the moor to the north.

In 1086 the *clerici Sancti Neoti* are recorded as holding the manor of *Neotestou*, but a note is added that the 'Count has taken all this land away from the Church, except for 1 acre of land, which the priests have'.[114] Perhaps before 1086 St Neot was a single manor, held by the clergy, headed by 'Godric the priest' (or *presbiter*). It appears that the Count of Mortain then took away the larger part of its lands, to create a separate manor: this was held by one Odo, along with other manors, on behalf of the count.

The small portion of the property that was left to the priests may have become a manor in its own right; the community is not recorded again. If Godric the priest held part of its estate, this could indicate a pattern whereby individual presbyters, or members of the community, held farms belonging to their church. Wrmonoc's ninth-century Breton Life of St Paul Aurelian describes homes (*domus*) in which individual clerics lived who may have functioned in a similar manner as a dispersed community.[115] Perhaps Cornish monasteries of this date did not have extensive living accommodation, but clerics gathered to pray in the church.

Gueriir and Neot

Asser's Life of King Alfred relates that the king went hunting in Cornwall and turned aside to pray for healing at a church 'in which St Gueriir lies in peace (and now St Niot lies there as well)'.[116] Gueriir may have been the original saint honoured in the church; the Life suggests that Neot was buried there after Alfred's lifetime. In French, *guérir* means 'to heal'; the Cornish equivalent is *gweres*. Gueriir may have been commonly invoked for healing, but perhaps he was remembered as a generic healing saint, rather than as a specific individual – he is mentioned nowhere apart from the incident described in the Life of Alfred. In the sixteenth century, Nicholas Roscarrock assembled as much information about St Gueriir as he could find.[117]

St Neot's church and holy well

The churchyard contains one of the finest early crosses in Cornwall, carved of granite, and richly ornamented with interlacing. It probably dates from the late ninth or early tenth century; its style resembles that of the tenth-century cross at Cardinham, described above. The church contains magnificent stained glass windows dating from the fifteenth and sixteenth centuries; they depict angels and saints, the Creation, the Flood and the legendary life of St Neot. One window portrays a crowned figure with children in his lap: its nineteenth-century restorer inserted an inscription that describes the figure as Brychan, but it is more likely to represent God the Father, or Abraham with the souls of the righteous in his lap.

St Neot's well is 400 m from the church (OS 183681), near the St Neot River (illus. 88). In his history of the parish (1833), William Michell writes:

> ... there was an arch of stones over it, with a large oak springing from the arch, and with doors to the entrance. [It] was remembered by some old inhabitants of the village lately deceased ... Weakly children used within living memory to be brought here.[118]

The well-house was rebuilt in 1862. Neot's relics were taken to Eynesbury, 18 miles west of Cambridge, according to the earliest Life of Neot. The Life was written in the eleventh century at or for the church of Eynesbury, which was renamed St Neots in his honour.

ILLUS. 88. St Neot's holy well.

Doniert's cross, St Cleer

St Cleer is 4 miles east of St Neot, on the south-eastern edge of Bodmin Moor. The remains of two late ninth-century crosses can be seen beside a minor road from St Cleer to Redgate, 1.5 miles to the north-west. One is a decorated cross-shaft; the other is the base of a cross with a knotwork panel on one side (illus. 89) and on the other a Latin inscription carved in Saxon minuscule. It reads: DONIERT ROGAVIT PRO ANIMA, meaning 'Doniert has requested [this cross, or prayers] for [his] soul'.[119]

Doniert may have been Dumgarth, king of Cornwall (*Dumnarth rex Cerniu*), who is recorded in a Welsh chronicle, *Annales Cambriae*, as having drowned in 875; he was perhaps a Cornish chieftain who was a vassal of the king of Wessex. He is the last recorded native ruler in Cornwall before the reign of the Saxon King Alfred who, according to his will, owned property in north-east Cornwall.[120] Doniert's cross stands 3 miles north of Liskeard, which is named *Lys Cerruyt* in about 1010, and probably means the *lys*, or court, of Kerwyd, who was perhaps a native ruler.[121]

Liskeard became an administrative centre of the Anglo-Saxon government in the early eleventh century. If Doniert is Dumgarth, as seems likely, he may have been the last king to rule from Liskeard before the Saxons gained control of Cornwall.[122] Doniert's cross appears to be in an isolated location today, but the site is above a ford over the River Fowey, at the crossroads of two major early routes. The road from Liskeard in the south to Camelford and Tintagel in the north was described as 'the great way of wagons' (*magnum iter plaustrorum*) in the mid-thirteenth century.[123]

ILLUS. 89 *(left)*. Cross-base of King Doniert (left) and carved cross-shaft (right).

ILLUS. 90 *(right)*. St Cleer holy well.

St Cleer's church is Norman; its dedication, *Ecclesiam de Sancto Claro*, is first recorded in 1212. The church is likely to be named after one of several French male saints named Clair.[124] The head of a small cross, rather crudely carved, stands outside the south door of the church; it has been dated to the eleventh century. Since the church stands within a very large curvilinear enclosure, and since a quite large aisled church was built here in Norman times, this may have been a significant local site.[125]

Downhill from the church is a fifteenth-century granite well-house (OS 249683), beside a wayside cross of the same date. The small granite building is the only Cornish well-house with an open porch-like design (illus. 90). Like that of Altarnun, the well is believed to have been a 'bowssening' or immersion pool. It would have had a reservoir beneath the well-house, with a sunken cistern to the west and a pool to the east, into which people could be tossed.[126]

St Germans cathedral

To conclude the chapter, we will consider six sites in south-east Cornwall. St Germans grew beside a tidal river that joins the Tamar, which flows southwards to the sea. Its earlier name was *Lanalet*; it was an important community and a bishop's seat from the early tenth century. At this time, the diocese of Sherborne was subdivided: as a result of the political expansion of Wessex, which now included all of south-west Britain, it had grown too large to administer effectively. Therefore, in about 909, a new see was created at Crediton, to serve Devon and Cornwall. But that too was found unwieldy, so some twenty years later, in the reign of King Æthelstan, a new see was created at St Germans, to serve Cornwall.[127]

In the tenth century, when the diocese was subdivided, bishops with British names are recorded in Cornwall, including Conan, to whom King Æthelstan gave the region 'as far as the Tamar flows'. Like Conan, his successors Daniel and Comoere had names that were Cornish, Welsh or Breton, but Comoere also had an Anglo-Saxon name, Wulfsige. By the end of the tenth century, the bishops of Cornwall all had Saxon names.[128]

ILLUS. 91. Norman west door, St Germans priory.

St Germans cathedral owned a large estate that supported the bishop's household and cathedral clergy. St Germanus of Auxerre was venerated here: a page survives from a mid-tenth-century manuscript that contains texts for the Mass on his feast day. It refers to *Lannaled* (St Germans), the 'famed and universally known place, where the relics of Bishop Germanus are preserved'.[129] By this time, St Germans was both a monastery, or minster, and a bishop's seat. In 1042 the bishop's see was moved to Crediton, but the monastery continued. The Anglo-Saxon cathedral was replaced by an impressive Norman church with an elaborate west door (illus. 91). In the twelfth century it became an Augustinian priory.

St Indract's well, St Dominic

Unlike the important bishop's seat at St Germans, the church of St Dominic was probably small, and unimportant; by 1283 it was known as the church of *Sancta Dominica*, an unknown female saint.[130] If one follows the River Tamar 10 miles upstream, high above its the west bank there is a holy well dedicated to St Indract (OS 417659) in St Dominic parish; it was restored in 1951 (illus. 92). There was a chapel at the site; some of its stones are incorporated into the walls of nearby Chapel Farm.[131]

ILLUS. 92. St Indract's well on the bank of the Tamar, St Dominic.

This is the only site dedicated to Indract outside Somerset; he had an important cult at Glastonbury, being buried beside the high altar. At Glastonbury, Indract was believed to have been Irish, and indeed his name seems to be an Irish one. His life story was presumably told and preserved at Glastonbury before it appeared in standard English legendaries. In the mid-fourteenth century, the chronicler John of Tynemouth included in his *Nova Legenda Anglie* material which he either heard or invented, claiming that Indract and Dominic were brother and sister. Before describing Indract's martyrdom, he relates that, on their way to Rome, Indract and his companions stopped at a place called *Tamerunta* (probably a copyist's error for *Tamertuna*, meaning '*tun* or settlement on the Tamar'). This implies that Indract was still honoured at St Dominic in the fourteenth century.[132]

In St Dominic parish, Indract's name appears as St Ildrayth (1351), St Ildreyth (1352), St Ildreith (1362) and St Ildract, confessor (1419). These Cornish variants of Indract's name date back to at least 1100, when Cornish was last spoken in this neighbourhood, on the eastern fringe of Cornwall.[133] Indract perhaps lived in the mid-ninth century, and, if Cornish was no longer spoken by 1100, this suggests a possible dating for the dedication of St Indract's chapel and holy well at St Dominic, some time in the tenth or eleventh century.

Looe Island

There are two chapels at Looe on the south Cornish coast, 12 miles west of the Tamar estuary, one on Looe Island (illus. 93) and the other on the mainland, half a mile to the north. Both were excavated by Time Team under the direction of Mick Aston in 2008, but neither site produced substantial evidence from before the twelfth century. The chapel on the island produced the earliest remains: a pre-Christian standing stone, a burial chamber that may have been prehistoric and an oval embankment surrounding the chapel, which may have enclosed a prehistoric settlement.[134]

Stone anchors were found of a type used by small trading boats from the Iron Age into post-Roman times.[135] A small hoard of eight Roman coins from the late third or early fourth century was discovered, and fragments of late Roman amphorae dating from the fifth to the seventh centuries. The enclosure may have surrounded an early Christian burial ground; two cist (or stone-lined) graves were found, one beneath the chapel's south wall.[136]

The chapel was built into solid bedrock on one side – a considerable feat of engineering; on the other side, it was supported by massive foundations. Pieces of the stone buttresses that supported the chancel arch lay on the surface of the soil. Glastonbury abbey acquired the island before 1144, and developed it as a centre for pilgrimage, together with a site on the mainland opposite. Pottery was found on the island dating from the early twelfth century to the late thirteenth century. The grave of one of the last clerics on the island, or perhaps of a thirteenth-century nobleman, was discovered in front of the altar.[137]

The chapel was visible to offshore shipping; it features on early maps and probably served as a beacon for traders sailing round this part of the coast, with its dangerous currents. It was dedicated to St Michael, and was intended to rival St Michael's Mount, on its tidal island further to the west.[138] St Michael was popular as a patron of islands and of high places, a remarkable early example being Skellig Michael on a rocky islet 9 miles off the Inveragh peninsula in Kerry, Ireland.

The short crossing to Looe Island is choppy, and limited by the tide, so pilgrims' boats were often wrecked. Michaelmas was close to the autumn equinox, when it is possible that pilgrims could have walked across to the island in safety at low tide. However, at a court in 1290, a jury of twelve local men agreed that pilgrims travelling to the island on St Michael's Day, 29 September, were in danger of drowning.[139] Perhaps pilgrims tried to cross too soon, or stayed too long on the island and were cut off by the tide. A chapel on the mainland opposite proved a more accessible place for pilgrims to pray and donate their offerings; it was known as Lammana, or '*lan* of the monks', and was built halfway up the hillside, level with the chapel at the crest of Looe Island.

ILLUS. 93. Looe Island from the mainland.

Lammana, opposite Looe Island

ILLUS. 94. 'Monks' house', Hannafore, Looe.

Lammana was excavated in 1935/36 by C.K. Croft-Andrew and a team of local archaeologists. Medieval documents suggest that a stone chapel was extended in the twelfth century after its acquisition by Glastonbury abbey; this later chapel was built of local stone, roofed with rough, heavy local slates to withstand storms, with green-glazed, crested ridge tiles.[140] In 2008, a box 1 m long was discovered in the chancel, in front of the altar: this was identified as a reliquary, perhaps containing the relics of a local holy man, since it was too small to serve as a grave. No bones were found in it; they appear to have been subsequently removed.[141] Croft-Andrew found two burials nearby, while Time Team uncovered a cist-grave in the chapel.

Lower down the hill, alongside the last modern house on Hannafore, a stone wall containing openings for doorways and windows had been named 'monks' house' by Croft-Andrew (illus. 94). In the excavations of 2008 it became evident that this was a two-storey building, perhaps a refectory or hospice for pilgrims, with two cells or bedrooms above for the resident community; there may have been other adjacent monastic buildings. A Glastonbury charter relating to Lammana, drawn up in about 1200, names two clerics who may have tended the property: the charter's witnesses were 'Elias, then prior of that place and his companion, the monk John'. This suggests that Lammana was a small priory.[142] Across the road, a steep, overgrown track leads to the ancient quay for boats to depart for Looe Island.

Pelynt's church

Pelynt, 3 miles west of Looe, was an early site. There is a barrow cemetery nearby; ten barrows still exist and others have been destroyed. Pelynt's church is built within a raised oval enclosure that may have been an Iron Age settlement; the churchyard is surrounded by a road that could have formed its enclosure ditch. Fragments of the head of an eleventh-century wheel-cross found at nearby Trelay Farm are displayed on the wall of the north aisle; these factors hint at an early medieval church.[143]

The name Pelynt consists of the prefix *plou* followed by a personal name, perhaps a male saint, Nenit or Nennyd, since Domesday Book refers to *Plvnent*; a saint with a similar name was known in Wales. *Plou* derives from the Latin *plebs*, meaning 'the people [of God]', or 'the parish'. The prefix is frequently found in Brittany: there are some hundred Breton settlements that begin with *plou* or one of its derivatives.[144] Pelynt is the only surviving Cornish parish whose name begins with *plou*.

In ninth-century Brittany, a *plou* (or *plebes* in Latin) was primarily a civil group, consisting mostly of peasant farmers, with a responsible officer (the *machtiern*, or hereditary local chairman) and priests; the term also referred to the group's territory, of about 30 miles, the size of a large parish. People carried out business in public meetings within the *plebs* and settled most disputes at a court within the *plebs*. It might have a focal church and a scatter of small religious communities. The church was served by a small group of local priests, most with hereditary property; they undertook a range of both secular and spiritual roles. In the Redon area, for example, priests constituted perhaps a third of those who owned property and used money.[145]

Pelynt's chapel and holy well

Although Nenit was considered to be a man, by the thirteenth century a female saint with the Latin name *Nonnita* was honoured at a chapel and well (now named St Nun's well) a mile down the valley, above the West Looe River; she and Nenit may have originated as the same person. The chapel stood within an Iron Age hill fort; the Giant's Hedge was incorporated into the earthwork's long eastern rampart. The Giant's Hedge (illus. 95) is thought to have been an early territorial boundary, stretching some 10 miles from Kilminorth, near

ILLUS. 95. The Giant's Hedge, south of Pelynt chapel.

Looe, westwards to Lerryn, above a tributary of the River Fowey.

In 1979 a brief survey of the earthwork revealed a chapel of uncertain date, on a slight platform within the round that formed the initial phase of the fort. The rectangular chapel faced west–east, and a small square building adjoined its northern side; this may have been a priest's dwelling, or that of a nun.[146] It is likely to be the 'Chapel of St Nenine the Virgin', described in 1241 as belonging to the nuns of Wilton abbey in Wiltshire; In 1409 the bishop appointed a chaplain for the chapel after the responsible authority, which was probably Wilton abbey, failed to do so. The chapel fell into disuse after the Reformation.[147]

ILLUS. 96. Granite bowl incised with wheel crosses, Pelynt holy well.

The well is lower down the hill in Hobb Park (OS 224564), where a spring emerges from the hillside. Inside the well-house, the water trickles into a heavy bowl of pink granite, incised with wheel crosses (illus. 96); it is unusual for such a bowl to survive. Although restored, the well-house retains its original shape, with a curved roof, a stone lintel, and walls of flat, unmortared stones. On either side of the entrance is a stone bench where pilgrims could sit and pray (illus. 97).

ILLUS. 97. The well-house, St Nun's well, Penynt.

A Welsh saint, Cuby

St Cuby is one of a group of Welsh saints whose Lives are to be found in a manuscript compiled around AD 1200; they combine legend and folklore with a limited amount of fact.[148] According to his Life, Cuby (or Cybi in Welsh) was the son of a Cornish chieftain named Selevan; he sailed to north-west Wales, and landed on Anglesey, where the chieftain, Maelgwn Gwynedd, gave him permission to build a church in a Roman fort at Holyhead (or *Caergybi*), in the north-east corner of Holy Island (*Ynys Gybi*), which is connected to Anglesey by a causeway.

The fourth-century fort may have been no more than a fortified landing place, and the church sits neatly inside it, well protected by its Roman enclosure wall with towers at each corner (illus. 98). In the south-west corner of the

ILLUS. 98. St Cuby's church (right) and burial chapel (left), inside a Roman fort, Caergybi, Anglesey.

churchyard is a second building, the *eglwys y bedd*, or chapel of Cuby's shrine. It dates from the fourteenth century and may have housed Cuby's relics. Excavation in 1992 identified the footings of an earlier building, possibly dating from the twelfth century. The chapel's chancel was demolished in 1832, when evidence was found of at least one burial inside the chapel, and early medieval long-cist graves outside it, within the fort.[149]

Cuby's church at Duloe

The unusual claim that Cuby was Cornish may be due to the fact that his Life was written in Wales, and it was typical to portray saints as arriving from overseas. St Cuby is patron of three other Welsh churches and two in Cornwall, one at Cuby, near Tregony, on the south coast and the other at Duloe; both were dedicated to him by the late thirteenth century. Duloe is 4 miles north of Looe and 4 miles south of Liskeard, on an exposed site. In 1286, the Cornish name for Duloe was *Lankyp* or *Lankep*, meaning 'church-site of Cuby'.[150]

Duloe was a holy place in pre-Christian times: on the edge of the village a stone circle was constructed in modern times from massive stones that may have formed a chambered tomb; the eight large white quartz stones were quarried at Herodsfoot, 2 miles to the north-west. A late Bronze Age burial urn was found at the site of the tomb, and a golden torc, or neck ornament, was discovered half a mile away.

Cuby's church at Duloe stands within a raised circular churchyard, 250 m south-west of the stone circle. There is a massive stone bowl or font inside the church, thought to date from Norman times (illus. 99). It is decorated with a gryphon on one side and a dolphin on the other. As we saw in chapter one, in early iconography Christians were sometimes represented by dolphins, and the mythical gryphon could symbolise evil, with its ferocious lion's body and an eagle's head and wings. The bowl may be a baptismal font, with its carvings representing the struggle between the forces of life and death, into which new Christians enter at baptism.

ILLUS. 99. Carving of a gryphon on the stone bowl in Duloe church.

The bowl was formerly inside St Cuby's holy well, half a mile east of the church, beside the road leading down the hill to Looe (OS 241579); it is so heavy that a team of oxen were required to transport it. The well's outer chamber contains a stone bench, and within the inner chamber steps lead down into a pool of clear water (illus. 100). People could have been immersed in the pool for baptism or for healing. In 1913 a large granite entrance was added to the well-house.[151]

ILLUS. 100. Pool inside St Cuby's well, Duloe.

Cuby near Tregony is another early Christian site: a memorial stone of red granite dates from the last third of the sixth century. It is built into the south-west corner of the church at ground level; its Latin inscription can be translated as '[The memorial of] Nonnita, Ercilivus, Ricatus, three children of Ercilingus'. Nonnita is a woman's name, the rest are men; their names are British. The second son's name, Ricatus, may mean 'kingly in battle'.[152] The name Nonnita means something like 'Our dear nun' – it is the name that Rhygyfarch gave to St David's mother, as we have seen. St Patrick's biographer, Tírechán, writing in the late seventh century, described him founding a church and entrusting its care to 'three brothers and a sister', as we saw on p. 140.[153] It is a possibility that the monument at Tregony commemorates something similar.

St Keyne's holy well

Keyne is described as one of the daughters of Brychan in twelfth-century Welsh genealogies, and several Welsh churches are named after her, although she does not feature in Hartland abbey's list of Brychan's children. According to her legendary Life, she became a nun and left Wales in search of solitude. She lived for a while at a place infested by serpents, which she turned into stone – this is probably intended to be Keynsham in Somerset, at a crossing of the Avon, where ammonites are found.

In her legend, Keyne continued to Cornwall, where she built many chapels; she met St Cadoc while he was on a pilgrimage to St Michael's Mount. This feature of her story is borrowed from the twelfth-century Life of Cadoc by Llifris of Llancarfan; it therefore helps to date her own Life. Devotion to Keyne flourished in the later medieval period; the church of St Martin-by-Looe was formerly dedicated to her.[154]

The village of St Keyne is 2 miles north of Duloe and 2 miles south of Liskeard; it is not mentioned until 1291. Its medieval church stands on high ground above the village, and Keyne's holy well is in a valley a mile south-east of the church, down a leafy lane (OS 248603). The stone well-house (illus. 101) was restored in 1932. Above the well there used to be four holy trees, which were described by various antiquarians. In 1602, Richard Carew wrote:

> … The shape, 4. trees of divers kinde,
> Withy, Oke, Elme and Ash,
> Make with their roots an archèd roofe,
> Whose floore this spring doth wash …[155]

These trees died, and new ones were planted in the early eighteenth century; these have also disappeared. An engraving of 1858 depicts the willow, oak, elm and ash towering above the well-house; their stature implies that they were considered to be as important as the well (illus. 102).[156]

There was a fanciful legend that they sprang from a single root, planted by St Keyne.[157] While this may be a recent tale, trees were held in honour in ancient times. There is a hawthorn beside the pool at Altarnun and a hazel tree at St Juliot's well, Lanteglos. Earlier in this chapter we saw that there was an oak above St Neot's well; Dirinon meant 'Oak tree of Non', while Kildare in Ireland means 'church at the oak tree'. In the Old Testament, we are told that God met Abraham 'at Shechem's holy place, the Oak of Moreh' (Gen. 12. 6); Abraham later built an altar at the Oak of Mamre (Gen. 13. 18), where God again appeared to him (18. 1).

The oak was considered a holy tree both in the Near East and in Europe because it was strong, durable and long-lived, although the British oak differs from its Near Eastern counterpart, which is an evergreen variety. The tree is a powerful symbol of the life of the cosmos, representing its growth and proliferation, its continual birth and rebirth.[158] While some conservative theologians in the early Church considered reverence for trees as pagan, others pondered the

ILLUS. 101. St Keyne's holy well.

ILLUS. 102. St Keyne's well and holy trees, from an engraving of 1858.

mystery of the tree of life which, for them, was also the tree of the cross.

Throughout the early Church at Easter, bishops preached about the mystery of the cross. A fourth-century Easter sermon, perhaps by Pseudo-Hippolytus, praises the tree of life:

> This tree, the plant of immortality, rears from earth to reach as high as heaven, fixing the Lord between heaven and earth. It is the foundation and stabiliser of the universe, undergirding the world that we inhabit. It is the binding force of the world and holds together all the varieties that human life encompasses.
>
> It is riveted into a unity by the invisible bonds of the Spirit, so that its connection with God can never be severed. Brushing heaven with its uppermost branches, it remains fixed in the earth and, between the two points, its huge hands completely enfold the stirring of the air. As a single whole it penetrates all things and all places.[159]

Such sermons were pondered in monasteries across the Christian world.

Notes

1 Sam Turner, *Making a Christian Landscape* (Exeter: Exeter University Press, 2006), p. 54.

2 Philip Payton, *Cornwall: A History* (Fowey: Cornwall Editions, 2004), p. 52.

3 Charles Thomas, *Tintagel: Arthur and Archaeology* (London: Batsford/English Heritage, 1993), pp. 83–84.

4 Turner, *Making a Christian Landscape*, pp. xv, 55.

5 Christopher D. Morris, 'Tintagel 1998', in *Council for British Archaeology South West*, vol. 2 (Winter/Spring 1999), p. 6.

6 Steven Morris, 'Inscribed Seventh-Century Window Ledge Unearthed at Tintagel', *The Guardian*, 14 June 2018.

7 *Ibid.*

8 Turner, *Making a Christian Landscape*, p. xvii.

9 Nicholas Orme, *The Saints of Cornwall* (Oxford: Oxford University Press, 2000), p. 154.

10 Turner, *Making a Christian Landscape*, pp. 50, 59.

11 *Ibid.*

12 Orme, *The Saints of Cornwall*, p. 190.

13 Nicholas J.A. Williams, '"Saint" in Cornish', *Cornish Studies*, 7, ed. Philip Payton (Exeter: University of Exeter Press, 1999), p. 222.

14 Eilert Ekwall, *The Concise Oxford Dictionary of English Place-Names*, 4th edn (Oxford: Oxford University Press, 1970), entry: Boscastle.
15 Nicholas Orme, *Cornwall and the Cross: Christianity 500–1500* (London: Victoria County History Publications, Phillimore, 2007), pp. 34–35, 70.
16 Lynette Olson and Oliver Padel, 'A Tenth-Century List of Cornish Parochial Saints', *Cambridge Medieval Celtic Studies*, 12 (1986), pp. 33–71.
17 Nicholas Orme, ed., *Nicholas Rosacrrock's Lives of the Saints: Cornwall and Devon*, New Series, 35 (Exeter: Devon and Cornwall Record Society, 1992), pp. 46–47.
18 St Patrick, *Confessio* 41, 42 in Thomas O'Loughlin, *Saint Patrick: the Man and his Works* (London: SPCK, 1999), pp. 77–78.
19 Tírechán, *Collectanea*, ch. 11, in Ludwig Beiler, 'Tírechán: Biography and Character Study', in *The Patrician Texts in the Book of Armagh, Scriptores Latini Hiberniae*, no. 10 (Dublin: The Dublin Institute for Advanced Studies, 1979).
20 Antoinette Clark Wire, *The Corinthian Women Prophets: A Reconstruction Through Paul's Rhetoric* (Minneapolis: Fortress Press, 2003), pp. 181–87.
21 Lucy Toulmin-Smith, *The Itinerary of John Leland* (London: G. Bell, 1907–10), vol. 1, pp. 177, 302.
22 Orme, *The Saints of Cornwall*, p. 154.
23 Nicholas Orme, *English Church Dedications, with a Survey of Cornwall and Devon* (Exeter: University of Exeter Press, 1996), p. 95.
24 Orme, *The Saints of Cornwall*, pp. 59–60.
25 Oliver Padel, *A Popular Dictionary of Cornish Place-Names* (Penzance: Alison Hodge, 1988), p. 96.
26 Ann Preston-Jones and Elisabeth Okasha, *Corpus of Anglo-Saxon Sculpture, vol. XI, Early Cornish Sculpture* (Oxford: The British Academy/Oxford University Press, 2013), p. 166.
27 Elisabeth Okasha, *Corpus of Early Christian Inscribed Stones of South-west Britain* (London: Leicester University Press, 1993), no. 22, pp. 141–45.
28 Preston-Jones and Okasha, *Corpus of Anglo-Saxon Sculpture*, pp. 165–66.
29 'Lanteglos Church, Camelford', Historic Environment Service of Cornwall County Council, 2007.
30 Jack Meyrick, *A Pilgrim's Guide to the Holy Wells of Cornwall* (Falmouth: Meyrick, 1982), no. 26, p. 29.
31 Mary Low, *Celtic Christianity and Nature* (Belfast: Black Star Press, 1996), pp. 98–99.
32 Historic England, 'The Long Cross, an Early Christian Memorial Stone and Medieval Wayside Cross, and a Post-medieval Guide Post 400 m North of Trelights', no. 1008164, 1994.
33 Peter Trudgian, 'Excavation of a Burial Ground at Saint Endellion, Cornwall', *Cornish Archaeology*, 26 (1987), pp. 145–46.
34 *Ibid.*, pp. 146–47.
35 Orme, *Cornwall and the Cross*, p. 17.
36 Orme, *Nicholas Roscarrock*, pp. 11–12, illus. pl. 14. The so-called 'Langdale Rosary' is now in the Victoria and Albert Museum, London, ref. no. M.30-1934.
37 Orme, *Nicholas Roscarrock*, pp. 71–73, 130–31.
38 Charles Thomas, *And Shall These Mute Stones Speak?* (Cardiff: Cardiff University Press, 1994), pp. 263–64, figs 16.4, 17.15, 17.17.
39 *Ibid.*
40 Padel, *A Popular Dictionary of Cornish Place-Names*, p. 124.
41 Historic England, 'Church of St Morwenna and St John the Baptist', no. 20505 25325, 2019.

42 John Harvey, ed., *William Worcestre: Itineraries* (Oxford: Oxford Medieval Texts, 1969), pp. 26–27.
43 Padel, *A Popular Dictionary of Cornish Place-Names*, p. 78.
44 Thomas, *And Shall These Mute Stones Speak?*, pp. 28–30; Elizabeth Rees, *Celtic Saints of Wales* (Stroud: Fonthill, 2015), pp. 110–12.
45 Orme, *The Saints of Cornwall*, pp. 158–59.
46 *Ibid.*
47 Orme, *Nicholas Roscarrock*, p. 125.
48 Historic England, 'St Clether's Chapel and Holy Well', no. 1018492, 2019.
49 *Ibid.*
50 Padel, *A Popular Dictionary of Cornish Place-Names*, p. 77.
51 *Discourses by Dio Chrysostom* (Oration 719), 'On the Philosopher', trans. H. Lamar Crosby (Cambridge, MA: Harvard University Press, 1951), vol. 5, Loeb Classical Library no. 376, p. 173.
52 Paull Franklin Baum, trans., *Anglo-Saxon Riddles of the Exeter Book* (Durham, NC: Duke University Press, 1963), Riddle 44, lines 1–6.
53 *Ibid.*, lines 7–13.
54 *Ibid.*, lines 14–18.
55 *Ibid.*, lines 19–22.
56 BM 2512, Benjamin Bruch, 'Word and Music in Medieval Cornish Drama', *Ars Lyrica*, 16 (2007), p. 9.
57 BM 4565, 2547, Bruch, 'Word and Music in Medieval Cornish Drama', p. 9.
58 Merv Davey, 'Cornish Bagpipes: Roots and Revival', *Chanter* (Spring 2006), pp. 21–31.
59 Jerry Sampson, 'Late Medieval Porch Galleries in North Somerset: *welcomyng Crist with songe into the chirch*', *The Consort*, 75 (Summer 2019), p. 17.
60 Richard Sharpe and John Reuben Davies, eds and trans., '*The Life of Saint David* by Rhygfarch', ch. 3, in *St David of Wales: Cult, Church and Nation*, ed. J. Wyn Evans and Jonathan M. Wooding, Studies in Celtic History 24 (Woodbridge: The Boydell Press, 2007).
61 Jane Cartwright, 'The Cult of St Non: Rape, Sanctity and Motherhood in Welsh and Breton Hagiography', in Wyn Evans and Wooding, *St David of Wales*, pp. 182–83, 203.
62 *Ibid.*, p. 205.
63 Oliver Padel, 'Local Saints and Place-Names in Cornwall', in *Local Saints and Local Churches in the Early Medieval West*, ed. Alan Thacker and Richard Sharpe (Oxford: Oxford University Press, 2002), pp. 315–16.
64 Crispin Paine, 'Portable Altar of Countess Gertrude', MAVCOR, https://mavcor.yale.edu/material-objects/portable-altar-countess-gertrude, accessed 11 July 2019.
65 Heather James, 'The Geography of the Cult of St David: A Study of Dedication Patterns in the Medieval Diocese', in Wyn Evans and Wooding, *St David of Wales*, p. 197.
66 Harvey, *Worcestre: Itineraries*, p. 62.
67 Bernard Tanguy, 'The Cults of Ss. Nonne and Divi in Brittany', in Wyn Evans and Wooding, *St David of Wales*, p. 207.
68 Paris, Bibliothèque nationale de France, fonds celtique 5.
69 Yves Le Berre, ed. and trans., 'Buez Santez Nonn hac ez map Deuy', in *Buez santez Nonn. Vie de sainte Nonne. Mystère breton*, ed. Yves Le Berre, Bernard Tanguy and Yves-Pascal Castel (Brest: Minihi-Levenez, 1999), pp. 113–94.

70 Richard Carew, *The Svrvey of Cornwall* (London: John Jaggard, 1602), ff. 122v–23r, facsimile edn, John Chynoweth, Nicholas Orme and Alexandra Walsham, New Series, 47 (Exeter: Devon and Cornwall Record Society, 2004).
71 Thomas Charles-Edwards, *Wales and the Britons 350–1064* (Oxford: Oxford University Press, 2013), pp. 168–69.
72 Thomas, *And Shall These Mute Stones Speak?*, pp. 263–64, p. 274, n. 21.
73 Benedicta Ward, *The Sayings of the Desert Fathers* (London: Mowbrays, 1981), p. 124.
74 John Cassian, *Confererences*, trans. Colm Luibheid (New York: Paulist Press, 1985), Conference 15. 3, pp. 176–77.
75 Orme, *The Saints of Cornwall*, p. 133.
76 Thomas, *And Shall These Mute Stones Speak?*, pp. 262–63.
77 *Ibid.*
78 Brian L. Harris, *Harris's Guide to Churches and Cathedrals* (London: Ebury Press, 2006), pp. 428–29.
79 Joseph Fowler, ed., *A description or briefe declaration of all the ancient monuments, rites, and customes belonginge or beinge within the monastical Church of Durham before the suppression*, Surtees Society, no. 107 (London: J.B. Nichols, 1842), ch. 13, p. 19.
80 *Ibid.*
81 For a recent translation, see Michael Swanton, *The Anglo-Saxon Chronicle, a Revised Translation* (London: Phoenix Press, 2003), entry: AD 891.
82 In ch. 4 of the Voyage of St Brendan (*Navigatio Sancti Brendani Abbatis*), perhaps dating from the ninth century, when Brendan was about to set sail, three monks came down to the beach and begged to be taken aboard. Brendan agreed, but foretold that two of them would meet a hideous fate, while the third would not return home. They had not been asked to set out by their abbot, and so were weak before the siren voices of temptation.
83 Michel Priziac, *Bretagne des Saints et des Croyances* (Grâces-Guincamp: Ki-Dour Éditions, 2002), pp. 185–86.
84 Orme, *The Saints of Cornwall*, p. 73.
85 Preston-Jones and Okasha, *Corpus of Anglo-Saxon Sculpture*, p. 124.
86 Raymond Wood, *A Guide to the Church of the Ancient Parish of St Tudy, North Cornwall* (1994), revised by St Tudy History Group in 2017, p. 3. https/s3.spanglefish.com/s/37629/documents/st-tudy-church-guide.pdf, accessed 11 July 2019.
87 O.J. Prestidge, *Jory's Meadow, St Tudy, Bodmin, Cornwall*, Stratascan Geophysical & Specialist Survey Services, 2014, https://archaeologydataservice.ac.uk/library/browse/issue.xhtml?recordId=, accessed 11 July 2019.
88 Turner, *Making a Christian Landscape*, p. 21.
89 Payton, *Cornwall: A History*, p. 45.
90 The Leofric Missal, Bodley 579; Exon Domesday, pp. 104–06; Wood, *A Guide to St Tudy*, p. 5.
91 Wood, *A Guide to St Tudy*, pp. 16–17.
92 Howard Williams, 'Hogbacks: The Materiality of Solid Spaces', in *Early Medieval Stone Monuments: Materiality, Biography, Landscape*, ed. Howard Williams, Joanne Kirton and Meggen Gondek (Woodbridge: Boydell and Brewer, 2015), pp. 241–68.
93 *Ibid.*
94 Priziac, *Bretagne des Saints et des Croyances*, pp. 73–76, 376–78.
95 Jacques Thomazy and Jacques Pensec, *St Tudy's Church* (Loctudy: Office de tourisme Loctudy, 2011), pp. 1–4.
96 Charles-Edwards, *Wales and the Britons*, pp. 23–24.
97 Historic England, 'Dupath Holy Well, 45 m NNE of Dupath Farm', no. 1013663, 1995.

98 Joanna Mattingly, 'A Note on Cornish-Breton Links', *Institute of Cornish Studies Associates' Newsletter*, 2nd series, no. 4 (May 1995).
99 Payton, *Cornwall: A History*, p. 100.
100 Padel, *A Popular Dictionary of Cornish Place-Names*, p. 65.
101 Orme, *The Saints of Cornwall*, p. 190.
102 Harvey, *Worcestre: Itineraries*, pp. 96–98.
103 Thomas, *And Shall These Mute Stones Speak?*, p. 265.
104 *Ibid.*
105 Meyrick, *A Pilgrim's Guide to the Holy Wells of Cornwall*, no. 28, pp. 30–31.
106 Orme, *The Saints of Cornwall*, p. 234.
107 Michael J. Swanton, *St Sidwell: An Exeter Legend* (Exeter: Devon Books, 1986), pp. 14–15, 18.
108 Christina Hole, *A Dictionary of British Folk Customs* (London: Paladin, 1978), pp. 135–36.
109 William Hone, *Everyday Book, Or, A Guide to the Year: Describing the Popular Amusements, Sports, Ceremonies, Manners, Customs, and Events, Incident to the Three Hundred and Sixty-five Days, in Past and Present Times*, vol. 2 (London: T. Ward, 1826), quoted in Hole, *A Dictionary of British Folk Customs*, p. 136.
110 Women's Institute Home Skills Publication, *Corn Dollies from the Start* (London: Bell and Sons, 1979), p. 12.
111 There are various video clips of 'Crying the neck' on YouTube, including 'Crying the Neck, Madron, 1991, final mp4', and 'A traditional slice of St Ives: crying the neck, 2016'.
112 Lynette Olson, *Early Monasteries in Cornwall* (Woodbridge: Boydell, 1989), p. 56.
113 Rosamond Faith, *The English Peasantry and the Growth of Lordship* (London: Leicester University Press, 1997), pp. 70–74.
114 Caroline Thorn and Frank Thorn, eds and trans., *Domesday Book: A Survey of the Counties of England, vol. 10: Cornwall; History from the Sources* (Chichester: Phillimore, 1979), 4. 28.
115 Olson, *Early Monasteries in Cornwall*, p. 23.
116 Asser, ch. 74, p. 55, trans. p. 89, in Simon Keynes and Michael Lapidge, *Alfred the Great: Asser's Life of King Alfred and Other Contemporary Sources* (Harmondsworth: Penguin, 1983), pp. 173–78, 89.
117 Orme, *Nicholas Roscarrock*, pp. 76–77.
118 William Michell, *Parochial History of St Neots, in Cornwall* (Bodmin: Liddell, 1833).
119 Preston-Jones and Okasha, *Corpus of Anglo-Saxon Sculpture*, p. 134.
120 Orme, *Cornwall and the Cross*, p. 3.
121 Padel, *A Popular Dictionary of Cornish Place-Names*, p. 110.
122 Preston-Jones and Okasha, *Corpus of Anglo-Saxon Sculpture*, p. 136.
123 Preston-Jones and Okasha, *Corpus of Anglo-Saxon Sculpture*, p. 135.
124 Orme, *The Saints of Cornwall*, p. 88.
125 Preston-Jones and Okasha, *Corpus of Anglo-Saxon Sculpture*, p. 133.
126 Historic England, 'St Cleer's Well and Cross', no. 1018205, 1998.
127 This in turn created a difficulty, which surfaced later in the tenth century, concerning whether the properties in Cornwall that had been given to Crediton, to help with its role of pastoral care in Cornwall, should now be passed to the new see at St Germans, or whether they had been given to Crediton in its own right.
128 Orme, *Cornwall and the Cross*, pp. 9–11.
129 Bodleian Library, MS Bodley 572, f. 1. See Orme, *The Saints of Cornwall*, pp. 127–28.
130 Padel, *A Popular Dictionary of Cornish Place-Names*, p. 79.

131 Meyrick, *A Pilgrim's Guide to the Holy Wells of Cornwall*, no. 28, pp. 38–39.
132 Oliver J. Padel, 'Glastonbury's Cornish Connections', in *The Archaeology and History of Glastonbury Abbey*, ed. Lesley Abrams and James P. Carley (Woodbridge: The Boydell Press, 1991), pp. 246–48.
133 *Ibid.*, p. 245.
134 Wessex Archaeology, 'Looe, Cornwall: Archaeological Evaluation, and Assessment of Results', ref. no. 68734, March 2009, pp. 1–6, 22.
135 www.channel4.com/history/microsites/T/timeteam/2009/looe/index.html, accessed 11 July 2019.
136 Wessex Archaeology, 'Looe, Cornwall', pp. iii, 1–6.
137 www.channel4.com/timeteam/2009, accessed 6 December 2019.
138 *Ibid.*
139 Wessex Archaeology, 'Looe, Cornwall', p. 23; www.channel4.com/timeteam/2009, accessed 11 July 2019.
140 Wessex Archaeology, 'Looe, Cornwall', pp. 5–6, 9–11.
141 *Ibid.*, p. 10.
142 *Helya tunc eiusdem priore, at eius socio monacho Iohanne. Ibid.*, pp. 14, 28.
143 Cornwall Historic Churches Trust, 'Pelynt, St Nun', www.chct.info/histories/pelynt-st-nun, accessed 11 July 2019.
144 Priziac, *Bretagne des Saints et des Croyances*, p. 554; Williams, '"Saint" in Cornish', pp. 219–41.
145 Grenville Astill and Wendy Davies, *A Breton Landscape* (London: UCL Press, 1997), pp. 55, 92–93, 98.
146 Information from a plan by Jeremy Milne for Cornwall Archaeological Unit, 1979.
147 Orme, *The Saints of Cornwall*, p. 207.
148 BM Cotton MS Vespasian A xiv, composed in Cemis, Pembrokeshire.
149 David Petts, *The Early Medieval Church in Wales* (Stroud: The History Press, 2009), pp. 90, 72.
150 Padel, *A Popular Dictionary of Cornish Place-Names*, p. 80.
151 Meyrick, *A Pilgrim's Guide to the Holy Wells of Cornwall*, no. 39, pp. 39–40.
152 Thomas, *And Shall These Mute Stones Speak?*, pp. 283–84.
153 Tírechán, *Collectanea*, ch. 11.
154 Orme, *The Saints of Cornwall*, pp. 162–63.
155 Richard Carew, *The Survey of Cornwall* (London: Iohn Iaggard, 1602), ff. 129v–30r.
156 John Blight, *Ancient Crosses, and other antiquities in the east of Cornwall* (London: Simpkin, 1858), p. 90.
157 Meyrick, *A Pilgrim's Guide to the Holy Wells of Cornwall*, no. 79, pp. 68–69.
158 Elizabeth Rees, *Christian Symbols, Ancient Roots*, 2nd edn (London: Jessica Kingsley, 1992), pp. 65–71.
159 Pseudo-Hippolytus, *De Pascha Homilia 6*, in Jacques-Paul Migne, *Patrologia Graeca 59*, Chrysostom, *Spuria* (Paris: Imprimerie Catholique, 1857–66). The sermon has also been attributed to Gregory of Nyssa and John Chrysostom. Trans. in James Boniface Ramsey, *Beginning to Read the Fathers*, 2nd edn (New York: Paulist Press, 2012), p. 81.

CHAPTER 6

Pre-Norman sites in central Cornwall

This chapter will focus on early Christian sites from Bodmin in east Cornwall to Truro and the Fal estuary in the west. As in the previous chapter, sites with evidence of a pre-Norman Christian presence will be examined, beginning in north Cornwall and continuing southwards. There are disadvantages to this approach, but the paucity of early Christian material means that only a few pieces of a very large jigsaw survive.

Yet Cornwall is a region rich in early Christian sites, many of which are within 5 or 10 miles of each another, in contrast to Welsh or Irish sites, which can be widely separated by mountains, forest or bog. There is some value, therefore, in considering Cornish sites as an interrelated network. My intention is to focus on the rather disparate 'pieces' of the jigsaw – at least, the more significant ones. A geographical approach to this task can enable us to glimpse some of the patterns behind the surviving evidence.

The first group of sites are close to each other, and they are linked, somewhat artificially, by the authors of two Lives of St Petroc: it was important that the saint whose cult they promoted should be seen to interact with other local holy men, regardless of factual detail. The major study of Petroc and his complex hagiography has been written by Karen Jankulak.[1] She focuses on Cornwall and Brittany, who shared his cult, and sheds light on the politically motivated twelfth-century account of the furtive translation of Petroc's relics to Brittany, which offers significant evidence of the relationship between the two regions.

We shall begin this chapter by examining Padstow, where Petroc's first Cornish monastery was said to be located, beside the River Camel on the north coast; this was a sheltered port for travellers from Wales. In chapter four, we saw how Samson and his companions set sail from Wales, and 'with a favourable wind, after a happy passage' they reached the Camel estuary near Padstow. From here, they continued up the River Camel towards 'a monastery which is called Docco', 6 miles to the east.

Padstow's early cemetery

The first indication of a Christian presence in Padstow is an early cemetery just beyond the northern boundary of the parish church of St Petroc. Excavation in 2001 revealed seventeen graves aligned broadly east–west, arranged in two rows, all of them lined and capped with slate; both rows of graves were fan-shaped. The western row probably marked the western limit of the cemetery;

it appears to continue the western boundary of the churchyard, which at that time extended further to the north. Three graves were excavated and bones from them were radiocarbon dated to the eighth or ninth century.[2]

They were long-cist graves, some with parallel sides and others tapering. There are a number of cemeteries with long-cist burials on the north Cornish coast between Perranporth and Tintagel, and a small cluster around the River Hayle, but a stronger preference for long-cist burials is found beyond the Cornish border, in northern and western Britain, with a concentration in south Wales, across the Bristol Channel from Cornwall.[3] This is one possible indication that early Christianity in Cornwall derived from that of Wales.[4]

The most interesting pottery fragment found at the site in Padstow was a sherd from a wheel-thrown cooking pot rarely found in Britain (Hamwic fabric 127), of sandy white clay with a sooty exterior, dating from between the eighth and the eleventh centuries. These pots are believed to have been made in the lower Seine valley; they indicate Anglo-Saxon trade with Normandy, especially with the area around Rouen. Eleven similar sherds were discovered at the port of Exeter.[5]

St Petroc's cult supplants that of Wethinoc

Domesday Book names Padstow as *Lanwenehoc* (or '*lann* of *Wethinoc*') after a local bishop, Wethinoc, whose cult was superseded by the more famous figure of St Petroc. A First Life of Petroc was probably written in the later eleventh century, perhaps in Cornwall; it is contained in one manuscript only, dating from the sixteenth century, at the abbey of St Méen-le-Grand, with fragments in other Breton manuscripts. A fuller Second Life is preserved only in the fourteenth-century Gotha manuscript, which was probably written in England, though it is unclear where.[6]

The author of the First Life was familiar with various locations in Cornwall that were named after Petroc, which he weaves into his narrative. He relates that Petroc, whose name means 'little Peter', landed at Padstow, where he found a hermit named Samson living by the shore; this is a reference to a late medieval chapel near the mouth of the estuary, dedicated to St Samson. The author relates that, at Padstow, a bishop named Wethinoc had a *cella* (apparently a monastery), which he and his followers left for Petroc's use, asking that the place be named *Landewethinoch* in his memory.[7]

St Petroc's monastery is first mentioned in the mid-tenth century, the date of the earliest manumission in the Bodmin Gospels, which will be described later. There is no clear indication of the extent of the monastery's lands until a hundred years later, when its possessions in 1066 are named in Domesday Book. By this time, the monastery was probably quite large, with at least one church, a cemetery, communal buildings, accommodation for clerics and a sizeable lay population. The skeletons in the cemetery include women and children, who may have either belonged to the monastic community, or lived in the town.[8]

The Anglo-Saxon Chronicle records that in 981 *Sancte Petroces Stow* (probably Padstow) was ravaged by Vikings.[9] By the eleventh century the monastery had moved to Bodmin, which was in a more central location within the community's lands, but they continued to own the town and monastery of Padstow until the Reformation. Petroc was believed to be buried at Padstow, but in the late tenth century Petroc's shrine, with his staff and his bell, appear to have been taken inland to Bodmin, perhaps because of Viking raids around the coast.

The author of the Second Life of Petroc states that he surrounded his lands at Padstow with an outer enclosure of 'very long ditches in the manner of a rampart, the ruins of which even now are apparent'.[10] The author seeks validation for the monastery by claiming that the saint himself had dug the ditches to demarcate the monastery's spiritual and legal boundaries. Bodmin became the chief centre of the monastery in the later medieval period: its community subsequently developed their own church as a centre for pilgrimage to Petroc's shrine.

St Petroc's church, Padstow

The earliest portions of St Petroc's church at Padstow date from the eleventh century; this suggests that the church existed in late Saxon times. There are three elaborate crosses and a coped tombstone in the area surrounding the church, dating from the late tenth to the eleventh centuries. This indicates an innovative sculpture workshop at the monastery, active both before and after the Viking raid. The workshop continued after the establishment of Petroc's second monastery at Bodmin; it was likely to have been influential, and was perhaps the source of other crosses found in mid- and east Cornwall. The cross in the grounds of nearby Prideaux Place displays a uniquely Cornish design of cross-head with four trefoil shapes, like that at St Breward, illustrated in the previous chapter (illus. 91).[11]

Together with Probus, St Buryan and St Keverne, this was one of four chartered sanctuary churches in Cornwall, perhaps from the reign of King Æthelstan until the Reformation.[12] At every church, criminals were protected from the law until they could hopefully reach the nearest port in order to leave the country; they were then stateless, however, and might be vulnerable, unable to find a home or work. In a chartered sanctuary church, people could continue to live and ply a trade within its precincts. It is interesting that Bodmin was not one of the four churches with chartered rights of sanctuary (beyond the normal rights which any church had), whereas Padstow was. These rights were granted before the monks' move from Padstow to Bodmin, which perhaps took place in the eleventh century.

The lower section of Padstow's church tower dates from the eleventh century; its wall is 2 m thick. During repairs to the wall at the base of an arch dated by Pevsner to the thirteenth century,[13] crumbling sandstone boulders from the beach were found. This could indicate that the church of 1100 was built of this soft material and therefore failed to survive; the present church dates from the fifteenth century.[14]

ILLUS. 103. Relief of St Antony of Egypt, Padstow church.

Set into the wall to the right of the altar, above a holy water stoup or piscina, is a relief of St Antony of Egypt, which may have been preserved from the earlier church, where it perhaps stood in a niche above the church porch for worshippers to see as they entered the building. Antony is bearded, and wears a hooded cloak; he holds a staff with a T- or *tau*-shaped handle that was traditional in Egyptian monastic life, and carries a hand bell and a book of the gospels, for he preaches the word of God (illus. 103).

At his feet is a pig; the emblems of a bell and a pig derive from the time of the Hospitallers of St Antony, founded in about 1100. They travelled on horseback throughout western Europe, caring for the sick in medieval towns. They rang small bells so that people might give them alms; the bells were also hung round the necks of animals, to protect them from disease. The Hospitallers raised pigs in order to support their work, and the Order's pigs were allowed to roam freely in towns.[15]

The 'wilderness' of Little Petherick

Little Petherick is 2 miles south of Padstow. The author of Petroc's First Life found a place for it in his story, and described the saint appointing a deputy to take charge of his monastery in Padstow, after which Petroc went with twelve companions to live in a wilderness nearby. In the Second Life, further details are added: the wilderness was a tidal creek in the estuary of the River Camel (colour plate 12), named *Nan Funttun*, meaning 'valley with a well' (*nans* + *fenten*).[16] The church was called *ecclesia de Nansfunten* in 1264 and *ecclesia de Nasfonteyn* in 1274.

The village is located at the limit of navigation on Petherick Creek and at its lowest crossing point.[17] Here, we are told, Petroc constructed a chapel and a mill; he lived on 'bread and water, with porridge on Sundays'. The church is built into the hillside; its dedication is first attested in 1327, when it is named as the 'Parish of *St Petrocus Minor*', in contrast to Petroc's major foundation at Padstow.[18] Four pinnacles that decorate the tower of Little Petherick church and a column in the north aisle were brought from a ruined chapel dedicated to the Welsh saint Cadoc, in nearby Harlyn Bay.[19]

St Cadoc's chapel and holy well

The author of Petroc's Second Life connects him into Welsh traditions, and claims that he was the uncle of St Cadoc; in this way he weaves his local knowledge of a nearby chapel dedicated to Cadoc into his story. The chapel adjoined a well and St Cadoc's Farm (OS 884749) in the parish of Padstow, approximately 1 mile south-east of Harlyn Bay (illus. 104). The land surrounding the chapel rises sharply northwards to St Cadoc's Farm, but more gently southwards to the village of St Merryn and east to the town of Padstow. This is the only Cornish example of a farm, chapel and holy well dedicated to St Cadoc; the complex was first recorded in 1302 as *villata Sancti Cadoci*.[20]

The late eleventh-century Life of Cadoc by Llifris of Llancarfan contains much unlikely detail, including an account of Cadoc's journey to St Michael's Mount on the south Cornish coast. On the way home he caused a spring to

ILLUS. 104. St Cadoc's Farm, Padstow.

ILLUS. 105. Pinnacles from St Cadoc's chapel, on Little Petherick's church tower.

arise, where Cornish people were cured of intestinal diseases such as worms. A small stone church (*ecclesiola*) was built beside the well; the story appears to refer to Cadoc's well in Padstow parish. Four hundred years later, when William Worcestre visited Cornwall in 1478, he heard that 'Cradok' was honoured at a chapel near Padstow, and that (intestinal) worms could be destroyed by drinking water from the well.[21]

This is an early site: to the north of the chapel, in the field immediately to the west of the farm, there is an Iron Age enclosure, with a cemetery of similar date at nearby Harlyn Bay. St Cadoc's chapel has not been excavated, but it is likely to have been established by the eleventh century. There is an adjacent cemetery, of unknown date; in 1954, the farmer's wife described a burial ground to the north-east of the chapel site where a grave had been found fifty years previously.[22] In about 1930 Charles Henderson drew a small sketch of the site, and indicated the cemetery's location with a note, 'bones found', to the north of the chapel.[23] Gilbert Doble drew a more detailed plan of the complex in 1937.[24]

The chapel was rebuilt in the fifteenth century: in 1445 Bishop Lacy of Exeter granted an indulgence (or remission from sins) to those who donated money for this purpose.[25] In 1537, at the Reformation, it became the property of the Crown and in 1545 the chapel and its surrounding land were granted to Nicholas Prideaux of Padstow, whose family still own the land.[26] The structure is currently a ruin; there are likely to be substantial remains beneath ground level. There is a fast-flowing stream to the south, spanned by a rare type of medieval packhorse bridge, constructed from a single arch of killas slate blocks.[27]

A post-hook fixed to a wall suggests that the chapel was later adapted for farm use as a penning area. Its stones were robbed; some ornamental pieces are now displayed on the farmhouse garden wall. When the site was cleared and surveyed in 2013, a stone arch was found, and granite window tracery, both from the fifteenth-century chapel; a section of ridge tile from the medieval roof was also found.[28] The chapel was elaborately embellished: some of its stonework can be seen in the entrance gateway of Prideaux Place, and, as we have seen, four pinnacles were removed to the nearby church tower of Little Petherick (illus. 105).

St Constantine's well chapel, Harlyn Bay

The author of the eleventh-century first Life of Petroc describes a wealthy man named Constantine hunting deer at Little Petherick. Petroc interrupted the hunt, saved the stag and converted Constantine. The author was again weaving local traditions into his story, for on the coast 3 miles north-west of Little Petherick lay St Constantine's well chapel (OS 865749). The small building of corbelled slate is 3 m long and 1.5 m wide; there are two stone benches along its inner walls and a channel for water in the floor between them (illus. 106), with a niche above the well at the south end. It is an early building, restored in 1390.[29]

In the early eighteenth century the antiquarian William Hals described the chapel as 'stronge built of stone and arched over; on the inner part wherof are places or seates for people to sitt and wash themselves in the streams therof'.[30] Over time, the well-house became buried by sand dunes; it was rediscovered and excavated in 1911. The tiny chapel can be seen, protected beneath a shelter, on the golf course in Harlyn Bay.

On rising ground 50 m away are the ruins of Constantine church, with its tower, chancel, nave and south aisle. It was rebuilt in the fifteenth century, but suppressed in about 1540, after which the church became buried by sand. At

ILLUS. 106.
St Constantine's well chapel, Harlyn Bay.

one time it was surrounded by a graveyard and houses. Its fine Norman font, of black catacleuse stone, was taken 2 miles inland to its mother church of St Merryn. There is also a cist-grave cemetery in St Merryn parish.

It was believed that St Constantine was a converted Cornish chieftain: the first named king of Dumnonia, Constantinus, was addressed as a Christian by the British monk Gildas writing in about 540. Gildas condemned his adultery and murder of two princes, but promised him God's forgiveness if he repented. Later tradition may have thought that the king did so, since the Welsh *Annales Cambriae* refer to 'the conversion of Constantine to the Lord'. There is another parish named Constantine 30 miles to the south, at the head of a creek in the Helford River estuary, 5 miles south-west of Falmouth. Domesday Book suggests that this south Cornish parish supported a community of clergy, but later it was simply a parish church.[31]

Early Christians at St Breock

Returning to the north Cornish coast, St Breock is 5 miles south-east of Padstow. Set in a deep, narrow valley near the Camel estuary, Brioc's church is built beside a fast-flowing stream. This is the only Cornish church dedicated to Brioc; it is first described as *Ecclesiam Sancti Brioci* in 1259. According to his eleventh-century Breton Life, he was a Welsh saint who founded a monastery at Saint-Brieuc in north-east Brittany. The Cornish parish is called *Lansant* (1259) and *Nansant* (1291); the first name is a variant of the second, which means 'holy valley', unless 'Sant' (or 'Sent' in other variants) is a personal name.[32]

A sixth-century inscribed stone now serves a gatepost on Nanscow farm (OS 968708), 1.5 miles west of Wadebridge, in the parish of St Breock. It reads

VLCAGNI F[ILI] on one side and SEVERI on the other, and means 'Olcán, son of Severus'. The father has a Roman name, and the son an Irish one. This suggests that elements of Roman culture spread from the native British population to the Irish Christians who settled among them in the sixth century.[33]

Mawgan Porth, a Saxon settlement

Six miles south of Padstow is the ancient harbour of Mawgan Porth; its name means 'Port, or harbour of St Maugan'. Excavations here in 1950–54 revealed at least three houses set around small courtyards; a coin of Æthelred II, minted at Lydford in Devon between 990 and 995, helped to date the site.[34] Mawgan Porth was probably inhabited between about AD 850 and 1050, when it was encroached upon by blown sand from the beach below. This late Saxon complex is the most complete tenth-century Cornish settlement to have been excavated. Its occupants were farmers and fishermen with no metal implements, who kept sheep and goats, horses and oxen, dogs, cats and poultry.[35]

More than 2,000 fragments of *bar-lug* pottery were discovered at the site: these were coarse household vessels with flat grass-marked bases and straight sides. Many are thought to have been cauldrons, whose lugs, or projecting handles, prevented their suspension rope from burning. *Bar-lug* vessels were produced in Cornwall from the seventh to the eleventh centuries. Other forms of bowls and platters were also found here.[36] The site has been preserved on the sloping green opposite the beach: the outline of some of the homes can be seen.

Above the village was a cemetery with about fifty long-cist graves lined with slate; its western portion contained many child burials. By the tenth century, English Christians were starting to be buried by their priest in the ground surrounding their local church, but in Wales and Cornwall the dead person's family and neighbours continued to carry out this task. The cemetery at Mawgan Porth was 30 m away from the small settlement. Its excavators postulated a lost chapel, but this could have been a lay cemetery without a chapel. In Ireland, burials not associated with churches continued into the late medieval period.[37]

St Maugan is commemorated in Wales and Brittany, and has an early dedication in south Cornwall at St Mawgan in Meneage, since in a tenth-century list of saints he is named next to St Keverne, who is honoured nearby.[38] Maugan also gave his name to Mawgan Porth and its inland settlement of St Mawgan in Pydar, 2 miles up the river, where the land is more fertile. Its church was in existence by about 1075; it belonged to the bishops of Exeter, and the name *Sancte Maucanne* occurs in an eleventh-century litany of saints used at Exeter cathedral.[39] Immediately inside the lych gate is St Mawgan's holy well, now dry (illus. 107).

The 'Runhol' cross at Lanherne

Over St Mawgan's churchyard wall, outside Lanherne convent, is a fine cross dating from the mid-tenth to the eleventh century, inscribed with the word

ILLUS. 107. St Mawgan in Pydar's church and well.

RUnHOL; the same word is found on a similar cross at Sancreed. The cross was brought from elsewhere: in the late eighteenth or early nineteenth century it was removed for safekeeping from the site of a chapel of St Gwinear on land owned by the Arundell family at Roseworthy, a hamlet west of Camborne, in Gwinear parish. The cross therefore originates from the neighbouring parish to that containing the Sancreed cross, which bears the same inscription. The Arundells brought the Gwinear cross to their property at Lanherne, 26 miles to the north-east.[40]

Runhol is an unusual word, which could mean 'paternal', or 'inherited' in Old Cornish: there are parallels in an Old Welsh gloss (*roenhol*) and an Old Breton gloss (*roinol*) of the same period. Or the word might be a noun meaning 'patrimony' or 'inheritance'. Some inscriptions on Welsh monuments relate to

ILLUS. 108. The 'Runhol' cross, Lanherne.

the donation or ownership of the land on which it stands.[41] For example, in a field on the parish boundary between Dyserth and Whitford in Denbighshire, north Wales, a highly decorated cross of similar date was originally named *Maen Machwyfan*, or 'stone of Cwyfan's field'. It stands in its original position, 2.5 miles east of the settlement of St Cwyfan in Dyserth, and appears to demarcate the land belonging to the local saint.[42]

The 'Runhol' cross is carved out of soft Pentewan stone from south Cornwall. It has a four-holed head; a stone ring links the four cross limbs. Its decoration is comprehensive and elaborate; the carving is neatly executed, although several irregularities or errors are visible in the design. On the front is a figure of Christ crucified, with his arms extended and his fingers visible (illus. 108). Protrusions may represent his rib cage, or the folds of his tunic – its lower hem is visible. His feet turn outwards and slant down, so they appear to stand on the upper curve of the pattern on the shaft beneath. Underneath this pattern is another panel containing a text arranged in four horizontal lines, which could represent two personal names. On the reverse of the cross-head are five round bosses in high relief, to symbolise the five wounds of Christ. They are arranged symmetrically, one in the centre and one on each arm. The word RUnHOL appears towards the bottom of the shaft, beneath an engraved line.[43]

A memorial stone at Rialton Priory

A large granite pillar dating from the first third of the sixth century was found in a farm building at Rialton Priory (OS 849629), a dependency of Bodmin, 2 miles east of Newquay. The slab of distinctive close-grained granite was probably brought from Hensbarrow Downs, 6 to 10 miles away: these are granite hills, now the focus of the china clay industry. The upper portion of the slab is missing, but the inscription reads BONEMIMORI [F]

ILLUS. 109. Rialton Priory well.

ILLI TRIBVNI, 'In loving memory of the son of Tribunus': this could either be a personal name, or mean 'tribune'.[44] In the late Roman army, a *tribunus* was a senior officer who commanded a cavalry group; the title survived in the East Roman army until the early seventh century.

Rialton Priory was not, in fact a priory, but one of the earliest duchy manors. The penultimate prior of Bodmin, Thomas Vivian, built the present priory house between 1508 and 1533, including its well-house (illus. 109).[45] In 1895 it was observed that 'the water is excellent and never failing', although the well 'has no legend or tradition connected with it'.[46]

A community at Crantock

The village of Crantock is a mile south-west of Newquay, on the opposite side of the Gannel estuary. Crantock is named after Carantoc, who is the subject of two medieval Welsh Lives that survive in a manuscript in the British Library, dating from around AD 1200. Carantoc is said to have lived in a cave above the church named after him at Llangrannog on Welsh coast. The first Life relates how he came from Ceredigion and founded one or more churches in Britain. Crantock is the most significant foundation named after him: in Domesday Book, Crantock is referred to as *Langorroc*, using a hypocoristic, or pet form of Carantoc's name.[47]

Crantock church is surrounded by extensive burial grounds, probably dating from the Iron Age into late medieval times; a second chapel once stood in the small field to the north. The burials extend far beyond the churchyard, which suggests that the wider community was also granted burial here. Tintagel, St Piran's and Phillack may also have had pre-Christian burial grounds.[48] Domesday Book states 'The canons of St Carantoc hold *Langorroc* as they held it in the time of King Edward'. By this time, Crantock was a minster staffed by canons, subject to a fixed (or 'canonical') way of life; they were priests who had not taken monastic vows, who could own property and mix freely with other people.[49]

In the thirteenth century there were ten canons at Crantock. This was an unusually large number: of the other pre-Conquest minsters that survived into this period, Probus had six canons and St Buryan only four.[50] In 1283 Crantock became the mother church of the area, including St Columb Minor and Newquay, which at that time was the hamlet of Towan, although since Crantock church was poor and remote it had little status or influence beyond its immediate neighbourhood. Canons were not required to live in the community as long as they arranged for others to do their duties, but Crantock's canons continued with some form of communal life, with a provost (later a dean), canons, vicars, clerks and choristers.[51]

We are given a glimpse of Crantock's oversight of churches in the surrounding settlements by Nicholas Roscarrock (*c.* 1549–*c.* 1634), who relates that each year seven churches in the parish used to bring their relics in procession to Crantock. He writes that Crantock church

> had of olde seaven churchyards belonging vnto it, And seaven Parishes did vse to com yerelie vnto it from there seaven severall churches, bringing with them Relickes & placing them on seaven severall stoanes like Aulters designed for it, as an olde Preist, an eye witness hath informed mee.[52]

This recalls Breton Pardons of today, with men carrying banners, statues and reliquaries, women in colourful costumes, priests in their most elaborate vestments, musicians, hymn-singing and, afterwards, partying into the night. Carantoc's holy well (illus. 110) is close to the centre of the village, where four roads meet around a medieval animal pound. The well-house dates from the seventeenth century; its beehive-shaped top, a more recent

ILLUS. 110. St Carantoc's well, Crantock.

addition, has now been removed. A stream flows from the well into the River Gannel.

Cubert's two holy wells

Cubert is a village 3 miles south-west of Newquay and 2 miles from the sea. An inscribed gravestone set into the outer wall of the tower indicates an early Christian presence. It was probably a pillar stone, and dates from the second half of the sixth century. The inscription reads CONETOCI FILI TEGERNOMALI, or '[the stone of] Conetocus, son of Tegernomalus'. The names are British; the name-element *Tegern* denotes a prince.[53] The first name

ILLUS. III. St Cubert's chapel and well-house, above Holywell Bay.

may contain the British word *cuno*, or 'hound', and suggests a fast-running warrior; the stone probably commemorates local chieftains.[54]

The parish may be named after a native saint or after the northern saint, Cuthbert, who was widely venerated in medieval England. It is likely to have had an earlier dedication, however, since the adjacent farm is named Lanlovey; the church is described as *Lanowyn alias Lanwoven alias Egloscubert* in 1622.[55] There are two holy wells in the parish, the first alongside a stream that flows into Holywell Bay, in Trevornick Holiday Park (OS 773588). The well is enclosed in a fourteenth-century chapel, with two arched doorways containing a forecourt with benches on which pilgrims could sit (illus. 111).

The second well is a series of freshwater pools in a cave in Holywell Bay (OS 766600). There are three caves, and in the furthest of these, at the northern end of the bay, a series of steps against the cave wall leads up to four or five shallow pools, formed by condensation dripping from the cave roof (colour plate 13). The rock is pink and white from calcareous deposits; in wet weather the rocks are too slippery to climb, but in dryer conditions one can clamber past the pools into a chamber in the cave roof. In earlier times, pilgrims flocked to the well: this suggests that sea level has altered, since the cave is now above water level only for an hour either side of low tide.

The well water was good for bowel conditions: William Hals (1655–1737), who compiled a History of Cornwall, noted that the well

> stands in a dark caverne of the sea cliff rock, beneath full sea mark on spring tide … The virtues of this water are, if taken inward, a notable vomit [an emetic to expel a harmful substance], as once I had experience of.[56]

The water also cured children's diseases: mothers brought sick or deformed children here, dipping them into the pools, and taking them up into the inner chamber. Cripples also left their crutches here; in 1895 Mabel Quiller-Couch noted the 'incredible numbers' of people who used to visit the sea cave.[57]

Perranzabuloe, a monastery in the dunes

One of Cornwall's chief medieval shrines was that of Piran at Perranzabuloe, from the Latin *in sabulo*, or 'in the sand'. The site is in the dunes, a mile from the sea (OS 772564), 7 miles north-west of Truro. Piran's Life was probably written in the south-west in the twelfth or thirteenth century, and survives in the fourteenth-century Gotha manuscript, but the account is borrowed from a Life of the Irish bishop, Ciarán of Saighir. Piran may have been an early Cornish cleric or nobleman who founded, or lived or died at Perranzabuloe.[58]

Piran was a popular Cornish saint, after whom two settlements on the south coast are named: Perranarworthal, meaning 'St Piran beside the marsh', in the Fal estuary, and Perranuthnoe, 4 miles east of Penzance. The earliest reference to Piran is a place-name marking the boundary of the saint's territory, *Carn Peran*, meaning 'rock, or tor, of Piran', recorded in a secular charter in 960: the saint was considered to own the land.[59] A cross is also mentioned as a boundary marker:

ILLUS. 112. Three-holed cross, Perranzabuloe.

it is referred to as *Cristelmæl*, which means '[?sign of] Christ's cross'. It was possibly a wooden cross that may eventually have been replaced by the present stone cross.[60]

All that can be seen at Perranzabuloe today is a three-holed granite cross (illus. 112); its decoration suggests a late eleventh- or early twelfth-century date. The cross may delineate the boundary wall of an early monastery, named *Lanpiran* in Domesday Book. Beside the cross, the outline of a roughly circular churchyard is still partly visible in the sand dunes; the wall enclosed both the cross and the church. The decoration on the cross is sophisticated but eroded, because of its exposed location on the dunes. It consists of panels created by lines of incised dots, a unique Cornish design. The holes in its head are so placed that the stonework between them creates a diagonal St Andrew's cross, another unusual Cornish feature. It could have been erected by St Piran's monastery, or possibly by that of St Petroc at Bodmin, who owned the adjacent land in 1086.[61]

Piran's oratory with its relics

Four hundred metres to the west is the site of a pre-Norman chapel, buried beneath the sand; the site is marked by a tall wooden cross. This was Piran's shrine; it has been excavated several times, most recently in 2014. The present building appears to have been constructed within a terrace in an already existing dune. Its walls are of unhewn, cemented stones, leaning inwards to minimise roof stress. The existing building is thought to date from the eleventh or twelfth century, though the chapel's east wall is earlier.[62] The site is surrounded by an extensive early cist-grave cemetery: a Roman coin and silver ring were found here.[63]

The skeletons of two adults and ten children were buried to the north-west of the chapel; tests on the bones of two of the children suggested a date of around 800. The adults were women, one aged at least forty-five and the other younger, between twenty and twenty-five years old. The children were very young, one less than six months old and the others aged between one and five. There might have been earlier burials cut into the sand beneath them. All but one were aligned east–west in the Christian tradition; some burials were marked with upright stones at the head and feet.[64]

Two skeletons with familial traits were perhaps close relatives; they appear to have been buried together. The bodies were probably wrapped in shrouds and placed in grave pits dug into the sand.[65] Evidently people from the wider community were buried at the monastery. During the first excavation of the oratory, in 1835, three Romanesque carved stone heads were found to adorn its stone arch, depicting a man, a woman and a catlike animal. The animal was carved on the keystone of the arch, with the human heads lower down on either side; they are now in the Royal Cornwall Museum, Truro.

Domesday Book describes the late Saxon monastery here:

> The canons of Sanctus Pieranus hold Lanpiran, which was always free in the time of King Edward. There are three hides. There is land for eight ploughs. There are two ploughs and two serfs and four villeins and eight bordars and ten acres of pasture.

This suggests that a larger church had now been built alongside the chapel.[66] Before the dunes encroached, Piran's oratory stood at the head of a small valley. Pilgrims drank from a spring that rose beside the chapel and flowed down to the sea. In the eleventh or twelfth century, a north door was constructed to facilitate their movement: they could now enter the chapel to venerate Piran's relics and leave by the door on the opposite side.

The saint's relics were widely honoured in the thirteenth to the sixteenth centuries. During a visitation of the manors belonging to Exeter cathedral in 1281, the following relics of Piran were to be seen:

> One box or reliquary bound with iron and locked, in which is the head of Saint Piran with other relics.
> One pastoral staff of Saint Piran, ornamented with silver, gold and precious stones.
> One silver cross in which are placed tiny relics of Saint Piran.
> One portable shrine in which is placed the body of Saint Piran.
> One bone cross of Saint Piran and one little bell of Saint Piran of copper.[67]

This is an early and detailed account of a Cornish saint's relics. The shrine containing Piran's body rested on the chancel floor and the reliquary containing his skull was placed in a niche above the altar. The bone cross was a pectoral cross, hung round the neck. On feast days, the relics were carried in procession around neighbouring parishes; in 1331, the parishioners were criticised for taking them to various distant places 'as previously'. In the sixteenth century, Nicholas Roscarrock wrote:

> I, who was borne … not far from Sct Piran, remember his reliques were wonte to be carryed vpp and downe in the country vppon occation and haue seene them so carryed in the tyme of queene Mary [Tudor].[68]

Piran's relics disappeared in the seventeenth century.

The chapel was overwhelmed by sand dunes in medieval times. Later, in the seventeenth century, tin mining caused the Penwortha stream to go underground. Drifting sand does not cross running water, and until this time the

Penwortha had protected the parish church from the encroaching dunes, but with the disappearance of the stream, the parish church, too, was gradually engulfed in sand; it was abandoned in 1804.

Early Bodmin

Bodmin lies on an ancient, possibly prehistoric, east–west route through Cornwall, now followed by the A30. It is also on a north–south route between Padstow and Fowey, recently named the 'Saint's Way'. There is little early evidence to support this name, but Bodmin is situated midway between the highest navigable points on the Camel and Fowey rivers, which in early times were probably only about 6 miles apart; the headwaters of both have now silted up. Grass-marked pottery dating from between the seventh and eleventh century has been found on the site of Bodmin's former priory and in the car park south of Fore Street. Tin was also mined during this period: at nearby Boscarne, a tin ingot was found and an early tin smelting site, together with the remains of oak shovels that were radiocarbon dated to AD 635–1045. They were probably used for tin-panning in the streams.[69]

The settlement is first named *Bodmine* in the Bodmin Gospel Book, in two manumissions that date from the second half of the eleventh century. Bodmin's name probably derives from the Cornish elements, *bod* and *meneghi*, which is likely to mean 'dwelling by church-land';[70] it is named *Botmenei* in the twelfth-century Life of St Cadoc.[71] Bodmin is the only large Cornish settlement recorded in Domesday Book, which notes that *Bodmine* was held by St Petroc's church, and states that 'St Petroc's has 68 houses and a market'. By this time, therefore, Bodmin was already a small town, one of only three in Cornwall at this period, the others being Liskeard and Launceston.[72]

Bodmin's monastery

It is likely that the Saxon minsters of Cornwall and west Devon developed out of earlier religious sites, housing small communities centred on their own saint's relics. They may have become more influential than other similar communities only after 800, mainly under Anglo-Saxon influence. In Cornwall, at both Bodmin (*Dinuurrin*) and Padstow (*Lanwenehoc*), the late saints' Lives suggest that the community of St Petroc displaced the local cults of St Uuron and St Wethinoc, perhaps in the early to mid-ninth century.[73] However, we have no knowledge of a monastery at Bodmin earlier than 1066, when it is named in Domesday Book, although it is likely to be somewhat older.

The monastery and the developing settlement of Dinuurrin may have been on the hill to the north of the present church. There are a number of place-names which include the element *berry* in this part of the town: they date back to at least the fourteenth century. The fifteenth-century chapel of the Holy Rood survives as Berry Tower. The word may derive from the Old English *burh*, as a translation of the Cornish *din* ('a fort'), which occurs in Dinuurrin. Before the mid-eighth century, *burh* meant 'enclosed or defended [monastic] place', but by the tenth century it meant 'defended [secular] site' or 'manor house'; eventually, it became our word 'borough'.[74] There is a possible defensive site at Castlehill, on the ridge east of the house of that name in the upper part of Castle Street.[75]

Bodmin's Augustinian priory

The monastery of St Petroc was re-established as a foundation of Augustinian canons in the 1120s or 1130s, an evolution found elsewhere in the south-west at this time, where former monastic settlements of secular canons became priories. At Bodmin a new priory complex was built to the south-east of the earlier monastic site. This may not have occurred immediately – excavations in the mid-1980s uncovered the north-west corner of the aisled priory church: it dated from the late twelfth or early thirteenth century.[76]

In his *Itineraries* (*c.* 1538–43), John Leland records in some detail what was then known about the monastery's evolution:

> The late Priory of Blake Chanons ['black canons', or Augustinians] stoode at the est ende of the paroch chirchyard of Bodmyne ... There hath bene monkes, then nunnys, then seculare prestes, then monkes agayne, and last canons regular in S. Petrokes chirch.[77]

The new priory church was an impressive structure, one of a substantial group of buildings that included a cloister, dormitory, chapter house, refectory and prior's lodgings; a graveyard also developed around the priory. It is likely that the former monastic church, on or close to the site of the present St Petroc's, was retained initially as the parish church.[78] Life at the priory continued until the dissolution of the monasteries in 1539.

St Petroc and Bodmin

There is no evidence that Petroc established a community at Bodmin, and it is considered more likely that Bodmin was founded as a daughter house of Padstow after his death. However, the authors of the two Lives of Petroc wished to consolidate their priory's position as a centre of pilgrimage, so they claimed that a monastery was established there by Petroc himself, who gave the town its alternative name of Petrockstow. According to their narrative, after leaving Padstow and its surrounding area, Petroc travelled inland with his companions to a remote location where a hermit named Vuron lived.

The 'remote location' is probably Bodmin, or Dinnuurrin ('*din*, or fort, of Vuron'). Vuron is named Guron in a tenth-century list of Cornish saints, though he may have been a chieftain, not a hermit. In Petroc's Life we are told how Guron welcomed Petroc and his three companions, setting out a table for them, with white bread. Like Wethenoc at Padstow, he left his hut to Petroc, and travelled a day's journey to Gorran, a mile from the south Cornish coast, 7 miles south of St Austell. This, we are told, is how Gorran became the centre of Guron's cult.[79]

Dwarfed by the splendid minster church of Bodmin is Guron's well, in a sixteenth-century well-house (illus. 113). Above its entrance is a relief of Guron

ILLUS. 113. St Guron's well-house, Bodmin.

ILLUS. 114. St Guron prays outside his cell: detail, St Guron's well-house, Bodmin.

kneeling beneath a tree: he prays before a crucifix carved over the door of his cell (illus. 114). The well is now dry; the spring has been channelled through pipes, and a large volume of water now pours into a trough beside the main street, below the well.[80] The author of the Second Life relates that Petroc eventually retired as a hermit, travelling northwards to the bleak open spaces of Bodmin Moor.

Petroc's relics

As we have seen, Petroc was believed to be buried in Padstow, but his relics, including his staff and his hand bell, were brought to Bodmin. His head-reliquary was constructed by Arab craftsmen in Sicily in the twelfth century, and is a small, house-shaped casket made of ivory plates bound with brass strips, decorated with delicately carved medallions (illus. 115). The shrine was initially kept in the monastery, but was later removed to the priory: this conferred legitimacy on the new priory and attracted offerings from pilgrims.

At least eight Cornish churches, chapels and wells are dedicated to Petroc, and he was even more popular beyond Cornwall. The Saxon kings encouraged the veneration of regional saints: religious, and therefore political, unity was strengthened when pilgrims travelled with a common purpose from one part of Britain to another. Petroc's feast day is listed in various cathedral calendars, and his supposed relics were venerated in many of them.[81] In 1478 William Worcestre visited Bodmin priory and wrote that Petroc's body rested in a beautiful shrine facing the Lady Chapel, at the east end of the church, and that the priory celebrated three feasts in Petroc's honour.[82]

Bishops in Bodmin

Dinuurrin was probably the seat of the only known bishop of ninth-century Cornwall: we hear of an early bishop named Kenstec, who was

ILLUS. 115. St Petroc's casket, Bodmin church.

consecrated between 823 and 870, whose seat lay in 'the monastery of Dinuurrin'. He professed obedience to Archbishop Ceolnoth of Canterbury, marking a stage in the incorporation of Cornwall into the English church. The terms of his profession are unusual in that he is described as a bishop in a monastery:

> … the humble Kenstec, elected though unworthy to the [or 'an'] Episcopal seat among the people in Cornwall in the monastery which in the language of the Britons is called Dinuurrin.[83]

Cornwall was under Saxon control by 838, so Kenstec's submission to Ceolnoth was probably an acknowledgement that the whole of Cornwall was now subject to Canterbury, and to the kings of Wessex.

It is possible that St Petroc's monastery at Padstow and later that of Bodmin were enlarged by the kings of Wessex: by 1066, this was the largest land-owning monastery in Cornwall. A charter to the diocese of Cornwall, which was based at St Germans, states that St Petroc's monastery was to be subject to the bishops at St Germans; the charter does not specify whether 'St Petrock's monastery' was at Padstow or at Bodmin, and we do not know when the monastery at Bodmin came into existence.

The Bodmin Gospels

The Bodmin Gospel Book is the only surviving manuscript from an early Cornish monastery.[84] It was copied in a Breton monastic scriptorium in the early ninth century and had arrived at St Petroc's monastery in Bodmin by the 940s, where it was used for swearing oaths on the altar in church. It is illuminated, though not elaborately: there are several large decorated initials in red and brown. Manumissions, or the formal liberation of slaves, were later recorded on its spare leaves and in its margins; most of the slaves were Cornish, while most of their owners had Saxon names, although by this date Cornishmen were taking Anglo-Saxon names, so their ethnicity is not necessarily revealed by their names.[85]

The Bodmin Gospels were unfinished when they reached Bodmin: the letters *IN* at the start of the word *Initium*, which opens St John's gospel on folio 50r, are only partially decorated, while folio 108v contains five empty roundels that were probably intended to depict Christ enthroned in majesty, surrounded by the four evangelists. The principal decoration appears in the canon tables (ff. 9r–13v), which are a concordance (like a modern spreadsheet) that indicates whether and where a particular passage in, say, Matthew's gospel also appears in those of Mark, Luke and John. The canon tables are decorated with interlace patterns and some zoomorphic designs, such as a bird-like creature on folio 13r.[86]

The original gospels are written in continental Caroline minuscule, the standard script used at the court of Charlemagne and throughout France at this time, unlike the Insular minuscule then used in Cornwall. The earliest manumissions of slaves are thought to date from the reign of King Edmund (941–46), by which time Cornish scribes mainly employed Anglo-Saxon minuscule. Some later additions contain early examples of Cornish Caroline script, including the form of the letters 'a' and 'g'. There are entries by many different scribes.[87]

A note inserted between the arches of the canon table on folio 13r informs us that the gospels were placed on the altar: the Gospel Book represented Christ and St Petroc, who validated the transactions. The note reads:

> This is the name of the woman Medguistyl with her offspring Bleiduid, Ylcerthon and Byrchtylym who were freed by the clerics of Saint Petroc on the altar of this St Petroc's for the souls of Eadred the King and for their souls, before these witnesses, Comuyre the priest ...[88]

We know little about the lives of ninth-century slaves such as this woman and her three children – we do not know where they came from, or how they came to be slaves.

The Gospels contain fifty-one grants of manumission, which occurred between 950 and 1100: these marginal notes form one of the most important records of early Cornish Christianity. Though they are written in Latin and Old English, many of the personal names are British, such as *Wurci* (cognate with the Welsh *Gwrgi*, meaning 'man-dog') and *Modred*, the name of King Arthur's ill-fated nephew.[89] Most of the manumission entries date from the tenth rather than the eleventh century, and therefore they probably record acts made at Padstow rather than Bodmin.

How manumissions were carried out

The manumissions recorded in the Bodmin Gospels demonstrate that the monastery was closely involved in Anglo-Saxon political life: we read of slaves who are freed for the benefit of the souls of the tenth-century Saxon kings. The earliest datable king is Edmund (939–46); others include Eadred and Eadwig, while slaves are also freed on behalf of the souls of bishops, nobles and others. Sometimes the saint's relics and once his bell are mentioned in the manumission entry.[90]

We also glimpse an organised urban settlement with its officials: one manumission dating from the second half of the eleventh century records an individual purchasing a female slave and her son 'at the church door in Bodmin', paying a toll to 'Ælsige the portreeve' (a bailiff, mayor or chief magistrate) and the hundredsman (presumably the head man of the hundred), before freeing the two individuals 'on Petroc's altar'.[91]

The details of this transaction, recorded in Old English on folio 8r, illustrate how manumissions were carried out with some solemnity, in the presence of at least eight clergy as well as civic officials:

> Here is made known on this book that Æelsig had bought a woman Ongynedhel and her son Gyðhicael from Thurcilde with half a pound at the church door at Bodmin, and paid to Æelsige the portreeve and Maccos the hundredsman four pennies for toll.
>
> Then Æelsig did what he had bought them for, and freed them on Petroc's Altar, free of any liability. On the witness of these good men: Isaac, the Mass-priest & Bledculf, Mass-priest & Wunning, Mass-priest & Wulfger, Mass-priest & Grifiuð, Mass-priest & Noe, Mass-priest & Wurþicið, Mass-priest & Æelsig, deacon … And if anyone should violate this freedom, may he lose Christ's protection. Amen.[92]

This manumission illustrates how people might buy slaves in order to set them free; in this case, a toll was paid to the king or his representative for doing so. The names of those in authority are Anglo-Saxon, including the freer of the two slaves and the portreeve and hundredsman. Æelsig(e) was a popular name, shared here by three people. Most of the names are Cornish, including those of the slaves, while two of the priests, Isaac and Noe (or Noah), had been given Old Testament names.[93]

Why were slaves liberated?

The liberation of slaves was rooted in Jewish-Christian beliefs concerning justice and equality. The Old Testament Book of Leviticus described how Jews were required to set free their slaves every fifty years, since they, too, had been slaves in Egypt: 'You will declare this fiftieth year sacred and proclaim the liberation of all the inhabitants of the land' (Lev. 25. 10). The ransom of slaves was considered a work of charity that wealthier Christians should carry out in imitation of Jesus who, quoting the prophet Isaiah, declared he had come 'to proclaim liberty to captives … to set the downtrodden free' (Is. 61. 1; Lk. 4. 18).

In his Letter to the Galatians, St Paul developed a theology of equality: 'there are no more distinctions between Jew and Greek, slave and free, male and female, but all of you are one in Christ Jesus' (Gal. 3. 28). While a prisoner in Rome, in AD 61–63, Paul wrote a short letter to a Christian named Philemon, after one of his slaves, Onesimus, had run away and sought protection with Paul. Paul asks Philemon to welcome him back, not as a slave but as

ILLUS. 116. Sixth-century memorial stone, Lanivet.

a brother; he goes further, and offers to pay whatever the slave might owe to his master:

> I know you have been deprived of Onesimus for a time, but it was only so that you could have him back for ever, not as a slave any more, but something much better than a slave, a dear brother … Welcome him as you would me, but if he has wronged you in any way or owes you anything, then let me pay for it. I am writing this in my own handwriting: I, Paul, shall pay it back. (vv. 15–19)

In the fifth century, St Patrick was captured and sold as a slave in Ireland. Towards the end of his life, his 'Letter to the Soldiers of Coroticus' addresses the fact that soldiers who were nominally Christian were also engaged in slave raids. He begs the tyrant's soldiers:

> Free the baptised servants of God and the handmaids of Christ – for whom he was crucified and died. The Church suffers and mourns for its sons and daughters … who were carried off and brought to distant lands … There freeborn men are offered for sale and Christians are made into slaves again, indeed slaves of the worst and most unworthy of men: the apostate Picts …
>
> Though it be very late, it may be they will repent of their impious actions – being murderers of the Lord's brothers and sisters – and release the baptised captives they have taken. Thus they would merit to live in God and be healed for this life and eternity.[94]

It took centuries before slavery was more generally perceived as immoral.

A sixth-century Christian at Lanivet

Some fifty years after St Patrick's death, a memorial was erected to a Christian at Lanivet, 2 miles south-west of Bodmin. A mid-sixth-century granite pillar stone, now inside the church, commemorates ANNICV FIL[I], or '[the stone] of Annicus, son of …' (illus. 116); the name is Roman. The letters are carved in Roman capitals, and framed with a cartouche; only the pillar's upper portion survives.[95]

Lanivet appears as *Lannived* in 1268; its name means 'church site, or *lann*, at *neved*'. The word *neved* indicates a pre-Christian holy place, as in Nymet (Devon), Nemet (Brittany) or *nyfed* (Welsh for 'shrine').[96] Derivations of the word *nemeton*, which often denote a sacred grove or a shrine, are widely found from Scotland to Galicia in north-west Spain and as far east as central Turkey. It is not known to whom Lanivet church was dedicated.

There is an Anglo-Saxon coped tombstone at Lanivet: this was a wealthy Christian form of commemorating the dead, perhaps the secular equivalent of a saint's shrine. It dates from the late tenth or eleventh century, and probably covered a grave, since it is over 2 m long. Like the hogback tombstones found in northern Britain, it has a well-defined roof with a crouching animal at each end, facing inwards; it is decorated with knots and fret patterns.[97]

There are two elaborate crosses in the churchyard – an eleventh-century four-holed cross and an eleventh- or early twelfth-century wheel cross. The second of these has five decorative panels on its east face, two including male figures, and six on its west side. It is possible that these fine crosses were taken for safety from Bodmin priory at the Reformation, since Charles Henderson (1925) records a Norman capital from Bodmin priory in Lanivet's chancel, and a document stating that in 1539 Lanivet's parishioners bought four of the bells from the dissolved monastery for £36.[98]

Luxulyan and a playing place

Luxulyan is in moorland 6 miles south of Bodmin and 4 miles north-east of St Austell. Originally dedicated to Sulien, Luxulyan's church stands within an oval enclosure, and may be built over a pre-Christian burial mound. It is referred to as 'Chapel of *Luxulian*' in 1282 and as *Lansulien* in 1343. It is named after a Breton saint, *Sulian* or *Sulien*, who is sometimes equated with another male saint, *Suliau* or *Suliac*.[99]

Sulien has eight dedications in western Brittany, including the similarly named Lossulien in the far north-west, near Brest.[100] The first element of the name Luxulyan, like the Breton *loc*, derives from the Latin *locus*, meaning 'the [holy] place'. It is the sole example of such a site in Cornwall, although the prefix appears in the names of some ninety Breton settlements.[101] The churches of Corwen and Cwm in mid-Wales are both dedicated to a pair of holy men, Mael and Sulien.[102]

By 1412 Luxulyan's church was dedicated to Saints Cyricus and Julitta, a widow and her son who were supposedly martyred around AD 304 at Tarsus in south-central Turkey. There are several dedications to the couple around the mouth of the River Fowey, dating from the thirteenth century onwards; perhaps their cult spread to that part of Cornwall from mainland Europe.[103] Luxulyan's holy well was dedicated to St Cyr, at least by the nineteenth century. The well is built into the wall below a house on the main street, on the hill below the church (OS 054580). The tall well-house with its elegant doorway dates from the fifteenth century (illus. 117).[104]

ILLUS. 117. St Cyr's well, Luxulyan.

Halfway between Bodmin and Luxulyan, at the summit of a low rise called Castle Hill on Innis Downs, a henge was later used as a playing place (OS 031627). It is 75 m north-east of Castle Hill Farm, and is close to the source of the Luxulyan River. Henges are ritual or ceremonial centres that date to the late Neolithic period (2800–2000 BC); they normally cover a flat area over 20 m in diameter. The henge at Castle Hill is an oval enclosure, with a high bank, a deep inner ditch and two entrances. Castle Hill is an unusual example of an early henge that was reused as a social and ceremonial meeting place much later, but possibly for similar reasons. It was identified as a playing place by the antiquarians William Copeland Borlase (1848–99) and Charles Henderson (1900–33).[105]

Medieval playing places, or *Plain an Gwary* in Cornish, were an early form of outdoor theatre, usually oval or circular, with an outer bank, where mystery plays were performed and various social, religious and political events were held. The site was partially excavated by Charles Thomas in 1962; some prehistoric flint flakes and medieval pottery fragments were found. Thomas concluded that the bank of the henge was remodelled in the thirteenth century to construct the playing place. Later, during the Civil War, the enclosure was used as a gun emplacement: there was evidence of cannon wheel ruts and cannon balls.[106]

Two Breton saints, Mewan and Austell

Five miles south-west of Luxulyan, two adjacent parishes are named after Mewan and Austell. Mewan, known as Méen in Brittany, was believed to be a relative of St Samson, and was one of his deacons at Dol; unlike most Breton saints, his life is well documented. A Latin Life of Mewan (*Vita Meveni*), attributed to Ingomar, was written at his own monastery in about 1084; in the Life, Austell is described as Mewan's godson.

The Cornish form of their names, *Megunn* and *Austoll*, appears in the early tenth-century list of forty-eight saints that has already been mentioned. The list survives on one of a group of fly-leaves used to bind a ninth-century Breton manuscript that included *De Moribus* by pseudo-Seneca and Jerome's chapter on Seneca from his *De Viris Illustribus* ('On Illustrious Men'). Its compiler knew the locations of places in Cornwall associated with these saints, since he grouped them geographically. Numbers 39 to 47 are saints of parishes close to St Austell, which suggests that churches in this area were in existence by the late ninth century.[107]

St Austell's church, a mile from the south coast, is first mentioned in 1155 or 1160 as *ecclesiam de Austol*, while that of St Mewan, in a village a mile south-west of St Austell, is mentioned in 1291 as *Ecclesia Sancti Mawani*.[108] According to Mewan's Life,

> The two servants of God, St Samson and St Mewan, with their monks, safely cross the sea and arrive in Letavia [Brittany]. Crowds of both sexes flock to hear them preach, among them Privatus, whose sick wife and daughter are healed by the prayers of the holy men.[109]

After following Samson to Dol, Mewan established two communities in the central forest region of Brocéliande. Ingomar recounts how this came about: Samson sent Mewan on a mission to Waroch, count of Vannes, in eastern Brittany. Mewan broke his journey at Gaël, where Caduon, chieftain of the region, offered him his fort and its surrounding forest, asking him to return and found a monastery. Mewan returned to Dol, and Samson gave him permission to make the foundation. Mewan's lifelong friend and relative, Count Judicaël of Domnonia entered the monastery at Gaël, where he died the following year.[110]

The Life relates that Mewan and his disciples built cells, small buildings and a church dedicated to John the Baptist beside the River Meu; this is likely to have been in the present village of Gaël. A gold ring decorated with glass beads of various colours was found at Gaël; it dates from between 570 and 670.[111] Mewan died there in about 548. Before his death, his godson Austell was grief-stricken, but Mewan promised his godson that he, too, would die a week later. Austell cried:

> 'Why, Father, do you leave me, your servant, desolate? Who will guard your feeble sheep from the wolf when the shepherd is taken away?' *[Mewan replied:]* 'Go on with your appointed labours and diligently perform your duties … You shall join me in the glory of the heavenly life'.[112]

The monastery of St Méen-le-Grand

Two miles north of Gaël, the monastery of St Méen-le-Grand, or 'St Mewan's great [monastery]', became the centre of Mewan's cult. It was rebuilt several times: the earliest surviving portions are a late eleventh-century wall and a twelfth-century tower. A series of frescoes dating from the first half of the fourteenth century depict St Mewan's life: they cover the vault and the north

ILLUS. 118. Scenes from the life of St Mewan, St Méen-le-Grand, Brittany.

wall, and are framed in elegant symmetrical panels.[113] In one of them, illustrated here (illus. 118), the upper portion depicts Count Judicaël as he escapes from the court of King Haëloch and takes refuge with Abbot Mewan; the crowned king is visible on the left. In the centre, Mewan stands in prayer, with his tonsured head and white habit. To the right, Judicaël removes his royal clothing, in order to receive the habit.

The lower panel depicts Mewan's death and that of his godson, Austell. To the left, Mewan is on his deathbed, with his anxious community behind him. In the central scene, Mewan lies in state in his coffin, with his crozier beside him. The grief of his mitred and tonsured brethren is evident from their facial expressions, as they pray beside the bier. On the right, the naked souls of Mewan and his godson rise from their bodies into God's presence.

Mewan's relics are found in many places in Brittany and Anjou, and his shrine at St Méen-le-Grand was a popular centre of pilgrimage. His cult spread throughout Brittany, where there are twenty-six dedications to him, and to other regions of France. Churches in Belgium are also named after him.[114] However, although Austell's name was also known at St Méen-le-Grand, there are no dedications to St Austell anywhere except at the single parish in Cornwall.

Probus, an early minster

Probus is 7 miles south-west of St Austell. In the early tenth-century list of forty-eight saints, *Propus* and *Latoc* feature: they are the patron saints of two adjacent churches, Probus and Ladock.[115] Domesday Book refers to canons at St Probus (*Canonici S' Probi*). The same two forms of his name, *Propus* and *Probus*, are used for a saint honoured at Sherborne (Dorset), where a papal grant of 1145 refers to *Propeschirche*, and another of 1163 describes the chapel of *Sancti Probi*.[116]

Like Padstow, Probus was one of Cornwall's four chartered sanctuary churches; its 'safe space' was demarcated by crosses. Probus was a small minster whose clergy lived in separate houses and might have been married with families. It had a small estate of only one hide:[117] this was an Anglo-Saxon term meaning 'family', and denoted a landholding sufficient to support a single family. Probus was one of only five Saxon minsters to survive the monastic reorganisation that followed the Norman Conquest; the others were Bodmin, Crantock, St Buryan and perhaps St Kew, which was re-founded in the twelfth century, apparently after a period of disuse.

The Normans established communities that followed the Benedictine rule, some of which were cells of French monasteries. Probus had six canons, whose superior was known as the dean, but King Henry I (1068–1135) gave the church of Probus to Exeter cathedral, and in 1268 the bishop of Exeter suppressed the office of dean of Probus, and reallocated its endowments to the cathedral. Probus was virtually reduced to a parish church, although it continued to support five canons who rarely went there.[118]

The Latin word *probus* means 'morally upright' and was an early Christian term for someone considered worthy or sufficiently mature for leadership in the Christian community. In the First Letter to Timothy, St Paul enumerates the qualities required for elders and deacons (1 Tim. 3. 1–13). A lengthy letter addressed to the Christians in Corinth, attributed to Clement I, bishop of Rome, and composed some time between AD 80 and 140, describes *viri probati* ('approved men'):

> [The Apostles] appointed those [ministers] already mentioned, and afterwards gave instruction, that when these should fall asleep [in death], other approved men should succeed them in their ministry … Blessed are those presbyters who, having finished their course before now, have obtained a fruitful and perfect departure [from this world]; for they have no fear lest any one deprive them of the place now appointed them.[119]

This is the earliest preserved letter outside the New Testament: in parts of the early Church it was included in the scriptural canon. This provides a possible context for the choice of the name Probus for the person honoured at this minster church. Similarly, *Iustus* (as in St Just) was a popular name for Christians during the post-Roman period, and some of its bearers also became saints.

Ruan Lanihorne and St Rumon

The remainder of this chapter will focus on sites around the Fal estuary, starting with its upper reaches. Settlements beside the long Fal estuary thrived in earlier times, where boats could penetrate deep into Cornwall. Ruan Lanihorne is alongside an arm of the River Fal, 4 miles south-east of Truro. Ruan is an abbreviation of Rumon; Lanihorne denotes the church-site of a person named Rihoarn.[120] This small settlement became a flourishing market town with a harbour, until it silted up in the seventeenth century; near the church, an old road leads down to the River Fal.

ILLUS. 119. St Rumon's well, Ruan Lanihorne.

Rumon's well is opposite the northern boundary of the churchyard, in a nearby field (OS 894421) (illus. 119). Rumon is a form of the Latin name, *Romanus*; he is listed in the tenth-century list of Cornish saints. A later tradition claims that Ruan Lanihorne was the site of his shrine until most of his relics were taken to Tavistock abbey in south Devon, where they are listed in about 1031.[121] The theft of his body, like that of St Neot, also taken to an English shrine, indicates the value which the Saxons accorded to Cornish saints.

Along with Petroc and Piran, only Neot and Rumon became widely known in England through relics, church dedications, inclusion in church calendars and collections of saints' Lives.[122] A Life of Rumon was composed at Tavistock, but it was based on a legendary Life of St Ronan of Quimper in western Brittany. On the Lizard, the small parishes of Ruan Major and Ruan Minor are dedicated to him, and two men are named *Rumun* in the Bodmin Gospels. In 1525, a widow named Marion Lelley willed her cow to the church property store of St Rumon at Ruan Lanihorne.[123]

ILLUS. 120. Inscribed pillar stone, St Clement.

Early inhabitants of St Clement

The village of St Clement is above the River Tresilian, a tidal tributary of the Fal. The village is 1.5 miles south-east of Truro, into which it extends, with its boundary running along St Clement Street. The parish was referred to as Moresk, after its manor; the earliest surviving reference to the 'church of *Sanctus Clemens*' dates from 1329.[124] St Clement's well is 300 m east of the church, down the track leading to the river, in a low stone well-house (OS 853438). It is described as *fontem Sancti Clementis* in a late twelfth-century charter, copied in the fourteenth century.[125]

A sixth-century inscribed pillar stone, now outside the church, was used to commemorate two different men (illus. 120). Its longer Latin inscription has been dated to the first third of the sixth century and reads: VITALI FILI TORRICI, or '[the stone] of Vitalis, the son of Torricus'. Vitalis is frequently found as a wealthy Roman's name – he was perhaps a landowner – while Torricus appears to be a British name. Above this inscription, a shorter one, in smaller letters, is incomplete; it may read IGNI OC, or '[the stone of] ...gnus, here', and perhaps dates from the last third of the sixth century.[126] In later medieval times, the stone was roughly trimmed, cutting short the second inscription; its front was dressed back to produce an unpierced cross-head. It is thought that it once stood in a field behind the well, named 'The Sanctuaries': this may have been an early burial ground.[127]

Old Kea

Kea is a large parish, 2 miles south of Truro, bounded on the east by the Truro and Upper Fal rivers. Its former parish church is at Old Kea, which is likely to have been the centre of Ke's cult in Britain. In Domesday Book the parish is named *Landighe* ('enclosure of thy *Ke*'); the name of its saint is also given in Latin as *Cheus*. This implies the presence of a religious community dedicated to the saint: a group of clerics may have lived here until the Norman Conquest.[128] Inside the church, the very large granite block that surrounds the font was perhaps the base of the medieval Kea cross, which stood at the forked junction at the top of the hill on the track down to Old Kea. Outside the church is a stone pillar, which may have been the shaft of a cross or a boundary marker.

From at least 1390 onwards, Ke is sometimes given the epithet *Colethek*, meaning 'Ke, the cherished'. The same epithet is found in Brittany, where variants of his name include Cai and To-Cai; Quay, Quai and Qué; and also Colledoc and Kecolledoc.[129] Ke's cult was widespread: Landkey in north Devon is recorded as *Landechai* in 1166, while an estate with a similar name, *Lantokay*, was apparently granted to Glastonbury abbey by the bishop of the West Saxons in 680; it is described on pages 55–57.

A largely legendary Latin Life of St Ke was written in Brittany and summarised in French by the Dominican, Albert le Grand, in 1637.[130] Elements in this Life are also found in the play *Bewnans Ke*, or 'The Life of Ke', which probably dates from the mid-fifteenth century.[131] When this became damaged, perhaps through frequent use, a copy was made by a good Latin scholar, which was then copied by a poor one in the mid- or second half of the sixteenth century. In the play, the saint is named Ke, while in the stage directions he is named Colodoc, or Keladocus, the Latin form of his epithet.[132]

The play was probably in three sections, performed on three consecutive days; fragments survive of parts one and two. This may have taken place in St Kea parish, where there were two rounds in a field named Plain Place, meaning 'Playing Place' (OS 814419); the earlier round survives, but the other has been ploughed away.[133] There was a holy well nearby, under an oak tree beside the road.[134] Fresh water would be useful to the crowds gathered for three days' entertainment.

In *Bewnans Ke* the saint is persecuted by a Cornish tyrant named Teudar; they engage in a long theological discussion. This resembles a sequence in *Beunans Meriasek*, a play based on the life of a Breton bishop, Meriadoc, the patron saint of Camborne. Later in *Bewnans Ke*, the scene shifts to King

Arthur's court, using material based on Geoffrey of Monmouth's *Historia Regum Britanniæ* (*c*. 1139). These plays in Middle Cornish were probably written by one or more priests from the College of St Thomas at Glasney in Penryn. From 1270, the parish of St Kea paid tithes to Glasney College.[135]

ILLUS. 121. Upper portion of Mylor's churchyard cross.

Mylor: St Melor's church and well

Four miles south of Old Kea and 5 miles north of Falmouth, Mylor is one of a number of sites around the Fal estuary that are most easily reached by sea; the church stands above the harbour. Its patron saint is referred to as *Meler* in the tenth-century list of forty-eight saints; his cult is likely to have spread from Brittany. The farmhouse beside the vicarage is named Lanwithick, meaning 'church site among the trees'. Surviving Romanesque elements suggest that the Norman church was built at the beginning of the twelfth century. Unusually, Caen stone from Normandy was imported for Mylor church and for nearby St Anthony in Roseland: this suggests that they were wealthy establishments.[136]

East of the south porch, Mylor's unique granite cross stands 5 m high; it may have been a pre-Christian monolith, with a sun-symbol consisting of three concentric circles carved at its top (illus. 121). The stone is taller than it appears, for it is planted 2 m deep; it was capped with a Christian cross in medieval times. St Mylor's well is in the churchyard, 50 m west of the church (OS 820353); the present structure probably dates from the nineteenth century, but medieval fragments of dressed stone lie near its doorway.[137] The existence of a spring may have determined the choice of site for the church and a settlement around it; the well water is still used for baptisms.

St Melor's Breton cult

In Brittany, two saints named Melor were honoured. The more significant was considered to be a murdered prince: the centre of his cult was at Lanmeur, near the north-west coast. His legend, derived from two lost Latin Lives, claims that a wicked uncle killed Melor's father, King Meliau, and cut off young Melor's right hand and left foot, so that he could neither ride a horse nor bear a spear, and was therefore barred from kingship. Eventually, the uncle ordered Melor's death: he was murdered at Lanmeur, where his relics were said to have been preserved until the ninth century.[138]

Statues of Melor with his prosthetic limbs can be found in many medieval Breton churches (colour plate 14). Perhaps adults with injured limbs, who could

ILLUS. 122. St Melor's church crypt, Lanmeur, Brittany.

not fight or work the land, found consolation by praying to one of the few saints who was disabled like themselves. Melor's tomb stood in the crypt of the parish church at the centre of Lanmeur; it was destroyed in the eighteenth century. There used to be two small windows through which the tomb could be venerated from outside.[139]

The crypt's low vault is supported by eight broad pillars, two of which are decorated with stylised plant motifs (illus. 122); they probably date from the tenth or eleventh century. A spring rises in a pool against one wall; the town was formerly known as *Kerfeunten*, after the spring. During excavations, two carved gold figurines were found, perhaps dating to the sixth century. There are some fifteen dedications to Melor in Brittany.[140]

St Just in Roseland

This church and its extensive grounds are in a tidal creek on the east side of the Fal estuary, opposite Mylor. It is one of a group of churches in the Roseland area whose saints, Iust, Entenin, Gerent, Fili and Rumon appear together in the list of forty-eight early saints, dating from around AD 900. They are honoured at St Just in Roseland, St Anthony in Roseland, Gerrans, Philleigh and Ruan Lanihorne, respectively.[141] 'Roseland' derives from the Cornish *ros*, meaning a promontory; this prefix is also found in early Irish, Scottish and Welsh place names. The English 'land' was a later addition.[142]

ILLUS. 123. Inner chamber of St Just's well, St Just in Roseland.

The Latin name 'Justus' was often used in the early British Church, and meant 'a just man'. In monastic communities, this was a familiar word that appears frequently in the psalms, which were chanted each week. Psalm 37 is a lengthy alphabetical psalm that reflects on good and evil, and encourages an upright life. A favourite phrase from the psalm was:

> The just man's mouth utters wisdom
> And his lips speak what is right;
> The law of his God is in his heart. (Ps. 37. 30–31)[143]

These were the words sung during the entrance procession for Mass on the feasts of most male saints, beginning with the phrase, *Os justi meditabitur sapientiam.*[144]

There is a well in the churchyard but, as often, St Just's holy well is further away, 80 m east of the church on the estuary path (illus. 123), at the head of the creek (OS 849358); its water is still used for baptisms.[145] While a reliable spring was vital to an early settlement, a suitable spot to construct a church might be some distance away. The well-house is medieval, with some rebuilding. A rectangular roofed chamber contains the spring, and there are remains of an outer chamber or porch, with side walls, a doorway and lower walling that may have formed a bench, topped with smooth flat stones. This would provide seating for pilgrims seeking a cure, since the water was believed in medieval and post-medieval times to have healing properties.[146]

St Mawes

St Just in Roseland was the mother church of St Mawes, near the southern end of the Fal estuary. In 1284, St Mawes was named *Lavousa* ('*Lan*, or church-site, of Mawes'); it did not become a parish in its own right. Mawes is known as Maudez in modern Breton; eleven parish churches in Brittany and at least sixty-three chapels are named after him. An impressive double well at Landebaëron in northern Brittany, 22 miles north-west of Saint-Brieuc, is jointly dedicated to Mawes and another Breton saint, Paezron, or Pedron (illus. 124).[147] They date to the seventeenth century; beyond the two well pools is a larger one in which villagers washed their clothes.

The earliest Life of Mawes was written in Brittany in the eleventh or twelfth century; it does not mention Cornwall.[148] Mawes was said to have settled on a small island, now Île Modez, where he taught his followers, seated on 'St

ILLUS. 124. Twin holy wells at Landebaëron in northern Brittany.

Maudez's Chair'. This is a feature in some saints' Lives; in Scots Gaelic, *suidhe* (the normal word for 'seat') can also indicate a natural rock formation where a saint was believed to have sat in prayer, or taught his followers.[149] In Wales, St Canna's Chair is a boulder at Llangan (Carmarthenshire), near the site of her former holy well; in Cornwall, St Germoe's Chair is in Germoe churchyard, near Helston.

When the Breton legends were repeated at St Mawes, elements of the Life of St Maudez were relocated to Cornwall. John Leland visited Cornwall in about 1540, when he was told that the saint had a Seat at St Mawes. Leland described

> a chapelle of [Mawes] and his chaire of stone a little without, and his welle. They caulle this sainct there St Maudite: he was a bisshop in Britain [*i.e.* Brittany] and painted [?on a wall] as a scholemaster.[150]

Nicholas Roscarrock (*c.* 1549–*c.* 1634) knew of the same tradition. He wrote:

> Sainct Mauditus was borne in Ireland & a Bishop who lived a most strict & austere life on the east syde of Falmouth in Cornwall, where there is at this present a church dedicated vnto him in a poore Fisher Towne bearing his name, In the churchyarde whereof there is a Seat of hard stoane which the inhabitantes call St Mawes chayre, in which hee vsed to sitt. There is also a well therevnto adjoyning bearing his name, which hee vsed to frequent in his life.[151]

ILLUS. 125. The well-house, St Mawes.

The well (illus. 125) can be seen in the steep street above the Victory Inn (OS 847332). South-west of the well, Holywell Cottage is thought to be built on the site of a fourteenth-century chapel dedicated to St Mawes, with a 'Chapel Yard', a quarter of an acre in size, on the slope above. In 1381 the rector of St Just in Roseland held a licence to celebrate Mass 'in the chapel of St Mawes, within his [*i.e.* the rector's] parish' (*in capella Sancti Mawdeti infra parochiam suam*). The licence was renewed in 1391 and again in 1427. The chapel was seized under the Chantry Act of 1545, but services continued until the reign of Elizabeth.[152]

By 1650 the chapel had been converted into a house, of which only a wall of Pentuan stone and an arch remained by the end of the eighteenth century. The wall can still be seen beside the old road; some of the chapel may survive in Holywell Cottage.[153] The adjacent Chapel Yard could have been a cemetery: Meyrick heard that human remains had been found when Holywell Cottage was built. The well is no longer used: its clear, cold water is now drawn from a standpipe beside the Victory Inn.[154]

Notes

1 Karen Jankulak, *The Medieval Cult of St Petroc* (Boydell, 2000).

2 Pru Manning and Peter Stead, 'Excavation of an Early Christian Cemetery at Althea Library, Padstow', in *Cornish Archaeology*, 41–42, 2002–03, ed. Graeme Kirkham and Peter Herring (2006), pp. 80–106, at pp. 80, 83, 92.

3 *Ibid.*, p. 89.

4 Lynette Olson, *Early Monasteries in Cornwall* (Woodbridge: Boydell Press, 1989), p. 105.

5 John Allan and Graham Langman, 'Appendix 3: The Pottery', in Manning and Stead, 'Excavation of an Early Christian Cemetery at Althea Library', pp. 97–99.

6 Karen Jankulak, *The Medieval Cult of St Petroc*, Studies in Celtic History, 19 (Woodbridge: Boydell, 2000), pp. 3–4.

7 Nicholas Orme, *The Saints of Cornwall* (Oxford: Oxford University Press, 2000), p. 215.

8 Manning and Stead, 'Excavation of an Early Christian Cemetery', pp. 80, 90–91.

9 Olson, *Early Monasteries in Cornwall*, p. 70.

10 Jankulak, *The Medieval Cult of St Petroc*, p. 45.

11 Ann Preston-Jones and Elisabeth Okasha, *Corpus of Anglo-Saxon Sculpture, vol. XI, Early Cornish Sculpture* (Oxford: The British Academy/Oxford University Press, 2013), p. 178.

12 Manning and Stead, 'Excavation of an Early Christian Cemetery', pp. 90–91.

13 Peter Beacham and Nikolaus Pevsner, *The Buildings of England, Cornwall* (New Haven: Yale University Press, 2014), 'Padstow', pp. 129–30.

14 'The Church in Padstow, St Merryn and St Issey', http://padstowparishchurch.org.uk/history-2, accessed 28 September 2019.

15 David Hugh Farmer, *The Oxford Dictionary of Saints*, 2nd edn (Oxford: Oxford University Press, 1987), pp. 22–23.

16 Orme, *The Saints of Cornwall*, p. 215.

17 'Little Petherick Conservation Area Character Statement', North Cornwall District Council, 1997, pp. 3–4.

18 Oliver Padel, *A Popular Dictionary of Cornish Place-Names* (Penzance: Alison Hodge, 1988), p. 137.

19 William Penaluna, *An Historical Survey of the County of Cornwall* (London: W. Penaluna, 1838), p. 148.

20 Orme, *The Saints of Cornwall*, p. 79.

21 John Harvey, ed., *William Worcestre: Itineraries* (Oxford: Oxford Medieval Texts, 1969), p. 72.

22 Steve Northcott, 'The Lost Chapel and Holy Well of St Cadoc: A Community-Based Archaeology Project', report no. 2013R002, May 2013, Archaeology Dept, Truro and Penwith College, pp. 8–9.

23 *Ibid.*, p. 10.

24 Gilbert H. Doble, *Saint Cadoc in Cornwall and Brittany*, 'Cornish Saints' Series, no. 40 (Truro: Dean and Chapter of Truro Cathedral, 1937). A second plan by Charles Henderson (without the note 'bones found') can be found in the Appendix.

25 *Ibid.*, p. 33.

26 Northcott, 'The Lost Chapel and Holy Well of St Cadoc', p. 9.

27 *Ibid.*, pp. 7–8.

28 *Ibid.*, pp. 11, 16–17.

29 Jack Meyrick, *A Pilgrim's Guide to the Holy Wells of Cornwall* (Falmouth: Meyrick, 1982), no. 125, pp. 99–100.

30 BL, Add. MS 29762, f. 171r.
31 Orme, *The Saints of Cornwall*, p. 95.
32 Padel, *A Popular Dictionary of Cornish Place-Names*, p. 59.
33 Thomas Charles-Edwards, *Wales and the Britons 350–1064* (Oxford: Oxford University Press, 2013), p. 169.
34 Sam Turner, *Making a Christian Landscape* (Exeter: Exeter University Press, 2006), pp. 79–80.
35 Craig Weatherhill, *Cornovia: Ancient Sites of Cornwall and Scilly* (Tiverton: Cornwall Books, 1985), p. 119.
36 Turner, *Making a Christian Landscape*, p. 79.
37 John Blair, *The Church in Anglo-Saxon Society* (Oxford: Oxford University Press, 2005), p. 464.
38 Lynette Olson and Oliver Padel, 'A Tenth-Century List of Cornish Parochial Saints', *Cambridge Medieval Celtic Studies*, 12 (1986), pp. 34, 47–48.
39 Michael Lapidge, 'The Cult of St Indract at Glastonbury', in *Ireland and Early Medieval Europe: Studies in Memory of Kathleen Hughes*, ed. Dorothy Whitelock, Rosamund McKitterick and David Dumville (Cambridge: Cambridge University Press, 1982), p. 198.
40 Historic England, 'Lanherne Cross, Standing Cross in the Grounds of the Convent, Lanherne', no. 1020866, 2019.
41 Oliver J. Padel, 'Old Cornish *runhol*', in Preston-Jones and Okasha, *Corpus of Anglo-Saxon Sculpture*, pp. 154–55.
42 Elizabeth Rees, *Celtic Saints of Wales* (Stroud: Fonthill, 2015), pp. 113–14.
43 Preston-Jones and Okasha, *Corpus of Anglo-Saxon Sculpture*, pp. 152–53.
44 Charles Thomas, *And Shall These Mute Stones Speak?* (Cardiff: Cardiff University Press, 1994), pp. 268–70.
45 Meyrick, *A Pilgrim's Guide to the Holy Wells of Cornwall*, no. 13, p. 111.
46 Mabel and Lilian Quiller-Couch, *Ancient and Holy Wells of Cornwall* (London: C.J. Clark, 1894), p. 191.
47 Karen Jankulak, 'Carantoc Alias Cairnech? British Saints, Irish Saints and the Irish in Wales', in *Ireland and Wales in the Middle Ages*, ed. Karen Jankulak and Jonathan M. Wooding (Dublin: Four Courts Press, 2007), pp. 116–48.
48 Turner, *Making a Christian Landscape*, pp. 49–50.
49 Nicholas Orme, *Cornwall and the Cross: Christianity 500–1560* (London: Phillimore, 2007), p. 14.
50 *Ibid.*
51 *Ibid.*, pp. 38–39.
52 Nicholas Orme, *Nicholas Roscarrock's Lives of the Saints: Cornwall and Devon*, New Series, 35 (Exeter: Devon and Cornwall Record Society, 1992), p. 66.
53 Thomas, *And Shall These Mute Stones Speak?*, pp. 282–83.
54 Weatherhill, *Cornovia*, p. 46.
55 Padel, *A Popular Dictionary of Cornish Place-Names*, p. 76.
56 BL, Add. MS 29762, f. 44r.
57 Quiller-Couch, *Ancient and Holy Wells of Cornwall*, p. 54.
58 Orme, *Cornwall and the Cross*, p. 19.
59 Oliver Padel, 'Local Saints and Place-Names in Cornwall', in *Local Saints and Local Churches in the Early Medieval West*, ed. Alan Thacker and Richard Sharpe (Oxford: Oxford University Press, 2002), p. 324.
60 Preston-Jones and Okasha, *Corpus of Anglo-Saxon Sculpture*, p. 190.
61 *Ibid.*, pp. 190–93.

62 James Glossop, St Piran Trust Report, Cornwall24.net: worldwide Cornish e-Magazine, 17 August 2015.
63 Preston-Jones and Okasha, *Corpus of Anglo-Saxon Sculpture*, p. 192.
64 *Ibid.*
65 *Ibid.*
66 A.A. Clinnick, *The Story of the Three Churches of St Piran* (Truro: A.W. Jordan, 1949), p. 2.
67 Exeter Cathedral Archives, D&C 3672A, f. 10r.
68 Orme, *Nicholas Roscarrock's Lives of the Saints*, p. 107.
69 Graeme Kirkham, Cornwall & Scilly Urban Survey, *Historic Characterisation for Regeneration: Bodmin*, Historic Environment Service Report no. 2005R064, 2005, pp. 13–14.
70 Padel, *A Popular Dictionary of Cornish Place-Names*, p. 55.
71 Eilert Ekwall, *The Concise Oxford Dictionary of English Place-Names*, 4th edn (Oxford: Oxford University Press, 1970), entry: Bodmin.
72 Kirkham, Cornwall & Scilly Urban Survey, p. 15.
73 Jankulak, *The Medieval Cult of St Petroc*, pp. 41–71.
74 Blair, *The Church in Anglo-Saxon Society*, pp. 285–87.
75 Kirkham, Cornwall & Scilly Urban Survey, p. 14.
76 Kirkham, Cornwall & Scilly Urban Survey, p. 16.
77 Davies Gilbert, *The Parochial History of Cornwall, founded on the manuscript histories of Mr. Hals and Mr. Tonkin* (London: J.B. Nichols, 1838), vol. 4, p. 261.
78 *Ibid.*
79 Orme, *The Saints of Cornwall*, pp. 131, 215.
80 Meyrick, *A Pilgrim's Guide to the Holy Wells of Cornwall*, no. 13, p. 21.
81 Orme, *The Saints of Cornwall*, pp. 217–19.
82 Harvey, *Worcestre: Itineraries*, pp. 86, 88.
83 Lynette Olson, 'Introduction', *St Samson of Dol and the Earliest History of Brittany, Cornwall and Wales*, Studies in Celtic History 37, ed. Lynette Olson (Woodbridge: The Boydell Press, 2017), pp. 12–13.
84 The manuscript, BL, Add. MS 9381, can be viewed online. http://www.bl.uk/manuscripts/FullDisplay.aspx?ref=Add_MS_9381, accessed 21 November 2019.
85 Chantry Westwell, British Library, Medieval manuscripts blog, 2014.
86 *Ibid.*
87 *Ibid.*
88 *Ibid.*
89 *Ibid.*
90 Padel, 'Local Saints and Place-Names in Cornwall', p. 323.
91 Kirkham, Cornwall & Scilly Urban Survey, p. 14.
92 Westwell, British Library, Medieval manuscripts blog.
93 *Ibid.*
94 Thomas O'Loughlin, *Saint Patrick: The Man and his Works* (London: SPCK, 1999), Patrick's Address to the Soldiers, para. 7, p. 97; para. 15, p. 102; para. 21, p. 105.
95 Thomas, *And Shall These Mute Stones Speak?*, pp. 265, 294–95.
96 Padel, *A Popular Dictionary of Cornish Place-Names*, p. 106.
97 Preston-Jones and Okasha, *Corpus of Anglo-Saxon Sculpture*, pp. 163–64.
98 *Ibid.*, pp. 159–63.
99 Orme, *The Saints of Cornwall*, pp. 238–39.
100 Michel Priziac, *Bretagne des Saints et des Croyances* (Grâces-Guincamp: Ki-Dour Éditions, 2002), pp. 165–66.

101 *Ibid.*, pp. 552–53.
102 Rees, *Celtic Saints of Wales*, pp. 91–93.
103 Orme, *The Saints of Cornwall*, pp. 101–02.
104 Meyrick, *A Pilgrim's Guide to the Holy Wells of Cornwall*, no. 112, p. 90.
105 Historic England, 'A Henge Re-used as a Medieval Playing Place, 75 m North East of Castle Hill Farm', no. 1006684, 2019.
106 *Ibid.*
107 Olson and Padel, 'A Tenth-Century List of Cornish Parochial Saints', pp. 59–60.
108 Orme, *The Saints of Cornwall*, pp. 67, 191–92.
109 Gilbert H. Doble, *Saint Mewan and Saint Austol*, Cornish Saints Series, 8, 2nd edn (Long Compton: King's Stone Press, 1939), pp. 5–11.
110 *Ibid.*
111 Pierre-Roland Giot, Philippe Guignon and Bernard Merdrignac, *The British Settlement of Brittany* (Stroud: Tempus, 2003), p. 246.
112 Doble, *Saint Mewan and Saint Austol*, p. 11.
113 Jacques Charpy, ed., *Patrimoine Religieux en Bretagne* (Rennes: Éditions Ouest-France, 1998), p. 91.
114 Priziac, *Bretagne des Saints et des Croyances*, pp. 326–31.
115 Olson and Padel, 'A Tenth-Century List of Cornish Parochial Saints', pp. 51–52.
116 Orme, *The Saints of Cornwall*, pp. 223–24.
117 Orme, *Cornwall and the Cross*, p. 14.
118 *Ibid.*, pp. 38–39.
119 St Clement of Rome, Letter to the Corinthians ch. 44. 2. Andreas Lindemann, 'The First Epistle of Clement', in *The Apostolic Fathers: An Introduction*, ed. Wilhelm Pratschler (Waco, TX: Baylor University Press, 2020), pp. 47–69.
120 Padel, *A Popular Dictionary of Cornish Place-Names*, p. 151.
121 Olson and Padel, 'A Tenth-Century List of Cornish Parochial Saints', p. 46.
122 Orme, *Cornwall and the Cross*, p. 20.
123 Gilbert H. Doble, *The Saints of Cornwall, Part 2: The Saints of the Fal* (Truro: Dean and Chapter of Truro Cathedral, 1962), pp. 120–34.
124 Padel, *A Popular Dictionary of Cornish Place-Names*, p. 69.
125 Orme, *The Saints of Cornwall*, p. 90.
126 Thomas, *And Shall These Mute Stones Speak?*, pp. 244–45, 270.
127 Historic England, 'Early Christian Memorial Stone and Wayside Cross in St Clement's Churchyard', no. 1015459, 2019.
128 Orme, *The Saints of Cornwall*, pp. 156–57.
129 Priziac, *Bretagne des Saints et des Croyances*, p. 297.
130 Albert le Grand, *Les Vie, Gestes, Mort et Miracles des Saincts de la Bretagne Armorique* (Nantes: Pierre Doriou, 1637), pp. 506–09.
131 The manuscript containing *Bewnans Ke*, NLW MS 23849D, was donated to the National Library of Wales in 2000.
132 Graham Thomas and Nicholas Williams, eds, *Bewnans Ke: The Life of St Kea, a Critical Edition with Translation* (Exeter: University of Exeter Press, 2007), pp. xxii, xliv, xlix.
133 *Ibid.*, pp. xxxiii, xli.
134 Meyrick, *A Pilgrim's Guide to the Holy Wells of Cornwall*, no. 74, p. 64. Meyrick notes that it 'was filled in when Mrs Doggrell slipped there some time back'.
135 Thomas and Williams, *Bewnans Ke*, pp. ix, xxviii, xli, xliii.
136 Orme, *Cornwall and the Cross*, p. 53.
137 Historic England, 'The Holy Well of St Mylor at approx. 50 m north of the Church of Saint Mylor', no. 1141639, 2019.

138 Florian Le Roy, *Bretagne des Saints* (Paris: Éditions André Bonne, 1987), pp. 208–11.
139 Alain Dag'Naud, *Guide des Lieux Insolites et Secrets de Bretagne* (Luçon: Éditions Jean-Paul Gisserot, 2002), p. 52.
140 Priziac, *Bretagne des Saints et des Croyances*, pp. 319–23.
141 Olson and Padel, 'A Tenth-Century List of Cornish Parochial Saints', pp. 44–45.
142 Padel, *A Popular Dictionary of Cornish Place-Names*, p. 150.
143 *The Psalms: A New Translation*, ed. The Grail (London: Collins/Fontana, 1963), p. 68.
144 *The Liber Usualis*, ed. The Benedictines of Solemes (Tournai: Desclée, 1950), p. 1200.
145 Meyrick, *A Pilgrim's Guide to the Holy Wells of Cornwall*, no. 69, p. 62.
146 Historic England, 'Holy Well 80 m East of St Just Church', no. 1020713, 2019.
147 Priziac, *Bretagne des Saints et des Croyances*, p. 341.
148 Orme, *Nicholas Roscarrock's Lives of the Saints*, p. 151.
149 William J. Watson, *The History of The Celtic Place-Names of Scotland* (Edinburgh: Birlinn, 1993), p. 260.
150 Lucy Toulman-Smith, ed., *The Itinerary of John Leland* (London: G. Bell, 1907–19), vol. 1, p. 200.
151 Orme, *Nicholas Roscarrock's Lives of the Saints*, p. 87.
152 Historic England, 'Holy Well Cottage', no. 1136576, 2002; Historic England, Pastscape, 'Chapel of St Mawes or Mauditus', 2015.
153 Historic England, Pastscape, 'Chapel of St Mawes'.
154 Meyrick, *A Pilgrim's Guide to the Holy Wells of Cornwall*, no. 71, p. 63.

CHAPTER 7

West Cornwall, the Scilly Isles, Guernsey and Jersey

In this final chapter, early Christian sites in western Cornwall will be examined, beginning in the Hayle estuary on the north coast. We shall continue westwards round the coast to Penwith, where inscribed stones and other early evidence of Christianity can be found. We shall then focus on the Lizard: it is named after a village at its southern tip. 'Lizard' derives from *lys ardh*, meaning 'court on a height': this indicates that it was a significant secular centre in early times.

Much of the eastern region of the Lizard was named Meneage, or 'land of the monks', and we shall explore some implications of this. On the Lizard's south and west coast, two small churches are named after the Breton saint, Guénolé. His own monastery of Landévennec in Brittany has been excavated, and we shall examine its development from a group of hermits into a community, in order to throw light upon the possible evolution of early Cornish monasteries.

Finally, early Christian sites on the Scilly Isles, Guernsey and Jersey will be described. The Channel Islands demonstrate a remarkable juxtaposition of prehistoric and Christian sacred sites, while the Scillies eventually became a centre for pilgrimage. After completing a survey of the significant, though disparate, surviving fragments of evidence of early Christianity in south-west Britain, we shall be in a position to at least glimpse the lives of the women and men who were the first Christians in the region. As it happens, some of our earliest evidence is to be found in west Cornwall, particularly around the Hayle estuary.

The Hayle estuary: a Roman port

The name Hayle derives from the Cornish *heyl*, meaning a river mouth, or estuary; its name was later transferred to the entire estuary.[1] It provided a safe harbour from prehistoric times and a focus for settlement, trade and shipping, since it is one of the few large natural ports on the north Cornish coast. In recent years a number of late Roman coins have been discovered at various sites in Phillack, a mile to the north of Hayle, with an unusual number from eastern Mediterranean mints, such as Heraclea in modern Turkey and the port of Alexandria in Egypt: these are rarely found in Britain. This suggests that the Hayle estuary might have been a Roman port, having direct maritime trade links with the Mediterranean in the fourth century AD.[2]

Until recently, such links were known to exist in post-Roman times, in the fifth and sixth centuries – there have been extensive finds in Cornwall of eastern

Mediterranean imported pottery from this later period – but the coin finds at Phillack are a century earlier. The coin from Heraclea is a copper alloy *nummus* (one of low value – a 'copper') from the reign of Constantine the Great, dating between AD 330 and 333, while that from Alexandria is a similar coin from the reign of Constantine II, dating from about 340. They might have been lost in Phillack or they could have been exchanged by seaborne traders who landed in the Hayle estuary.[3]

The small Iron Age hill fort at Carnsew on the north-west side of Hayle commands the entrance to the estuary. The fort may have remained in use until late Roman times: a hoard of several thousand coins, apparently deposited in the late third century, was found in a bronze container a little to the west of the fort. The estuary continued to be an important trading centre, especially in the fifth to the seventh centuries. It has been suggested that Carnsew fort may have been a centre of secular power within the post-Roman kingdom of Dumnonia, with a significant role in the distribution of Mediterranean imports to western Cornwall.[4]

Early Christians at Carnsew fort

At the foot of Carnsew fort, on its eastern side, a Christian memorial slab was discovered in 1843; it is now in Hayle Heritage Centre. The granite pillar was associated with a long-cist grave that was lined and covered by flat slabs, and contained sand, charcoal and ashes; the grave was covered by a mound of stones.[5] The style of the inscription on the pillar suggests that it was carved in the late fifth or early sixth century, considerably earlier than other Cornish memorial stones; its phrasing recalls monuments found on mainland Europe. It refers to a woman whose name, Cunaide, is possibly Irish; this is one of two Cornish inscriptions that commemorates a woman, the other being at Tregony.[6]

On the upper part of the narrow pillar, two mineral veins form a natural cross: their position may have been deliberately borne in mind when the stone was selected and shaped. The exposed face bears a lengthy shallow inscription of ten lines in capital letters across the width of the stone; it reads [HI]C [PA]CE [-] REQUIEVIT CUNAIDE HIC [IN] TUMULO IACIT VIXIT ANNOS XXX III. This can be translated as 'here in peace lately went to rest Cunaide. Here in this grave she lies. She lived 33 years'. The wording resembles that found on monuments in Gaul, and suggests the presence of a group of Christians in the Hayle estuary, perhaps from northern Gaul.[7]

Christian leadership in northern Gaul

We know almost nothing about Christian leadership in Cornwall during this early period, but texts from northern Gaul describe bishops, communities and solitaries; they might provide us with parallels for Britain. During the second half of the fifth century, a soldier named Sidonius Apollinarus (*c.* 430–*c.* 489) became bishop of Clermont-Ferrand in Gaul. He wrote poems and letters, and in a poem that he wrote to an older monk, Faustus of Riez (*c.* 410–*c.* 495), he describes the different locations where hermits live – in the African desert, in marshes such as those with which he was familiar around the mouth of the River Loire, in caves or on Alpine mountain slopes.

There are a number of early hermits' caves around the British coastline, including a dramatic Welsh example at St Govan's Head, Pembrokeshire, where a tiny chapel is wedged on a narrow cleft halfway down the cliff; it may date from the eleventh century, but its foundations are earlier.[8] There are a number of hermits' caves in Scotland around the Fife coast, where the soft rock eroded in various places to create caves: at Pittenweem, East Wemyss and at Caiplie, near Anstruther, for example. At Caiplie there are two caves, close to the beach, with early crosses inscribed on their walls (see colour plate 15).[9]

Faustus may have been born in Britain; he was abbot of the highly esteemed monastery of Lérins on the island of Saint-Honorat in southern Gaul, in what is now the French Riviera. Faustus later became bishop of Riez in Provençe. His British contemporary, Patrick also appears to have trained as a monk in Gaul, for he tells us: 'I was all set to … go to Gaul, to visit the brethren and see the face of my Lord's saints'.[10] It appears that, at this early date, Gaulish monasteries could offer British monks a more thorough formation than could be acquired at home.

Sidonius and hermits

In the poem to Faustus, Sidonius recalls the great models of sainthood from which the abbot can take encouragement. Faustus had a reputation on account of his austerity, and Sidonius does not conceal his admiration for Faustus. The poem of Sidonius is of particular interest for its account of the various locations in which hermits might be found, and for its assumption that an abbot such as Faustus might also be a hermit. It was accepted that some abbots would spend Lent alone: St Cuthbert's Isle off the larger island of Lindisfarne (Northumberland), inaccessible except at low tide, is a later example of such a hermitage chosen by an abbot (see colour plate 16).

Sidonius writes to Faustus:

> Whether you stay, roughly clothed, in the inhospitable wilderness beside the sun-baked Syrtes [a shallow sea off the north African coast], or whether you choose a green, slimy marsh, or clefts of rock, with deep sunless caves in perpetual gloom, or if you choose the Alps, whose steep mountain ranges stretch far into the distance, yet all these will tremble before you, great hermit, as you snatch a brief sleep on the chilly ground, and with all their cold they can never overcome the warm glow that Christ has put in your heart.
>
> For this is the way that you are urged to live by the Prophet Elijah and John the Baptist, by the two great Abbots Makarios … Again, you are called to this by Antony [of Egypt], who wore nothing but a tunic made of palm leaves from the kind hand of [God] his Master.[11]

Sidonius uses the Latin word *tesqua* to describe these different kinds of wilderness. This word often appears in pre-Christian literature, but was rarely used by Christians. The only other time that *tesqua* appears in a Christian

ILLUS. 126 *(opposite).* Llanllŷr, Ceredigion: contract stone, whereby Ditoc's 'little desert' is gifted to a monastery.

context is a century later, when St Isidore of Seville (*c.* 560–636) explains its meaning in his *Etymologies*: '*Tesqua* is called by some a hut and by others a rough and wild place'.[12] Thus he describes it as both a hermitage and a *desertum*, or 'empty place'.

A Welsh hermit

The word *tesqua* occurs once in Wales, in its diminutive form *tesquitus*, meaning 'a little desert', on a pillar stone at Llanllŷr (OS 542560), 5 miles north of Lampeter in Ceredigion. The pillar dates from between the seventh and the ninth century, and the word *tesquitus* is used to describe the marshy desert dwelling of a hermit named Ditoc, in the broad valley of the River Aeron. Its Latin inscription is one of the few surviving examples of a *contractus*, or a text used as a charter. The stone commemorates Ditoc, who by now had probably died, and describes how the plot's owner, Aon, gifts the land to the monastery of an Irish saint, Modomnóc (illus. 126).

The inscription is carved in round half-uncials, neatly picked. It reads downwards: TESQUITUS DITOC/ MADOMNUACO/AON FILIUS ASA/ITGEN DEDIT, or 'The small hermitage of Ditoc [which] Aon, son of Asa Itgen gave to [Saint] Modomnóc'. The names on the monument are Irish, which might have been expected in the Irish-speaking kingdom of Dyfed, south of the River Teifi, but is less common north of the Teifi, in Ceredigion; this suggests that Ditoc was an Irish hermit living in exile outside Pembrokeshire. Sadly, the second half of the memorial slab was broken up and recycled as building stone before its value was recognised.[13]

The variety of vowed life

Isidore of Seville informs us that the dwelling of a single vowed person was also considered to be a monastery. In his *Etymologies* he observes:

> A monastery *(monasterium)* is the dwelling of one monk, for *mónos* is Greek for 'alone' *(solus)*. It is the dwelling of a solitary *(solitarius)*. 'Convent' *(coenobium)* seems to be a compound of Greek and Latin. It is the habitation of a

> number of people living in common, for *koinos* in Greek means 'common'.[14]

Isidore's *Etymologies* were well known in early British monasteries from the mid-seventh century onwards: Bishop Aldhelm draws on them in his Riddles (or *Aenigmata*), and some thousand manuscript copies of the *Etymologies* survive from the medieval period.

The Greek and Russian Orthodox Churches retain Isidore's concept that a monk may live alone, in the 'cell of his heart'. The Russian metropolitan archbishop, Anthony Bloom (1914–2003) considered himself primarily as a monk: he made monastic vows in 1939, although he did not belong to a community. He was ordained a priest nine years later and consecrated as bishop nine years later still. Though common in the Orthodox Churches, this type of monastic life is described scornfully in the Rule of Benedict:

> They live in twos or threes, or even singly, without a shepherd, in their own sheepfolds and not in the Lord's ... whatever enters their mind or appeals to them, that they call holy; what they dislike, they regard as unlawful ... In their works they still keep faith with the world, so that their tonsure marks them as liars before God.[15]

Despite these strong words in the Rule of Benedict, this freer form of vowed life was more prevalent in Europe than the newer monastic life that the Rule was designed to promote. It may have been the norm in pre-Saxon Britain.

We do not know where Patrick trained in Gaul, but the monastery at Lérins, of which Faustus was abbot, played a central role in promoting the semi-solitary life of the Egyptian Desert Mothers and Fathers. The *Ratio de cursus qui fuerunt eius auctores* (or 'Explanation of the liturgies, about who were their authors'),[16] written before 767 by an Irish monk living in Italy, tells us that Egyptian monastic life spread from the island of Lérins to Ireland and elsewhere, and that many monks and future abbots trained at Lérins.[17] Another important figure in the evolution of semi-solitary monastic life was John Cassian (*c.* 360–433), who studied monastic life in Egypt and established two monasteries in Marseilles, one for men and the other for women.

Early Christianity at Phillack

Returning to the Hayle estuary, Phillack may have been the site of an early monastery; its church is sheltered by sand dunes in the river mouth beside Hayle's East Pool. While Carnsew fort may have been a centre of secular power, Phillack was perhaps a complementary religious centre. The church was the focus for more than a hundred early cist burials, found within the current churchyard and beyond. A stone carved with the *chi-rho* symbol for Christ dates from the fifth century: it may have come from a larger tombstone, and is now set into the outside wall of the church, above the entrance. It resembles similar carvings in mainland Europe and the eastern Mediterranean.[18]

During excavation in 1973 along the southern curve of the churchyard wall, a number of pre-Norman long-cist graves were found, some cut into the bedrock. Close to them, part of the rim of a vessel of imported red slipware from Phocaea (a city on the west coast of Anatolia, Turkey) was found, dating to the late fifth or early sixth century.[19] Finds of imported pottery of this date reflect links with the eastern Mediterranean: perhaps Cornish tin was traded for wine, oil, and pottery. Contact with the Mediterranean probably facilitated the early development of Christianity.[20]

An inscribed grave marker stands outside the vestry at Phillack; the coarse granite slab is likely to date from the first third of the seventh century, and its inscription reads CLOTUALI MOBRATTI, or '[the stone] of Clotualus Mobrattus'. These are British names, the first meaning 'worthy of fame' and the second perhaps an epithet 'great in judgement'. The pillar stone may commemorate someone important in the tribe; it suggests that Phillack with its harbour was a significant settlement in post-Roman Cornwall.

A possible monastic site

The concentration of early medieval evidence suggests that Phillack was an early Christian centre and burial site from the fifth century onwards, perhaps comparable with early Welsh monasteries of a similar date. Life at two such monasteries, Llanilltud Fawr and Ynys Pyr (or Caldey Island), where St Samson received his training, was described in chapter four. Of the two, Llanilltud Fawr was larger, more intellectual and the burial place of kings, while Caldey was smaller and more eremitical. If there was a monastery at Phillack, its material remains suggest a lifestyle containing elements of both these Welsh communities: a large cemetery, early monuments and a chieftain's burial are reminiscent of Llanilltud Fawr with its collection of inscribed stones, but, as at Caldey, there is no surviving evidence at Phillack of scholarship or of outstanding leaders, although much Cornish documentary evidence has either been lost or never existed.

The Cornish-language name for the two churches at Phillack and Hayle was Egloshayle; as we have seen, the name applied to the entire Camel estuary. Phillack was recorded as *Egglosheil* or 'church on the estuary' in about 1170, as preserved in a thirteenth-century document.[21] The prefix *eglos-* derives from the Latin *ecclesia*, meaning 'church community'; churches with this prefix are generally considered to date from about the tenth century, but the archaeological evidence at Phillack indicates that this is an exception. The names of most known early monastic sites contain the element *lan*, rather than *eglos*: the prefix *lan-* was used from about the sixth century until the twelfth, at the latest.[22]

Phillack continued as a high-status church in the tenth and eleventh centuries, with several examples of Anglo-Saxon sculpture, including a coped hogback tombstone. A fine wheel-head cross just inside the churchyard dates from the late eleventh century: it depicts the crucified Christ (illus. 127). The wheel-head is pierced by four holes; unusually, only the upper two holes fully pierce the head. Another unusual feature is that its shaft is square in section, not rectangular. The proportions of the monument and the figure of Christ resemble those

ILLUS. 127. Wheel-headed cross, Phillack.

of the 'Runhol' cross at Lanherne, illustrated on page 193, which originally came from the neighbouring parish of Gwinear. The 'Runhol' cross may have been its model.[23]

On its west face, Christ is carved with arms outstretched and wearing a tunic; his legs and out-turned feet extend down onto the shaft. The east face is decorated with five raised bosses, one on each limb and one at the intersection of the limbs, to represent the five wounds of Christ. Much of the rest of the cross is decorated with plaitwork. A rectangular granite slab with a crucifixion incised on it may have formed part of an altar; it perhaps dates from the eleventh or twelfth century.[24] The present church is Norman.

In the tenth-century list of forty-eight saints, the settlement's patron saint was named *Felec*. By the thirteenth century, *Felec* was equated in Latin documents with the female saint, Felicity, but in vernacular records the original spelling of *Felec* reappeared in the fourteenth century and was frequently used from the early sixteenth century onwards.[25] Phillack's holy well is south of the church, across the road (OS 845397). In the tenth-century list of saints, *Felec* and *Guidian* are paired: each is a local saint, honoured at only one site. *Guidian* is likely to be the patron of St Gothian's chapel at Gwithian, the neighbouring parish 2 miles north of Phillack, where a sequence of church buildings and burials from early medieval times onwards lies beneath the sand dunes.[26]

Anta and Euny of Lelant

Situated on the western side of the entrance to the Hayle estuary, Lelant means 'church site of Anta'; it is named *Lananta* in about 1170, in a charter granting it to the Benedictine priory at Tywardreath, near Fowey.[27] The present church dates from about 1100 and its rectangular graveyard, raised 1.5 m above the surrounding land, may preserve the rectangular platform of a Roman coastal fort that was positioned to control access to the estuary. However, it appears that this was not the original site of Anta's church:

ILLUS. 128. Head of a medieval wayside cross, Lelant churchyard.

during the laying of a railway cutting closer to the shore in 1875, a cist-grave cemetery was uncovered, dating from the fourth or fifth century AD, and what may have been a pre-Norman chapel was found, 300 m north of the present church. Erosion or blowing sand may have caused the inhabitants to move further inland.[28]

In 1170 Thomas Becket, archbishop of Canterbury, referred to Lelant as 'the church of Saint Euni' (*Sanctus Eunius*). We hear nothing more of the earlier saint, Anta, until about 1496, when a chapel at a spot later known as Chapel Ainger or Black Rock had been built in his or her honour on the rocks of Lelant's shoreline at the entrance to the Hayle River; it was erected by the guild of St Anta, as a guide for boats entering the estuary.[29] By contrast, Euny was venerated in at least five locations in west Cornwall: his earliest dedication appears to have been at Lelant.

By the fifteenth century, Euny was thought to be buried at Lelant, since William Worcestre noted in 1478:

> St Euny, brother of St Erth, lies in the parish church of St Euny near Lelant village, upon the sea-shore, three miles from St Michael's Mount.[30]

The term *merther* often indicates not a martyr but a shrine where a saint was buried, and two churches are named Methereuny – the parish church at Redruth and a tenth-century chapel in Wendron parish – although this term was not used at Lelant.[31]

The parish of Lelant was prosperous; it included St Ives, which had no church of its own. In the churchyard, the wheel-head of a medieval granite wayside cross survives; on its south face, a figure of Christ is carved in relief, with outstretched arms, his head inclined to one side; his body terminates abruptly at the lower edge of the cross-head, although originally the figure would have extended onto the shaft (illus. 128). The cross may once have stood on Trencrom Hill, 2 miles south-west of Lelant.[32]

Ia of St Ives, a Breton nun

St Ives is on the western shore of St Ives Bay, its harbour sheltered by a headland known as St Ives Island, where the Hayle estuary broadens out to the sea. An engraving from about 1840 conveys an impression of its location (illus. 129).[33] In 1284 St Ives was named *Porthya*, or 'Ia's harbour', while St Ives Bay was described in 1288 as '*roda* of *Sancta Ya*': *roda* is an English term meaning 'a road, or shipping lane'.[34]

ILLUS. 129. St Ives harbour, from an engraving, *c.* 1845.

St Ia is described as an Irish nun in a legendary Life of Gwinear composed by the Breton cleric Anselm in about 1300, but she is more likely to have been a Breton saint. A single Breton parish is named after her, that of Plouyé, or 'parish of Ia' in Finistère, some 30 miles from the west coast of Brittany; in 1337 its name was *Ploehie*. This is a large and probably early parish, at a pre-Christian site: close to the church, a tall Gallo-Roman pillar, perhaps dating from 300 to 200 BC, commemorates a Gaulish warrior (illus. 130). The church was rebuilt in the eighteenth century; it has a very large churchyard.

As we have seen, St Ives was a daughter church of Lelant, 2.5 miles to the north-west; perhaps because it was initially a dependent chapel of Lelant, there are no early references to the site; its present church was built between 1410 and 1434. In 1478, William Worcestre was told that Ia was buried here; he also observes:

> St Ives, sister of St Erth and [St Euny], lies in the parish of St Ives town, upon the north coast, about twelve miles from the western end of the kingdom of England; her feast-day is held on 3 February.[35]

John Leland, who visited Cornwall in about 1540, refers to Ia's 'legend', meaning a written Life; it has not survived.

Venton Ia (or Ia's well) is located in St Ives below the cemetery, near Porthmeor Beach (OS 514407). It consists of two recesses each containing a trough of water (illus. 131), and was restored in the late seventeenth century. In 1923 Sabine Baring-Gould wrote:

ILLUS. 130. Gallo-Roman column, Plouyé churchyard, Brittany.

> Venton Eia (S. Ia's well), on the cliff overlooking Porthmeor. – This ancient well, associated with the memory of the patron saint of the town (S. Ives), was formerly held in the highest reverence. Entries occur in the borough records of sums paid for cleansing and repairing it, under 1668 and 1692–3. On the last of these occasions the well was covered, faced, and floored with hewn granite blocks in two compartments. It is still known as 'the Wishing Well', from the old custom of divination by crooked pins dropped into the water.[36]

A plaque over the well notes that until 1843 the well was the main water supply to Downalong, the old name for this area of the town.

Fenton Ia, Troon

Nine miles east of St Ives, a smaller site with earlier structural remains is also named after Ia: a chapel and holy well named Fenton Ia was recorded in 1429, 1.5 miles south-east of Camborne. It is in a wooded gorge, on the east slope of a rushing stream, half a mile west of the village of Troon, near Chytodden Farm (OS 658381). Excavation in 1966 revealed a small square chapel with a stone floor and perhaps a timber superstructure, dating from the mid-tenth century. It was rebuilt in the twelfth century and extended in the thirteenth, when it may have served as a chapel for the residents of Troon.[37]

Excavation revealed a possible well in the chapel floor; otherwise, the 'holy well' may have been the stream itself, or a spring that is no longer visible. A 'cell' on the opposite bank of the stream might be the remains of a hermitage, or could have been a structure associated with the chapel. A tenth- or eleventh-century carved stone was said to be the altar frontal from the chapel; it is now at Camborne church, together with a twelfth-century cross from the site.[38] Thus St Ia appears to have been venerated from at least Saxon times.

Senara's cliff-top chapel at Zennor

Four miles west of St Ives, the church of Zennor, or *Senar* in Latin, is named after a local female saint – she has no other known dedications. In a charter of about 1210, contained in the Charter Roll of 1235, she is referred to as *Sancta*

ILLUS. 131. St Ia's well, St Ives.

Sinara; Senara may have been a nun. The churchyard follows the oval outline of an Iron Age enclosure, which is superimposed on an earlier field-system. It is a typical isolated rural Cornish church site, beside a road, with a farm and a few cottages; later this type of site was described as a 'churchtown'.[39] In about 1170, Robert Fitzwilliam, lord of Cardinham, gave the church to the prior and convent of Tywardreath, near Fowey.

A mile to the west of Zennor, on the isthmus connecting the mainland with Gurnard's Head, a spring is named in documents as a holy well, with the footings of a small chapel 100 m west of the spring (OS 434382). The chapel is in an artificially dug hollow which forms an oval enclosure 2 m deep, on the edge of the cliffs overlooking Treen Cove; its ruined walls are 0.5 m high. It is referred to in local records as 'Chapel Jane': its name may derive from the Cornish word *ynyal*, meaning 'wild, desolate'. Excavations in 1964 and 1966 produced pottery dating from about 1100 to about 1325; the chapel remained in use until at least the early sixteenth century.[40]

Charles Thomas, who assisted with the excavation, considered that the chapel may have been pre-Norman, in view of its small size (2 m by 5 m), its unmortared masonry and its remote situation; it may have started as a hermitage, or perhaps a well chapel, like that of Fenton Ia at Troon, which also stands within the remains of an oval enclosure.[41] At Chapel Jane, a large granite altar slab was probably set on a ledge in the east wall; an altar stone was found outside the north wall; some internal wall plaster survived. There was a stone bench against the north wall and a door in the south wall. The chapel was later enlarged westwards; the south door was blocked, and a new one inserted in the west wall. Over the extension, there may have been a tower with a light to guide ships. Parishioners of Zennor held an annual pilgrimage and feast at the chapel until the beginning of the nineteenth century.[42]

St Helen's oratory, Cape Cornwall

Eight miles south-west of Zennor there is another cliff-top chapel at Cape Cornwall, named after St Helen (OS 352318), although it does not seem to have been associated with St Helen before the eighteenth century. Cape Cornwall is a small headland a mile west of St Just in Penwith: until 200 years ago, it was believed to be the most westerly point in Cornwall. Pottery found in cist graves on the Cape have been dated to the late Bronze Age, while the presence of a hill fort on the cliffs at Kenidjack, just north of the Cape, suggests that the area was important in the Iron Age.

The chapel (see colour plates 17, 18) is a small building 6 m long by 4 m wide. It is constructed in a variety of styles – huge rounded boulders and mortared drystone walls of rubble, with finely dressed square granite stones at the external angles of the walls. The gable is topped with a rough cross of coarse granite that was found nearby. There are two square-headed windows in the west wall and a doorway to the south-west. To the south and west of the chapel is a level platform, where a dwelling is likely to be buried beneath the turf. An enclosure formed of a stone and earth bank adjoins the chapel and also surrounds the dwelling.[43]

A stone with a *chi-rho* monogram was found near the chapel: the slab was in the form of a rough cross-head, dating from about AD 500, but was subsequently lost. The two strokes of the *chi* each extended diagonally from one angle of the stone cross to the opposite one, dividing the face of the stone into four almost equal parts.[44] It was drawn by John Blight, who wrote:

> ... on the isthmus, the remains of an ancient chapel within its original enclosure, may still be seen... The building, with some modern additions, is now used as a cattle shed: it was known as St Helen's Oratory. In a water course near the ruins a small stone cross was found, supposed to have been the gable cross attached to this structure.[45]

A shaped boulder with a stone basin carved out from it, perhaps to contain holy water, was also found at St Helen's chapel and taken to the church at St Just.

Early Christians at St Just in Penwith

A mile west of Cape Cornwall, early monuments provide evidence of Christians living at St Just in Penwith in the sixth and seventh centuries. A memorial stone in the church dating from the mid-sixth century reads SENILVS [H]IC IACIT, or 'Senilus lies here'. The stonemason appears to have made an error, and omitted NI from the dead person's name but, realising his mistake, he inserted the missing letters, though smaller, above the text (illus. 132). On an adjacent face of the pillar stone, he carved an upright cross with T-shaped ends and a rounded loop, or *rho*, at the top, resembling a shepherd's crook; it is contained within a rectangular cartouche (illus. 133).[46]

A later memorial stone dating from about AD 700 was found near Carnyorth Farm on Boslow Common, 2 miles south-west of St Just (OS 392330). On one face of the four-sided stumpy stone, the name TAETUERA is inscribed in large, straggling half-uncial style: it illustrates the evolution of lower-case letters. Taetuera appears to be a primitive Cornish name: Charles Thomas has suggested that it may denote a priest.[47] An equal-armed cross with each arm ending in a T-shape is carved on another face of the pillar.

As we saw in the previous chapter, the name Justus, 'a just man', was a popular name for a Christian leader. The first surviving reference to the church of St Just in Penwith is in the Taxation of Pope Nicholas IV (1291), where it is described as *Ecclesia Sancti Justi*.[48] In 1478 William Worcestre heard that St Just was buried here. By now, he was held to be a martyr:

> St Just, martyr, lies in the parish of St Just; it is five miles west of Penzance, upon the coast of the westernmost part of England.[49]

Inside the church, the shaft of a cross dating from the first half of the tenth century now acts as a lintel over a recess in the north aisle. With its elaborate interlace patterns it resembles those in east Cornwall at St Neot and King Doniert's stone at St Cleer; however, it is some 60 miles south-west of the crosses at St Neot and St Cleer, and any relationship between them is unclear.[50]

Across the town square from the church, *Plain an Gwary* was a circular arena for performing medieval Cornish miracle plays. In 1769 the

ILLUS. 132. Memorial to Senilus, St Just in Penwith.

PHOTO: PAUL JOHNSON.

ILLUS. 133. Cross carved on the memorial to Senilus, St Just in Penwith.

PHOTO: PAUL JOHNSON.

antiquarian William Borlase noted six stone steps for seating; these are now replaced by a grassy bank. With its early Christian monuments, particularly that inscribed to Senilus, containing a *rho* symbol for Christ, there is likely to have been an early religious community at St Just that was of local importance in the far west of Cornwall.[51] However, as at other early Cornish sites, there is no evidence to indicate what type of community existed here, or who St Just might have been.

An early Welsh community at Llansadwrn

There is a possible parallel, however, on Anglesey, where the village of Llansadwrn, 3 miles west of Beaumaris, is named after an early Christian called Saturninus: this is a diminutive form – a sign of affection or of honour – of the name Saturnus.[52] Together with his wife, he may have founded a Christian community at the site. Sadwrn's unique tombstone, dating from the sixth century, was formerly in the churchyard and is now set in the chancel wall.[53] It is carved in Roman capitals and, unusually, commemorates his wife as well. The village church is surrounded by an oval bank, dating from early times; the tombstone is the earliest on Anglesey.

The couple's followers, who presumably erected the memorial, remembered them as inspiring leaders: the husband is described as blessed (*beatus*) and his wife was holy (*sancta*). It reads: HIC BEATUS [-] SATURNINUS SE[PULTUS I]ACIT ET SUA SA[NCTA] CONIU[N]X. PA[X VOBISCUM], or 'Here lies blessed Saturninus and his holy wife. Peace be with you both' (illus. 134).[54] This suggests a local couple who perhaps led a house church, a century after St Patrick and his family were doing so on their small estate near a village. Perhaps Justus or Senilus performed a similar role at St Just in Penwith.

What sort of Christian community might we find in early Cornwall in the sixth to the eighth centuries? As we saw in chapter four, the author of St Samson's Life describes how he inspired his family, including both men and women, married and single, to join him in spreading the Good News of the gospel. Over the centuries, religious life became increasingly formalised, but there is now a return to a more flexible form of living by so-called 'new communities' that include vowed men and women, married couples and individuals, living in small groups, for longer or shorter periods of time. They are sometimes ecumenical: an example of this is Chemin Neuf (or 'New Path'), founded in Lyons by a French Jesuit in 1973. Archbishop Justin Welby invited Chemin Neuf to form a community at his London residence of Lambeth Palace in 2014: in its combination of commitment with flexibility, it might resemble some early Christian communities in Cornwall and Wales.

ILLUS. 134. Memorial to Sadwrn and his wife, Llansadwrn, Anglesey.

A community at St Buryan

St Buryan is 5 miles south-east of St Just, and 2 miles from the south Cornish coast. Excavation has shown that the circular churchyard lies within a Romano-British earthwork, perhaps an enclosed farm; its surrounding ditch was found when the road was widened in 1984.[55] The saint's name first appears as *Berion* in the tenth-century list of saints; it was probably the principal pre-Norman church of Penwith. It is first recorded in a charter dating from the first half of the tenth century, which appears to confirm the status of a pre-existing religious community.[56] The twelfth-century martyrology of Exeter cathedral states that the son of the eighth-century Cornish King Gereint was cured of paralysis at Berion's intercession.[57]

If it is dedicated to a female saint, the early community could have been a women's monastery, either large or small. Hermits, particularly women, often lived in twos or threes throughout the medieval period: we learn from her autobiography that the Saxon nun, Christina of Markyate (*c.* 1096–*c.* 1135), who lived near St Albans in Hertfordshire, spent the first half of her vowed life among a network of small groups of hermits.[58] Even if St Buryan had been a larger community it might not have lasted, since women had few rights. Irish laws, for example, rarely allowed women to own land or pass it on. A nun might be given land for a monastery only for her lifetime; when she died, the land reverted to the men in her family who had given it to her.[59]

Alternatively, St Buryan might have been a community of both men and women, as could be found in sixth-century Brittany. In such monasteries, men and women lived separately, but came to church to chant the offices together and celebrate eucharist. They were often led by an abbess: she might be a royal widow, and therefore older and more experienced than the other monks and nuns, many of whom could be teenagers. At this time, women might be married at the age of twelve and men at fourteen, so they had to choose celibate religious life at a young age. Double monasteries were a north European form of religious life of which Theodore, the Greek archbishop of Canterbury, disapproved. On his arrival in England in 669, he found a number of them, often established by a woman of the local royal family.[60]

St Buryan is re-established

As we have seen, the monastery at St Buryan appears to have been re-founded in the mid-tenth century. A late copy of a charter claims that the grant was made by King Æthelstan in 943, though in fact he died four years earlier.[61] However, its wording appears genuine: the grant of land was 'in the place which is called *Ecclesia Sancte Beriane*' and is made 'to the honour of God and blessed Berian'. Typically, the land was granted not to human owners, but to the saint. In Domesday Book, St Buryan is listed as one of only twelve Cornish land-holding churches: the 'canons of *S. Berrione*' held the manor of *Eglosberrie* (or 'church of Buryan').[62]

It was claimed that Berion was Irish, but it is probable that she was either Cornish or Breton: the large parish of Berrien in Finistère may be named after her. However, the name of this Breton parish may mean *ber* (or 'raised plateau') of an owner called *Rien*, a name found elsewhere in Brittany.[63] Until the Reformation, St Buryan's church was served by canons under the authority of a dean; it became the mother church of two smaller parishes, Sennen and St Levan. However, community life at St Buryan church gradually ceased to exist: there were only four canons, including the dean, and by the thirteenth century these rarely or never went to St Buryan; poorly paid chaplains and clerks deputised for them in their absence.[64]

Early sculpture at St Buryan

Beside the path leading to the church, the remains of a coped, or roofed, tombstone can be seen; it dates from the late tenth or the eleventh century. It is decorated with a trailing plant that resembles the vine tendrils carved on the fine coped tombstone at St Tudy, illustrated in chapter five.[65] Inside the church, part of a twelfth-century arcade survives, with arches and a pillar, in the north wall of the later chancel (illus. 135).

The upper portion of a fine wheel-headed cross stands to the south of the church. It dates from the mid-tenth to the early eleventh century; it is well executed, and boldly carved, and the figure is well proportioned. The wheel-head is pierced by four small holes to create an equal-limbed cross: the lower limb is shaped to accommodate the lower half of the figure of Christ, who reigns from the cross, a triumphant warrior, clothed in a knee-length tunic, with arms outstretched to save (illus. 136).[66] The Saxons held fighting in high regard and, according to their theology, Christ was a young warrior hero, as we learn from the Saxon poem, 'The Dream of the Rood'.[67]

ILLUS. 135 *(left)*. Romanesque arches in the chancel, St Buryan church.

ILLUS. 136 *(right)*. Churchyard cross, St Buryan.

In the medieval period the four minster churches of St Buryan, Padstow, Probus and St Keverne were chartered sanctuary churches. Seven medieval crosses depicted on a sixteenth-century plan of St Buryan may mark the extended zone of sanctuary, which was about halfway between the church and its parish boundary; an inner circle of crosses marked the approach to the churchyard. The parish contained twenty-two crosses, most of which were on routes converging at the church, at intersections with tracks or streams. These were way-markers: none of them stood at the tenth-century charter-bounds of the parish. Many fields still retain the names of Cross Field or *Park an Grouse*.[68]

Berion's holy well is in a field a mile north-west of St Buryan (OS 393251), in the hamlet of Alsia; it provided the villagers with drinking water, and was also a healing well. Mothers came with weak and rickety children, to bathe them in the well: rickets was a common disease in childhood, caused by vitamin D deficiency, often as a result of swaddling babies and thus denying them sunshine. A nineteenth-century miller's daughter from Alsia recalled that village women fought with pilgrims to prevent them from dipping their babies into the well and contaminating the water.[69]

St Levan, a coastal hermitage

The hamlet of St Levan is on the coast, 3 miles south-west of St Buryan. This is an early landscape: *Salamun* is mentioned in the tenth-century list of forty-eight

ILLUS. 137. Fissured rock and twelfth-century cross, St Levan.

saints, and the names of a number of nearby hamlets and farms contain prefixes such as *Tre-* ('farmstead, or hamlet') and *Bod-* ('dwelling'). Names beginning with *Tre-* are likely to date from between the sixth and the eleventh centuries; those starting with *Bod-* may have been given during the earlier part of this period. The church is named *Selevan* in 1545: the saint's name derives from King Solomon in the Old Testament.[70] This may have been a monastic name, describing a wise and peaceful person: 'Solomon' originates from *shalom*, the Hebrew word for 'peace'. The Irish surname Sullivan also derives from Solomon.

The church is within a small curvilinear churchyard, in a sheltered hollow above the cliffs; its comparatively isolated setting suggests that Selevan may have been a hermit. The church was built beside a pre-Christian holy stone: a large fissured rock in the churchyard. Six tall, elegant crosses can also be seen in the churchyard, three at either door of the church. One of these stands almost 3 m tall, and the heads of two others survive. The finest cross, between the south door and the fissured rock, has a figure of Christ on the cross carved in relief, though it is not so well proportioned as figures on earlier crosses, below which are incised bold zigzag patterns (illus. 137); on the opposite face is an unusual carving in relief that resembles a slender medieval processional cross. The cross stands on a rough granite base in its original position; it dates from the twelfth century.[71]

Selevan's chapel and well

Across the road, a track leads down to a well-house and a spring (OS 380219), above Porthchapel, or Chapel Cove. The well-house is a small building, 1.5 m by 2 m, with an east doorway (see colour plate 19). It is constructed of granite boulders, set into a single granite floor slab. A spring wells up beside it, covered by granite lintels, and flows through a channel into the well-house. It overlooks the sea, which turns turquoise and azure as it pounds the white shingle of Porthchapel. Describing the well in about 1750, William Borlase observed:

> ...the water is reckon'd very good for eyes, toothach and the like, and when people have wash'd they are always advis'd to go into this chapel and sleep upon the stone which is the floor of it.[72]

Pilgrims were advised to sleep at the well in order to receive healing; this common practice was also recommended at nearby Madron. At this time,

Selevan's well was still roofed. It is possible that, together with the well-chapel of Constantine near Padstow, this is one of Cornwall's earliest Christian buildings.[73]

A flight of some fifty stone steps leads down from Selevan's well-chapel past a two-roomed structure, 30 m east of the well, also edged with granite boulders. The steps recall a similar feature at Kewstoke near Weston-super-Mare (Somerset), described in chapter three. Excavation of the small building at St Levan, carried out in about 1931, revealed a roughly flagged stone floor. It was built on an east–west axis, and one room may have been a chapel. The building and the flight of steps leading down to the cove may date from the seventh or eighth century.[74] This would have been a sheltered spot for a hermit, with easy fishing in the cove below, although it is also subject to dangerous currents.

Crosses at Sancreed

Returning inland, Sancreed is 2 miles north of St Buryan. The church is named *Eglossant*, meaning 'church of Sancred' in about 1176, as preserved in a thirteenth-century text.[75] The oldest part of the churchyard is a circular *lan* site, surrounded by a wall. It is higher inside than outside because of burials over centuries: this is likely to have been an early Christian graveyard.[76] We hear nothing of St Sancred until Nicholas Roscarrock, writing in the early seventeenth century, recorded a legend that Sancred became a hermit to atone for accidentally killing his father:

> Ther is a church dedicated to this sainte by the name of Sancred and a well also called of him in the hundreth of Penwith in Cornwall. I haue hard that they haue by tradition ther that he killed by misfortune his owne father, with which he was so moved as, abandoning the world, he became a hogherd and liued so exemplarly as he was after esteemed a sainte.[77]

Outside the church, a tall granite pillar commemorates a sixth-century Christian, but all that survives of its inscription is FILIVS [H]IC, or 'X, son of … [lies] here'.[78] The pillar was later inverted and in the late tenth or eleventh century it was shaped into a round-headed cross with a figure of Christ at the top. The monument may have been completed later still, with a tall fleur-de-lis in a vase added below the figure of Christ, perhaps in the late twelfth or thirteenth century.[79] A lily in a vase was a medieval symbol of Christ born from the womb of Mary.

Outside Sancreed church, another fine cross dates from the late tenth or eleventh century. On its south face, Christ crucified is carved at the top, with outstretched arms, and a halo around his head. He wears a tunic and has a band around the waist; his legs extend onto the top of the shaft and have out-turned feet. The middle panel of the shaft bears interlaced knots, and the lower panel contains an inscription in two horizontal lines. It is carved in an early medieval form of script derived from Roman-style capitals and reads RUNHOL; as we saw in the previous chapter, this may mean the 'patrimony' or 'inheritance' of

ILLUS. 138. Sancreed holy well.

the person or the saint commemorated here. The east side of the cross is decorated with a snake-like creature with an interlaced body and tail.[80]

The impressive range of its early Christian monuments implies that Sancreed served as a Christian focus for this upland part of Penwith, although no documentation survives to indicate an early monastery, unlike nearby St Buryan. Sancreed parish was in a significant location, crossed diagonally by two ancient routes: one led from St Just in the north-west to Paul and Mousehole (a departure point for Brittany) on the south-east coast and the other led from Sennen in the south-west, past Chapel Euny well to Madron and the Penzance area, on Penwith's north-east coast.[81]

Sancreed's holy well is across the road, 300 m south-west of the church (OS 414292), in an enclosure, down a steep flight of nine granite steps (illus. 138); the well is fed by a spring. The steps and well are roofed by granite lintels covered with earth; beside the well is an ancient thorn bush hung with clouties, or rags that represent prayers. There are remains of a small rectangular chapel, 3 m from the well.[82] The chapel walls are constructed of granite moorstone, with a doorway in the south side. The complex is thought to date from the eleventh or twelfth century.[83]

ILLUS. 139. Beehive hut adjoining the *fogou*, Carn Euny.

PHOTO: PAUL JOHNSON.

Carn Euny's ancient village

Two miles west of Sancreed, the ancient village of Carn Euny was inhabited from about 400 BC to AD 400. Ten stone houses date from between the second and fourth centuries AD: seven single-roomed round houses, and three larger 'courtyard houses'. This is a type unique to west Penwith: a drystone wall forms an oval courtyard, with a round house built into the wall opposite the entrance and lean-to structures along either side, which were probably store rooms, workshops or animal shelters. There was evidence of spinning, weaving and grinding corn; imported amphorae sherds suggest contact with the Roman world well before the conquest of AD 43, and it is likely that trade with Brittany, Wales and Ireland also flourished. The village was abandoned some time after the fourth century AD.[84]

An earlier *fogou* adjoins one of the courtyard houses; *fogou* is Cornish for 'cave'. This is a curved underground passage, 30 m long, excavated from the rock and lined and roofed with slabs of stone. *Fogous* are found in west Cornwall and in other parts of Britain, Ireland and Brittany where they are known as *souterrains*, from the French for 'underground'. They may have been used for storage or refuge, or for a religious purpose. Attached to the *fogou* at Carn Euny is a large corbelled beehive hut, roofed with massive stone slabs (illus. 139).[85]

Chapel Euny's twin wells

The twin wells at Chapel Euny, half a mile away (OS 399289), probably formed the water supply for the Romano-British village; the two wells are situated on either side of an ancient track. The more elaborate well (colour plate 20) has steps leading down to it and the second well is surrounded by four large granite slabs. A stream flows from the wells; the water is rich in iron, sulphates, calcium and arsenic. William Borlase visited the wells at Chapel Euny in the 1750s and wrote:

> It has a chapel adjoining it, dedicated to St. Euinus; the ruins of which, consisting of much carved stone, bespeak it to have been formerly of no little note. The Water has the reputation of drying humours, as well as healing wounds and sores.[86]

The lost medieval chapel was of an unusual design: an estate plan of 1778 shows a rectangular chapel facing east, with a long side room to the north that partially adjoined it; both were contained within a roughly oval enclosure. The chapel was in ruins by the nineteenth century, and dressed stone from it appears to have been moved to a new position round the top of the second well.[87]

In 1881 Robert Hunt described how children were brought to the wells for healing:

> On the first three Wednesdays in May, children suffering from mesenteric [intestinal] diseases are dipped three times, against the Sun [anticlockwise], and dragged three times round the well over the grass in the same direction.[88]

This is one of at least five cult centres named after Euny, who appears to have been a Cornish saint. The location of St Euny's twin wells on Sancreed's parish boundary, beside the early track leading from Sennen, past Chapel Euny to Madron and Penzance, suggests that Chapel Euny was an early feature in the landscape.[89]

Madron's noble warriors

Madron is 5 miles north-east of Chapel Euny, in moorland a mile north-west of Penzance. The church is dedicated to Madern, who may have been unique to this village, where people were named after him; even today, Maddern is a common surname in the area. Madron's raised churchyard was oval until it was extended in the 1820s. Although it is only a village today, Madron was the mother church of Penzance. Three inscribed memorial stones in the neighbourhood provide insight into the early community who worshipped here.

A thin slab of fine white granite inside the church, perhaps originally a pre-Christian standing stone, was reused in the seventh century to mark a Christian burial. It is 2 m tall and carved in an original style, with an incised cross at the top, its three arms decorated with trefoils. Below the cross, an ornamented cartouche encloses an inscription of three lines, to be read downwards. The first word, VIR, is unique in insular inscriptions: it appears to mean 'my husband' and suggests that a widow commissioned the monument for her late husband. The complete inscription reads VIR QUONFAL FILIUS VENNORCIT, or '[stone of my] husband Quonfal, son of Vennorcit'. Both are British names of highborn warrior chieftains: Quonfal is probably to be read as Conmael (or *Cunomaglus* in Latin), meaning 'Hound Lord', while Vennorcit means 'Fair Slayer'.[90]

A mile east of Madron, near the village of Gulval, a sixth-century inscribed stone at Bleu Bridge stands beside a track that leads east from the Penzance-Zennor road (OS 476317). The tall granite pillar is inscribed QUENATAVCI [H]IC DINVI FILIUS, or 'Quenataucus [lies] here, the son of Dinuus'; the names on this monument are also British. This is an example of a stonemason misjudging the size of his lettering: he began with over-large letters, so at the end of the vertical first line he had to place the horizontal 'I' of QUENATAVCI above the 'C', and squeeze in a tiny IC for [H]IC [IACIT].[91]

Two miles north-west of Madron, near the road from Madron to Morvah (OS 427353), a third early Christian granite memorial stone refers to two men of high class. It is known as *Mên Scryfa* (Cornish for 'inscribed stone') and stands 300 m beyond the *Mên-an-Tol* (or 'hole stone'), which may have formed part of a Bronze Age chambered tomb. The memorial may be a reused standing stone; it is believed to be in its original position. From the style of its lettering and the inscription, in two lines running downwards, it is considered to date from the mid-sixth century. It reads RIALOBRANI CVNOVALI FILI, or '[the stone] of Rialobranus, son of Cunovalus'. The names mean 'Royal Raven' and 'Valiant Hound', so the stone probably commemorates local sixth-century chieftains.[92] We can guess that Valiant Hound was fleet of foot.

These memorial stones commemorate individuals, but they are likely to indicate that much of this area was Christian by the sixth or seventh century. In early cultures, embracing a new belief system was a corporate act, not an individual one. In the Acts of the Apostles, Cornelius of Jaffa is baptised after being told that Peter 'has a message for you that will save you and your entire household' (Acts 11. 13). In Philippi, Lydia invites Paul to lodge with her 'after she and her whole household had been baptised' (Acts 16. 15). Philippi's jailer 'was baptised then and there with all his household' (Acts 16. 33).

In sixth- and seventh-century Britain, when a secular leader became Christian, his people were also baptised. In his *Ecclesiastical History of the English People*, completed in about 731, Bede relates how Archbishop Paulinus came from Canterbury to Northumbria and baptised King Edwin (586–633) at York on Easter Day in 627. Edwin's family and his nobles were baptised in their turn, and Paulinus spent the next six years, until Edwin's death, evangelising the region. Bede describes how Paulinus used Edwin's royal country seat at Yeavering for this purpose:

> So great was then the fervour of the faith… that [Archbishop] Paulinus at a certain time coming with the king and queen to the royal country seat, which is called Adgefrin [or Yeavering], stayed there with them thirty-six days, fully occupied in

catechising and baptising; during which days, from morning till night, he did nothing else but instruct the people, resorting from all villages and places, in Christ's saving word; and when instructed, he washed them with the water of baptism in the River Glen, which is close by.[93]

Madron baptistery

St Madern's baptistery is a mile north of the church, along a track. Before reaching it, one passes the spring, which rises in a marshy area surrounded by ancient sallow willows. Tied to the branches are hundreds of clouties, or strips of cloth: these are symbolic prayers for healing or in gratitude for a cure. In 1894 Madron well was said to be Cornwall's only ancient cloutie well.[94] By the 1980s this practice had begun at the wells of Alsia and Sancreed, and now it is widespread.[95] Cloutie wells almost always have a tree growing beside them, where rags are tied.

The pieces of cloth are often dipped in the well and then tied to a branch while a prayer is said to the spirit of the well – in Christian regions to God, but elsewhere to the local nature spirit. The sacred trees at British and Irish cloutie wells are usually hawthorn or blackthorn, though ash trees are also common.

ILLUS. 140. Eastern end of Madron baptistery, with altar, granite step and benches against the walls.

PHOTO: MARGARET REES.

This pre-Christian custom is still practised across Europe, Asia, Africa and South America.[96]

A channel conveys the spring water to Madern's chapel with its baptistery, 75 m further along the track (OS 445327). There are foundations of a solid stone building with a granite altar, stone benches along the side walls, a granite step raising the chancel from the nave, and a baptismal basin built into its south-west corner (illus. 140). A rectangular cavity in the altar was designed to contain a portable altar stone in order to celebrate the eucharist. The chapel is likely to be pre-Norman with twelfth-century additions, including the seats, altar and chancel division.[97]

The baptistery was partially demolished at the Reformation; in 1652 Francis Coventry noted a great thorn tree, whose branches formed a leafy roof over the chapel.[98] Each year, parishioners used turf to repair a green bank alongside the altar, which they called 'St Madern's Bed'. Sick people came to bathe in the well and sleep on the bed, and many were cured, including a cripple who recovered so completely that he enlisted in the army and was killed in action at Lyme Regis (Dorset) in 1644.[99] In 1750 the water from Madron spring was channelled down the long hill to form the first water supply for Penzance.

St Michael's Mount

St Michael the archangel's chief shrine in Cornwall was St Michael's Mount, on a tidal islet opposite Marazion, 2 miles east of Penzance (illus. 141, 142). Small amounts of Mediterranean pottery dating from the fifth to the seventh centuries have been found on the island: these fragments of imported post-Roman vessels suggest an elite residence, perhaps secular or monastic, or both. There was a chapel on the mount in the later medieval period, and another with associated buildings on the mainland opposite; it is not known which site is earlier.[100]

Both St Michael's Mount and Marazion are in the parish of St Hilary, 2 miles to the east. This church is partly enclosed by a rampart and may occupy the site of a Roman fort. Inside the church, a stone dating from the early fourth century records road maintenance in the time of the emperor Constantine the Great. It may have been associated with a Roman-controlled mining area around Godolphin Hill, a little to the east.[101] By the seventh century, the area had become Christian: in St Hilary churchyard a seventh-century memorial stone is inscribed NOTI NOTI, or '[the stone] of Notus, [son] of Notus'.[102] *Notus* can mean 'of note, notable', and could imply a prominent father and son.

A religious community probably existed on St Michael's Mount before the Norman Conquest; it was large enough to be recognised by the Saxon authorities and their Norman successors, and so to feature in documentary records. Domesday Book records that its manor of Truthwall was exempt from paying royal tax by 1086: this was a privilege typical of early Cornish monasteries and minster churches.[103] At this time it was one of twelve Cornish land-holding churches, in which the saint was considered to be a tenant-in-chief of the king.

ILLUS. 141. St Michael's Mount at high tide.

PHOTO: PAUL JOHNSON.

The mount and its priory were granted to the abbey of Mont Saint-Michel in Normandy, either by Edward the Confessor in a doubtful charter dating from about 1033 (he had not become king by this date), or by Robert, count of Mortain, in about 1070.[104]

Mont Saint-Michel was claimed to have been established in about 708 as a chapel on a tidal island, after Aubert, bishop of Avranches, had a vision of St Michael. St Aubert's chapel is on a rocky outcrop at the north-west of the mount, and his well inside its well-house is down by the shore, to the north. Under Charlemagne, the chapel was replaced by an abbey; in the tenth century, a group of Benedictines replaced its former canons. Between 1017 and 1144 the monks built a Romanesque abbey at the summit of the mount: the previous Carolingian building was incorporated as one of its crypts.[105]

Their Cornish daughter house developed at the same time: the church was built or rebuilt in 1135. Its monastery was staffed by a prior and a few monks from Mont Saint-Michel. It was apparently intended that thirteen monks should live there, but there were probably six or less. From the eleventh to the sixteenth century it was Cornwall's most frequently recorded pilgrimage centre; a legend arose that the mount was the site of one of the archangel Michael's three earthly appearances.[106]

St Michael's Mount became separated from its French mother house in 1383, after which it adopted St Aubert's foundation legend and claimed that the archangel instructed St Aubert to found his monastery at the Cornish site.[107] In the early seventeenth century Nicholas Roscarrock recounts how he climbed the mount and saw, at a high place on the rocks, the 'chair' on which the archangel sat:

ILLUS. 142. St Michael's Mount at low tide.

PHOTO: PAUL JOHNSON.

> There is a place in the west of Cornewall called St Micaeles Mount … severed from the land by the full sea and at low water by a plane Sand, a flight shott in brea[d]th, on which yow maye goe to it drye shodd. In the mayne Rock of that Mount there was a Seat which I haue seene, nether easie to clymbe vnto nor to sytt in, which is called St Michaels Chayre, where they saye he hath made his appearition, which caused it to be frequented as a great Pilgrimage.[108]

While one might think of a saint sitting to teach or pray, it is difficult to imagine an archangel doing so.

A Cornish nun at Breage

Breage is 3 miles west of Helston, and a mile from the coast. As an early religious centre, Breage might have functioned in relation to Helston, which was a seat of secular power, perhaps as early as the sixth century. Helston appears as *Henlistone* in Domesday Book, a name derived from the Cornish *hen lys*, or 'ancient court' with the later addition of the English *tún*, meaning 'farm, or manorial estate centre'.[109] Breage church is built within an oval graveyard and was named *Egglosbrec*, or 'church of Brec', in about 1170. Later legendary Lives relate that Brec came from Ireland together with Germoc and other saints honoured in nearby settlements, but she seems unique to Cornwall, and is honoured only at Breage. In 1478 William Worcestre heard that she was buried in the church:

> St Breage, virgin: the feast-day is held on 1 May; she lies in the church of that saint, four miles from St Michael's Mount.[110]

A Latin Life of Brec was composed in the fourteenth or fifteenth century, probably at or for Breage church, since it refers to places in the parish and depicts her as senior to neighbouring saints.[111] Breage was the mother church of Germoe, and in 1246 the earl of Cornwall also assigned the chapels of Cury and Gunwalloe to Breage. The head of an elaborately carved cross stands in the churchyard, though its decoration is largely eroded. This is because it is carved not from granite but from softer red sandstone, which might have come from the Roseland peninsula or from further afield. It is a wheel-head cross with five bosses on each side of the head; it dates from the tenth or eleventh century (see colour plate 21).[112]

ILLUS. 143. Roman stone recording road maintenance, Breage church.

The area surrounding Breage was occupied in Roman times: a third-century stone, perhaps recording road maintenance, fifty years earlier than that at St Hilary, was found about 300 m from Breage church, in which it now stands (illus. 143). It is inscribed IMP [C] DO NO MARC CASSI; when complete, it would have read '[to] the Emperor Caesar, our Lord Marcus Cassianus Latinius Postumus, pious, fortunate, august'. Postumus reigned between AD 258 and 268; this is the only stone dedicated to him to survive in Britain. It was probably associated with tin mining, like the similar stone at St Hilary. Christianity may have reached this area quite early, through contact with traders from the rest of the Roman empire.

Tin production appears to have intensified in Cornwall during the third and fourth centuries, at a time when the use of pewter objects was increasing, and when the Roman administration was less able to obtain tin from Spain. Four tin ingots were found at Praa Sands on the coast, 2 miles south-west of Breage. The ingots were probably associated with timbers that were radiocarbon dated to AD 600–790, which suggests that tin mining continued after the Romans departed. A larger group of ingots was found offshore at the mouth of the River Erme in south Devon, 6 miles south of Ivybridge: they resemble those from Praa Sands, and were found close to a post-Roman site of similar date. They had presumably come from a ship wrecked on the rocks in the Erme estuary.[113]

'Dear little Germoe'

Germoe is 2 miles west of Beage; it is first recorded in about 1176 as 'Chapel of *Sanctus Germoch*'.[114] The suffix *-oc* is an early hypocoristic, or pet name, meaning something like 'Dear little X'; St Germoc is not known elsewhere. In the first surviving list of Cornish churches, dating from 1291, one-fifth (about forty of them) were chapels that belonged to a larger church. Germoe is one such chapel: its parishioners paid tithes to the larger church and were expected to attend it – Breage, in this case – on certain occasions.[115]

In the mid-sixteenth century John Leland visited Germoe, where he observed that Germoc's tomb could still be seen, together with his 'chair' in the churchyard and his well outside it: 'S. Germochus a chirch … his tumb is yet seen ether …. S. Germok there buried'. Germoe is one of a number of quite minor Cornish churches at which the body of its patron saint was venerated.[116] The church contains an early Norman font, on which two faces are carved in relief (illus. 144); the church fabric dates from the twelfth century onwards.[117]

ILLUS. 144. Norman font, Germoe church.

PHOTO: GILLIAN JOHNSON.

Germoc's 'chair', noticed by Leland, is not a rough boulder but a small stone building in the churchyard, entered through a double archway and containing three seats in a recess (illus. 145). Above the central seat, a head is carved: by this time Germoc was believed to have been an Irish king. The unique building is likely to date from the early thirteenth century.[118] It might have been used during the Palm Sunday procession, during which, in medieval parishes, the priest and people paused at points round the churchyard to read the account of Palm Sunday from the gospels. Germoc's well is 3 m south-west of the church, beside the road (OS 584294).

St Corentin of Cury

Cury is 6 miles south-east of Breage, near the west coast of the Lizard; as we have seen, it was incorporated into Breage parish in 1246. 'Cury' is probably a pet form of the name of St Corentin, a Breton bishop. He is first mentioned in Wrdisten's late ninth-century Life of Guénolé; this is the only English church dedicated to him. It was named *Egloscuri*, or 'church of Cury', in 1219 and *ecclesia de Sancto Corentino* in 1284.[119] Cury's church stands within a raised oval enclosure in an exposed position, 60 m above sea level; there is a tall post-Norman cross in the churchyard.

The church is Norman with a fine Romanesque doorway (illus. 146). Its arch is decorated with a row of beads and another of lozenges; this encloses a tympanum, or sculptured panel, decorated with overlapping circles.[120] A wall-painting in Breage church, dating from the mid-fifteenth century, depicts Corentin as a bishop with his mitre, vestments and staff, accompanied by a fish, of which

ILLUS. 145. St Germoc's 'chair', Germoe churchyard.

he was said to have eaten a slice each day. The mural bears an inscription, *S[anc]te Quorentine ora pro nobis*, or 'St Corentin, pray for us'.[121]

ILLUS. 146. Norman doorway into Cury church.

Corentin, bishop of Quimper

In Brittany, Corentin is honoured as the first bishop of Quimper. According to his Life, written in the 1230s, Corentin was a hermit at Plomodiern in western Brittany on the slopes of the Ménez-Hom range, until King Gradlon asked him to become bishop of Quimper. On the outskirts of Plomodiern, a steeply roofed well-house is built over the spring beside which Corentin is said to have lived; a statue of the bishop stands on a niche inside the well-house. A damaged corpus of Christ on the cross is suspended from the ridge tiles, and two other saints flank the well-house. In front is a pool in which pilgrims could bathe; it is now dry (illus. 147).

Quimper is 20 miles to the south, at the mouth of the River Odet. Corentin's monastery may have been situated half a mile downstream from the present cathedral, at the church of Locmaria, near the river but on higher ground, in the eastern quarter of the Gallo-Roman town. Locmaria is an apsed Romanesque building that may have remained the bishops' seat until their successors moved upstream. A sherd of Samian ware engraved with a Christian symbol in fourth-century style was found near the church. In the ninth century there was a double community of monks and nuns at Locmaria who followed the Rule of Columbanus; later, they adopted the Benedictine Rule. Often, these two rules were combined. There is a chapel of St Columbanus near the church, surrounded by the foundations of Roman buildings.[122]

St Guénolé of Landewednack

Six miles south-east of Cury, at the southern tip of the Lizard, Landewednack commemorates the Breton saint Guénolé; the church is named *Ecclesiam Sancti Wynewali* in 1279. More Cornish churches and chapels are dedicated to Guénolé than to any other saint. They also include Gunwalloe on the west coast of the Lizard, Towednack, 2 miles south-west of St Ives, Gwynwala in Camborne and St Winnols in St Germans, but the sites are small, and perhaps date from no earlier than the tenth century; the Anglo-Saxon kings who ruled Cornwall in the late ninth and tenth centuries had close contacts with Brittany. Some of the sites may date from even later.[123]

ILLUS. 147. St Corentin's well, Plomodiern, Brittany.

ILLUS. 148. Norman arch over the doorway, Landewednack church.

Guénolé was considered to have been the first abbot of Landévennec, on the west coast of Brittany; he is thought to have lived in the sixth century, although the earliest information about him dates only to the ninth century. Landewednack (*Lan to-winnoc*) and Towednack (*To-winnoc*) preserve pet forms of Guénolé's name: *to* means 'thy' and *oc* is a diminutive term of endearment. Landewednack is the most southerly church in mainland Britain; it stands within a curvilinear graveyard surrounded by a wall constructed from boulders. The earliest feature of the church is a twelfth-century Norman doorway; its arch is decorated with zigzag patterns, crosses within circles and other designs (illus. 148). A medieval cross marks the road down to the church, which stands above Church Cove, a narrow rocky cove with a slipway for boats.

The monastery at Landévennec

No early Cornish monasteries have been excavated, but that of Landévennec has produced remarkable evidence that provides a useful parallel to the evolution of monastic life in Cornwall. Landévennec's early texts are also valuable: its scriptorium was especially productive in the second half of the ninth century, when its abbot Wrdisten produced at least three versions of the Life of St Guénolé, including a *Vita major* of Guénolé 'at the unanimous request of his brothers'. It is written in poetic Latin prose, with sections in verse, and is the earliest surviving complete example of a saint's Life in metrical prose, a genre that had become popular under Charlemagne.[124]

It appears that Guénolé took part in the migration from Devon and Cornwall to Brittany. He settled with some disciples on the small island of Tibidy, which is in a sheltered spot at the mouth of the River Faou; it is now connected to the mainland by a causeway. The monks then sailed across the broad river mouth to Landévennec, where there was more land to grow food. The first monastery at Landévennec was on the site of, or beside, a Gallo-Roman villa, now lying beneath the modern village; it is likely that a noble family gave their property to the founding monks.[125]

Excavation indicated that the monastery was established in the late fifth century, at which time the villa was probably still habitable. Only the church and cemetery of the first monastery have been discovered; the monks may have lived and worked in the existing villa buildings, or they may have lived singly in simple huts. In the following centuries, Roman material from the villa was recycled: Roman roof tiles were reused, as were *tubuli*, or flues from the wall shafts of the heating system in the bath suite. In the tenth-century abbey choir, Roman cut stones were used as bases for pillars, and Gallo-Roman bricks became floor tiles.[126]

Evolution from eremitic to community life

Communities of hermits such as those who first lived at Landévennec were subject to canonical regulations. In 405 the Council of Vannes decreed that monks could leave their community and withdraw to a solitary retreat (*solitarias cellulas*) with their abbot's approval, but they must live within the boundary of the monastery and under its authority. The early acts of Landévennec describe a central complex surrounded by satellite hermitages, all named 'monasteries'. Over the next three centuries, the monks gradually evolved a more communal lifestyle.[127]

At the end of the sixth century, the monks moved from their original villa site, which was on the north side of a small valley, to the present site at the bottom of the valley, where the monks could utilise the lower course of the stream for their water supply. In the mid-seventh century, they built a mill on the south side of the stream, with a farm and workshops. Cattle farming and agriculture were undertaken from the late sixth or mid-seventh century. These developments indicate the vitality of the monastery and the generosity of its benefactors; they also indicate how the monastery was growing away from its earlier eremitic origins.[128]

The first chapel may have been a wooden building on stone foundations. It was enlarged and rebuilt in stone in the late seventh or early eighth century; both the oratory and graveyard remained on this site until the fourteenth or fifteenth century. The original enclosure is preserved on the seashore side; it probably consisted of a wooden fence, or boarding, built on stone foundations. In the mid-eighth century, the farm on the southern slope was moved further back, and replaced by a building which appears to have housed kitchens and perhaps a refectory: these bordered the stream.[129]

Landévennec becomes a Benedictine abbey

An edict issued by Louis the Pious in 818 imposed the Benedictine Rule on the monastery, which continued to evolve. A large church was built, linked to a new eastern enclosure, bounded by a strong wall with a fortified gateway. The oratory was rebuilt and connected to the church as an additional chapel. The relics of St Guénolé were transferred from the ancient oratory into the chancel of the new church. Here they became a focal point for pilgrimage: people could file past the saint's tomb in an orderly manner.[130]

The new building was extended over the stream and up its south bank, to connect with the farm buildings; it housed a new refectory and kitchens. The whole monastery had now become an enclosed square with a central court, bordered by galleries with colonnades. The later Romanesque and Gothic abbeys built on the site retained this plan. The stream now ran through the monastery building; its channel was covered by large slates (illus. 149). In the ninth century a well was dug, near what was now the east end of the church (illus. 150); this was useful, since it could provide water for the baptismal font at the entrance to the choir.[131]

ILLUS. 149. Stream crossed by a ninth-century slate bridge, Landévennec.

'Like the Egyptian monks'

The gradual evolution of the monastery from a sixth-century Gallo-Roman estate occupied by eremitical monks to a ninth-century Benedictine abbey is also reflected by the range of manuscripts in the abbey library, which include the *Apophthegmata* (or 'Sayings') of the Desert Fathers, the Rule of Caesarius of Arles, the Rule of Columbanus and the Rule of Benedict. In his Life of Guénolé (*c.* 860), Wrdisten recalls that the original monks of Landévennec followed the Desert Fathers, living *sicut Aegyptii monachi* ('like the Egyptian monks').[132]

Although monastic life at Landévennec and elsewhere gradually evolved from a semi-solitary to a more communal model, Christian monks and nuns have always tried to live alone (*monachos*) in the cell of their heart, while at the same time loving and caring for others. The Egyptian Desert Mothers and Fathers lived as hermits, though normally in groups, and often near to cities, where they could help the poor. In the Wadi Fayran, 15 miles north-west of Mount Sinai, on the ancient road to St Catherine's monastery, hermits lived in caves in the rock face, alone, yet in close proximity (see colour plate 22). On the opposite side of the track, the mud walls of a fourth-century church stand

ILLUS. 150. Ninth-century well at the east end of Landévennec's church.

on a *tel*, or raised mound, beside which a few Orthodox nuns still live in an early women's monastery.

The spread of Guénolé's cult

In about 913, Landévennec was burnt and sacked by Vikings. The monks took their manuscripts and relics, including Guénolé's hand bell and Wrdisten's Life, to Picardy, where they established a monastery near Boulogne. They brought some of Guénolé's relics to the Benedictine abbey of Mont Blandin in Ghent for safety, and returned to Landévennec thirty years later, when the situation became peaceful once more. They rebuilt the monastery and continued to live there until the French Revolution, by which time there were only four monks left. A new foundation was made, and in 1965 the new Benedictine abbey church was consecrated.

Guénolé was surprisingly popular from Saxon times onwards in England. One reason for this was that the Benedictine monk St Dunstan (909–88) was exiled to Mont Blandin in 955 for two years; he appears to have returned with relics of Guénolé, and the monks of Ghent gave further relics to Leofric, bishop of Exeter. Glastonbury (of which Dunstan was abbot), Abingdon and Waltham all possessed relics of Guénolé, and his name occurs in English litanies of the tenth and eleventh centuries. In England he was known as Winwaloe or Winnol. In Norwich, a local rhyme about weather in the first three days of March runs:

> First comes David, then comes Chad,
> Then comes Winnol, roaring like mad.[133]

This refers to the respective feast days of the three saints. The church of East Portlemouth on the south Devon coast near Salcombe was dedicated to Winwaloe from at least 1450, and two Cornish inland sites were named after him: Poundstock church by 1333 and a chapel at Rosecraddock in St Cleer by 1448.[134] These may have acquired their dedications through secular Norman landowners who possessed property on both sides of the English Channel.

A monastery at St Keverne

St Keverne is on the east side of the Lizard, a mile from the coast. Its saint is called *Achobran* in the early tenth-century list of saints, and the church is named *Sanctus Achabranus* in Domesday Book, which also refers to the group of canons who served it by 1066 (*Canonici Sancti Achebranni*).[135] It possessed a large parish, and may have housed Keverne's shrine. Although it was the only religious house on the Lizard to be recorded in Domesday Book as holding land, after 1066 it lost its property to the Norman count of Mortain, who appears to have granted much of the estate to the Benedictine abbey of Mont Saint-Michel.[136] In 1235 it was given to the Cistercians of Beaulieu in Hampshire; it thus remained a monastic establishment, though its life was expressed in various forms, for a very long period.

The eastern sector of the Lizard peninsula was well populated in early times: there are some sixty-three rounds, or enclosed farmsteads, in the region, and many settlements with the prefix *tre* (or hamlet), particularly around St Keverne itself. This prefix is thought to have been used between the sixth and the eleventh centuries. St Keverne's property included the parishes of St Martin and St Anthony in Meneage, Manaccan and the eastern half of St Mawgan in Meneage.[137] Manaccan, 3 miles north-west of St Keverne, stands in a raised circular graveyard at the centre of the village; its saint was regarded as female. The church is referred to as *Ecclesia Sancte Manace* (1308) and *Manachan* (1395): these employ a feminine form of the word 'monk', so the parish could be named after a nun.[138]

'Meneage' derives from the Cornish *manach*, or monk; the name 'Meneage', or 'monks' land' may indicate the area over which the monastery of St Keverne had jurisdiction. The first recorded use of the element *manach*, in a charter dated 967, is in the estate of *Lesmanaoc* to the west of St Keverne, now Lesneage. With its prefix *lys-*, this may have been St Keverne's civil or agricultural centre.[139] Although *manach* means 'monk', by Saxon times the canons of St Keverne would have lived in separate houses rather than sleeping in a dormitory; they did not hold property in common and they could have been married, with families.[140]

In the south-west, St Keverne's feast day was considered a significant one: a deed of William Brewer, who was bishop of Exeter from 1224 to 1244, was dated 'St Keverne's day', in the fifteenth year of Brewer's consecration.[141] St Keverne was later equated with the Irish bishop, Ciarán of Saighir. The name *Funten-Keran*, or 'Kieran's fountain', appears in about 1300; it is likely to be the well 100 m along Well Lane (see colour plate 23), opposite St Keverne's church square (OS 790214). In the sixteenth century, several men were named Keverne or Kieran(us) in the parish or nearby.[142]

St Keverne was one of four chartered sanctuary churches of Cornwall; its sanctuary zone was still recognised in the sixteenth century. Keverne was identified with St Piran by John Leland, who wrote in his *Itinerary* (1538):

> Within the land of Meneke or Menegland is a paroch chirch of St Keveryn otherwise Piranus; and ther is a Sanctuary with x or xii dwelling howses and thereby was a sel [cell] of monks but now goon home to ther hed hows. The ruines of the monastery yet remenith.[143]

Their 'head house' was the Cistercian abbey of Beaulieu, some of whose monks lived in a priory at Tregoning on the outskirts of St Keverne. Canon Diggens, vicar of St Keverne from 1896–1913, observed that Leland was here describing the parish manor of Tregoning, where there were traces of a range of buildings, human remains and many sculptured stones. He adds: 'The cattle shed is of great age, and from portions of the windows it has been assigned to the fourteenth century'.[144]

St Mawgan in Meneage

The saint of this church, 6 miles north-west of St Keverne, *Maucan*, is paired with *Achobran* (or Keverne) in the early tenth-century list of saints; this hints that St Mawgan in Meneage was possibly Maugan's chief cult centre, with St Mawgan in

ILLUS. 151. Sixth-century pillar stone, St Mawgan in Meneage.

Pydar a secondary dedication. The church is 4 miles south of the Helford River and close to Mawgan Creek; in medieval times, this parish was the second largest on the Lizard, the first being St Keverne. Maugan's cult may be an early one because, although various churches and chapels are named after him in Wales and Brittany, none of them became important in later medieval times.[145]

An early granite pillar stone (illus. 151) stands 2 m high on the village green in what is probably its original position, south of the churchyard, at a point where three roads meet, including the main road leading to the church. The pillar dates from the last third of the sixth century and is inscribed CNECVMI FILI GEN[A]IVS, and is likely to read '[the stone] of Cunegumus, son of Genaius'. The first element of the British name Cunegumus means 'hound', and can indicate a swift warrior, while the first element of his father's name, Genaius, is often found in Gallic names, such as the fourth-century saint, Genesius of Arles.[146]

The pillar stone may have stood at an entrance to the large outer enclosure of a monastery; its probable dimensions are indicated by field boundaries. The church, with its smaller oval churchyard, stands near the south-eastern edge of the larger enclosure, not at its centre: this is on account of its topography, on top of a small hill. The monastery is likely to have been in existence by the seventh century.[147] It was in an excellent location, close to a spring, and with the possibility of fishing in nearby Mawgan Creek, and in the Helford River, 4 miles to the north.

There has been no excavation at St Mawgan in Meneage, but a monastery of similar date at Whithorn in south-west Scotland was excavated between 1984 and 1991. At Whithorn, the church was surrounded by a graveyard, monks' cells and a few communal buildings. Beyond these were the homes of the families who worked as smiths, stonemasons and farmers, forming a monastic village. At the outer edge of the site, cultivated fields belonged to the community. Opposite is an artist's impression of how a monastery at St Mawgan in Meneage might have looked in AD 700, viewed from the south, with the Helford River in the background (illus. 152); it is based on the identification of its outer boundary proposed by Ann Preston-Jones,[148] and utilises tracks and a water course shown on the OS map of 1888.

St Anthony in Meneage

The final Cornish site that we shall consider is St Anthony in Meneage, beside the Helford River, 3 miles north of St Keverne. It was known as *Ecclesiam Sancti*

ILLUS. 152. Artist's impression of a monastery at St Mawgan in Meneage, AD 700, looking north to the Helford River.

DRAWING BY: ANNETTE WELLS.

Antonini by 1260 or 1270; Anthony appears under his Cornish name, *Entenin*, in the tenth-century list of saints, where he is placed next to *Iust*. This indicates that the list's compiler was referring to his church at St Anthony in Roseland, which is near that of St Just in Roseland. The only other site dedicated to Entenin is a holy well, Ventontinny ('*fenten*, or spring, of Entenin'), in the parish of Probus. Entenin's cult did not spread far: his two coastal churches are 6 miles apart by sea, and Probus is 10 miles north of St Anthony in Roseland.[149] Since Entenin's three minor sites are relatively close to each other, he is likely to have been a local holy man.

Often in west Cornwall, a farm beside a church preserves the site's earlier Cornish name. The farm next to the church at St Anthony in Meaneage is called Lantinning (formerly *Lanyntenyn*), meaning 'the *lan*, or church-site, of Entenin'. Entenin's name derives from Latin, which was spoken during the

Roman occupation of Britain; the evolution from the Latin Antoninus to the Cornish Entenin is likely to have occurred between the fifth or sixth and the eighth centuries.[150] Antoninus is a diminutive, meaning 'little Anthony': it may be a term of endearment. Perhaps Entenin was named after St Antony of Egypt, who was considered a model for monks.

ILLUS. 153 *(opposite).* Medieval cross on the track to St Loy's Cove.

PHOTO: PAUL JOHNSON.

The enclosure surrounding his church at St Anthony in Meneage is unusually large for a small parish, and suggests an early cemetery, and perhaps a monastery. The church is at the western edge of the Dennis promontory, a name derived from *dinas*: it was the site of an Iron Age hill fort in a strategic position at the mouth of the Helford River. Fragments of Romano-British pottery were found at the fort, and the church may have been established under the patronage of its chieftain.

In the early 1970s, when a car park close to the church was under construction, what might be an early carving of a *chi-rho* symbol, or possibly a practice piece, was found. It is about 15 cm wide and is carved on a boulder 1 m by 0.7 m; it can be seen inside the churchyard entrance.[151] The remains of a cross with a human face carved on its shoulder, beneath the cross-head, stands against the church wall; it is likely to date from Norman times.[152] St Entenin's holy well is at the upper end of the churchyard (OS 783257): it consists of a rectangular pool inside a seventeenth-century stone well-house, and was used for baptisms.

The Scilly Isles

Finally, we shall consider some island sites: the Scillies, Guernsey and Jersey. The Scillies form an archipelago of about eighteen islands, five of which are inhabited; they are in an isolated location 28 miles south-west of Cornwall. Their archaeology suggests a relationship with Penwith: while most Cornish secular sites from the Roman period are rounds, in parts of Penwith and the Scilly Isles 'courtyard houses' have been found in which, as we have seen, an oval courtyard contains a round house built into the wall opposite the entrance, with outbuildings along either side.

Courtyard houses may have continued in use until the fifth and sixth centuries on the mainland, and even later in the Scillies: a courtyard house at Halangy Down on St Mary's, Scilly, may have been occupied into the seventh or eighth century.[153] Limpets were the inhabitants' main source of protein: some 110,000 limpet shells were found at Halangy Down, together with granite beach pebbles battered at one end, which perhaps were used to dislodge limpets from the rocks.[154]

By this time, Christianity had spread to the archipelago. A memorial pillar dating from the second half of the sixth century has been found on the island of Trescoe: it is built into the jamb of the south door of the ruined Benedictine priory of St Nicholas in Trescoe Abbey Gardens. The remains of its inscription read: ...THI FILI COL[I]NI, or '[the stone] of ...thi, son of Colinus'. Colinus

ILLUS. 154 *(opposite).* Head of medieval cross on the track to St Loy's Cove.

PHOTO: PAUL JOHNSON.

is a Latinised British name; the stone is earlier than many others on the Cornish mainland.[155] The priory was granted a charter in the twelfth century.

On the Scillies, early buildings once thought to be hermits' chapels are now considered to have been churches for the islanders; they probably date from the eighth to the tenth century. The church on St Helen's (formerly known as St Elidius), and perhaps that on Samson, seem to have been preceded by early cemeteries.[156] The low walls of a building known as St Theona's chapel can be seen on the uninhabited island of Teän; it, too, appears to have been preceded by an early cemetery.

The remains on St Helen's, which is now uninhabited, include an eighth-century chapel and a circular cell associated with St Elidius; the chapel was replaced by a small church dating from the eleventh or twelfth century surrounded by graves, and twelfth-century living cells. During medieval times, the relics of St Elidius were entombed in a Purbeck marble shrine; it became a popular centre for pilgrimage. On the Cornish mainland, the chapels of St Helen at Cape Cornwall and of St Loy (*Eligius* in

ILLUS. 155. St Loy's Cove: departure point for pilgrims to the shrine of St Elidius in the Scillies.

PHOTO: GILLIAN JOHNSON.

Latin), 2 miles south of St Buryan, appear to have been departure points for pilgrims sailing to the shrine of St Elidius. A series of medieval crosses served as way-markers, or signposts, along the track from St Buryan to St Loy's Cove (illus. 153–55).[157]

Guernsey churches at pagan sites

Guernesy is 75 miles south of the English coast and 30 miles from Normandy; its earliest settlers were Neolithic farmers who built tombs and erected monuments around the coast from about 5000 BC, and there is evidence of early Christianity at a number of these sites. It is likely that Christianity was brought to Guernsey by the Romans, who settled on the island: a well-developed trading network is suggested by the discovery of amphorae for marine transport, often of wine, from Spain and from the area around Herculaneum in southern Italy.

Buildings excavated at La Plaiderie, in St Peter Port on Guernsey's east coast, appear to have been Roman warehouses, which were in use between AD 100 and 400. A wrecked cargo vessel dating from the third century AD was discovered in St Peter Port harbour: it was probably at anchor or grounded when a fire broke out. A few early Christian artefacts are known: a cross thought to date from the eighth century was discovered in 1978, built into a farmhouse wall at Les Messuriers in St Pierre du Bois, in the west of Guernsey.[158]

'The grandmother of the cemetery', St Martin

Near the south-east coast, the settlement of St Martin derives its name from the fact that it was granted in 1048 by William, duke of Normandy, to the abbot of Marmoutier, which St Martin had founded in the late fourth century. St Martin's parish church stands on the site of a Neolithic tomb, at which two springs emerge. One, La Fontaine de la Bellouse, was considered to have healing powers. The present church dates from the late twelfth or early thirteenth century.[159]

At the churchyard gate is a granite menhir 1.6 m tall carved by Neolithic settlers; it was dressed and smoothed to create a female figure with breasts, folded arms and a girdle (illus. 156). In late Roman times, between AD 200 and 300, her facial features were re-carved; she was given curls, and a short buttoned cape falling around her torso. Later, an attempt was made to cut her in two, but the granite proved too tough. She is known as *La Gran'm*ère *du Chimquière*, or 'the grandmother of the cemetery'.[160]

An even larger, and perhaps earlier, menhir in the form of a female figure stands outside the church of St Marie de Castro, in Castel. The church stands on the edge of high ground, overlooking the flat region of north Guernsey; its name derives from the *castrum*, or stronghold, of a Norse pirate. The giant

ILLUS. 156 *(left). La Gran'mère du Chimquière*, St Martin church, Guernsey.

ILLUS. 157 *(right).* Incised cross on a prehistoric menhir, St Saviour's churchyard, Guernsey.

menhir was discovered under the chancel floor in 1878; it is 2 m high and perhaps dates from the tenth century BC.[161] During excavation in 1999, quantities of Roman tile and pottery confirmed the existence of a Roman building on the site; several early Christian burials were also found. A smaller menhir was found at St Saviour's church, west of the island's centre. It now serves as a gatepost at the north-east entrance to the churchyard, and has an incised cross on both faces (illus. 157).

ILLUS. 158. Stone commemorating a Christian woman, St Michel du Valle, Guernsey.

St Michel du Valle

The church of St Michel du Valle, on Guernsey's north coast, is on a small hill about 220 m from the shore, and 7 m above sea-level; the hill was a tidal islet until the nineteenth century, cut off from the mainland at high tide. The church is within a semicircular enclosure, and a number of cross-marked stones are built into the body of the church. Between 1027 and 1035, half of Guernsey was given by Duke Robert of Normandy to the abbey of Mont Saint-Michel; this church is listed among the properties of Mont Saint-Michel in 1155.[162]

There are megalithic remains in the vicinity, and a stone 1 m tall from a dolmen, or megalithic single-chambered tomb, can be seen outside the west door of the church. Between the eighth and tenth centuries AD, a deeply incised cross was carved on its west face (illus. 158). Above the arms of the cross, an *alpha* was carved to the left and an *omega* to the right; a second *omega* can be seen at the top of the stone. They symbolise Christ, the beginning and the end of all things.

Beneath the arms of the cross, at the left edge of the stone, a capital D stands for *Dominus*, or 'Lord'. Beneath the cross, most of a woman's name can be seen; it reads [...]NSF[R]IDA. Some Frankish and Saxon names include the element *frid*, such as the Anglo-Saxon name *Osfrida*.[163] The church lies close to '*L'Ancresse* Common'; this may refer to an anchoress, or solitary nun.[164] The area is first described in 1563 as 'A poynte of the Lande called Ancrese'.[165]

A hermitage at St Helier, Jersey

The larger island of Jersey, to the south-east of Guernsey, is 10 miles wide. Its chief port, St Helier on the south coast, was believed to have been named after an early hermit, but the eleventh-century Passion of St Helier is largely legendary, and the name is likely to derive from that of St Hilary, bishop of Poitiers (*c.* 315–*c.* 368): in Latin, the two names are *Helierus* and *Hilarius*.[166] The abbey of St Helier was established in 1155 on a tidal islet at the eastern end of St Aubin Bay, but in 1179 it was annexed to that of St Mary of the Vow, near Cherbourg in Normandy. St Helier was subsequently downgraded to a priory, which came to be administered by six Augustinian canons.

On a smaller islet, a twelfth-century hermitage chapel (illus. 159) was built around a cave on an outcrop 27 m high; it is reached by a flight of sixty-five steps. Inside, the chapel is plain and whitewashed, with two square cavities for an aumbrey and a piscina, to house the vessels for the eucharist, and to wash them. In 1887 it was joined by a short causeway to the larger islet on which the abbey stood; the island is now named Elizabeth. At low tide one can walk along the 1,000 m causeway from the mainland to both islands.

ILLUS. 159. St Helier's hermitage chapel, Jersey.

A Roman column capital at St Lawrence

ILLUS. 160. Roman capital used as a Christian memorial, St Lawrence, Jersey.

The church of St Lawrence is west of the island's midpoint, a mile north of St Aubin Bay. In 1198 the church was given by King John to the abbey of Blanchelande in Normandy. It contains a number of cross-marked slabs, perhaps of early medieval date, in its western walls, and a broken Roman column with a Doric capital was found beneath the church floor. In the seventh or eighth century, this was re-worked to become a piece of church furnishing, perhaps a reading desk, which was intended to be viewed from its ornamented side. An inscription was carved on its only remaining plain surface, perhaps soon afterwards, since the carving technique of both the decoration and the inscription is similar.[167]

The column might have come from one of the sites producing Roman material on Jersey; however, the stone used is a type of granite not found in the Channel Islands, but known in Normandy and Brittany. The column's flattened back is decorated with a double-interlace design, and a larger version of this interlacing forms a double knot on the column capital beneath (illus. 160). It may have been carved in Jersey, but similar decoration is found on Merovingian and Carolingian sculptured monuments, so the column could have been brought here from mainland Europe, at an unknown date.[168]

The inscription employs contractions for several words, and reads USDI|LAU [L]:SER|RIGOND. This can be expanded to read UIRGO SACRATA DEI LAULA SERRIGOND, meaning '[the stone of] Laula, a virgin consecrated to God, [from] Serrigond'. Alternatively, it might read 'Laulus, a man consecrated to God, [from] Serrigond', or perhaps 'Dilau, a most holy man, [aged] 50, [from] Serrigond'. Such a place is not known: it could refer to a small locality, or to the home of the dead person. Medieval spellings for Sark, a small island between Jersey and Guernsey, include *Sargia*, *Serc* and *Cerqueyo*; *Serrigond* perhaps reflects a pre-Norman form of Sark.[169]

The Fishermen's Chapel at St Brelade

The old town of St Brelade is situated above a sheltered harbour at the south-west end of Jersey; the church stands on a rocky shelf overlooking St Brelade's Bay. There is evidence of both prehistoric and Roman activity in the churchyard, which was formerly roughly circular, with the cliff forming a third of its boundary. Outside the church, sanctuary steps of granite lead down to a slipway

ILLUS. 161. St Brelade's sanctuary steps, Jersey.

on the beach below (illus. 161). Its saint is also patron of the Breton village of St Broladre, which was on the old shoreline of Brittany before the sea receded. St Broladre is 7 miles north-east of St Samson's monastery of Dol-de-Bretagne; Broladre is said to have been a disciple of Samson. St Brelade has also been equated with Branwalader, and sometimes with St Breward.[170]

The Norman parish church at St Brelade stands alongside a smaller building named the Fishermen's Chapel, which is likely to have been the earliest church on the site; the present chapel dates from the twelfth century and is decorated with fourteenth-century wall-paintings. It was perhaps named after a late medieval fishing guild. It was excavated and restored by Warwick Rodwell in 1982–88; the graveyard between the two buildings was also examined. In the cemetery, Neolithic flints were found on the rock shelf, and megaliths that were no longer *in situ*; a standing stone was discovered, extending under the south transept of the main church, where it had apparently been used as the threshold of an earlier timber church. Similar stones had been recorded in the foundations of the chancel of the main church.[171]

The topsoil that lay beneath the chancel of the Fishermen's Chapel contained the remains of timber structures and domestic debris from an aceramic period. A timber building with a clay floor pre-dated the Fishermen's Chapel; this could have been the original church. Cutting through the timber structures was a series of shallow, ledged graves. The chapel was superseded in the early Norman period by the new and larger parish church, on flatter ground, further back from the cliff edge.[172] Like the churches described on Guernsey, this is a site where pre-Christians met to pray and honour their dead: on a small island, designated sacred spaces tend to remain the same for millennia.

Where next?

We have now completed a survey of significant early Christian sites in south-west Britain – a survey, but not a synthesis. Our knowledge of Saxon sites is considerable, since a wealth of early texts survive and also a number of buildings, or at least their foundations, but pre-Saxon evidence is still fragmentary. Apart from inscriptions, early texts are few. Almost no insular monasteries have been excavated in south-west Britain, except in restricted circumstances: a women's monastery at Lamyatt (Somerset) was examined in 1973, but the site had already been poorly excavated at an early date and subsequently robbed, while in 1993 a promising early monastic site at Carhampton (Somerset) was excavated in a brief rescue dig during which torrential rain filled the trenches. Two further short excavations at Carhampton did not examine the deeper, early Christian, levels of the site.

A number of extensive early Christian cemeteries have been uncovered, the work having been funded by companies prior to developing the land for other uses, but funding for the excavation, or even geophysical surveys, of monastic sites is less readily available in our market-led economy. In 2015, before EDF Energy began to build two new nuclear reactors at Hinkley Point, a considerable sum of money was allocated to excavating an early cemetery beneath the site, although it does not significantly increase our knowledge.

It is tantalising that only 12 miles to the west, no funding has so far been available to excavate the monastic village at Carhampton, or even to publish the meticulously documented account of its initial rescue dig, although it is the only known eighth-century monastic site in the south-west whose members made a living by smelting iron for export. However, further work is shortly to be carried out on the earliest layers of this complex monastic site.

A prime area for discovering more about early Christianity in the south-west could be the Lizard, in the area that medieval Christians named Meneage, or 'monastic land'. Churchyards can rarely be disturbed, but in 2002 Ann Preston-Jones identified what appears to be the wider monastic enclosure at St Mawgan in Meneage: this could usefully be examined. St Anthony in Meneage might be explored in a similar way. The site of an early hermitage that deserves excavation is St Levan, near Land's End, with its baptistery, its ancient flight of steps and presumed living quarters. It could be that, in the next decade or so, more vital pieces of evidence will be found concerning early Christianity in south-west Britain, so that the partially complete jigsaw may reveal more of its design.

Notes

1 Oliver Padel, *A Popular Dictionary of Cornish Place-Names* (Penzance: Alison Hodge, 1988), p. 94.

2 Caitlin R. Green, 'Phillack and the Hayle Estuary in the Late Roman and Early Medieval Periods', www.caitlingreen.org/2018/05/phillack-and-the-hayle-estuary.html, accessed 22 November 2019.

3 *Ibid.*

4 *Ibid.*

5 Elisabeth Okasha, *Corpus of Early Christian Inscribed Stones of South-west Britain* (London: Leicester University Press, 1993), p. 116.

6 Charles Thomas, *And Shall These Mute Stones Speak?* (Cardiff: Cardiff University Press, 1994), pp. 192–93.

7 *Ibid.*

8 Elizabeth Rees, *Celtic Saints of Wales* (Stroud: Fonthill, 2015), pp. 19–20.

9 Elizabeth Rees, *Celtic Saints of Scotland* (Stroud: Fonthill, 2017), pp. 96, 98, 115.

10 Patrick, *Confessio* 43, in Thomas O'Loughlin, *Saint Patrick: The Man and his Works* (London: SPCK, 1999), p. 78.
11 *Carmina XVI* in William Blair Anderson, *Sidonius: Poems and Letters*, Bks 1–2 (Cambridge, MA: Harvard University Press, 1963), p. 250, modernised.
12 *Tescua quidam putant esse tuguria, quidam loca praerupta et aspera*, Etym. XX, in *The Etymologies of Isidore of Seville*, trans. Stephen A. Barney, Wendy J. Lewis, Jennifer A. Beach and Oliver Berghof (Cambridge University Press, 2006).
13 Mark Handley, Celtic Inscribed Stones Project (CISP), 'Llanllŷr, Ceredigion, Wales', 2001; Rees, *Celtic Saints of Wales*, pp. 14–16.
14 Etym. XV, in *The Etymologies of Isidore of Seville*, trans. Barney *et al.*, iii. 10. iv. 5, 6.
15 St Benedict's *Rule for Monasteries*, ch. 1, in *RB 1980: The Rule of St Benedict in Latin and English with Notes*, trans. Timothy Fry (Collegeville, MN: Liturgical Press, 1980).
16 BL, Cotton Nero A.II, ff. 37–42.
17 Constant J. Mews, 'Apostolic Authority and Celtic Liturgies', in *St Samson of Dol and the Earliest History of Brittany, Cornwall and Wales*, Studies in Celtic History, 37, ed. Lynette Olson (Woodbridge: The Boydell Press, 2017), p. 123.
18 Green, 'Phillack and the Hayle Estuary'.
19 Thomas, *And Shall These Mute Stones Speak?*, pp. 197–98, 285.
20 Nick Cahill, *Hayle Historical Assessment, Cornwall Archaeological Unit* (Truro: English Heritage and Cornwall County Council, 2000), p. 22.
21 Padel, *A Popular Dictionary of Cornish Place-Names*, pp. 81, 138.
22 Oliver Padel, 'Local Saints and Place-Names in Cornwall', in *Local Saints and Local Churches in the Early Medieval West*, ed. Alan Thacker and Richard Sharpe (Oxford: Oxford University Press, 2002), p. 307.
23 Ann Preston-Jones and Elisabeth Okasha, *Corpus of Anglo-Saxon Sculpture, vol. XI, Early Cornish Sculpture* (Oxford: The British Academy/Oxford University Press, 2013), pp. 193–94.
24 *Ibid.*, pp. 194–96.
25 Padel, 'Local Saints and Place-Names in Cornwall', p. 337.
26 Sam Turner, *Making a Christian Landscape* (Exeter: Exeter University Press, 2006), p. 158.
27 Padel, *A Popular Dictionary of Cornish Place-Names*, p. 108.
28 Thomas, *And Shall These Mute Stones Speak?*, fig. 18.8.
29 Cahill, *Hayle Historical Assessment*, p. 22.
30 John Harvey, ed., *William Worcestre: Itineraries* (Oxford: Oxford Medieval Texts, 1969), p. 114.
31 Padel, 'Local Saints and Place-Names in Cornwall', p. 358.
32 Historic England, 'Wayside Cross 2 m South of St Uny's Church, Lelant', no. 1017629, 1997.
33 'St Ives. Cornwall', engraving (*c.* 1845), from Thomas Dugdale, *England and Wales Delineated* (London: L. Tallis, 1835–60).
34 Padel, *A Popular Dictionary of Cornish Place-Names*, p. 100.
35 Padel, 'Local Saints and Place-Names in Cornwall', p. 359.
36 Sabine Baring-Gould, *A Book of Cornwall* (London: Methuen, 1923), ch. 2, The Holy Wells, Venton Ia.
37 Historic England, 'The Remains of the Chapel of St Ia and Adjacent Cell', no. 1441204, 2017.
38 Preston-Jones and Okasha, *Corpus of Anglo-Saxon Sculpture*, pp. 65, 234–35.
39 Nicholas Orme, *Cornwall and the Cross: Christianity 500–1560* (London: Phillimore, 2007), p. 16.

40 Vivien Russell and Peter A.S. Poole, 'The Excavation of Chapel Jane, Zennor', *Cornish Archaeology*, 7 (1968), p. 43.
41 *Ibid.*, p. 53.
42 Historic England, 'Medieval Chapel Called Chapel Jane', no. 1004631, 2019.
43 Historic England, 'Medieval Chapel Called St Helen's Chapel with a Dwelling and Enclosure at Cape Cornwall', no. 10045, 2019.
44 Susan Pearce, *The Kingdom of Dumnonia – Studies in History and Tradition in South Western Britain AD 350–1150* (Padstow: Lodenek Press, 1978), pp. 66–67.
45 John Blight, *A Week at the Land's End*, 2nd edn (Truro: Lake and Lake, 1876), p. 155.
46 Thomas, *And Shall These Mute Stones Speak?*, pp. 286–87.
47 *Ibid.*, pp. 287, 291–93. His father's name is not given, perhaps because he had renounced earthly ties.
48 Nicholas Orme, *The Saints of Cornwall* (Oxford: Oxford University Press, 2000), p. 154.
49 Padel, 'Local Saints and Place-Names in Cornwall', p. 355.
50 Preston-Jones and Okasha, *Corpus of Anglo-Saxon Sculpture*, p. 156.
51 *Ibid.*
52 Ifor Williams, 'The Personal Names in Early Anglesey Inscriptions', in *The Beginnings of Welsh Poetry. Studies by Sir Ifor Williams*, ed. Rachel Bromwich (Cardiff: University of Wales Press, 1980), pp. 16–24, at p. 19.
53 Molly Miller, *The Saints of Gwynedd* (Woodbridge: Boydell Press, 1979), pp. 6, 8, 11.
54 Victor Erle Nash-Williams, *The Early Christian Monuments of Wales* (Cardiff: University of Wales Press, 1950), pp. 61–63.
55 Nicholas Johnson and Peter Rose, *Cornwall's Archaeological Heritage* (Truro: Cornwall Archaeological Unit, 1990), p. 19.
56 Preston-Jones and Okasha, *Corpus of Anglo-Saxon Sculpture*, p. 127.
57 Orme, *The Saints of Cornwall*, p. 78.
58 Charles H. Talbot, *The Life of Christina of Markyate*, ed. Samuel Fanous (Oxford: Oxford University Press, 2009).
59 Mary Low, 'Canaire of Inis Cathaig', in *The Radical Tradition: Revolutionary Saints in the Battle for Justice and Human Rights*, ed. Gilbert Markus (London: Doubleday, 1993), p. 27.
60 Patricia Rumsey, *Women of the Church* (Dublin: Columba Press, 2011), pp. 143, 145.
61 Peter Sawyer, *Anglo-Saxon Charters: An Annotated Handlist and Bibliography* (London: Royal Historical Society, 1968), charter no. 450.
62 Padel, 'Local Saints and Place-Names in Cornwall', pp. 320–21.
63 Michel Priziac, *Bretagne des Saints et des Croyances* (Grâces-Guincamp: Ki-Dour Éditions, 2002), pp. 163, 181.
64 Orme, *Cornwall and the Cross*, pp. 38–39.
65 Preston-Jones and Okasha, *Corpus of Anglo-Saxon Sculpture*, p. 128.
66 *Ibid.*, p. 127.
67 Elaine Treharne, 'The Dream of the Rood', in *Old and Middle English c. 890–c. 1400: An Anthology* (Malden, MA: Blackwell, 2004), p. 108.
68 Ann Preston-Jones and Andrew Langdon, 'St Buryan Crosses', *Cornish Archaeology*, 36 (1997), pp. 107–28.
69 Jack Meyrick, *A Pilgrim's Guide to the Holy Wells of Cornwall* (Falmouth: Meyrick, 1982), no. 19, p. 25.
70 Padel, *A Popular Dictionary of Cornish Place-Names*, p. 109.
71 Preston-Jones and Okasha, *Corpus of Anglo-Saxon Sculpture*, pp. 239–40.
72 BL, Egerton MS 2657, f. 10r.
73 Sam Turner, ed., *Medieval Devon and Cornwall: Shaping an Ancient Countryside* (Oxford: Windgather Press, 2006), p. 32.

74 Charles Thomas, 'Christians, Chapels, Churches and Charters – or "Proto-parochial Provisions for the Pious in a Peninsula" (Land's End)', in *Landscape History*, 11 (1988), pp. 19–26, at p. 25.
75 Orme, *The Saints of Cornwall*, p. 230.
76 Nicholas Orme, ed., *Unity and Variety: A History of the Church in Devon and Cornwall*, Exeter Studies in History no. 29 (Exeter: University of Exeter Press, 1991), p. 14.
77 Nicholas Orme, *Nicholas Roscarrock's Lives of the Saints: Cornwall and Devon*, New Series, 35 (Exeter: Devon and Cornwall Record Society, 1992), p. 113.
78 Thomas, *And Shall These Mute Stones Speak?*, p. 286.
79 Preston-Jones and Okasha, *Corpus of Anglo-Saxon Sculpture*, p. 244.
80 *Ibid.*, pp. 198–99.
81 Ann Preston-Jones, *Sancreed Churchyard, Cornwall: Repair and Restoration of Medieval Granite Wayside Crosses* (Truro: Cornwall County Council, Historic Environment Service, 2005), p. 10.
82 Meyrick, *A Pilgrim's Guide to the Holy Wells of Cornwall*, no. 170, p. 132.
83 Blair, *The Church in Anglo-Saxon Society*, p. 375.
84 'Carn Euny, Sancreed, Penwith', *Cornwall's Archaeological Heritage: A Field Guide to Accessible Sites* (Truro: Cornwall County Council, Historic Environment Service, 2005).
85 *Ibid.*
86 William Borlase, *Natural History of Cornwall* (Oxford: W. Jackson, 1758), pp. 31–32.
87 Caitlin Green, tweet, https://twitter.com/caitlingreen/status/970762852368863234, August 2018.
88 Robert Hunt, *Popular Romances of the West of England* (London: J.C. Hotten, 1871). Mesenteric disease is tuberculosis of lymph glands inside the abdomen; it was a children's illness caused by drinking milk from cows infected with tuberculosis. It is now uncommon, because milk is pasteurised.
89 Preston-Jones, *Sancreed Churchyard, Cornwall*, p. 10.
90 Thomas, *And Shall These Mute Stones Speak?*, pp. 290–91, fig. 17. 3.
91 *Ibid.*, p. 271.
92 *Ibid.*, pp. 283 (fig. 17. 5), 286.
93 Bede, *Ecclesiastical History of the English People*, trans. Leo Sherley-Price, rev. Ronald E. Latham (London: Penguin Classics, 1990), bk 2, ch. 14.
94 Mabel and Lilian Quiller-Couch, *Ancient and Holy Wells of Cornwall* (London: C.J. Clark, 1894), p. xxvii.
95 Cheryl Straffon, *Fentynyow Kernow: In Search of Cornwall's Holy Wells* (Penzance: Meyn Mamvro, 1998), pp. 40–42.
96 Francis Jones, *The Holy Wells of Wales* (Cardiff: University of Wales Press, 1992), p. 94.
97 This is the view of Charles Thomas, but others' opinions vary: 'The date of the well chapel is uncertain, but the structure resembles others that are likely to be late Saxon, such as St Helen's Oratory, Scilly' (Turner, *Making a Christian Landscape*, p. xvi); 'Madron's chapel is likely to date from the eleventh or twelfth century' (Blair, *The Church in Anglo-Saxon Society*, p. 375). Pevsner dated it to the fourteenth century: see Nikolaus Pevsner, *The Buildings of England: Cornwall*, ed. Enid Radcliffe, 2nd edn (New Haven: Yale University Press, 2002), p. 111.
98 Orme, *The Saints of Cornwall*, pp. 170–71.
99 *Ibid.*
100 Turner, *Making a Christian Landscape*, pp. 43, 54.
101 Cornwall Historic Churches Trust, https://www.chct.info/histories/st-hilary-st-hilary/, accessed 7 October 2019.
102 Thomas, *And Shall These Mute Stones Speak?*, pp. 289–90.
103 Lynette Olson, *Early Monasteries in Cornwall* (Woodbridge: Boydell, 1989), pp. 89–90, 92.

104 Padel, 'Local Saints and Place-Names in Cornwall', pp. 320, 329.
105 Jean-Paul Benoît, *Mont Saint-Michel* (Luçon: Éditions Jean-Paul Gisserot, 1991) pp. 2, 6–10, 26.
106 Orme, *Cornwall and the Cross*, pp. 35, 61.
107 Orme, *Nicholas Roscarrock's Lives of the Saints*, p. 156.
108 *Ibid.*, p. 92.
109 Padel, *A Popular Dictionary of Cornish Place-Names*, p. 96.
110 Padel, 'Local Saints and Place-Names in Cornwall', p. 354.
111 Orme, *The Saints of Cornwall*, pp. 71–72.
112 Preston-Jones and Okasha, *Corpus of Anglo-Saxon Sculpture*, pp. 122–24.
113 Turner, *Making a Christian Landscape*, pp. 74–75.
114 *Ibid.*, p. 87.
115 Orme, *Cornwall and the Cross*, p. 30.
116 Padel, 'Local Saints and Place-Names in Cornwall', pp. 342, 345.
117 Historic England, 'Church of Saint Germoe', no. 1142197, 2019.
118 Historic England, 'St Germoe's Chair', no. 1310470, 2001.
119 Orme, *The Saints of Cornwall*, p. 96.
120 Pevsner, *The Buildings of England: Cornwall*, p. 61.
121 Orme, *Nicholas Roscarrock's Lives of the Saints*, p. 125.
122 Pierre-Roland Giot, Philippe Guignon and Bernard Merdrignac, *The British Settlement of Brittany* (Stroud: Tempus, 2003), p. 239.
123 Orme, *The Saints of Cornwall*, pp. 29, 257–58.
124 Bernard Merdrignac, 'The Process and Significance of Rewriting in Breton Hagiography', in *Celtic Hagiography and Saints' Cults*, ed. Jane Cartwright (Cardiff: University of Wales Press, 2003), p. 185.
125 Annie Bardel, 'The "First Bretons" at Landévennec: From the Sixth to the Ninth Century', in Giot, Guignon and Merdrignac, *The British Settlement of Brittany*, pp. 166–67.
126 *Ibid.*
127 *Ibid.*, p. 167; Giot, Guignon and Merdrignac, *The British Settlement of Brittany*, pp. 215, 249.
128 Bardel, 'The "First Bretons" at Landévennec', pp. 168, 170.
129 *Ibid.*, pp. 168, 171.
130 *Ibid.*, p. 171.
131 *Ibid.*
132 Giot, Guignon and Merdrignac, *The British Settlement of Brittany*, p. 215.
133 David Hugh Farmer, *The Oxford Dictionary of Saints*, 2nd edn (Oxford: Oxford University Press, 1987), pp. 442–43.
134 Nicholas Orme, *English Church Dedications, with a Survey of Cornwall and Devon* (Exeter: University of Exeter Press, 1996), pp. 112, 157.
135 Orme, *The Saints of Cornwall*, pp. 159–60.
136 Turner, *Making a Christian Landscape*, p. 95.
137 *Ibid.*, pp. 29, 86, 95.
138 It would not be extraordinary to omit the saint's actual name. In the village where I have lived for twenty years, despite the fact that I call myself Liz, I am known as 'the Nun', which is how I am likely to be remembered, if at all.
139 Turner, *Making a Christian Landscape*, p. 117.
140 Orme, *Cornwall and the Cross*, p. 14.
141 Padel, 'Local Saints and Place-Names in Cornwall', p. 348.
142 Orme, *The Saints of Cornwall*, p. 160.

143 Charles Henderson, 'The Ecclesiastical History of the 109 Parishes of West Cornwall', *Journal of the Royal Institution of Cornwall*, 3, part 2 (1958), pp. 211–382, at pp. 256–57.

144 Canon Diggens Archive: 'The Manors of St Keverne', St Keverne Local History Society, 2018, http://www.st-keverne.com/History/diggens/d20.php, accessed 22 November 2019.

145 Orme, *The Saints of Cornwall*, pp. 182–83.

146 Thomas, *And Shall These Mute Stones Speak?*, p. 284.

147 Ann Preston-Jones, 'Decoding Cornish Churchyards', in *The Early Church in Wales and the West*, ed. Edwards and Lane, pp. 120–21.

148 *Ibid.*, p. 121.

149 Padel, 'Local Saints and Place-Names in Cornwall', pp. 332–34.

150 *Ibid.*, pp. 308, 334.

151 Information from Anthony Jenkin, churchwarden at St Anthony in Meneage, 30 August 2019.

152 Preston-Jones and Okasha, *Corpus of Anglo-Saxon Sculpture*, p. 108.

153 Paul Ashbee, 'Halangy Down, St Mary's, Isles of Scilly: Excavations 1964–1977', *Cornish Archaeology*, 35 (1996).

154 Paul Ashbee, 'Excavations at Halangy Down, St Mary's, 1967–1968', *Cornish Archaeology*, 7 (1968), pp. 24–32.

155 Thomas, *And Shall These Mute Stones Speak?*, pp. 271, 273, fig. 16.10.

156 Charles Thomas, *Exploration of a Drowned Landscape: Archaeology and History of the Isles of Scilly* (London: B.T. Batsford, 1985), pp. 180–87.

157 *Ibid.*, p. 204.

158 Peter McGregor Eadie, *The Channel Islands: Blue Guide* (London: A. & C. Black, 1987), p. 21.

159 Marc Trickey, *Guide to the Parish Church of St Martin in the Island of Guernsey* (Guernsey, 1988), p. 1.

160 Chris Catling, *Guernsey; Herm, Sark, Alderney* (London: APA Publications, 1999), p. 27.

161 Victor Coysh, *The Visitor's Guide to Guernsey, Alderney and Sark*, 3rd edn (Ashbourne: Moorland Publishing, 1994), p. 139.

162 Wendy Davies, Jonathan Koch, James Graham Campbell, Mark Handley, Paul Kershaw and Gwenaël Le Duc, *The Inscriptions of Early Medieval Brittany* (Oakville, CT, and Aberystwyth: Celtic Studies Publications, 2000), pp. 307–13.

163 *Ibid.*

164 Richard Coates, 'Thoughts on L'Ancresse, Guernsey', *Nomina*, Society for Name Studies in Britain and Ireland, 23 (2000), pp. 75–78. Coates demonstrates that the name derives from the Greek for 'anchorite', but is unaware of its feminine form, 'anchoress'.

165 Report of Royal Commissioners, Hatfield House, Salisbury MSS 297/2 (1563).

166 Anthony Mathieu Bellows, *St Helier: The Man and the Myth* (St Helier: Société Jersiaise, 2002).

167 Davies *et al.*, *The Inscriptions of Early Medieval Brittany*, pp. 298–306.

168 *Ibid.*

169 *Ibid.*

170 Priziac, *Bretagne des Saints et des Croyances*, pp. 185–86.

171 Beth Lloyd, *Parish Church of St Brelade and the Fishermen's Chapel* (Andover: Jarrold, 2003), pp. 13–14.

172 Warwick Rodwell, *The Fishermen's Chapel, Saint Brelade, Jersey, its Archaeology, Architecture, Wall Paintings and Conservation* (Saint Helier: Société Jersiaise, 1990).

Index

PLATE I. Mosaic floor, Frampton Roman villa, courtesy of Dorset Natural History and Archaeological Society.

PLATE 2. Baptismal pool beneath St Joseph's church, Nazareth. Photo: Garo Nalbandian.

PLATE 3. St Congar's Walking Stick, Congresbury, Somerset.

PLATE 4. Brean Down, Somerset, viewed from the south.

PLATE 5. Steep Holm, in the Bristol Channel, viewed from the east.

PLATE 6. Harbour at the south-eastern end of Lundy Island, opposite Hartland Point, Devon. Photo: Monica Watson.

PLATE 7. View down steep cliffs to the sea at the south-western end of Lundy Island. Photo: Monica Watson.

PLATE 8. Foundations of early buildings at Tintagel, Cornwall.

PLATE 9. St Julitta's chapel, Tintagel, Cornwall.

PLATE 10. Wheel-head cross, St Juliot, near Boscastle, Cornwall.

PLATE II. View up the hillside to St Clether holy well, Cornwall.

PLATE 12. Little Petherick creek, near Padstow, Cornwall.

PLATE 13. St Cubert's well in a cave, Holywell Bay, Cornwall.

PLATE 14. Statue of St Melor in Lanmeur church, Brittany.

PLATE 15. View from a hermit's cave, Caiplie, Fife.

PLATE 16. Remains of a medieval chapel on St Cuthbert's Isle, Lindisfarne. Photo: Ros Marsden.

PLATE 17. St Helen's oratory, Cape Cornwall. Photo: Gillian Johnson.

PLATE 18. St Helen's oratory, showing oval enclosure. Photo: Gillian Johnson.

PLATE 19. St Levan's baptistery, above Porthchapel, Cornwall.

PLATE 20. One of Chapel Euny's twin wells, Penwith, Cornwall.

PLATE 21. Sandstone cross-head, Breage church, Cornwall.

PLATE 22. Hermits' caves in Wadi Fayran, Sinai.

PLATE 23. Kieran's fountain, St Keverne, Cornwall.